BERLIOZ
and His Century

BERLIOZ and His Century

An Introduction to the Age of Romanticism

With a new Preface

Jacques Barzun

The University of Chicago Press

This Phoenix edition, as revised and adapted by the author, is published by arrangement with Little, Brown and Company from *Berlioz and the Romantic Century,* copyright 1949, 1950 by Jacques Barzun, renewed 1978.

The University of Chicago Press, Chicago 60637

Phoenix edition 1982
Printed in the United States of America

99 98 97 96 95 94 93 92 91 5 4 3 2

Library of Congress Cataloging in Publication Data

Barzun, Jacques, 1907–
Berlioz and his century.

Rev. ed. of: Berlioz and the romantic century. 3rd ed. 1969.
Includes bibliographical references and index.
1. Berlioz, Hector, 1803–1869. 2. Composers—France—Biography. I. Title.
ML410.B5B2 1982 780'.92'4 [B] 81-16072
ISBN 0-226-03861-0 (pbk.) AACR2

Contents

To the memory of Tom S. Wotton (1862-1939): foremost Berlioz scholar of his time

WHY BERLIOZ? (1982)

Among Goethe's lighter works there is a ballad called "The Sorcerer's Apprentice," which tells the story of the mishap that occurred when the magician's helper, left alone, changed a broom into a creature and ordered it to bring water to fill a tub. The water kept coming in floods and nearly swamped the house, because the apprentice did not know the magic word with which to stop what he had started.

I find that tale fitting my mood as I am asked to write a new author's note for the fourth reissue of my book on Berlioz. Not that I am looking for any magic to stop it; but, like the apprentice, I did not know what I was unleashing when, some fifty years ago, I began work on what I believed would be "a long essay" on a composer I loved and admired. The essay became two large volumes, published after eighteen years of search and research here and abroad. Parts of the original sources from Central Europe—letters, programs, scores, pamphlets—were scattered or destroyed during the Second World War, and their message survives by the happy accident of my finding and using them earlier.

Soon after my volumes came out, I was urged to reduce the "life, times, and works" to a "life" by itself, which is what the reader now has in hand. But the demands did not stop there, nor even with the duty to see the book through the press, from time to time, in various normal transformations of format and contents. From the first, I was summoned to nurture the subject I had brought back on the stage. I had to write (and even recite) program notes for his chief works as they reentered the repertory one by one; to turn his texts and librettos into English; to provide jacket copy for the long-playing discs that followed the concerts; to retranslate *Evenings with the Orchestra,* which existed in an English edition full of mistakes and barbarisms; to gather and edit a group of unpublished letters in private hands; to attend and be vocal at conferences and symposiums where the new race of Berliozians held their tribal meetings; and to keep up an endless correspondence with inquiring strangers and scholars.

No one should suppose that I am complaining. Rather, I am *ex*plaining why, at this point and in this place, I do not once more go over the reasons why a book about the life of Berlioz deserves the reader's interest: I have uttered them often enough. Besides, W. H. Auden put them all in one terse sentence: "Whoever wants to know about the nineteenth century must know about Berlioz." And to know about Berlioz—well, here he is, high and (I hope) dry, while the swirling waters continue to rise about the apprentice's limbs. Let it be a lesson to all brash young magicians.

J. B.

PREFACE TO THE REVISED EDITION (1956)

Berlioz is now established among American listeners on the firmest possible basis—the direct knowledge of his works. Thus when a new edition of Grove's *Dictionary of Music and Musicians* appeared in 1954 containing in its article on Berlioz some of the old clichés about the noise and grandiloquence of the *Requiem,* one of the editors of the New York *Times* Book Review could confidently write a little note of reproof qualifying the opinion in Grove as untenable: he knew the *Requiem,* he had heard it.

Twenty years before, the authority of an earlier Grove and of kindred writers was unquestioned. Their words filled the textbooks and program notes, predisposing the newcomer against the rare performances of Berlioz, making it embarrassing for anyone to avow a liking for the music and difficult to document an admiration for its creator: the unfavorable preconceptions, as is so often the case in cultural history, were buttressed by large blocks of factual error and conventional opinion. The change in attitude was brought about by the long-playing disc which, beginning about 1950, supplied almost overnight a genuine repertory, not only of Berlioz but of western music as a whole. Our culture has been deeply affected by this sudden recovery of music, an understanding of which is now less and less a specialty, more and more a part of our intellectual life.

It so happened that by the same year 1950, I had finished and published the study of the composer which I had begun some twenty years earlier, not guessing that the demonstration it attempted would be borne out, thanks to technology, by conclusive proof through the ear. My first intention, in the late 1920's, had been to disentangle from false criticism the figure of an artist whose work struck me as original and powerful. But I very soon saw that I could not do this without recreating for the reader the musician's physical and mental surroundings, so generally misconceived in popular and scholarly literature. And I had barely embarked on this task when it became apparent that my aim and duty were enlarging still farther: Berlioz was not merely a composer mis-heard by our critics and neglected by our conductors; he was not merely an extraordinary artist fighting the usual losing battle with his contemporaries and early posterity; he was also an archetype whose destiny, when retold, was the story of an age; he was the incarnation of a style and spirit that we can no more expunge from the history of western man than one can expunge a stretch of years from one's own past.

This increasing purpose and its fulfillment account for the form and size of my two volumes entitled *Berlioz and the Romantic Century*. They were meant to provide, in an expected absence of Berliozian melody, a continuous narrative of his life, a description of his twelve great works, and an enveloping extract of the cultural history of Europe from, roughly, the rise of the First Napoleon to the fall of the Third.

This combination of life, work, and times was from one point of view easy to fashion, for Berlioz is representative of his age in no symbolic or indirect sense. He was not simply an artist in a room thinking great thoughts and keeping his sensibility attuned to the European spirit in travail. He was a man of action, working in the practical ways of the organizer and leader of men. As conductor, manager, and critic, he came in contact with nearly every notable of his time, from Schumann, Wagner, and Bettina von Arnim to Metternich, Guizot, and Frederick William IV. His travels, which took him twice to Russia, covered every country where living art was being made during the critical half century between the death of Beethoven and the rise of the Russian and Impressionist schools.

And as a mind of a high order, articulate and penetrating in equal degree, the ideas and feelings then prevailing found somewhere in him a reflecting surface, the glancing lights from which are still undimmed. His abundant writings, his admirable letters, are to the connoisseur a source of fact, wisdom, and humor. In short, as W. H. Auden has said, "Whoever wants to know about the nineteenth century must know about Berlioz."

But to "know" in this sense, after a long course of misinformation, requires the abandonment of a large set of accepted ideas, and since nature abhors a vacuum, a new set has to be supplied. Otherwise confusion, not corrected vision, is the result. The new set of ideas is what the psychologists used to call the "apperceptive mass"—the notions we must carry about with us before we can perceive. It was this mass that I offered in my first *Berlioz,* and the book was accordingly massive, to a degree I was the first to point out and deplore. Now that hearers find in Berlioz a musical idiom they spontaneously enjoy, it is no longer necessary to prove by a close dialectic what will be readily granted on inspection—for example, that the man who could compose the *Romeo and Juliet* symphony was a great artist. This changed view permitted the present edition of *Berlioz*—shorn of its supplements and apparatus, and detailing without polemics the events and achievements of the composer's life.

The simplified account is still complex enough to provide the reader with a broad view of Romanticist Europe and to define its genius. But for critical essays on Berlioz' works; for a full bibliography, iconography, and discography; as well as for discussions of the scholarly problems and desiderata in the study of Berlioz' musical and literary works, the reader will have to go to the larger work. To that source also the student must have recourse if he wants to find the detailed reference for each important statement.

In recasting the text, I have naturally taken the opportunity to correct the errors that occurred in the previous edition. Some were pointed out to me by readers whom I hereby thank; others were the perverse but familiar effect of strained attention, by which recognizable blunders leap to the author's eye only when the book is printed and bound. Slips will no doubt still remain, given the extent and variety of the materials drawn upon. I comfort myself with the thought that the appearance of Mr. C. H. Hopkinson's great *Bibliography of the Musical and Literary Works of Berlioz,* fifteen months after my book, did not upset any significant assertion or inference in it.

Before concluding—or rather, before beginning—and while I am on the subject of error, a word more is in order about the causes that for a century and a quarter perpetuated the absurdest nonsense about Berlioz and conspired to keep him in the half-light of ambiguous fame. The case is remarkable but not unique in the history of cultural criticism, and as such it is instructive. "How many great artists," exclaims André Gide, "win their case only on appeal!" Why should this be and why was it so for Berlioz?

The main answer is that Berlioz was caught in the general determination to keep Romanticism under. This is easily tested by a parallel: "It is long since Delacroix has been out of fashion," wrote a critic half a dozen years ago, "but I consider him to be by all odds the greatest French painter of the century. It has always amused me that the people who say that the subject does not count object to Delacroix's romantic subjects . . . The important question is, can the painter get away with it, and Delacroix could. He was one of the rare dramatic artists who is a real painter—one with Giotto, Michelangelo, Tintoretto, Rubens—a great colorist, a great master." [1] Substitute Berlioz for Delacroix in this passage and you have the standard situation of the Romantic master caught in the subsequent counter-revolution. Anti-Romanticism has unfortunately had a long despotic reign. It is but recently that one has been able to laugh with impunity at the disfiguring passion of the calm classicist defending his gods. Consider, for example, the remarks of that distinguished and musical New Yorker, George Templeton Strong. Writing in his *Diary* in the late sixties, when Berlioz was still alive, he refers to "the Berlioz eructation called the Roman Carnival overture." Other Berlioz works are variously: "flatulent," "pyrotechnic," "rubbish," "flagrant" (*sic*), the work of "a tipsy chimpanzee." He hopes after hearing the *Symphonie Fantastique* that "Berlioz' dream came true and he was hanged at the end." Falling in with contemporary opinion, Strong has the explanation for all this: just as "Shelley and the Romantics drove out plain sense" from poetry, so now Berlioz, Liszt, and Wagner are doing the same to music. The spirit of Templeton Strong outlasted him and is only beginning to abate.

The second cause of misprision before the long-playing disc was the inaccessibility of Berlioz' music to men of letters. For it is writers and writers alone who confer lasting fame. They do not do this arbitrarily or without confirmation and support from the "experts." But the experts need reverberators. Berlioz received the accolade of every one of his artistic peers, from

[1] Leo Stein, *Appreciations*, N.Y., 1947, p. 198.

Schumann and Wagner to César Franck and Mussorgski, but this does little for a reputation as long as the applause is echoed only by the happy few who make it a point to know things at first hand. The academic experts rarely venture on an independent judgment, though they rationalize admirably after consecration. The result is that no general conviction prevails that an artist *is* until hosts of people who modestly follow the drift of opinion begin to see the name repeatedly referred to in a tone of respect. It must crop up in all relevant connections, in newspapers and literary essays, in program notes and dictionaries, until the strangeness wears off and the mind automatically registers an "Oh, yes." The value of this assent, culturally, is that it acts as an open sesame before the locked doors of indifference and skepticism. It is quite literally: recognition. When an uncommitted yet representative witness, for example, Mr. Brooks Atkinson, can say: "In my library, the supreme masterpiece is Berlioz' *L'Enfance du Christ*," and can go on to speak quite simply of its moving moments and of "the mystery of Berlioz' genius," then the genius in question ceases to be questionable.

Before that time, almost any affirmation is unsafe. In my writings on Berlioz down to 1950, I was particularly careful to advance no unsupported claims, and to avoid altogether the gushing vocabulary which is usual about dead artists—the "dear master" style that creates an aura of deference and eulogy. Yet when my book appeared the mere recital of what Berlioz had done struck so strange a note that the unprepared felt it as exaggeration. So much truth could not have been overlooked; so many creditable deeds were incredible. The useful phrase "special pleading" was invoked in consequence, as it generally is in the rear-guard action against any recovery of rights. For such a recovery disturbs not only rooted habits of mind but certain monopolies. Only for acknowledged geniuses may special pleading be used—and its use is common practice. In Terry's book on Bach's orchestra, for instance, "the master" is praised for wanting ever more expressive instruments, in greater quantities and louder volume—what a pioneer he was! As against this, when Berlioz first brings into being, then wishes to extend, this same musical power that Bach aspired to, it is special pleading to show the reasonableness of the attempt. In the latest Grove we are told, apropos of Beethoven's sacred music, that besides the artist in him there was a visionary idealist who did not care if he strained the singers' voices or not. When Berlioz once or twice puts such a strain on a singer, it is special pleading to suggest that he legitimately hoped someone might some day have the ability to carry out his intention.

But I am wrong to say it is special pleading: it *was*. For now the tide has turned and Berlioz is on his proper pinnacle, where he can be treated like everybody else, without pleading of any sort; secure, not indeed from criticism, but from blind animus. The bogey of Romanticism being largely dispelled, Berlioz' musical and other ideas are helping the public to revise its idea of what Romanticism itself means. Berlioz' style, of a rich sobriety, inspired but controlled, strong but delicate, and faultless in the one quality of pulse and movement, is enabling more and more hearers to say to themselves, "if this is Romanticism, then I am for it."

The work and personality of Berlioz are of course by no means synonymous with all of Romanticism—any more than Byron's or Balzac's, or Keats's, or Wordsworth's. But the Berliozian quality of fire and reason is a main ingredient of it, which we misconstrue to our loss. Moreover, now that the nineteenth century has taught us music as an art, and the twentieth given us the means of revising conventional judgments, it is clear that Berlioz' importance is far from being solely, or even chiefly historical. It is intrinsic. Berlioz, like all great artists, interprets his time and transcends it. He was able to interpret it because he transcended it. We go to his works for the manifestation of this ever-renewed mystery and find, in César Franck's words, *"une oeuvre faite de chefs-d'oeuvre"*—a life's work made up of masterworks.

J.B.

CHAPTER 1

TIME, PLACE, PERSONS

There is a harmony between men's lives and their names: a poetic justice. Hector Berlioz could not have pursued his high-fevered career under the name of Georges Jourdain.—THOMAS BURKE, 1929

The year 1803 opened with renewed preparations for war. Europe had been under arms for a decade, but the previous eight months had seen a truce between Bonaparte dictating to France and Great Britain leading the Allies. Now another hundred thousand Frenchmen must join the colors, a new fleet was being built, and the First Consul moved on three continents. Though he was losing India, he held title to Louisiana and had an army in Haiti. President Jefferson was alarmed, and shortly negotiations were begun to buy the future American Middle West from France, whose master was planning the invasion of England with barges and balloons. By the end of the year his army on the Channel had been designated for the Battle of Britain. Yet in retrospect the time would mark its men with other signs than those of war: a new century inheriting the Enlightenment, a new order growing out of the mightiest revolution in history, a new conception of life most vividly embodied in the headlong career of Napoleon.

Just before the year ended and only a few days before Louisiana became American, on Sunday, December 11, at five o'clock in the afternoon, Hector Berlioz was born in the small town of La Côte St. André, thirty-five miles northwest of Grenoble. At that time and place, the date of his birth was set down as the nineteenth Frimaire of the year XII, for

France was still nominally a republic and used the emancipated calendar. The child's given names, Louis and Hector, of themselves suggest a period of transition, for Louis is Christian and Hector fulfills the revolutionary behest that parents remember the heroes of antiquity in naming the future heroes of the First French Republic. The revolution, it is true, had at no time been very violent in the southeastern province of Dauphiné. Insurrection had been characteristically prompt and self-controlled. Two years before the nationwide upsurge of the Third Estate, the magistrates of Dauphiné had defied royal encroachment in a fashion resembling England's resistance to "ship money." Again, nearly a year before the outbreak of the revolution, Dauphinois lawyers and notables had held unauthorized assemblies of their own, and in a twelve-hour session at Vizille had "passed" most of the reforms which were later to shed glory on the National Assembly.

Moreover, considering itself a recent acquisition of the French crown—only five centuries old—the Dauphiné still felt stirrings of particularist feeling. Its local heroes were Bayard, the outspoken Knight without fear or reproach, and Lesdiguières, the invincible defender of Protestantism. At La Côte itself Servetus had preached before his exile to near-by Geneva, and from the same village came another Protestant family which was to produce the nineteenth-century economist and historian Sismondi. During the Terror, isolation in mountainous country and moderation in carrying out new laws had spared the region the worst of civil strife; so that by the turn of the century, and in the Berlioz family especially, party feeling had died down. It had not been replaced by enthusiasm for Bonaparte. The household was mildly royalist.

Hector's father, Louis Berlioz, was a physician descended from a long line of residents at La Côte who have been traced back with certainty to 1600. In the attempt to go farther, the name Berlioz (in which you must sound the *z* after the long *o*, all Parisians to the contrary notwithstanding) has been the subject of much profitless speculation on the part of race-thinking critics. The ending in *-oz* is common enough in the southeast, but the root *Berl* has been taken by some to signify Germanic descent. Others, finding the name in Savoy, argue for an Italian origin and so "vindicate" the Latin genius. Finally, there is mention of more than one Berlioz in an ancient roll of noble Crusaders, from which still others deduce a racial superiority of caste.

The simple fact is that three centuries in a narrow corner like La Côte St. André would suffice to acclimatize any alien strain, whether of slave or master race, and turn its representatives into the variable cultural product which you may call at once Dauphinois, Frenchman, and European. The desire to make Berlioz' musical genius come out of either Germany or Italy via the chromosomes of possibly tone-deaf farmers and artisans of La Côte is as childish as it is unhistorical. Where was German music at the time of the Crusades? And why did Berlioz grow up with a particular distaste for Italian music? The effect of time, place, and living persons is a truer aid to understanding the art and temper of the man than all the verbalizing of modern nationalists.

Engaged from the first in the locally important tanning industry, the Berlioz clan had gradually risen in station until by the middle of the eighteenth century its descendants were men of property and education. So much so that Hector's grandfather, the lawyer and tax official, Joseph Berlioz, found himself on a list of suspects during the Terror and suffered the confiscation of his goods. This was the time when the name Côte St. André sounded counterrevolutionary and had to be changed to Côte Bonne-Eau, in allusion not to its waters but to its fine liquors. Joseph Berlioz gave no further cause for suspicion and he eventually got back his property, both at La Côte and near Grenoble, where at Les Jacques he had a large estate overlooking the great valley and mountain screen of the Grésivaudan.

It was this same Joseph Berlioz who rebuilt at La Côte the house which still stands, and which in 1935 was made into a museum in honor of his grandson. It is a solid, flat-fronted stone house with sloping roof. The spacious rooms are well-proportioned and, except for wainscoting, bare of ornament. From the upper stories one has a superb view of the whole plain, framed within a silver-blue edging of mountains. Behind the house is a courtyard and beyond, a quiet garden with a small stream. When Berlioz was born, the grandfather lived in the house, a widower retired from professional life, but still busy as the largest landowner of the place—virtually a country squire. His physical appearance, as one can judge from a painting, was largely reproduced in his grandson Hector—a thin, high, hooked nose, fine lips with a sardonic curl at the corners, deep-set eyes and a sturdy build.

The son of the suspect, Hector's father Louis, born in 1776, seems by contrast a milder man. For a time, it is true, he was politically at odds with his father. The "noble words Liberty and Equality," the doctor tells us in a diary, had aroused his youthful zeal, which was enhanced by "the success of the citizen armies and the republican evocations of Athens and Rome." He became "quite wild, like many others." But events disillusioned him. He grew very self-contained, although generous feeling and independence of mind were characteristics that remained and influenced Hector, his first-born.

Louis Berlioz had studied medicine after giving up law, which was his father's choice for him. The young man taught himself by reading and attending lectures in the metropolis when available. Wartime schooling, then as now, is a chancy thing, but finally, two months after Hector's birth, Louis Berlioz went once more to Paris, defended his thesis, and obtained his degree. His age was twenty-seven.

All the while he had pursued other intellectual interests, notably music, and had learned English and Italian to keep up with contemporary literature and philosophy. Even beyond the small community of five thousand souls which he tended, he would have stood out as an unusual man. A great reader, who also wrote voluminously for his own use and pleasure, he could combine the meditative life with action in a manner which we shall find again in his son. The doctor was among the first to practice hydrotherapy and he developed and described other original methods of cure in a prize-winning essay chosen by the Montpellier Faculty in 1810. When rivals used his discoveries without acknowledgment, he remained unruffled and said only, "Let the truth prevail."

Dr. Berlioz soon enjoyed the trust and respect of his neighbors. He overcame their prejudices so quietly that he gained both their affection and the power to help them; and his interest in the welfare of the poor took the practical form of supplying them with housing and hygienic facilities at his own expense. He died a universally beloved public benefactor, a counterpart of Balzac's famous *Médecin de Campagne*.

Hector's mother was cast in a different mold. Whereas her husband was a gently skeptical philosopher, bred on Voltaire and Rousseau, poetry and natural science, Madame Berlioz was a passionate, devout, one-idea'd woman—the daughter of a Grenoble lawyer named Marmion. She was considered a beauty, tall, slim, and remarkable for her fine coloring and glowing health, though in spite of her apparent vitality she suffered from an obscure liver complaint. Friends and family, as is their wont, called it hypochondria, which did not improve the sufferer's irritable temper. Disappointed perhaps at the narrow life afforded to one of her sociable gifts, and driven by the demon of aggressive piety, Marie-Antoinette Berlioz was capable of turning every event of the day into an occasion for outcry—to the point of rousing even the patient doctor to a sudden burst of anger.

The household atmosphere might accordingly be charged with electricity, and although the bolts did not destroy the tight bonds of French family life, the boy Hector undoubtedly sensed the strain. A nightmare he tells of having had in early manhood pictured the attempt of three burglars to kidnap his father: Hector perhaps felt that the doctor had been his protector. What is certain is that although the boy was attached to his mother, he never felt for her a completely trusting affection. She lacked moral gentleness, and she was moreover puzzled from the start by her son's character and inclinations.

Besides the young couple with their first child, and Dr. Berlioz' aging father, the house at La Côte came to shelter five more children, of whom two girls, Nanci and Adèle, survived to maturity.[1] The house was also a center for the visits of an extensive *cousinage* scattered among the neighboring hills and reaching as far as Grenoble, where both sides of the family had property.

In this ensemble, an infrequent but distinct note was struck by Mme. Berlioz' younger brother, Félix Marmion. As an officer in training at the Paris Polytechnic School, he was the only Bonapartist of the family, and thereby at odds both with his sister and with her strongly anti-imperialist father-in-law: more wrangling—this time political—for the boy Hector to grow resistant to. The young lieutenant nevertheless remained an important link between La Côte and the outer world of great events and distant places. His campaigns took him as far as Prussia and Poland; he fought for four years in Spain; he was shot, enfevered, sabre-cut. Because of his royalist family he did not rise to a captaincy until the Bourbons' first restoration in 1814.

In spite of handicaps, Félix Marmion was gay, gallant and reasonably vain. Sociable like his sister, fond of music and competent on the violin, but even fonder of using his fine voice on a large repertoire of parlor songs and light opera selections, we can see him as a representative guardsman, in costume and character. Yet the coloring went deeper than the scarlet coat. Like so many of his generation, he was truly enamored of the Napoleonic way of life—that mixture of recklessness, rapid motion, and obsession with glory—which men as different as Balzac, Vigny, and the two Dauphinois, Stendhal and Berlioz, found so gripping and so rich in artistic suggestion.

The young Hector's first acquaintance with imperial institutions was of a different kind. At the age of six, he was sent to the seminary—an agency of mixed monastic and military discipline, designed to form all over France a Napoleonic Youth. There Hector presumably learnt by heart the catechism which told of the Emperor's goodness and divine mission, and he was set to play the drum in uniformed parades with his fellows. Fortunately, a rescript of 1811 abolished this infant prison and Hector was returned to his family, not to leave it again until he went to Paris ten years later.

The doctor took charge of his son's education and made a success of it. Music, mathematics, Latin, history, French literature, astronomy, and geography formed the course of study. Geography occupied a special place, for one of the usual responses to the feeling of mountain fastness is a passion for travel. In Hector it was matched by a thirst for stories of remote parts, and luckily the doctor's library contained many travel books, including the voyages of Bougainville and other explorers, whose daring had enlarged the eighteenth-century horizon. These, with more recent authors—such as Bernardin de St. Pierre and Chateaubriand—gave Hector glimpses of wild America and the south seas—regions which Voltaire and the Encyclopedists had used to prove human diversity and preach tolerance. While still a boy Hector became a cosmopolitan, and he remained true to this vision of earth and mankind.

The great book in the child's curriculum was Virgil's *Aeneid*. It was ideally suited to develop Hector's visible inclinations—the romance of travel, the love of nature, the quick sympathy with varied emotions, and the cultivation of a delicate ear. Indeed the effect of so much art once proved too much for the pupil's peace of mind. In translating for his father the passage that tells of Dido's despair after her desertion by Aeneas, the boy was choked by strong feeling and only saved by his father's adroit overlooking of the trouble and ending of the lesson.

The happy chance of a domestic education helps to explain why Berlioz seems so fully himself so young. Though not a prodigy, he undoubtedly acquired a conscious inner life earlier than most. No one can guess or explain all that goes into the making of an artist, but one element is surely the power to feel intensely and remember past feelings undimmed. It is as if the first impressions of childhood were there forever, fresh and producible, not to be worn away by worldliness. What Berlioz felt about Dido at eleven, he still knew at fifty-five, and the music he then wrote for her death scene echoes these early pangs.[2] This capacity to experience is an instinct which education, and particularly French education, carefully uproots or overlays, so that it takes years of disapprenticeship, or else the sturdy gift of a dunce, for the artistic nature to recover itself.

Berlioz was spared that struggle; he learned without losing sensitiveness. But he paid for the privilege. The home-reared child escapes narcotic schooling but stays too sheltered. Two years older than his oldest sister, with whom he was not especially congenial, Berlioz had too little of that rough-and-tumble with equals and contemporaries which toughens the outer, social skin. Study and solitude were his chief resource, besides the associations—usually with older companions—that music brought him. His relation with his father was close and tender, but even that was hardly free or demonstrative enough. To the end of their days Berlioz never addressed either parent otherwise than as *vous*. One's elders exacted a heavy toll of the staple Respect, and made behavior run ahead of emotions, so that childish impulse had to play hide-and-seek through the forms of a premature *savoir faire*. The same was true of religious belief, on which Hector's mother dwelt obsessively. Lacking a proper guide, Hector had to give himself wholly or not at all, and to be trusted in return before he could feel at ease. Then the pent-up feelings, gay or sad, would overflow, much to everyone's astonishment. His favorite within the family was his second sister, Adèle, who was lively and tender and unconventional like her father and himself. But owing to the difference in their ages, Hector could scarcely count on her companionship until his second return from Paris when he was twenty-five and she fourteen.

Despite all this, young Berlioz was not a hothouse plant. On the contrary, his broad shoulders and muscular physique made of him an indefatigable walker and climber. Though he had what is called the nervous temperament, his health can be described as robust, for "nerves," until they are overstrained, mean simply energy and responsiveness, not debility. One proof of Hector's health in childhood is that he remained a candid, open, and affectionate character despite the quietism of his father, the tantrums of his mother, and the opportunities of moping afforded by his freedom from school discipline.

As an adolescent, it is true, he went through a period of melancholy marked by religious fervor and a hopeless love affair. But these manifestations are by no means abnormal. Only their intensity at the time and their aftereffects betray an unusual nature. The story of the boy's infatuation is familiar to the readers of the *Memoirs*. During one of the vacations taken by the Berlioz family at Meylan, the maternal grandfather's house near Grenoble, there was an outdoor party where the military uncle and some neighboring young ladies were brought together. The officer was spirited and duly attentive, but he did not fall in love with either of the prizes submitted to his inspection: as someone has remarked, "he had been in Spain." It was his unhappy nephew Hector who conceived in secret a violent passion for Estelle Duboeuf, seven years his senior, and naturally disposed to treat Hector as a child. Rather wickedly, however, she teased her helpless and embarrassed admirer in order to amuse the company and possibly to awaken the captain to a sense of opportunity.

What the child saw was a tall, rather determined young woman of nineteen, with black hair and a somewhat provocatively cold glance. That she wore pink slippers—the first he had ever seen—remained indelibly fixed in his memory; which suggests how he kept his eyes shyly lowered. Yet perhaps the dominant fact was her association with the most beautiful landscape he knew—the Saint Eynard, which one climbs halfway to reach Meylan, and the broad valley of the Grésivaudan, crossed by two rivers and ringed with snow-capped peaks—a majestic panorama. Turning the experience at once into poetry, he christened her his *Stella Montis*, Estelle of the Mountain, an unattainable star, who centered in herself his need to adore, his vague but insistent wish for self-expression, and his religious feeling at the sight of nature. The varied consequences of this early attachment, unfolding through half a century, show it to have been something more than a laughable episode. It was rather the situation of another and equally romantic boy-poet, Dante, with a differently cast Beatrice.

What Berlioz does not tell us about this same formative period, is the rapid succession of deaths within the family. Between his sixth and ninth years, three members of the older generation died, including his maternal grandmother and a cousin on his father's side who lost his way and perished in a swamp. In 1815, within two days, his grandfather Joseph Berlioz died and his own eight-year-old sister Louise Virginie; and again, in 1818, his younger brother Louis-Jules-Félix. Then, in Hector's sixteenth year, occurred the presumable suicide of his friend and mentor, the son of his music teacher Imbert. It happened during vacation time, after a solemn and mysterious farewell taken by the older boy. The younger, returning and finding his friend gone, was never able to learn the exact truth.

These were but the beginning of a series of sudden losses that kept shattering his life until the end. If it is true, as one biographer supposes, that in playing about the house the boy sought to harden his feelings by handling the doctor's wired skeleton and staring at anatomical plates, it is even more certain that the succession of deaths, emphasized by the ritual black drapery, the visits of condolence and the restraint on laughter and games, played a part in the grown man's sense of life's fragility. His whole generation, as Musset and Vigny were to remark, had grown up in the atmosphere of war and sudden death and in the belief that extinction must be redeemed by heroism. Despite young Berlioz' true religious faith —perhaps because of it—this series of shocks, complicated as they were by the conflict between his infidel but loving father and his devout but harsh mother, left him subject to bouts of anxiety during which life seemed remote, outside himself.

Hector moreover seems quite early to have felt at one with the poets, who are traditionally cast by Fate for sorrow. His father's teaching and his own developing gifts made the identification natural enough, but the sentimentalism carried over from late eighteenth-century literature made melancholy worse. Reading the memoirs of Voltaire's protégé, Marmontel (which about the same time were bringing tears to the eyes of the young John Stuart Mill), responding to the gentle wails of the versifiers of the period, or to the grave accents of Chateaubriand's *Genius of Christianity,* strengthened in Hector the link between dark thoughts and artistic feelings.

From Chateaubriand's great work on what may be called

the poetry and passion of the Christian religion, the boy copied out in a notebook still extant a revealing passage about André Chénier. This fine poet had been executed by Robespierre in 1794 but his fame waited upon a proper edition of his works in 1820. In that year, the seventeen-year-old Berlioz, writing out the words and music of a song attributed to Chénier, made a note: "The author of these words was a young man who fell a victim to the French Revolution. This unhappy youth" (here Berlioz is quoting Chateaubriand), "on climbing the scaffold could not help exclaiming, as he struck his forehead, 'To die! when I feel something—there!' " The remark is doubtless apocryphal but the Keats-like fear is of the time and mood, and we shall find it again embodied in musical sound. For a youth endowed with imagination, the Red Terror did not seem very far in the past.

Nor was the Napoleonic legend very far in the future. Berlioz was eleven when, after the Emperor's first abdication, La Côte St. André was occupied by the Austrians. There was a short resistance to their inroad by partisans of the exiled Emperor; then came the usual resentment against the foreign troops; and shortly Napoleon returned from Elba. The incredible but lively apparition passed through Grenoble where he proclaimed himself a revolutionary soldier—an echo of his first glorious return from Italy in 1797—and on his journey north he drew near enough to La Côte so that his cannon were heard there. His defeat after one hundred days was like the fifth act of a tragedy. Everything after it was an anticlimax, and most of it proved sordid: a second Austrian occupation, followed by the appalling incidents of the White Terror. In Dauphiné an insurgent named Didier, whose chief crime was incompetence, was turned by popular hysteria into a formidable peril. He and twenty-four others were either slaughtered or guillotined, while the whole province quaked under false alarms.

Dr. Berlioz, never a party man, kept as aloof as he could, though higher authorities looked to him (as chief citizen) to take the lead in a regime of repression. Against his will, he was made Mayor. From then on the events as Hector saw them turned to tragicomedy. His father discovered a falsification in the accounts of his predecessor, who was also a royalist. Notifying his political friends, Dr. Berlioz silently withdrew. He did not forsee the slanders and squabbles which broke out and divided his unhappy town. By a twist of circumstance, the leader of the opposite faction was a friend of the family's, the father of Hector's closest companion, Charbonnel. The doctor gained nothing but worries from this brief tenure of an office he had not sought, and his son registered one more reason for his contemptuous dislike of politics.

Two years before, Waterloo had seemed to settle some uncertainties, including the survival of Hector's uncle, Captain Marmion; but the Bourbon Restoration, begun in blood and fear like the century, still had the overwhelming past to sort out, to forget, and, if possible, to turn to creative uses.

CHAPTER 2

MUSIC ON THE MOUNTAIN

I live not in myself, but I become
Portion of that around me; and to me,
High mountains are a feeling. . . .

Then stirs the feeling infinite, so felt
In solitude, where we are least alone;
A truth, which through our being then doth melt
And purifies from self: it is a tone,
The soul and source of music. . . .
BYRON, Childe Harold's Pilgrimage

The beginning of Berlioz' musical vocation was his discovery of an old flageolet in a bureau drawer. His father had played it in his own youth, and he taught Hector the fingering. Berlioz' inclination, it is clear, was marked even before he left for the seminary. Dr. Berlioz went on to teach his boy in a very lucid and logical way—as the pupil looked back on it—how to read notes and sing at sight. Soon the doctor bought Hector a flute, together with the standard method of Devienne. Then, wishing to provide more expert instruction, he arranged to have a local musician, one Imbert, give Hector two lessons a day.

Imbert was a violinist from the Lyon orchestra who had been brought to La Côte in order to lead the players of the National Guard and teach the children of the well-to-do. The revolution had encouraged the use of music—the singing of secular hymns and marching with military bands—as aids to propaganda for republicanism and war. This interest had continued under the Empire, and Imbert had been chosen by a local committee because he was versatile. He was guaranteed twelve pupils. Moreover his son had a gift for playing wind instruments and this would strengthen the chamber ensemble of amateurs. La Côte, without being a musical center, was at least not a tuneless dell.

Under Imbert's tuition the Berlioz boy developed his excellent voice and made rapid progress on the flute. In company with his teacher's son, he also tried his hand at other instruments—his clarinet is still extant. Then in 1819 came the mysterious disappearance of young Imbert. The father preferred to leave and was replaced by an Alsatian named Dorant. He taught Hector the guitar and attempted to do the same for the elder sister Nanci—but to no avail. In the Berlioz family, as we shall see, musical talent went with the male sex. There can be no doubt that Hector had great natural aptitude: his singing soon gave pleasure at social gatherings, and he entertained with complicated virtuoso pieces on the flute, such as Drouet's concertos. At neighboring dances he provided music on the guitar. Dorant shortly had to notify Dr. Berlioz that his lessons might just as well stop—the pupil knew as much as the master.[1]

Still, performing ability is by no means uncommon; creative power is another thing. What is worthy of remark at this stage, is not Berlioz' quickness and facility as an executant, but his spontaneous and persistent desire to compose. His eagerness for new music, not always easy to obtain, led him to improvise variations, supply accompaniments to well-known airs, or transform duets into larger scores. Notebooks have been preserved in which his earliest attempts to achieve variety and expressive force testify to an artistic instinct. He wrote at least two original quintets and one sextet, of which we know nothing except perhaps some of their melodies: two are known with certainty to have survived.

Certain biographers, finding that throughout this period there was no piano at La Côte, have concluded that Hector cannot have been properly initiated into the secrets of music. The fact is that there were very few pianos anywhere in the first two decades of the nineteenth century. The spread of the instrument for domestic use came after 1815, as the result of superior technology and many inventions. The first one in Berlioz' vicinage was bought by General de la Valette in 1818, and by that time Dr. Berlioz, like Pascal's father with the geometry book, withheld from his son the instrument that might too soon fix his career. The deprivation must not be regarded with the eyes of a much later period, when music and piano had become almost synonymous terms, and when highly organized music teaching had induced the belief that the art had to be learned learnedly through textbooks and the classics, Mozart, Haydn, and Beethoven. When Berlioz was born, Mozart was still considered a dangerous innovator and was little played in France; Haydn was still alive and very incompletely known; Beethoven was a synonym for cacophony and madness, whom even the younger German composers looked on with distrust. The classical tradition, in short, had not yet crystallized. And with respect to musical studies it is Berlioz, actually, who illustrates the "traditional" way to begin. He began, that is, like Haydn, Lully, Handel, Wagner, Elgar, and the great majority of musicians—with only local help and mother wit. Before the age of standardized, purchasable culture, the rule was to be self-taught or ill-taught, at least at first; young Mozart was an exception. Our institutional minds find it hard to believe that if all textbooks and teachers were annihilated, the art of music could be rediscovered, but we should make the effort to recall that *in the beginning* there was no G clef, no sonata form, not even an alphabet in which to say A B C D.

Apart from the merits and deficiencies of the musical establishment at La Côte, the place offered other musical resources that young Hector turned to profit. He himself has recounted with much charm what he called his first "musical impression." He was twelve and a half years old and celebrating his First Communion, on the same day as his sister, at the convent where Nanci was being educated. There, amid a cluster of young girls in bridal veils, he stood entranced by their voices, by the beauty of the spring day, and by the liturgy. He did not know that the motet sung on that occasion was based on an air from Dalayrac's opera *Nina, or the Woman Crazed with Love*. It was sweet and sad, and possibly appropriate to an act of wholesouled devotion. The church certainly afforded him many such "impressions," and long before he reached Paris Berlioz was at home in one ancient musical tradition. One thinks at once of Luther or of Thomas Hardy, reared on the hymns and dance tunes of a pious farming people—the purest source of many an artist's devotion to music. It has yet to be shown that the piano music of houses of ill fame, such as the young Brahms was forced to play and listen to, is a better start for a musical career.

After Sunday mass at La Côte, the string players repaired to the doctor's house where, with the aid of Hector and his friends, the company enjoyed a couple of hours of secular music. They played quartets by Haydn, Pleyel, and Catel, in addition to pieces by Berton, Boieldieu, or Martini, arranged or disarranged to suit the occasion. It was under the inspiration of such models and the demands of this chamber ensemble that by himself Hector composed six-part medleys now lost, and several original works for strings, including a flute quintet. This last proved too difficult for the group, but furnished one melody for a later work.

Apparently no one in the boy's entourage was qualified to help him in his creative efforts. His father, it is true, looked at what he wrote and gave his special approval to that flute melody, but these ambitious attempts to compose chamber music must have presented innumerable problems. The boy persevered. On seeing full-size sheets of score paper, he had exclaimed about the wonderful things one ought to be able to write for so many voices, and in his search for knowledge he had unearthed two treatises on harmony—Rameau's, which proved unintelligible since it was not meant for beginners but for theorists; and Catel's, the standard treatise of the period—with the aid of which he exercised his ear. But he did not receive much light of reason, for the book was true to its genre as then understood.

Yet this self-teaching was not valueless. The boy practiced the mental hearing of chords and their inversions on that essentially harmonic instrument, the guitar. Whatever mannerisms this may have left in his later handling of harmony, it gave to his musical idiom a character of unsought originality which is in pleasant contrast to the strainings after freedom of those who have to transcend a more common upbringing.

Limitations, as critical purists often remind us, have great virtues. In young Berlioz' circumstances, the virtue was the tremendous spur given to thinking about music, which presented itself to the boy composer in the form of real problems instead of lessons set. Suddenly, by dint of thinking and hearing, he caught the idea of voice-leading. The ultimate advantage of self-training is doubtless proportioned to the student's natural endowment. Without prejudging the result in Berlioz' case, we may note in passing the considered opinion of Bernard

Van Dieren, himself a great composer, that Berlioz had, "with the sole exception of Mozart, the most stupendous native gifts of the last few centuries."

In any case, this first phase of Berlioz' initiation into music was only half experimental, for he was not cast by fate on a desert island like Robinson Crusoe; or rather, like Crusoe, he had some aid from civilization. On the one hand, he had ready-made models in the printed music of the day (including some sheets from Gluck's *Orpheus*), and on the other, he worked under the natural restraint of the musical circle for which he wrote. What he produced, though no doubt clumsy and full of technical malpractice, could not be wholly without shape or meaning, or he would have lost the regard of his players, all of whom were older than he and ready to ask that he stop wasting their time. It is a fair guess that the quintet of his composition which the group found too difficult was made so not by its incoherence, but by its originality: at a further guess, it was the rhythm that undid them.

When Berlioz at fifteen finally gathered together some pieces of his own and offered them by letter to the Paris publishers, his folly was only relative. He was following an impulse which his subsequent history shows to have been sound: he knew that he was meant for music. This being so, if he managed to get some things published, however few or modest, he would have an argument against the career of medicine which his father was choosing for him. The source of melody was in him and it bubbled up with a force independent of his will. We know this not only from the operation of the gift in later years, but also from a remark he drops concerning his earliest tunes. There must have been a good many, for he says: "My youthful essays in composition were of a melancholy cast; almost all my melodies were in the minor mode. I was aware of the defect but struggled against it in vain."

At the time, no doubt, he was not aware that the character of these melodies was in the highest degree unusual: his musical utterance was completely fresh and underivative. In him the talent that makes a man think in sounds took the form not alone of producing melodies, but of creating a new idiom, a new *melos*—an accomplishment which in the history of music has been reserved to very few. Concertgoers familiar with the *Symphonie Fantastique* will remember the theme of the largo introduction of the first movement. This melody dates from Berlioz' twelfth year, and it is enough to show that even then the turn of his musical mind was perfectly distinct. Composed to fit some contemporary verses, the tune resembles nothing in the fashionable romances of the day. Hector had found in his father's library the works of the poet Florian, who is still read for his charming fables, but whose more ambitious and sugary pastorals were the works in Berlioz' hands.[2] He set several episodes, but one especially appealed to him—"*Estelle et Némorin.*" The boy identified the heroine with *his* Estelle, and himself even more easily with the lovesick swain. The melody came with its hesitant pauses and plaintive intervals, rising passionately at the conclusion of the first quatrain:

Je vais donc quitter pour jamais
Mon doux pays, ma douce amie,
Loin d'eux je vais trainer ma vie
Dans les pleurs et dans les regrets! [3]

The other boyhood melody that recurs in Berlioz' mature work is the second subject of his *Francs-Juges* overture. Its family likeness with still another, the *idée fixe* of the *Symphonie Fantastique,* has suggested to T. S. Wotton that the three occurred together, two being variants or accompaniments of one of them. If these three melodies did grow from a common germ, we are confronted with an extraordinary fact: the Estelle melody cited above is *sui generis* in the Berliozian manner; the *idée fixe* is its derivative but has something Beethovenian about it; while the *Francs-Juges* second subject makes one readily think of Weber or Schubert. Now Berlioz' first tune needs nothing to account for it except his genius, but the other two require a miracle to explain how a boy aged perhaps fourteen could, in his rural isolation, chime in with the melodic idiom of two composers of whom he had not heard a single note, nor even yet the name. The historian is tempted to see a traveling *Zeitgeist* at work, with ruled paper in his portmanteau.

Fortunately, it is not necessary to find material causes for the products of art. It suffices to point out the elements, their interaction and coincidences. Church music, we saw, was one of these elements in Berlioz' background and contemporary song writing was another. But music lived outdoors as well in Berlioz' corner of old France. The hunts met frequently and observed the ancient and complex ritual of horn calls—a rich source of melody, echoes of which will be found in later Berlioz scores. Again, shepherds in the mountains could be heard singing or piping to their flocks the traditional *ranz des vaches;*[4] countrywomen—and even Mme. Berlioz—sang folk tunes, as did artisans plying their trade. French folk tunes, it is well known, have long intermingled with church music through their use in the sequences or hymns, which unlike the liturgy have rhythm and marked melodiousness. One of the chants Berlioz particularly liked, the psalm "When Israel came out of Egypt," is thought to be a folk song as old as Charlemagne. Berlioz' fondness for modal effects in his own music is therefore grounded in a double national tradition. And possibly, on his way through Grenoble at the time of the Peninsular Campaign, the boy also heard the Spanish prisoners singing their native songs in the twilight.

In short, an ancient popular art shaped his early taste. Had Berlioz been born in the same place with the same gifts three centuries before, it is clear that he would have been an anonymous maker of tunes while tanning leather or pruning vines —and no less a musician. The force of early memories and natural influences must not be exaggerated, even in the study of a mind as precociously formed as Berlioz'. But it is worth considering a little further the emotion he felt at his First Communion and in similar circumstances. In speaking of the church ceremony, he himself uses the phrase, "my first musical impression," and this may seem like a slip of the pen; for the child had had musical *impressions* and even musical training before that day. The drum he played at school must have had the power to impress, his flute playing also, and since we are speaking of childish feelings, we should not forget the local brass band, conducted in public in the *halles* of La Côte years before Imbert's time by one Bouchmann.

What Berlioz means about the ceremony is that it was his first experience of a complete musical *occasion*—one might almost say his first musical drama. Its impressiveness lay in the use of appropriate music for a meaningful ceremony in man's life. The memory he kept so vividly as to write of it with emotion thirty-five years later reveals an instinctive choice. From the outset he felt that music was one of the necessities of existence, not a decoration or an artificial pleasure. Hence there must be fit occasions, of which church ritual was one kind, when music could be enjoyed for itself, though in a setting. This is, properly speaking, the dramatic view of music. It is equidistant from the two more usual views—the first, that music is to comfort man at any time, a gentle accompaniment to sociability. This might be called the courtly or monarchical view. The second is that music exists in a prepared vacuum as an object of contemplation, to which one "subscribes" annually as one of The Arts. This is the modern institutional view. Berlioz' instinct was true to the oldest of the three traditions. Young Hector had every chance to follow the bourgeois version of the courtly idea—music for sociability—and to become just another French composer of parlor songs and light opera. Instead, he found music closer to nature than to the parlor, and he obeyed his temperament in following the muse to her native haunts, where religion had already become her ally.

We know from a second autobiographical description that the rural festival of Rogation Days greatly moved the sixteen-year-old youth. The rite, it so happens, was first established in the very region of Berlioz' birth by the fifth-century bishop of Vienne, Mamertus. Designed to end a local blight, the ceremony may have been a revival of pagan practices. It is a fertility prayer and consists of a procession to invoke the aid of the saints. Three days are devoted to the blessing of all the fields of the parish, which is dotted with improvised outdoor altars embellished with flowers. Green boughs simulate an apse, and bright blossoms surround the images and relics laid on the covered trestles. Women and children follow the priest singing the litany of the saints: it is another occasion for popular art ranging from rustic decoration to song.

In alluding to this scene, the mature Berlioz recalls the musical effect it had upon him once when he experienced a violent attack of his lifelong "homesickness." The adolescent boy was in fact near home, lying in the fields reading a novel. But sudden melancholy seized him, filling his soul with the conviction that "home" was elsewhere. He could see the "slight motion of the grain field under the soft morning breeze"; he heard "the call of the quail to their mates, the bunting singing his joy high up on a poplar; while the mountains, struck by the early sun, flashed back the light in tremendous beams. . . ." The youth surrendered himself to nature only too completely. "Life," he adds curiously, "was evidently outside me, far away, very far."

When the grown man recorded his frequent indebtedness to nature for artistic inspiration, it was in the same contradictory mood of isolation and communion. Paralyzing at the moment, the sight of field and mountain was, when recollected, the source of another and a truer life than his own. "I am but a heavy clod, bound to the earth," said he, but "nature sings." Like Weber and Beethoven, Berlioz associated certain movements in his music with landscape, possibly with a particular sight of a familiar scene.[5] In the *Symphonie Fantastique,* the pastoral adagio is marked "In the fields"; in the second symphony, *Harold in Italy,* the opening is "In the mountains," and still later, in the *Corsair* overture and *Les Troyens,* it is the sea which is, not indeed depicted, but adumbrated. When such an ideal analogy obtains between nature and the work of an artist, we are bound to ask about the characteristic aspect of his native grounds. In Berlioz the answer to this question is especially instructive.

La Côte St. André, that is, the actual ridge named after Saint Andrew, is a steep elevation of eight hundred feet stretching east and west, perpendicular to the Rhone valley. The village clings to its northern slope, sheltered from the sirocco, and overlooks the large plain of Bièvre, where Hannibal is said to have encamped before crossing the Alps. From any point of vantage in good season, the foreground shows the green of field, meadow, and vineyard. In summer the soil is dry, yellow like near-by Provence; contours are clear and sharp. The sky is of a deep blue, thick enough to cut. To the south and west, the horizon is bounded by the purple heights of the Cévennes; to the east by a double screen, of hills first, and then of dimmer peaks in the distance which are the Dauphiné Alps: one is looking towards Grenoble and Savoy.

These shapes and colors are as much a lure to discovery as a barrier to vision. On whatever spot they dwell, high or low, the Dauphinois are perforce climbers; though tillers of the soil, they are not stationary beings rooted in an acre, and for Berlioz among them, excursions began young. The family had its livelihood at La Côte but its pleasure at Les Jacques and at Meylan, both near Grenoble, on opposite sides of the great valley through which flow the majestic Isère and the hurtling Drac.

The sights there are of vasty heights, intersecting valleys, piled-up forests, clouds massed and dispersing, saw-tooth edges, pointed ice caps. Color is always changing, from the gray-green poplars lining the river bank and ruffled by sudden gusts, to the bare rock walls that kaleidoscope the effects of sun and sky. The voices, louder than man's, are of mountain torrents, sudden storms, and shifting winds. All these, with the sharp dips of temperature or light, constituted for Berlioz one meaning, the earliest and most impressive, of the word nature.

The forms of space, which are common to nature and the graphic arts, can obviously affect the mind of the budding musician as well as of the painters, particularly forms like those just described, whose relations are in perpetual movement—contrapuntal, if the metaphor may be allowed. There is at any rate, a striking correspondence between Alpine scenery and Berlioz' sense of form: sharpness of definition in his melodic line, as well as the protracted, nonrepeating length of that line; brusque interruptions and changes of mood; balance by asymmetry rather than by identity; sensitiveness to coloring and to the simultaneity of contrasting effects (light in one patch while darkness invades the rest); and above all, perhaps, a sense of scale which achieves the heroic and grandiose without giantism.

These unmistakable features are without doubt among the causes of distaste which Berlioz' music inspires in perfectly sincere listeners. They may not word their objections in the language of geology—since Berlioz is not painting scenes but at most following an ingrained type of design—but it is this underlying pattern that displeases, for it does not appear in the same alluring guise to everyone.

In the period of his adolescent *Sehnsucht,* at any rate, Hector was not pondering esthetic problems. As far as he knew, he was heading the opposite way—toward a medical career. Dr. Berlioz had both reasoned with him and bribed him. If before going to Paris the boy applied himself, with his cousin Alphonse, to a first course of human anatomy, Hector would be given a flute of the latest model, "with all the keys." The boy, overcome by shyness and fear and temptation, yielded and went off in solitude to purge his soul of conflicting emotions.

Then with Alphonse Robert he bent over the life-size plates spread out under the doctor's finger and handled the driest of "dry preparations." But somehow this new knowledge came hard. It gave Hector creepy feelings to recollect or imagine the last struggles of the dying. Alphonse, who was a good violinist and with whom Hector talked music on their rambles together, was entirely at ease, competent, retentive. He was to become a distinguished Paris physician in whose life music was a diversion. Dr. Berlioz hoped for precisely this as a future for his son.

But before Hector could be admitted by the Paris Faculty he had to have his bachelor's degree, and in March, 1821, he went to Grenoble to pass his examinations. His success there speaks well for the thoroughness of his father's teaching in science and the liberal arts. Shortly thereafter, for the festival of Corpus Christi, Hector gathered his best instrumentists to accompany the cortege. Later that evening they played at his house for twenty guests. There was dancing and jollification in honor of the eldest son who would soon leave the paternal roof. A second son, Prosper, was not quite one year old and his brief musical role was reserved for a later day.

The remainder of the year passed quietly. On the Fifth of May, a date which soon concerned poets and subsequently Berlioz as composer, Napoleon died at Saint Helena. During the summer months at La Côte Hector finished an interesting guitar accompaniment to the romance *"Fleuve du Tage,"* the first "composition" of Berlioz' youth that is still extant. In October he got his passport for inland travel, and with Alphonse took the dusty diligence that was to bring him in about a week to the capital.

CHAPTER 3

OPERA AND CONSERVATOIRE

And ever as he went he swept a lyre
Of unaccustomed shape. . . .

SHELLEY

The music-haunted youth who arrived in Paris early in November 1821 was still within a few weeks of reaching his eighteenth birthday. Though he was not to grow beyond middle height, he had not yet attained his full stature, and his pale face showed only an adolescent fuzz. His hair, always abundant and overhanging a broad forehead, was of a fiery blond color—not red. His eyes were deep-set and of a clear blue that seemed to darken with changing thoughts; his nose prominent and high-bridged; his mouth wide, thin and even-lipped as befitted a flutist, all these features being mobile and expressive, like the energetic bearing of the whole body.

We can guess at his first impressions of the capital from the feelings that the mingled prospects of medicine and music must have aroused. There may also have been a touch of distaste for the city, such as his compatriot Stendhal had felt two decades before. "The surroundings," said that other self-aware Dauphinois, "seemed to me horribly ugly; there were no mountains at all!" And when he opened his window on an inner court there were not even trees. Yet the Paris of 1800 or 1820 was a city of modest size, from which it was easy to escape into the country. Montrouge was recommended to patients in need of fresh air, and as we shall shortly see, game could be snared within walking distance of the student's lodgings.

The capital had lost something of its animation since the days of the great Emperor. The Triumphal Arch was unfinished and looked in ruins; the "Marseillaise" and most other warlike symbols were prohibited. Not more than three years had passed since Madame de Staël's book on the revolution had made it possible to speak of that event in favorable terms. The restored Bourbons, while committed to a charter of liberties, lived in fear of all new ideas, whether liberal or Bonapartist, or simply modern and alien. And though Louis XVIII had brought back something of the stability and the elegance of the old regime, France was still feared by Europe as the incurable enemy of peace; even French culture was subversive. From time to time these fears seemed justified by outbursts of the old violence, as when the Duc de Berry was murdered in February 1820. Oddly enough, this incident had musical consequences: the duke was stabbed in the Opera House; the awkward architecture of the lobby interfered with his being helped, and he bled to death while the show went on and crowds milled around. The archbishop made it a condition of administering the last rites that the theater be torn down; and this led to the building of the new house which was to entice Berlioz away from medicine.

On first arriving, Berlioz and his cousin took up quarters in the rue St. Jacques, on the left bank. Hector's allowance of one hundred and twenty francs a month was for the time a generous budget which enabled him to live like what he was —a son of the landed gentry about to enter a profession. But his first practical taste of medicine was not alluring. The lectures interested him, but when his cousin bought a "subject" and Berlioz had to join him at the dissecting room, "the sight of that human charnel house, those scattered limbs, grinning heads and open skulls; the blood-soaked filth through which we walked, and the revolting odor of the place, with its sparrows fighting over bits of lung, and rats gnawing bones in the corners, so filled me with horror that I leaped out of the nearest window and ran breathless all the way home as if pursued by Death and all her train." [1]

His mind in a whirl, he contemplated "a thousand follies" in order to escape his fate. But twenty-four hours' reflection gave his will a chance to overcome his sensibility. He returned to the task and pursued it faithfully for about a year. To fortify himself, he would turn the most repellent of his duties into occasions for humor, singing grotesquely appropriate words from famous airs as he dissected. The macabre humor of the medical student in fact never deserted him and the vocabulary of the morgue remained a part—not the most attractive—of his literary fantasy. But distaste did not keep him from making friends with one of his teachers, Amussat, to whom he remained attached throughout the years to come.[2] The lectures of Gay-Lussac on experimental electricity also held Berlioz' attention and laid the foundation of his lifelong interest in science. For pleasure, too, Berlioz attended courses in literature and history at the Collège de France.

What he reports to his sister Nanci about the historian Lacretelle does not show the lecturer as profound, but it does show the boy's naive appreciation of drama: "The first day he made upon us all, I may say, a cruel impression by recounting the assassination of Henry IV; then, after depicting in lively colors the trouble and disorder of the beginning of Louis XIII's reign, he gave me great pleasure by contrasting with it the composure of the Minister Sully in his retreat . . . Called to the court by Louis XIII, this worthy man brought laughter and ridicule upon himself by appearing in old-fashioned dress; whereupon Sully, approaching the throne and looking with disdain at the wretches, said, 'Sire, when your father the King of blessed memory did me the honor of bidding me to court, he took care beforehand to dismiss the buffoons and mountebanks . . .'

"As for the Opera, now, that's another thing. I don't think I can give you the least notion of it. . . ."

The jump from the history lecture to the Opera is a faithful reflection of the writer's mind: Hector had not let many days elapse before pursuing his Muse; he had become a concert- and operagoer. Nor was he alone in flirting with art while destined for a paying profession. The early 1820's was the time when the geniuses whose works were to fill the first half of the nineteenth century in France were finding themselves and one another. They were fighting their families for the right to be artists, and sitting at the feet of a few pioneering elders. At Chateaubriand's country house or at Nodier's Arsenal Library in Paris, those destined to be—in Henley's phrase—the "glorious boys of 1830" were nursing their talents. Within the next few years Berlioz would meet Victor Hugo, Vigny, Balzac, Delacroix, Gérard de Nerval, Sainte-Beuve, and the brothers Deschamps.

Meanwhile, like them, he was fulfilling Stendhal's assertion that the only hope of art lay in the youths who came to Paris from the provinces in their late teens, with their heads full of antiquated ideas but with their convictions unblunted. This notion was part of Stendhal's witty defense of Shakespeare in the name of energy and realism in drama. But having endured twenty-five years of war the older citizens of France had no use for energy and drama. In 1822 they hissed Shakespeare and pelted the English actors who brought his works to Paris. The gifted, ambitious boys like Berlioz were as yet too young and bewildered to make a stand or even to know exactly where they stood. All they knew was that the postwar world offered them little scope, and those who had energy without special talents, as Balzac observed, could only choose dissipation and intrigue.

In music, as it happened, the "antiquated ideas" that young Berlioz harbored were not wholly out of fashion. After Napoleon's restriction on theaters and the Bourbons' shutting down of the *Conservatoire,* music was enjoying a renaissance. Just as Berlioz was setting foot in Paris a moderately progressive musician, François Habeneck, had been made director of the newly built Opera House. Another, Antoine Choron, had opened a school whose performances of sacred music formed the taste of a whole generation; while the elder Garcia was beginning to train a new group of singers of whom we shall hear further. Instrumental music, it is true, was less favored, caught as it was in the transition between the private patron's orchestra and the establishment of regular public institutions. But chamber music was rather more readily available, and at several smaller theaters—the Odéon, the Gymnase, and the Nouveautés—French comic opera was trying to resist the invasion of the Italians and their precocious maestro, Gioacchino Rossini.

Both because of the brightness and verve of his music, and because of the zeal of many Frenchmen for importations, Rossini soon became a Parisian idol. Literary men took him up and although his lively scores violated dramatic truth, he was hailed as the Raphael and Michelangelo of music—that is, as a lyrical and a dramatic genius combined. As always happens in the revolutions of opera, past beauties seemed feeble when compared with the latest "effects." Rossini enchanted the ear with his famous *crescendo,* his sparkling melodies and bubbling violin triplets. The truth was that a new clientele—indeed a new social class—was learning music, and learning it at the best of public schools, the one that relies on visual aid.

This "school" in two senses did not find favor with young Berlioz, whose taste in its broad outlines was already set. All he knew impelled him in the opposite direction, toward an older master—Gluck. For what Berlioz had heard and played and pondered at La Côte came from the French disciples and imitators of Gluck, and Berlioz' background of dramatic thought was classical and religious. To him the Italian plots lacked true musical "occasions," and mishandled those afforded. The few pages of Gluck's *Orpheus* that he had conned at home had not ceased to stir him, nor had he forgotten what he had read somewhere on the composer's life, on his orchestral effects, on the grandeur of the tragic poems he had composed.

Fortunately the French repertory did not succumb to the new Italian opera until about 1830, so that in these important years for Berlioz he was able to hear and to study at repeated performances, not only Gluck's *Armide, Orphée, Alceste,* and the two *Iphigénies,* but also the works of the Gluckist school—Salieri's *Danaides,* Catel's *Bayadères,* Méhul's *Stratonice,* Sacchini's *Oedipe,* Berton's *Virginie,* Kreutzer's *Abel,* and what is more: Spontini's *Vestale.*

Certain features made these spectacles particularly impressive. The Opera and Opéra-Comique numbered a few singers of unusual merit: Mme. Branchu, short and no longer young, but a great artist noted for her dramatic delivery and her mastery of dynamics; the baritone Martin; Dérivis with his powerful bass, and Adolphe Nourrit, a young tenor whom Garcia had trained and whom Berlioz was later to befriend. Stage effects, moreover were improving. Daguerre's diorama, a partly transparent painting for use with special lighting, encouraged the imaginative treatment of scenery, in place of the stiff eighteenth-century sets with their symmetrical balance and fixed vanishing point. About the same time gas lighting replaced the Argand lamps, the house was darkened during the show, and the practice established of lowering the curtain between the acts so as to preserve the unity of mood while shifting scenes.

But for Berlioz the opera meant something more than a

show. It meant the revelation of the orchestra as an instrument of dramatic music. This power was first disclosed to him at a performance of *Iphigeneia in Tauris,* probably late in November 1821. Having just told his sister that he could give her no notion of what opera was like, he goes on:

Short of fainting, I could not feel a stronger impression than that of seeing Gluck's masterpiece *Iphigeneia.* Imagine first of all an orchestra of eighty musicians who perform with such perfect ensemble that one would think it was a single instrument. The opera begins. You see a vast plain (I tell you, the illusion is complete) and farther still, the sea. The orchestra presages a storm; black clouds descend on the plain—the theatre is only lighted by flashes, in the most telling and truthful fashion. There is a moment of silence; no actor on the stage; the orchestra is dully murmuring; it seems as if you heard the soughing of the wind (you know how in winter you can hear it speak!). Gradually, the excitement grows, the storm bursts, and you discover Orestes and Pylades in chains, led by the barbarians of Tauris who sing a fearful chorus: "We must have blood to atone for our crimes." It's about the limit of what one can stand: I defy the hardest-hearted being a stay unmoved at the sight of these two wretches longing for death as their greatest hope . . . and when it turns out that it is Orestes' sister Iphigeneia, the priestess of Diana, who must sacrifice her brother, why, don't you see, it is ghastly.

I can't describe to you even approximately the feeling of horror one feels when Orestes, overwhelmed, falls down and says, "Calm is restored to my breast." Half asleep, he sees the shade of his mother whom he has killed; she is hovering about with other shades holding infernal torches above his head. And the orchestra! It's all in the orchestra. If you could only hear how all the situations are depicted in it, especially when Orestes is calm: there is a long hold in the violins suggestive of tranquillity—very *piano;* but below, the basses murmur like the remorse which, despite his calm, throbs in the heart of the parricide.

But I forget myself. Farewell, dear sister; forgive me these digressions and be assured that your brother loves you with all his heart. Give my love to everybody at home.

Dated two days after Berlioz' eighteenth birthday, this letter doubtless conceals from both sender and recipient the inevitable decision to give up medicine for music. At the same time it reveals the intentness with which the aspiring composer spied out the relation between dramatic and orchestral thought. Hector soon found out that the library of the Royal Conservatoire was open to the public, and he used it before and after each performance to analyze the scores with his special purpose in view. He copied out passages, compared editions, in short mastered his subject. That is how he came to lead, in behalf of Gluck and his other favorites, a kind of claque actuated by purely artistic motives. As he gained self-confidence he appointed himself the censor of musical morals: the anecdotes are often quoted of his standing up in the pit and shouting, "It's a piccolo, you wretch!" when the part was played on the ordinary flute; and again, "Where are the trombones?" when they missed their entrance. His battle against arrangers and perverters of musical truth had begun.

Berlioz thus opened his public career very young, having himself provoked the first skirmishes. Yet however it may look to us, the actions of this barely citified mountaineer were neither unique nor meaningless. Not only his friends—young men of good family—but other artists and even casual strangers responded to these protests against routine or convention. As a phase of Hector's inner life, the matter is equally clear. He felt a strong daemonic impulse—his genius—which he tried to repress for reasons of conscience: his family trusted him to pursue an established career. But that family had also bred in the boy a shyness which only an effort of will could conquer. Until his personality was formed, the struggle of these elements was doubtless an ungainly sight; and balance was achieved rather slowly because, unlike the ordinary youth, he was not exclusively concerned with himself but with his art. As Bernard Shaw said of his own similar predicament: "I had not then tuned the Shavian note to any sort of harmony, and I have no doubt [others] found me discordant, crudely self-assertive, and insufferable."

None the less the young men whom Berlioz gathered together into a Gluckist party all felt his personal charm and the strength that comes of knowledge allied to conviction. The mild poet Humbert Ferrand became his earliest confidant; the aristocratic Augustin de Pons, the politically influential Albert du Boys, the devout musician d'Ortigue; another poet (who knew English) Thomas Gounet, and another cousin, Auguste Berlioz, soon formed a loyal band. They shared their leisure hours in discussion at one another's rooms or at "choice dinners" when they were in funds. Three of the group remained Hector's friends for life.

Meantime, Berlioz also led the social life of a well-connected youth. Friendly families in Paris—as well as the Marmion uncle who moved freely from his regimental base at Beauvais—saw to it that Hector frequented the fashionable houses and was invited to dances. "You may think," wrote Berlioz to his sister, "that these affairs are very different from ours—not at all. The only difference is that instead of having sixteen people there are sixty, and the floor is so crowded that . . . one must always study where to put down one's feet. Dress is uniformly white for the ladies and black for the men. The orchestra! You probably imagine it superb. Well! it does not begin to compare with ours. Just think: two violins and a flageolet. Isn't it pitiable? two violins and a flageolet, and those three wretches could only play contredanses taken from the ballets I've heard at the opera: you can imagine the contrast. . . .

"The next day we went to hear Martin in *Azémia* and *Les voitures versées.* That was my compensation. I absorbed all that music. I thought of you, sister, and of the pleasure you would have hearing all this . . . I tell you I would have thrown my arms around Dalayrac had I been near his statue when I heard the air—for which one cannot find a fit adjective—'Thy love, oh sweetest daughter.' I felt nearly the same impression as when at the Opera I heard in *Stratonice* 'Pour your grief into your father's bosom.' But I cannot undertake to describe such music to you." [3]

Just one year after the beginning of his medical studies, politics for the first and last time served Berlioz' interests: the medical school was shut down. For the past ten months governmental repression had gone on, liberal plots were discovered everywhere, and purges finally reached the seats of learning. Lecturers were dismissed regardless of their subject matter: the brilliant young historian Guizot lost his chair—but the brilliant young musician found his freedom. When anatomy resumed its rights after three months, Berlioz was dissecting chords, not corpses.

At the library of the Conservatoire he had met a student slightly older than himself named Gerono, of whom little is to be said except that he was the go-between who brought together Berlioz and his teacher Lesueur. It is likely that even before the end of his medical studies, Berlioz had begun to set to music a poem by the popular Millevoye, "The Arab Mourning His Steed." When he decided to approach Lesueur, he submitted this work, adding to it—a characteristic touch—another piece in the form of a three-part canon: professors, he doubtless surmised, like to look on technique bare.

Lesueur's report was encouraging and, in retrospect, very farsighted: "There is a good deal of warmth and dramatic movement in your cantata but you do not yet know how to write, and besides, your harmony is so full of faults that it would be useless to point them out. Gerono will do you the kindness to inform you of our principles of harmony, and as soon as you know them well enough to follow me, you can be one of my pupils." Either Gerono was a genius at teaching or else it was the pupil who had the genius to learn, for in a few weeks Berlioz had sufficiently mastered "our principles" (derived from Rameau) to sit at the professor's feet.

Jean-François Lesueur, then a man of sixty-two, was with Cherubini the most celebrated teacher-composer in France. A grandnephew of Louis XIV's court painter, Lesueur began at sixteen the career of church musician. He rose to the headship of the chapel of Notre Dame before the revolution, and there put into effect his original views about sacred music. The controversy that ensued led him to write two essays, after which he retired from his post to a country retreat, but not for long. During the revolution he returned to active life as a composer of operas, one of which was highly successful and earned him official rewards. He took part in the foundation and direction of the Conservatoire in 1795, became Bonaparte's First Chapel-Master, and achieved further success with his grand opera, *Les Bardes,* in the year of the coronation. His eminence saving him from reprisals by the Bourbons, he was reinstalled as teacher of composition in the Conservatoire from 1818 to his death in 1837.

Lesueur and Berlioz soon found they had much in common and became full of respect and devotion for each other. They admired Napoleon and revered Virgil; they shared a natural bent toward dramatic music and religious subjects, as well as a fondness for folk melodies; both had a detailed knowledge of Gluck's scores. Lesueur was an inquiring mind who had studied plainsong and developed a theory of ancient Greek music which for a time his pupil adhered to. In both men musical passion was not incompatible with an intellectual interest in history, modern literature, and classical scholarship. Lesueur moreover knew at first hand the difficulties of the composer's career in a centralized state, and he was generous enough to want to help the young. Finally, his artistic integrity and firm character also found echoes in the soul of his new pupil.

Of this new connection the Berlioz family at La Côte did not hear for some time. The dutiful son had been sending home books and knickknacks as ordered, and in his letters had only once expressed to his father a desire to devote himself entirely to composition. Dr. Berlioz answered with kind but strong arguments about the trials and uncertainties of success in the arts. Hector had therefore kept up his attendance at medical lectures, while working steadily at composition. What time was left, Hector spent at the library reading scores and at various theaters hearing them. Arising from this, musical partisanship was plunging him into a third career, that of musical journalism.

It was the age of faith in the printed sheet so intimately described in Balzac's *Lost Illusions.* One of those sheets, *Le Corsaire,* was a daily devoted to all the arts, including ladies' fashions, yet with a special interest in music. This was shown in its masthead by an allegorical female head garnished with violins and flutes. Music was then deemed a lively topic for newspapers because it combined personal news and lively feelings. Accordingly in the *Corsaire* for August 12, 1823, Berlioz' first essay appeared. He had been aroused by an anonymous dialogue in which the Italian opera was praised at the expense of the French. The admirer of Gluck in this tendentious conversation was called *Crifort,* which is to say "Loud Noise," whereas the champion of Rossini took pride, as the custom was, in the name of *Dilettante*—so to say: "true connoisseur." Berlioz' anonymous victim had shown his amateurishness by imputing "love of noise" to his opponents—the eternal and unprovable complaint of those who dislike a particular musical idiom. So "Hector B.," as he signed his reply, carried war into his territory by exaggerating Rossini's faults and restating Gluck's methods and intentions.

The readers of the *Corsaire* could not suspect that this confident champion of Gluck was a provincial fellow of nineteen who had been in Paris barely a year and a half, and to whom before that date all opera scores were but a distant mirage. The modern reader is more astonished still. For here is the full-fledged Berlioz, his musical creed already clear in outline: though angered, he is punctilious; he shows concern about the minutest details of performance and the grading of sonorities, even to the placing of instruments in the hall; he discusses style in orchestration; expresses alarm at the rise in concert pitch and its effect on the singers; deplores the instrumental crudities of the Italians, which ruin voice production or obscure the melodic line; finally, he argues the possibility of creating drama in music by treating the orchestra as a collection of independent groups of timbres.

Lesueur's teaching can hardly be credited with so much influence so soon, unless we assume, as we should, a pre-existing harmony of views in the disciple. The article winds up with an aggressive confession of faith, backed up by cool self-assurance: "Rossini's operas taken together can hardly bear comparison with one line of Gluck's recitative, three measures of melody by Mozart or Spontini, or the least chorus by Lesueur . . . I have read the scores and looked into the matter before passing judgment." If in our mind's eye we see the callow youth, this effusion has a flavor of comedy; but Berlioz's already mature prose commands our respect. Precise, witty, and well-paced, the somewhat stilted period style hides the faults of overinsistence and naivete.

Berlioz was aware of inexperience in everything but his feelings. It therefore struck him as logical to gain experience and express those feelings in one operation which would test his creative powers. In short he must find a librettist who would give him something to compose, and afterwards, a chance to hear the result. This empirical attitude was in keeping with his upbringing, his character, and his epoch. There were, it is true, other motives to the search for a libretto. Like his post-napoleonic contemporaries he believed not only in art but in glory, and all agreed with Milton that love of fame was a noble failing. Finally, Hector also felt he must persuade his father that music could be a career.

The son therefore wrote to the composer Kreutzer a sincere but laughable letter of extravagant praise on first hearing the opera *Abel's Death*. This bid for an interview having remained fruitless, Berlioz next wrote to Andrieux (an academician whose lectures he was attending) asking him point-blank for a libretto. His curiosity aroused, the old gentleman came in person to deliver his answer and found the would-be composer in chambers, cooking his lunch. The conversation, flavored with the odor of fried onion, brought out the fact that Andrieux was a Gluckist, though not so fanatical as Berlioz. The elder teased his host and ultimately confessed that he felt too old to write an operatic love story. At his age he should be thinking rather of a requiem mass. Undaunted, Hector approached Gerono, and recalling his old love for Florian's *Estelle* persuaded his friend to base a plot on the romance. The thing was done and the music written—"as ridiculous a score," said Berlioz later, "as the text and rimes of Gerono." At the same time or soon after, Berlioz himself fashioned and composed a series of scenes based on a current drama, *Beverley, or the Gambler.*[4]

In the end, Berlioz had recourse to his master—or at least to his master's principles, which suggested a sacred text, presumably from the Vulgate, but chosen with an eye to situations at once dramatic and musical. Berlioz chose *The Crossing of the Red Sea,* wrote his own words, which he then set as effectively as he could.[5] Lesueur looked at the score and thought well enough of it to arrange for its performance. All was made ready for December 28, 1823—virtually a celebration of Berlioz' twentieth birthday. One hundred players and as many voices were to gather in the Church of St. Roch, and Valentino, of the Opera, would conduct.

Hector at once notified his father, but soon had to admit discomfiture: the performers, unpaid, had not shown up in expected numbers at the first rehearsal, and those that came were discouraged by the mistakes in the parts copied out by amateur hands. Valentino did his best to rally them, but the difficulties proved too great. As the conductor left, he assured the composer of his help at the first opportunity. Berlioz had learned a lesson about the military character of musical leadership: morale and materiel must be in perfect order for effective mass action.

Meantime, Berlioz had published a second article in *Le Corsaire*—again on the dilettanti—in which a new theme emerges: his dislike of imitative music. He inquires why the admirers of Italian opera "can hardly breathe from sheer emotion" at the pathos of Rossini's *Gazza ladra,* and yet are unmoved by Gluck. Berlioz answers with irony: "Because they sing so badly at the Opera, content as they are to be dramatic and sometimes sublime. How ridiculous is Madame Branchu in the role of Clytemnestra! Why, she does not add a single note to her part, not even in the aria of Jove and his thunderbolts, though on the first verse a 12-note roulade would admirably depict lightning and on the second a little *martellato* ['hammered' notes] would prettily stress the crushing of the

Greeks. On the words 'burning ships' a chromatic scale of trills would imitate the whirling flames:—those are the things the *dilettanti* expect from singers, and as long as Madame Branchu will confine herself to making her audience shudder and weep, the *dilettanti* will say she howls. . . . As for the orchestra at the opera, it is fashionable to call it noisy, without inquiring whether it is the composer's or the performers' fault. . . . The objectors never read the scores—for a very good reason which is easily surmised . . ."

The day after this blast, Berlioz was reaping the fruit of his continued labors as a medical student: he had passed the preliminary degree of Bachelor in the Physical Sciences, and so informed his father. But his real reward came later that spring, when the Opera revived *Orpheus.*

In June 1824, after two and a half years of music and medicine in Paris, Berlioz went back to La Côte for a summer visit. He undoubtedly hoped to clear up his ambiguous situation, but from the first it was plain that the word music must not be breathed in Mme. Berlioz' presence. She was sure that all players and artists were doomed to perdition. If his father could be brought to give his consent, his mother would have to be disregarded. Strengthened by Lesueur's encouragement, Hector bent his efforts on persuading the doctor, but he seems to have underestimated his parent's perplexity as well as misjudged his replies. For after a month of conversations, Hector wrote to his teacher that Dr. Berlioz was reconciled to the idea of a musical career. He also wrote to his closest friend, Humbert Ferrand, with whom he had planned an opera, that all was going well, "Father entirely sides with me."

The fact is that Dr. Berlioz was still undecided, paternally as well as maritally ill-at-ease. He wanted to preserve his happy relation with an affectionate and so far dutiful child. And Lesueur's uncommon interest in the boy weighed with him no less than his own knowledge of Mme. Berlioz' prejudiced views. Besides, Dr. Berlioz was himself interested in music and when Hector imparted some of Lesueur's theories about ancient Greek harmony, he was captivated: father and son talked about music a great deal of the time.

Nor had Hector given up working. He had brought with him his oratorio on the crossing of the Red Sea, and fragments of a mass begun during the last six months. As was to be his lifelong habit, he composed as fast as he could in the flush of inspiration, then revised and put the work aside. After a space, he took it up again and kept on revising. Now in July 1824, in an affectionate letter to Lesueur, he reports that upon rereading the *Credo* and *Kyrie* of his mass, he feels quite frigid about them, so he will turn to the oratorio. Parts of it seem "terribly messy" but he goes to work in hopes of getting an improved score performed in the fall.

Hector's long talks with his father at last aroused the curiosity not of Mme. Berlioz, but of her eldest daughter, Nanci, who as the keeper of a diary felt certain obligations to research. Her confiding brother disclosed the great secret, telling her apparently that all was settled to his satisfaction. Knowing her mother and seeing Hector in a new guise, Nanci was alarmed. "He is unshakable." Soon everyone felt it. Hector, who had been so full of verve earlier in the vacation, and told such good stories that "even Mother laughed," was now a center of emotional tension. Adèle, aged ten, and Prosper, the unruly boy of four, would still trail after the big brother from Paris who knew so many tricks to amuse them, but finally the storm burst. By mistake or not, Nanci revealed to her mother the young man's purpose and his belief in the doctor's acquiescence. Mme. Berlioz made a scene, but to everyone's surprise, doubtless including his own, Hector remained calm, polite, indifferent. Meals were a trial, though Dr. Berlioz drew on a reserve of gaiety to cover up the rift. Nanci records in her diary: "My brother is a great source of grief to me. . . . If only he would show a little sensibility, if only he would stay with us a little longer. But he is as inflexible as a rock." And the day after his departure: "he has left. . . . We have all been weeping, Mamma especially."

Not yet twenty-one, Hector had been forced into declaring his independence, not without strain. "Showing a little sensibility" was what he would have preferred, but he had been given no chance compatible with his convictions. His father was still a bulwark, though understandably not so "unshakable" as himself. His mother now opposed both and counteracted the doctor's good will. Nanci, unmusical and somewhat obtuse, could only utter pleas for family harmony. It was the first skirmish in a protracted struggle.

Despite this sudden hardening, Berlioz' self-confidence was not blind. He had heard enough from Lesueur to guess how steep must be the artist's path in a country where success depends on personal favors, official appointments, and political considerations. Even before, in his letter to Kreutzer, the nineteen-year-old boy had had a glimpse of the nature of public opinion: "And what will happen to me, if some day my music expresses passion: they will not understand me since they do not honor you." Moreover, he knew how much hard study lay ahead, which made him all the more impatient to begin.

Yet he was also conscious of some advantages, and these he shortly had to turn into arguments. He had no sooner returned to Paris in August than the blow fell: a letter came from La Côte, the result of what would nowadays be condemned as a parental crime: Hector had left with his parents a note addressed to his cousin Alphonse; someone, probably Mme. Berlioz, had opened it and read of Hector's set purpose, with an account of the family discussions. The doctor seems to have felt misrepresented and he now scolded. Hector's reply was a model of respectful wisdom and pointed reasoning; as so often happens in real life, the son sounds old enough to be his father's father.[6] After begging that Dr. Berlioz will take back the "cruel remarks" contained in his letter, and saying that he cannot think the message to Alphonse can be interpreted as unkind or disrespectful to his own parents, Hector meets the issue:

> I am voluntarily driven towards a magnificent career (no other epithet can be applied to the career of an artist) and I am not in the least heading for perdition. For I believe I shall succeed. Yes, I really believe it. There is no longer any point in being modest about this, since I have to prove to you that I am not drifting haphazard. I think, indeed I am convinced, that I will attain distinction in music; everything points that way from outside, and from within the voice of nature is stronger than the most rigorous dictates of reason. I have every conceivable chance in my favor if you will back me. I begin young, and I shan't have to give lessons, like so many others, to support myself. I have some solid knowledge and the rudiments of other branches, enough to be able to go deeper into them. And certainly I have experienced passions sufficiently strong not to mistake their accents whenever it will be necessary for me to depict or give them voice.

After this remarkable declaration, he goes on to calculate the income he may some day expect, so as to pacify at once the well-meaning provincials. It is a heart-rending calculation that Balzac would find worthy of his *Eugénie Grandet:* ". . . Make it but a mere twelve hundred francs; that's enough for me even though music should never bring me anything. In fine, I want to make a name for myself, I want to leave on this earth some trace of my existence, which is by no means an ignoble feeling—and so strongly do I feel it that I would rather be Gluck or Méhul dead than what I am in the bloom of manhood."

Dr. Berlioz had objected, with the speciousness of anger, that Hector was not learned in the "accessory branches" needed for music—the ancient languages and mathematics. This explains the boy's reference to his present stock of knowledge, and he takes pains to make the matter clear: "As M. Lesueur was telling me again yesterday [no doubt in a consultation upon the doctor's tirade] . . . he began by being a great musician before being a learned musician. He acquired his general information at college like everybody else, and only later saw how it bore on music . . . If I haven't gone in for Greek, Hebrew, and mathematics, I assure you it won't lessen my chances as a musician.

"This is the way I think, the way I am, and nothing in the world will change me. You could cut off my allowance or force me to leave Paris, but I do not believe you will want to make me lose the best years of my life . . . Farewell, dear Papa; read my letter over and do not ascribe it to some excited impulse. I have perhaps never been so calm. I kiss you as well as Mamma and my sisters. Your respectful and tender son.—H. Berlioz."

"Voluntarily driven" at the beginning of the letter is a phrase worth noting, not only for its accuracy as regards Berlioz' inner balance of will and reason, but because it is a spontaneous expression of the true Romantic life, which was then the only acceptable course for youths of spirit. Four months before, Delacroix, aged twenty-six, had written in his journal: "Glory is no empty word to me. The sound of praise intoxicates with a true happiness. Nature has put this feeling in all hearts. Those who give up glory, or who cannot obtain it, do well to exhibit for this mere vapor, this ambrosia of great souls, a disdain which they term philosophic." [7]

That same spring Byron had died at Missolonghi. Later in 1824, the poet-statesman Chateaubriand was dismissed from office, a sacrifice to prudence as against glory. To his young admirers, who resented the indignity, each of these events was a reminder of how life should be spent—in self-dedication to a cause and in the pursuit of glory.[8] Difficulty or even defeat was no deterrent but rather the final test of devotion. Hence Balzac's youthful heroes write treatises on the will and Stendhal's Julien Sorel rises by the deliberate study of passion. The driving impulse must be worthy and sustained, and the acceptance of death (as Berlioz spontaneously said) must go with it.

While Berlioz tried to make his family share these views, other young artists were combating the same stand-pat, play-safe policy of their own parents and governors, thus pursuing the age-old struggle between society and the creative mind. In the process the Philistine was beginning to sit for his portrait: "A philosopher" writes Delacroix with irony again "is a citizen who eats four meals a day as agreeably as possible, and for whom glory, virtue, and nobility of feeling are to be regarded only insofar as they interfere neither with these four indispensable functions nor with one's other bodily comforts." The death of Louis XVIII in that same year 1824 recalled not the life of glory but of "philosophy." Politically, after a brief hope, it meant only a change for the worse. Charles X, who succeeded, proved to be reaction incarnate; his brother in dying had prophesied quite truly that his heir would not end his days in the royal bedstead. The repressive measures that ensued were in fact a signal for everyone with a spark of independence to start struggling for liberation—liberation from pettiness as much as from oppression.

It took six years in politics, but in culture the battle was joined in this year of change of kings. The French Academy had reached the word "Romanticism" while revising the Dictionary, and appointed one Auger to report on it. Primed by a decision taken in high political circles, he declared war on "the new schism, Romanticism," and attacked the "barbaric poetry," which some were trying to establish "in violation of literary orthodoxy." This was aimed at Nodier's coterie of young poets, at Stendhal's praise of Shakespeare, at all those who admired Madame de Stael's book on German literature or the works of Chateaubriand. But as yet the new forces were scattered. By a paradox, the Romanticists were still royalist in politics, while the political liberals championed academic art. Both groups, however, numbered Bonapartists, and Chateaubriand himself could call the Restoration a regime bottomed on tired revolutionaries, whom he himself served for lack of any real alternative.

Though Berlioz had family ties with the "Ultras" who triumphed under Charles X, he was an admirer of the Emperor, and was already as detached from religious orthodoxy as his own father, the Voltairian doctor. With all generous young men, Hector felt that the poetry of life lay elsewhere than in politics or the church.[9] The chance to do great deeds being denied by historical circumstances, art could at least embody the spirit of greatness. This feeling also made him impatient with the amusements of society which he occasionally had to endure. He and his fellow music student, Louis Schloesser, would escort Lesueur's three daughters to balls, would dance the first cotillion (waltzing was still deemed rather immoral) and since there were usually more gentlemen than needed—bless the dowry system!—would retire to a corner out of the noise and confusion. On Friday nights there was a standing invitation to the house of friends who prided themselves on their musical evenings. But when Hector went it was to drink tea, which he had learned to like and which "helped him to swallow their music."

His real business in Paris, his reason for being alive, was to compose. He accordingly was working again at the score of his Mass. Much of what he wrote was in the style of Lesueur, as was natural, since the two men stood in the relation of master and apprentice for long hours every day. But Hector also read scores at the Conservatoire (despite a brush with the Director, Cherubini, over library rules) and by study was strengthening earlier ideas of his own. We know that while still at La Côte, he had read and reread Chateaubriand's *Genius of Christianity*. This book, which modern critics mention all too casually as "a romantic account of religion" was in fact a little treatise on esthetics, and one reason Berlioz understood Lesueur's principles of dramatic and religious music so readily was that he had been prepared for them by a far greater master.

In Chateaubriand, Hector had found a vindication of the arts based on their religious uses, and a vindication of Christianity based on its awareness of human passions. When Chateaubriand compared together all the great poets from Dante and Virgil to Milton and Voltaire, Berlioz could gain insights into the character of great lovers, from his cherished Dido to his other favorites, Paul and Virginia; he could even find a description of feelings that he may have thought exclusively his own—the vague longings of young manhood. Chateaubriand also said pregnant things about music (which confirmed Hector's emotional response to the psalm *When Israel*) and described the requiem mass as a dramatic masterpiece. Citing Pergolesi's *Stabat Mater,* the critic pointed out that the recall of musical themes to suggest man's return to grief was "a perfect imitation of nature." Again, a sentence such as: "The reasoning spirit, by destroying the imagination, undermines the bases of the fine arts" was to a lively mind a complete lesson in Romanticism, for what it implied was the Gothic as against the neo-classic principle in poetry and the arts. Even Chateaubriand's treatment of bells contained a social philosophy for musicians: "It is, on the face of it, a rather marvellous thing to have found a way, by the single stroke of a hammer, to cause a thousand hearts to feel the same sentiment in a given minute. . . . Besides, considered as harmony, bells indubitably possess a beauty of the first order, which artists call *grandeur*. The noise of thunder is sublime in the same way, by its greatness, and it is thus with the winds, seas, volcanoes, cataracts, and the voice of a whole people."

Read by a future creator of large works for national occasions, these remarks were not lost. One proof that Berlioz' mind was impregnated with Chateaubriand's ideas is that under the pressure of necessity, Hector imagined the sympathy to be mutual. He had never met the noble poet, recently Minister of Foreign Affairs, but he knew a number of young men in his entourage, and through them knew of Chateaubriand's generous attitude toward young artists. Rather than face the master, Berlioz wrote him a letter asking for nothing less than a loan to permit the production of his first finished work, now known as the *Mass of 1825*.

What had led to this bold step was quite simple: Berlioz' well-connected friend, Albert du Boys, had obtained for Hector two audiences with the King's Superintendent of Fine Arts, the Vicomte Sosthènes de la Rochefoucauld. This gentleman was a simon-pure royalist, the largest land-owner in France, a celebrated breeder of horses, and the only statesman who ever used his power in a vain effort to extend the area covered by the ballerinas' traditional costume. Though he was a devotee of Rossini, the Superintendent meant to be fair, so he granted Berlioz permission to use the Opera orchestra at his own expense. Its leader, Valentino, was still willing to conduct and Prévost to sing. But Berlioz remembered his first fiasco and was determined that the orchestra should be paid and the parts correctly copied. For all this he needed twelve hundred francs, which his father would certainly not advance. Here was Chateaubriand's role. Would he lend that sum to a vaguely recommended young artist? The year before, Hector had thought of approaching a well-known actor and asking him to launch one of his songs at a benefit, but on the very doorstep the applicant had been overcome with shyness and had run away. Now he addressed Chateaubriand in a dignified way, which elicited the dignified reply quoted in the *Memoirs:* Chateaubriand did not have the required sum at his disposal, nor had he any influence left in the ministry. But his words generously implied that the petitioner was a fellow craftsman with whose predicament he sympathized.[10]

This autograph document was Berlioz' New Year's gift for 1825. Though just turned twenty-one, he was not the sort to take youth as a pretext for doing nothing, but he began to feel that he had already weathered a good many trials: there seemed to be no way to begin. Nonetheless, having revised and polished the Mass until both Lesueur and he were satisfied, he set himself to copying the parts—a drudgery which took three months. He must have spent rather full days and nights, for he had meanwhile received from Humbert Ferrand the text of a cantata on the Greek Revolution, and the music for it was being put on paper. Since this new work had a topical interest (Byron—Missolonghi—the Philhellenic societies) its completion ought not to be delayed. Already life was passing, pressing, dwindling, as he dreamed of its potential uses. To give up now, and by failing to make his mark be forced to resume the medical apron, could not be borne even in thought. He must produce his Mass.

Augustin de Pons, another of Hector's wealthy friends who happened to be musical, came to the rescue and lent the twelve hundred francs. Everything was set in motion, rehearsals were begun, the newspapers notified, critics invited, the family kept posted, and finally on July 10, 1825, the church of St. Roch, which thirty years before had heard Bonaparte's "whiff of grapeshot" (and still bore its marks), heard something equally important and rather more appropriate.

The performance was a success. Dizzy with excitement, Berlioz heard his imaginings come to life and take effect on an appreciative audience. But he kept his ears open to criticism as well as to compliments, and more especially to the faults that only he could detect by comparing the actual sounds with his intentions. His next thought was to escape friends and inquisitive strangers, and to learn what his master thought of the work as performed. The old man had hidden behind a pillar and gone straight home to await his protégé. "By heaven," he told Berlioz, "you shan't be a doctor or an apothecary or anything but a great musician . . . There are too many notes in your work, but every intention carries, and makes itself felt even through the exuberance of ideas."

Several newspapers spoke of the Mass "by M. Lesueur's pupil," but the composer waited for further notices before despatching news of victory to La Côte. Then he wrote to his mother, telling her of the "rather brilliant reception of the work," and after "laying its success in homage at her feet," added diplomatically: "Despite your wish to see me take up other studies, your affection toward me is too great for a thing that has caused me so much joy to cause you any pain." He also pointed out that although he relished the approval of the amateur public, what he wanted was "the suffrage of artists, the opinion of those who know, and I was lucky enough to obtain it."

To Du Boys, who had started the ball rolling, he let himself go about M. Sosthènes: "Would you believe it, he gave me permission to have the musicians of the Opera, provided I paid for them. The good man! He permitted me to spend a thousand francs, if I had them, and he gave the musicians full and complete liberty to take the cash!" Nevertheless, Berlioz adds in a jubilant P.S. that the Mass has been requested by another chapel master for a performance in July, no longer at his expense. "The musicians will be fewer, only about sixty, but that will be enough for the size of the church." [11]

Some days later at the Opera, Berlioz, sitting as an habitué next to the head of the claque, was taken to task by this eminent man, usually known as Auguste.[12]

"Why didn't you tell us you made your debut at St. Roch's the other day? We'd have gone in a body."

"I didn't know you liked religious music as much as that."

"We don't like it at all. What an idea! But we would have warmed up your audience to the Queen's taste."

"But how? You can't applaud in a church."

"I know, but you can cough, blow your nose, move your chair, scrape your feet, hum and haw, lift your eyes to heaven —the whole bag of tricks. We could have done a sweet job for you, and given you a real success, just like a fashionable preacher."

For the next few days Hector tasted the pleasures of notoriety—met Mme. Branchu at her daughter's wedding, and was taken by other artists into the circle of their awareness. But this whiff of fame did not turn his head. He knew how applause and newspaper notices and the mutual admirations of the artistic world come and go. He also knew that the Mass needed retouching. The best thing in it, the vision of the Last Judgment on the words *Et iterum venturus* was a movement of some value and he must go over it. What the public liked best was the *Gloria,* "a show piece in light style. You might have known they'd prefer it."

But music was a pleasant sort of trouble, which Hector now accepted as synonymous with life. He was committed to art in every way and not merely through that disturbingly large debt to De Pons. Hence when that same year the new German music of Carl Maria von Weber broke upon Paris in an adaptation of *Der Freischütz,* its reception became at once part of his concern. From its new orchestral and operatic style Berlioz had much to learn, but he quickly saw that in addition to being badly sung Weber's work had been mutilated. The man responsible for this desecration was the powerful "XXX" of the *Journal des Débats,* Castil-Blaze.[13] Berlioz watched his chance to attack him directly in the pages of the *Corsaire.* The opportunity arose over Gluck's *Armide,* which the great critic had found "lacking in emotion," full of arias that "stopped short of full development," and built throughout on "a system of declamation which one no longer accepts." This dogmatism gave Hector his chance. After a technical refutation of the other's carping about consecutive fifths, Berlioz winds up: "But who is this 'one' who no longer accepts Gluck's system? It is M. XXX. Who is it that finds half the music of *Armide* ridiculous? M. XXX. Who finds the poem inferior, the main role unmusical, the settings tawdry and the ballets stale? Still M. XXX. But who then is this implacable critic, this universal corrector of taste? He must be some great composer, a lyric poet, or at least a member of the Academy? Not at all: he is more than all these. He is M. Castil-Blaze."

This was the first blast against the man who would shortly be called to account by Weber in person for making a musical hash out of *Freischütz* and *Euryanthe,* and by Weber's publishers for appropriating the receipts of these successful manglings. Young Hector had fired the first shot and carried the war against musical misrepresentation from the opera pit to the printed page. When Weber, dying of tuberculosis, passed through Paris on his way to staging *Oberon* in London, Berlioz could feel qualified to bring him a tribute of praise from the new generation. No one in France would understand Weber more thoroughly, or more naturally resemble him as man of action. But by ill luck, Berlioz missed him at every turn—at Lesueur's, at a music shop, at the Opera. A few months later, *Oberon* failed and Weber was dead.

Meanwhile Berlioz continued to write music and to seek performance. He had finished his "Heroic Scene: The Greek Revolution." He and Ferrand published the text and solicited officialdom. On their behalf Lesueur approached his colleague Kreutzer who was in charge of concerts at the Opera, but was gruffly challenged: "What would happen to us if we helped newcomers?" Undaunted, the poet-librettist and the composer went on to their next project, an opera based on the history of the Vehmic Courts, or secret "vigilantes" of late medieval Germany. It was entitled *Les Francs-Juges,* and an idea of its *Freischütz*-like atmosphere may be gathered from the opening stage directions: "A cavern showing 12 stone seats around a circular table draped in black, covered with daggers and symbolic objects." [14] But an opera is a laborious thing and Ferrand was not so abundant a poet as his friend was a musician. Berlioz therefore wrote songs, placed a few in magazines, and published others at his own expense. Finally he entered the preliminary competition for the Rome Prize and was not admitted.

This brought on a family crisis. Though Hector had begun to pay off his debt for the Mass by cutting his expenses and by giving music lessons, he had not been able to keep the facts from his family: Cousin Alphonse had inadvertently given him away. The doctor paid De Pons a sum which he thought the full amount, but which was only about a third, Berlioz having prudently minimized the total. At the same time the father set a date for the end of his son's musical studies. Only a notable success could save Hector, and now at the official trial he had failed. Dr. Berlioz immediately cut off all funds. The double blow to pride and pocketbook would surely quash musical inclination forever. But at this point Lesueur intervened, writing direct to the doctor that no doubt was possible about his son's divine gift and future success: "Music streams out of him through all his pores." He urged the parable of the buried talent. Dr. Berlioz replied huffily and ordered Hector home, where the prodigal was uncanonically received with studied coolness. No one spoke. An attempt at discussion between father and son ended in deadlock. Hector went numb and could not eat. The father lay awake at night. At last, one morning, the doctor summoned his boy to the office to say he might return to Paris as a music student. Only, he must leave La Côte without telling this to his mother.

Hector instantly came back to life and burst to poor Nanci, who records that "he talked to her too long for comfort," and that Mme. Berlioz immediately suspected her son's gaiety. Shortly before leaving he tried to avoid his mother, in vain. She forbade him to leave La Côte, but on seeing his stony expression, she turned from fury to entreaties, begging him on her knees not to disgrace himself and them. *"La considération avant tout."* [15] Those who have to do with theaters, she cried, are "disgraced in this life and damned in the next." [16] Seeing him adamant, she cursed him and fled to a neighboring cottage. As the time for taking the coach drew near, Hector, his father, and the other children, all weeping, sought her out, but she eluded them and Hector had to leave unblessed and heading for perdition.

Little wonder that when the young man thought of these scenes, of his debts, and of the risks and reckoning to come, he found himself subject to violent "inner storms." He analyzed them with a medical student's attention to physiological detail: when an idea seizes him, he tells Nanci, he is consumed by it, he has chills and fever, and his brain reels until his other ideas absorb the new one. Then he seeks to impart his vision, but everyone is cold and uncomprehending, and the discovery paralyzes him. But only for a time. When he recovers aplomb he knows that he has powers and can produce something that shall be "great, passionate, energetic, and true." He also knows that what makes men cold to his insights is that everyone is wrapped up in his own cloud of perceptions and illusions, which few transcend. He notes moreover that "these bouts of mine are always more violent when I am far from the place where the objects of my emotion are to be found, because the impossibility of verifying the facts necessarily creates illusions or exaggerated realities."

This cool self-criticism, which checks but does not destroy passion and spontaneity, was already apparent in Hector's first letter to Lesueur written in his twentieth year, and it remained perhaps Berlioz' most significant trait. Puzzling to some, and even repellent, its recurrent expression in Berlioz' mind, art, and behavior actually defines a kind of temperament. Stendhal and Delacroix occur at once as men identically compounded of fire and reason, but there were many others among the future great men of this creative period: Hazlitt, Shelley, Büchner, Heine, Dumas, Chopin. Indeed, if one looks into the early life of almost any productive mind, one finds a very similar mixture of emotion and melancholy wisdom. Many a self-possessed genius, an Olympian in later life, began as an untamed youth: Goethe, for example, or Wordsworth; and from the classic centuries: Racine, Pope, Voltaire, and Dr. Johnson.

But the roots of reason and order have to be there from the beginning, and it is important to notice their presence in Berlioz at this early date. From the first he displayed a rational conservatism, a prudent regard for the significant proprieties, which in any man doubles the offense of his revolutionary acts. Never a bohemian like Balzac, nor a dandy like Musset, Berlioz more nearly resembles Vigny in aristocratic self-control, but Berlioz had perhaps more to control, and his blend of passion and deliberateness varied in keeping with the claims, now of intellectual good breeding, and now of his daemon. The self-taming process was not always comfortable, and the aftermath of each crisis was likely to be a bout of melancholy, "the evil of isolation" (as he termed it) in short *ennui.* Ennui was simply energy quelling itself, waiting for an outlet—not merely an explosive discharge—and seeking fulfillment through coherent expression in lasting forms.

Since the Spring of 1826, Berlioz had been at work on a libretto furnished him by a friend, Compaignon de Marchéville, and based on Scott's *Talisman.* The opera was to be called *Richard in the Holy Land* and Berlioz was taking his usual pains to make his collaborator provide language and plot suitable for music. The correspondence dragged on for a year and the project came to nothing. Before its abandonment by August 1826, Berlioz had registered as a student at the Conservatoire, and thanks to Lesueur's recommendation was allowed to take Reicha's class in counterpoint and Lesueur's class in composition concurrently instead of in sequence. Lesueur naturally felt that his pupil—indeed his disciple—was far enough advanced to carry the work easily; and since it was absolutely necessary to win the Rome prize as a certificate of merit, Berlioz must learn another set of "our principles" with Anton Reicha.

This Czech musician was a conscientious master who had been a childhood friend of Beethoven's in Bonn, had met him (and Haydn) again in Vienna, and had come to Paris in 1808. He had written successful operas and chamber music, and after ten years had taken Méhul's place at the Conservatoire. His subject was fugue and counterpoint, which he taught, wisely enough, in combination with harmony, as the notebooks of his later pupil, César Franck, indicate. Reicha also showed some interest in instrumentation, and had tried out new combinations of strings and winds. Berlioz found him clear, concise, and sometimes critical of the sanctity of rules. He was willing to argue even when reasons were hard to find. It is true, Lesueur and Reicha did not agree in their systems; nor did Cherubini, the head of the Conservatoire, agree with the other two.[17] As for reconciling the rules with the practices of Gluck and Weber, let alone with one's musical instincts, that was an impossibility.

None the less Berlioz did the prescribed exercises, continued to live as an intimate—almost a son—of Lesueur, and on the side kept on composing *Les Francs-Juges.* All this on a very much reduced allowance in order to pay off De Pons. With his childhood friend Antoine Charbonnel (the son of Dr. Berlioz' political opponent of 1817), Hector kept cheaper lodgings and developed the virtuosity of the housewife. But this foretaste of poverty was nothing to the destitution which followed. For De Pons grew restive and wrote to Berlioz' father for the remainder of the money due. The doctor, shocked by the true amount, paid, but for the second time stopped Hector's allowance.

Music lessons—solfeggio, flute, guitar—were the only resource, but the young musician could hardly live on less than one franc a day, and lessons did not bring in that much. He tried to get a place as flutist in an orchestra, but all the desks were filled. He was even ready to go abroad, but agents reported no openings. Finally Hector landed a job as chorister in the Théâtre des Nouveautés, after astonishing the manager by his knowledge of the whole opera repertoire. He could sing at sight, so the appalling rehearsals of the nonsense given in that playhouse, the lowest kind of musical farce, were pure torture—"it will make me into an idiot and give me cholera morbus"—but the thirty francs a month with his days largely free for his classes meant the difference between victory and defeat.

When Charbonnel, a student of pharmacy, was not running after the girls, he proved handy with snare and shotgun and brought home game from Montrouge, which eked out the cheap staples open to their budget. Hector meanwhile was thinking of the prize competition—"that deadly system," as Balzac calls it "which we owe to the Pompadour's brother." [18] For this, too, Berlioz must save money, since those who enter it are *en loge* (incommunicado) for two weeks and must put up money for their board. Correspondence with La Côte was limited to letters from Adèle and Nanci, to whom Hector gave sardonic glimpses of his plans. The younger girl need not worry about the forwarding of her mail if he should go abroad—whether as prize winner at Rome or flutist in Australia—for "the only country to which letters are not forwarded is the country from which no traveller returns."

In June, Berlioz again took the preliminary test for admission to the prize contest. He wrote his fugue and Cherubini passed it. The subject of the finals was a "lyric scene" or brief cantata, "The Death of Orpheus at the Hands of the Bacchantes." The theme seemed most auspicious and Hector let himself go, hoping by a display of knowledge and imagination to carry the day. But the first prize went to one Guiraud, and Berlioz did not even receive a second prize.[19]

The score of *The Death of Orpheus,* lost until twenty years ago, was quite fittingly chosen by the national libraries of France after one hundred and three years, as one of the publications commemorating the centenary of Romanticism. *Orpheus* corresponds in Berlioz' career to Victor Hugo's *Cromwell* of the same year, 1827. There is in both that touch of defiance which goes with the first conscious innovation—in Hugo, the famous preface, in Berlioz, on the rejected manuscript, the no less famous note: "This work declared 'unplayable' by the Music Section of the Institute—Played on July 22, 1828."

What had happened at the Institute was that the pianist assigned to perform the competing cantatas for the judges had floundered over Berlioz' score. It was taken for granted that these prize pieces, though required to be written for voice and orchestra, could be easily reproduced on the piano. And most of them, having been first conceived in a keyboard way, lost nothing by reduction to their embryonic state. But on this point Berlioz' *Orpheus*—and this is the epoch-making fact—differed completely from all the rest. It had been not only scored but conceived for orchestra—and an original orchestra at that. From the point of view of Berlioz' success, the pianist's failure was ominous. It is true that even had the performer managed his reduction at sight, other aspects of Berlioz' originality would doubtless have alienated the jury. For applying his dramatic instinct to the musical problem, Berlioz had extracted from the rather dull scene a "Monologue and Bacchanale," and he wrote those two words down as the subtitle of his work. The fact was that Berlioz had produced *en loge* his first characteristic work.

CHAPTER 4

FAUSTIAN MAN

Au son de ton harmonie
Je rafraichis ma chaleur
Ma chaleur, flamme infinie
Naissante d'un beau malheur.
RONSARD, "To his Guitar" (*c.* 1550)

The summer of 1827, the prelude to a feverish autumn for Berlioz, began with depressing calm. Charbonnel had gone back to his parents at La Côte and Hector's other friends had scattered too. He meanwhile continued drudging at the Nouveautés, singing the choruses of lyric gems entitled *The Game of Hide and Seek, The Widow's Man,* or *The Bride's Engagement Ring.* Relaxed tension brought on illness. Sore throat developed into quinsy, and after a few days' discomfort Berlioz lanced the abscess himself. News of this reached La Côte, presumably through Charbonnel, and Dr. Berlioz with kindly words restored the mercurial allowance.

This temporary disorder was undoubtedly of nervous origin, for anyone less fundamentally healthy than young Berlioz would scarcely have been able to stand the blows of the next half dozen years. The first and heaviest shock occurred in early September 1827, when an English troupe of actors led by Kemble came to Paris and revealed Shakespeare to young France. Five years before, a similar attempt had proved disastrous. So soon after Waterloo, national pride had been offended by the "invasion," and Shakespeare had been scorned as "an aide-de-camp of Wellington." The hissing was followed by rioting; and a young actress was wounded (while curtsying) by coins hurled at her from the pit by the most polite people on earth. When Desdemona appeared lying on a couch, a voice called asking why the usual bedroom appliances were missing. Thus the wittiest nation of Europe in 1822.

Now in 1827 the enthusiasm for Shakespeare and his actors showed the effect of Nodier's influence, of the young Romantics' articles in *Le Globe,* of Villemain's public lectures, and of Stendhal's attacks on the Academy. Political passion, moreover, had shifted from foreign to home affairs. So everyone in Paris who had a name or hoped to have one went to the Odéon to see *Hamlet* and *Romeo* as well as *Jane Shore, The Rivals,* and *Venice Preserved.* Though the plays were given in English, people read Letourneur's prose Shakespeare, or simply responded to voice and pantomime just as in the twenties of this century the English-speaking world did at the Moscow Art Theater. Kemble, though fifty-two, was "sensational" as the Prince of Denmark; but the great revelation was a young Ophelia of twenty-seven named Harriet Smithson. She was tall and well-proportioned, had a striking face and beautifully modeled arms, and a moving voice. Her deep blue eyes were large and expressive: She was enchanting to hear and to behold.[1] On this point, the most critical witnesses were at one—Delacroix, Hugo, Vigny, Dumas, and Sainte-Beuve as well as ordinary critics on both sides of the Channel.[2]

They agreed also that she had a genius for tragedy, though few who knew her antecedents could have predicted any such triumph for her. Born in 1800 in Ennis, Ireland, the daughter of a theater manager, she had received a very strict religious upbringing and had gone on the stage only from necessity. To save her from the evils of the profession, she was put under the guardianship of her brother who exacted references from Abbott, her manager, and when she traveled, it was with her mother and a hunchback sister as chaperones. For three years she toured Ireland, then went to London where her native accent seriously damaged her prospects, even in comedy. On the Continent it passed unnoticed and chance opened to her the half-dozen roles ideally suited to her talents: Abbott had coached her in the traditional business of Ophelia merely in order that Kemble, whose leading lady was needed for the Queen, could play Hamlet.

On the opening night (September 11) as Ophelia played the mad scene, she seemed to have forgotten her part. Blind to her surroundings, she walked as in a trance; she stopped, her face vacant, arms hanging. She paused, and the whole house was gripped by an absolutely new dramatic emotion. Her song, without art or expression, rose amid the silence, her veil fell, she burst into tears and then slowly walked away. At the end of her second scene, the audience also wept; men sobbed or left hurriedly. The remainder of the play insured the success of the English actors; that night *Hamlet* ended to the sounds of an ovation.[3]

Though seven scenes, eight characters, and seventeen hundred lines had been cut, the play cast a new spell on spectators accustomed to the solemnities of French tragedy. Shakespeare's world had, in Dumas's phrase, "the freshness of Adam's first sight of Eden." Berlioz, also present, was overwhelmed: "I had to acknowledge the only dramatic truth. . . . I could at the same time gauge the great absurdity of the ideas Voltaire had spread in France about Shakespeare . . . and the pitiable narrowness of our old poetics, decreed by pedagogues and obscurantist monks. I saw, understood, and felt that I was alive and that I must 'arise and walk.'" Berlioz saw as in a flash that Shakespeare's "open construction" by scenes and glimpses, leaping over time and space to sum up a character or a situation, was precisely what the dramatic musician needed for his purpose. And what made him feel doubly alive was that he had fallen in love, virtually at first sight, with Ophelia.

He later compared this passion for Harriet Smithson to a bolt of lightning that had struck into his heart as into a virgin forest, and there is no reason to suppose that this was other than literal. He had not been so deeply moved since his unhappy childhood love for Estelle. During his student days we do not hear of any casual love-making nor so much as a flirtation. He was too busy, anxious, fastidious. Moreover, he had been so stupidly teased about the Estelle episode by his family, especially by his mother, that he undoubtedly carried his heart in wraps though appearing to wear it on his sleeve. And just as his boyhood love was linked with the sublimities of nature, heightened by the Virgilian tale of Dido, so this first adult passion was linked with the sublimities of drama, couched in Shakespeare's poetry. As the living sign of Shakespeare's power, Harriet brought devastation of spirit along with inspiration.

In less than half a year, two more such electric experiences were to befall Berlioz, the "virgin forest" of whose soul by then resembled a blasted heath. But these were artistic shocks, from which recovery is sure, and they came in the course of a great intellectual battle, crowned by victory. As if heartened by Shakespeare, the artistic youth of France were feeling their gathered strength and setting off explosive charges all around the academic fortress: Victor Hugo published *Cromwell* with a preface-manifesto, Delacroix exhibited his "Death of Sardanapalus," Rude was starting out as an independent sculptor in Paris, and Sainte-Beuve preached Ronsard and sixteenth-century romanticism. In the circle to which Mérimée told his tales of Spanish passion and Stendhal his witty anecdotes of Italian character, came Hazlitt who was at work on his Life of Napoleon. All idolized Shakespeare, and Gérard de Nerval brought out that Shakespearean offshoot, his translation of Goethe's *Faust,* Part I.

It was this poem which worked further havoc in Berlioz' mind. Everything about the "marvellous book" struck home—the theme, the form, the realistic variety, and the Nature philosophy. He read it constantly and urged everyone to read it. More than Werther and René, already a generation past, the figure of Faust seemed to embody the will of the moment, for Faust was more complete. Learned, passionate, curious, tender, courageous, bewitched, and desperate, he stood for genius in all its greatness and misery. The "two souls within his breast" showed him at once a sufferer and a doer:

Unresting action proves the man.

Yet Faust was a critic of himself no less than a critic of life, and his pilgrimage was a perpetual act of choice. To searchers like the young artists of the new era, it was wonderful to find a fable in which Experience and Wisdom were not shown as already bottled and labeled by the old for the use of the obedient young, but were purchasable solely with risk and effort. Without knowing that Goethe had begun the work at the same time as some ballad plays, Berlioz immediately felt that *Faust* was made for music. Nerval had translated the songs in verse, and already appropriate melodies were spinning in Berlioz' brain.

Besides this whirl of ideas there were practical matters to attend to, notably rehearsals. On November 22, in the midst of a political riot, Berlioz' Mass was given again in the great church of St. Eustache. Conducting for the first time in his life, he had the satisfaction of successfully leading his favorite portion—the fanfare followed by chorus for the Last Judgment—which at the earlier performance had been spoiled. He was so excited at the end of the movement that he had to sit down and literally shake it off. The performance convinced him that only this one section had any merit, the rest being a "clumsy imitation of Lesueur's style" which he might as well destroy.[4]

He knew moreover that the English players were about to leave: could he bring himself to Miss Smithson's attention? More and more distracted by his all-too-distant love (which so affected him that his friends noticed a Romeo-like jaundice and peakedness in his looks) Hector had resolved on a bold plan: he too would brave the public; he would give a concert of his own works. For this he must use only the best and latest of his compositions, as well as the ablest musicians in Paris. The *Francs-Juges* overture was just finished and Berlioz had another, unplayed, with a title and motto drawn from Scott, *Waverley*. With the "Greek Revolution" and the *Resurrexit* from the Mass, his concert would show enough quantity, quality, and variety.

In the midst of this projected one-man show or "festival"—a thing as yet unattempted by any musician in France—a ministerial decree established the *Société des Concerts du Conservatoire*. Its purpose was to give regular seasons of classical music by drawing on the best players in both the Opera and the Conservatoire. Habeneck was put in charge, and it was stipulated that the repertory should include works by new or neglected composers—those that neither Kreutzer's routine programs at the Opera nor Choron's oratorio society normally took up. In March 1828 Habeneck opened his series with the Third, Fifth, and Seventh symphonies of Beethoven.[5] The result was an artistic furore almost as great as had followed the advent of Shakespeare. On Berlioz the effect was exactly comparable. He saw in a flash what had been missing from his background and his teaching. Lesueur never really swallowed Beethoven, and Cherubini never acknowledged the virtue of symphonic form: "I've tried it and it doesn't strike me as good." Berlioz on the contrary soon convinced himself by a study of the scores that Beethoven was the transcendent modern who could not be transcended.

Berlioz' state of mind when this last thunderbolt fell and supercharged him is impossible to describe. He himself tried to give an idea of it, first in intimate letters to friends, and later in the *Memoirs,* where he ushers in the Shakespeare-Goethe-Beethoven sequence with the remark that here was "the great drama" of his life, that is, his moment of storm and stress. He tells what he did and how he felt, and from this retrospect biographers have tried to reconstruct the drama and judge it. One writer thinks Berlioz was close to madness; another argues that because Berlioz accomplished a good deal of practical work in that same half year, the report of his excitement must be exaggerated, or must at the time have been a pose. This is the old dispute about Hamlet feigning or being mad. It is impossible to make intelligible in print the paroxysms of love combined with the torments of emotional and artistic maturing. When Berlioz tells us that he suffered insomnia for long periods, that he walked for hours to tire out his ennui, after which he would drop into a stupor, now in a field covered with snow and again at the table of a cafe where he slept so long that he was thought dead, all we can say is that however unprecedented the detail, these are the sorts of things that passionate men have been known to do.

These odd actions of Hector's came in bouts. The salient trait of his temperament, which we find reflected in his music as well as in his calmest letters and most tightly knit articles, is swiftness in associating ideas. Under stress this speed became a headlong rush which on paper seems sheer vibration. For example, on June 28, 1828, Berlioz wrote a perfectly sensible letter to Ferrand about the music of the *Francs-Juges,* as well as about another theatrical project. But before sending the letter, some thought evidently swamped the writer in despair and he set off on a walk at the double quick to a suburb ten miles away. On coming back exhausted he pulls out his letter and blurts out his thought: "How alone I feel. My muscles are palsied as in those about to die. O my friend send me something to work on, a bone to gnaw. How beautiful the country was today. So much light. All the living beings I met coming back seemed happy. The trees were gently astir and I was alone in the vast plain. Space, absence, forgetfulness, pain, and rage assailed me. Despite all my efforts, life escapes me, I only catch shreds of it."

He intersperses a report of fresh troubles with his family, which doubtless intensified his feeling of isolation. The doctor had once again snipped the lifeline and Hector exclaims, "Money, money, always money. . . . I might be all right if I had a great deal of it." Then after considering death which, he sagely observes, is far from equivalent to happiness, he winds up: "Yet my blood flows through my veins as before; my heart beats as if full of joy. Come to think of it, I am in excellent form. Let us cheer up, by gad, cheer up!" The next day, he soberly closes the incident while reassuring his friend: "Do not worry about these unfortunate aberrations of my heart; the fit has passed."

Perhaps Berlioz should have destroyed these chaotic confessions instead of sending them to his bosom friend, but the nineteenth century in general and Berlioz in particular held to the belief that friendship is graced by frankness, and he acted on it.

This naïveté did not prevent him from adroitly overcoming the very crass obstacles put in the way of his projected concert. To secure the use of the hall at the Conservatoire, Berlioz needed Cherubini's permission. Luigi Cherubini, a Florentine who had settled in France before the revolution, was in 1828 a somewhat embittered man of sixty-eight. He had been disappointed as an opera composer and his affections were concentrated on a very few friends (including Ingres). His musical passion had been replaced by a great love of botany and as cofounder, now Director, of the Conservatoire, he proved to be an able administrator verging on the martinet. All rules were sacrosanct: he considered Bach a German barbarian because of his harmonic freedom, just as he considered Berlioz a criminal for entering the building through the wrong door. And the new Concert Society seemed equally subversive. To play Beethoven and encourage young students to have their own works performed would endanger all authority. He told Berlioz he would have the seats and music desks removed from the stage and the flooring *demolished.*[6] But Berlioz was not to be intimidated and he had friends at court. Cherubini therefore promised him the use of the hall if—if the Superintendent of Fine Arts also agreed. Berlioz had a successful audience with the Vicomte, whereupon Cherubini declared that he had never consented, since Berlioz' concert would interfere with the scholastic schedule. This was to underestimate Berlioz' resourcefulness. He penned three letters to officialdom, each text a model of persuasion and tact, and thereby checkmated Cherubini. Later, in a separate note, of a diction exquisitely relaxed to mark the change of mood, Hector topped his victory by asking the Vicomte, as a private patron of the arts, to attend his concert. The same Berlioz who was a mad lover and explosively confessional friend could also handle worldly weapons—it was a question of what he was giving his mind to.

To make the concert a Parisian event so that it might reach the ears of Miss Smithson, Berlioz had to make sure of the newspapers. This was all the more necessary that to take such a step while still a student at the Conservatoire was unprecedented. The last century did not feel as we do about youth and made no effort to bring out new composers; the only avenue to success was through a government commission or through the Opera. In announcing his concert, Berlioz drew attention to these conditions and pointed out the risk he was taking: "For four years I have knocked at every door, to no avail. I cannot obtain a libretto to set, nor secure the production of the one I have on hand. I have tried in vain all the usual means of gaining a hearing, except one, which I am now resorting to. Perhaps I should take as my motto Virgil's line, 'To the vanquished, the only salvation is to hope for none' . . . My concert, I know, will have all the disadvantages of musical programs that are made up of only one man's work, but at least good judges will be enabled to decide whether that work shows any promise."

The concert on May 26, 1828 was a triumph. Commenting upon it, the *Figaro* took up Berlioz' motto from Virgil and capped it with another, "Fortune favors the brave." The *Waverley* overture, said the critic, had deserved the three salvos of applause that greeted it, and the second part of the "Greek Revolution" was equally admirable. What mattered even more to Berlioz was the impression he had produced on his performers. From the first rehearsal they had been enthusiastic, and their gossip established him in the world of professionals —his first conquest of the kind in a long series. Already in 1828 the electric quality in Berlioz' art was evident to all, though diversely judged. The *Figaro* spoke of "a superabundance of verve which at first excites enthusiasm and then tires attention," and the influential theorist and composer, F. J. Fétis in the *Revue Musicale* concluded, "M. Berlioz has genius. His style is energetic and sinewy. His inspirations are often graceful. But still more often he spends himself in combinations of an original and passionate cast, which border on the wild and bizarre and are only saved by the fact that they come off."

The critics generally preferred the Greek scene to the

Resurrexit and the *Waverley* overture to the *Francs-Juges*—a fair index of what Berlioz was adding to tradition, for the *Resurrexit* contained the core of great movements in later works, and the *Francs-Juges* overture represents the native Berlioz at twenty-four. "One marvels," says a critic looking back after a century, "at the daring and ingenuity of the young musician . . . who could handle such a broad canvas. In it you can find twenty original ideas—enough to make all his confrères green with envy. You may say 'Obvious effects!' True, but they were not obvious before Berlioz invented them and set the pattern."

In the 1820's the first hearing of this overture was understandably called volcanic and terrifying. As always happens with unfamiliar art, listeners ascribed the shocks experienced in one or two places to the whole. They forgot the quiet introduction in F minor (much admired by Bernard Shaw), which is based on a theme derived from the second subject. This in turn was the flute melody of the boyhood quintet, treated here as a march of knightly character. Several striking novelties and their masterly incorporation make the work a genuine tour de force for a young dramatic musician working without knowledge of Beethoven.

The concert gave Berlioz the reassurance he required but it brought him little else. He had had to go into debt again and to explain himself at home, where the object of his struggles was still a mystery. Dr. Berlioz understood neither the conditions of music in Paris nor the special difficulties of genius. He evidently thought that if everything Lesueur said of Hector was true, the boy should by now be self-supporting. Why did medicine and agriculture still have to pay the piper? Hector tried to show in one hurtling epistle that innovation was at a discount and natural enmity to talent at a premium, while the public was no reliable arbiter. Berlioz knew even then how much opinion is swayed by habit, and how far his unwillingness to make concessions was a handicap: "I avoid like the plague those commonplaces which all composers (Weber and Beethoven excepted) serve up at the end of their pieces. They strike me as a kind of charlatanism which says, 'This thing is about over: get ready to applaud' . . . Those wretched conventional phrases make every piece resemble every other."

It was many years before the doctor finally understood. At the moment he could only give another puzzled yank at the pursestrings. Lesueur had to advance the money for Hector's entry in the approaching Rome Prize, and this determined the young man to compromise in order to win: he would for once compose like *ces messieurs* of the Institute. At the same time he would try other means to secure his independence. The favorable review of his concert in the new daily, *Le Figaro,* gave him an opening to its editor, Victor Bohain, who was also a dramatist and theatrical manager. He had written a *Faust* ballet, which Berlioz agreed to set in a manner that the Opera might accept.

Meanwhile the English players pursued their conquest of France, playing with continued success for Miss Smithson in the large provincial towns. They then returned to Paris, were joined by Charles Kean, and gave *Richard III* and the *Merchant of Venice*. Berlioz saw his idol again, and ventured backstage but was not admitted. He sent messages which were not delivered; he only managed to find out that neither his name nor his recent success had penetrated as far as the insulated world of the foreign company.

Gloomy but undaunted, Berlioz went *en loge* in July, after the usual elimination contest with its obligato fugue. The cantata subject, *Herminie,* by the symbolically named poetaster, Vieillard, retold a scene from Tasso's *Jerusalem Delivered.* It depicted the love of Erminia, an infidel, for the Christian warrior Tancred, who is wounded while storming the gates of her city. Berlioz may well have seen something appropriate to his own situation in a subject by Tasso, the poet driven mad by love and thwarted ambition. At any rate, in musical matters Berlioz was always thoroughly master of himself, and bent as he now was on getting his prize, he produced a perfectly ordered and acceptable piece. He subdued his ideas to others' implied specifications, writing for what he termed "a modest middle-class orchestra," which would sound "interchangeable with its own piano reduction." He even kept the strings going steadily, so that his judges could understand what he was doing at all points. For Erminia's song he used the Estelle theme of his boyhood (later the *idée fixe* of the *Symphonie Fantastique*), developing it to a considerable extent, but being careful to introduce into its accompaniment phrases in the comic opera style of the day. As in his previous effort, he used a leitmotif, but made sure that its form remained simple and visible. At the very end, however, his decision to be conventional wavered. Instead of ending his piece with a cadence twice repeated, holding the high note and adding an eight-bar ritornello, he conceived a dramatically and musically more interesting close—an instrumental coda which as it were takes Erminia into battle. The gentle decrescendo lets us hear once again the theme of her prayer sung by flute, clarinet, and horns; then the horns drop out while the strings and bassoon continue the march theme to a final very soft pianissimo.

This inspiration was his undoing. After mixed counsels, he was given a second prize. Cherubini apparently spoke for him, and others—outside any of the musical cliques—wondered why a young composer who had won some acclaim in the City was not worthy of a first prize in the Grove. For according to custom the artists of the Institute met first in professional "sections," then as a committee of the whole for the final vote: painters and architects judged scores on the same footing as musicians judged canvases and busts.[7]

The second prize being purely honorific, Berlioz was still in debt, to Lesueur among others, and without word from his father. After consulting with his teacher, he took the not unusual step of writing to the Minister of Fine Arts, Comte de Martignac, asking for a grant-in-aid. Lesueur added a covering note which said that the request was founded on the most brilliant promise; Berlioz—was "born for music" and would in ten years be a great composer and the leader of a school. Without waiting for the reply, Hector decided to go home and plead with his parents again.

He left late in August 1828 hoping to stay less than a month. To his amazement, his second prize had done more to justify him than anything he had said or done singlehanded. There is indeed no place like home for such touches of subtle flattery. Their "prize-winning boy," "not twenty-five years old," "chosen by the Institute," was feted from house to house as far as Grenoble and back; but though he acted his role with affability and showed the native humor and gaiety which, as he once said, "sweeps away all cobwebs," Hector's mind was elsewhere. The songs of *Faust* were in his mind's ear, and on September 14, while riding in a carriage not far from where Estelle used to live, he composed the haunting melody for Gretchen's song of the King of Thule. Two days later he writes to Ferrand to come soon and bring with him a copy of *Faust* if he has one, so that together they can read Shakespeare and Goethe—those "mute confidants of my life." Except for tramping in the rain with his little sister, Hector felt alienated from the family and its concerns; it was the family, rather, who sought a *rapprochement*. Like a magician (now you see it, now you don't) the doctor restored Hector's allowance—luckily, as it turned out, for the Minister of Fine Arts "did not see his way clear to, etc. . . ."

Back in Paris by early October 1828, Berlioz resumed the struggle to establish himself. This crucial prize-giving had denied him the reward he had earned by seven years of hard work. According to any reasonable standard, his cantata should have won the prize; he had unquestionably learned all that the Conservatoire had to teach. With his immense capacity for work, to by-pass the prize and go his own way would at this stage have been of incalculable benefit to his health, morale, and artistic output. But the state of music in Paris made this impossible. Outside the subsidized theatres there was no livelihood for a serious composer, and these monopolies were hard to breach. Hence the *Faust* ballet was Berlioz' first care. Bohain's three-act scenario having been "accepted" by the Opera and partly set by the composer, the latter requested the inevitable Sosthènes to commission the score: "If you wish to know my qualifications, here they are: I have set to music the greater part of Goethe's poems [in *Faust*]. My head is full of the theme and if nature has endowed me with any imagination, I doubt whether I can find a subject more congenial to it." [8] *Faust* being as much in vogue as Shakespeare and more so than Beethoven, its musical prospects were good. Indeed the Opera had accepted not one but three librettos. The Théâtre des Nouveautés had successfully launched an opera based on the poem, and adaptations without music were numerous. Scribe, Boieldieu, and Meyerbeer all tackled the drama, but made no headway with it.

Though Bohain's likewise never saw the light of day, what Berlioz had written to the Vicomte was strictly true. While in his native mountains he had begun composing a sequence of eight scenes (comprising nine songs) to the verse portions of Gérard de Nerval's translation of the drama. All other means failing, Berlioz would publish the score at his own expense, dedicating it, in memory of past favors, to the Superintendent of Fine Arts.[9] Finished by February 1829, the work was issued two months later and despatched to Goethe with a modest but fervent letter on April 10. Goethe was charmed by the missive, which he deemed most gentlemanly, and also by the attention, which matched Delacroix's sending of his lithographs. These last, Goethe felt, "shed a new light on his own poem." He might have found a similar enlightenment in Berlioz' music had he been able to hear it, but he consulted his old friend Zelter—Mendelssohn's teacher—who replied damning the work as a series of grunts, snorts, and expectorations.

Berlioz sent out other copies of his work, which elicited considerable interest. Adolph Marx, of Berlin, termed Berlioz a disciple of Beethoven, and invited him to contribute to his musical journal. Fétis termed the score highly original, too much so for his taste, but full of talent and ease. He then served notice on the theater managers that they must make use of the composer, who was "destined to the highest success" provided he received encouragement.

As none of these calls brought down the walls of Jericho, Berlioz could only keep on trying all things. He had never been so busy: composing, attending the statutory number of classes at the Conservatoire; finding and teaching pupils—among them a Spanish heiress who paid regularly and well; and finally, for ends of his own which may be guessed, learning English. ("It takes a whole evening in a public course to learn what a private tutor could tell you in fifteen minutes.") Since the libretto of *Les Francs-Juges* had been definitely turned down, he was recasting parts of the music into a single scene entitled "The Warriors of the Breisgau." And fresh inspiration to compose came from reading translations by his friend Gounet from Thomas Moore's *Irish Melodies.* Soon, Berlioz had nine new songs, of which one, the *Elégie,* in honor of the Irish patriot, Robert Emmet, was perhaps the first modern composition written to a prose text. Berlioz entitled the collection *Mélodies Irlandaises,* thus naturalizing in France the term *mélodie* to denote a song.

Despite much activity, this second half of 1829 brought little change in Berlioz' state of mind. He was feverish and depressed by turns. At one point he secured the post of musical director in a new theater, only to lose it when the backer-manager withdrew. His debts to several friends preyed on his mind, and he took on additional hack work, such as the proofreading of Rossini's *William Tell,* for which he received two hundred francs. There was compensating pleasure in proofreading the Beethoven symphonies and preserving them from Fétis's numerous "corrections," at the cost of antagonizing the critic. Berlioz' *Faust* score meanwhile earned him very flattering comments by established composers, such as Onslow and Meyerbeer, but the publisher was postponing payment of the slim royalties. To add to Berlioz' distress, his friend Ferrand was ill, and dilatory in his replies as always: more than once Berlioz had had to supply his own lines for the libretto of the *Francs-Juges*. Now for divers reasons, Ferrand was being urged by his parents to drop Hector's acquaintance, and knowledge of this having got back to Berlioz hurt and disquieted him.

In addition, he had perforce taken to regular journalism as a source of income and a means to power. Although the pressure for copy was great and the pay nonexistent, he was Paris correspondent for Marx's Berlin paper, as well as frequent contributor to a new weekly, *Le Correspondant*. Despite its strongly royalist and religious bias, this periodical accepted Berlioz' unorthodox views on music. In the issue for April 11, 1829, for instance, he expounded his lifelong tenets regarding the proper treatment for fugal style and the compatibility of dramatic ideas with religious in sacred music. In the same place not long after, Berlioz began a short serial biography of Beethoven, who had died two years before. It is a careful piece of work, giving details which Berlioz had in part gathered from living acquaintances of the master—Reicha, Fétis, Cherubini, and even the gruff Kreutzer. After a century of Beethoven scholarship, this sketch and these recollections have dwindled in value, but one passage has kept its significance about both Berlioz and Beethoven. The writer is speaking of a recent concert at which the C-sharp Minor Quartet was given by Baillot's ensemble:

About two hundred persons were in the hall listening religiously. After a few minutes, the audience grew restless; people began to talk, each telling his neighbor of his increasing discomfort and boredom. Finally, unable to stand such weariness of spirit, nine tenths of the audience got up and left, complaining aloud that the music was unbearable, incomprehensible, ridiculous—the work of a madman defying common sense.

Silence was at last restored at the request of a few, and the quartet was concluded. Thereupon the voice of condemnation broke out again. M. Baillot was accused of making fools of the public by presenting extravagant nonsense. A few Beethoven devotees apologized, pleading the composer's mental derangement. "What a pity that such a great man should have produced deformities after all his masterpieces!"

Yet in one corner of the room there was a small group—

and I must confess, whatever one may say, that I was among them—whose thoughts and feelings were altogether different. This tiny fraction of the audience, suspecting what was going to happen, had huddled together so as not to be bothered in their contemplation. After a few bars in the first movement, I did indeed fear I might be bored, though I kept listening. Shortly the chaos seemed to unwind, and just when the public's patience gave out mine revived, and I fell under the spell of the composer's genius. . . . Here is music, then, which repels almost all those who hear it and which, among a few, produces sensations wholly out of the ordinary. Whence this enormous discrepancy?

Berlioz is sure that musical ignorance is not the answer. He knew that the most distinguished theorist-composers in his entourage were against Beethoven, but while he derived from *Freischütz* and Opus 131 "new sensations," they only wondered what the world was coming to.[10] Each generation, says Berlioz answering his own question, fears change; and the envious oppose what is new, knowing their own incapacity to create. Berlioz' sketch of Beethoven, fortunately published *after* his third prize attempt, amounted in fact to a declaration of war upon his elders. In the last installment, he calmly asserted that the Ninth Symphony, which he had read but which no one in Paris had heard, so far from showing a great man struggling with dementia, was on the contrary a starting point for the music of the present.

To this declaration the standard rebuttal, the eternal rejoinder, was that Beethoven's predecessors Haydn and Mozart had done all that could be done, and had thus left to Beethoven only the bizarre, the contorted, the "rocky ways" of music. Everyone forgot, everyone always forgets, that earlier still it was Mozart who was accused of treading the rocky ways. This historical view is here in point, for Berlioz was perfectly aware even then that he belonged in the sequence. Critics would in time come around to Beethoven, but only to say that he had accomplished all that music can do "along that line," which of course explains why Berlioz had to follow the rocky ways.[11]

Between his return to Paris in October 1828 and the publication of his Beethoven biography in the summer following, Berlioz' imaginings of love had gone through several stages dimly discernible in the record. Having managed to communicate with Harriet Smithson early in 1829, Hector had been led to suppose, or had deceived himself into supposing, that the actress took note of his suit and would test its sincerity by a few months' delay. Two months later, Berlioz, who by coincidence lodged in a house opposite that in which she came to live, discovered that she had left, this time not for the provinces but for Holland, perhaps never to return. For several weeks he put her out of his mind; then in June the sight of English newspapers praising her dramatic genius rekindled his flame and made him a prey to new self-torture.

All the while, he had been revolving in his mind a large-scale symphonic work on the theme of *Faust*. During these eight months he had evidently perfected himself in the art of living on two different planes. His personal existence, divided between love-longings and the struggle for position, had the breathless, incoherent, obsessive character which the usual accounts of his life like to stress. His artistic inner life, on the contrary, was as steady, coherent, and progressively successful as if he had been a recognized genius in mid-flight. The schemes, hopes, and disappointments suggest a desperate gambler, which is what, for the time, Dr. Berlioz and the Institute made of him. But the music, the penmanship of letters and scores, the style of musical articles, the work at the Conservatoire—not to speak of the course in English—imply a very different being, whose characteristics are deliberate care, self-control, judgment, method, and an almost academic love of minutiae.

This craftsman's delight in the thing well done was nothing new. When in the throes of adolescence at La Côte, Berlioz had managed to make his notebook of romances as neat and systematic as a legal document. Throughout life his manuscripts were clear and even handsome, for where music was concerned patience never deserted him, not even in the most trying circumstances of the battle still ahead of him. Hence in Berlioz it is more than usually misleading to read the outward event into the work of art. If the two are connected it is deep down, invisibly, and not in the direct way of an offprint which the casual onlooker may read.

Berlioz' love for his unattainable Harriet undoubtedly dwelt with him, influencing his musical inspiration just as Estelle earlier had moved his childish heart and spurred his melodic invention. But other children and other youths have had unhappy loves and composed nothing at all, hence the relation of life to art is not one of simple cause and effect. Again, Hector's love for Miss Smithson seems clearly theatrical in both senses of the word. It is as if Berlioz had *wanted,* rather than had been brought, to love her. In this he was following the very respectable French tradition of the *amour de tête,* which is a form of idealism or true Platonic striving after an imagined perfection. The composer's fancy lighted on a woman who was charming to behold, possessed of talent, praised by others, living the life of art, and intimately associated with the thought of Shakespeare. It is even possible to conjecture that Berlioz was spiting his family by choosing an actress—or again, that Mme. Berlioz had unwittingly given him a taste for tragic scenes.

This heady passion, in a young man who had as yet had little or no personal attention from women, clearly drew on the emotional resources he had mentioned to his father when he spoke of his musical career; so that far from ascribing the music of these years to the love affair, it would be more plausible to explain the love by artistic passion. At the moment their joint effect was only to stiffen his ambition and sharpen his sense of loneliness. Yet even while he believed that his infatuation would kill him, Berlioz recognized that contrary to all maxims he could apparently love without hope. He has not a shred of hope left, he says as he gets ready for his third try at the Rome Prize in July 1829, but all the same he is copying the orchestra parts of his *Faust* scenes and of his remodeled *Francs-Juges.* The words of this operatic scene are to be translated into German for a possible production by Spohr in Kassel. Berlioz may have already sensed that Germany rather than Paris was his proper battleground, and after Rome (where the prize would compel him to go) he would spend a year in the land of Weber and Beethoven. Meantime he is trying to assure a good reception for the *Irish Melodies* which are in the press, and there is the usual tension preparatory to going *en loge.*

The subject for the 1829 competition was *The Death of Cleopatra,* the words being from the same Vieillard as the year before—feeble but malleable. From his knowledge of Shakespeare Berlioz could of course conjure up a greater Cleopatra, worthier of his music, but quite apart from the musical problem, the politics of the award was ticklish for both sides. It was impossible for the candidate to write a cantata more unlike himself than that of the previous year; it would be a parody.[12] On the judges' side it was understood that a Second Prize normally matured into a First, yet they resented their "pupil's" growing reputation as well as the divided counsels he brought into their midst. The worst of it was that Lesueur was too ill to attend, and at the meeting the performer once again failed to do Berlioz justice: this time it was the singer who was called to a rehearsal of *William Tell* and sent her neophyte sister. Without proper rehearsal, she freshly murdered Cleopatra, and despite the protests of Ingres and Pradier at this accidental unfairness to the candidate, the jury decided to give no awards, reserving the right to give two the following year.

The music of Berlioz' *Cleopatra* is as interesting as that of his *Orpheus,* freer and still more assured than that of *Herminie.* Rich in melodies—some were too good to waste and Berlioz used them again—the three arias range from antique declamation in Gluck's style to the Shakespearean vision of Cleopatra dreaming that her shade greets those of all the Ptolemies. This section bears a motto from *Romeo and Juliet,* "How if, when I am laid into the tomb . . ." written in English—which probably strengthened the judges' belief that young Berlioz positively declined to be understood. The last section is a subtly scored death scene, here and there suggestive of the love-philter music in *Tristan,* thirty years ahead.

The day after the announcement of the blank result, Berlioz met Boieldieu, the amiable composer of the opera *Dame Blanche,* who had sided with the majority and now tried to explain himself: "My dear fellow, why did you do it? We *wanted* to give you the prize, thinking you would be a better boy than last year. . . . I don't say your work isn't good. But how can I pass judgment on what I do not understand? There are so many things I've had to hear over and over again before I liked them. I couldn't help saying to my colleagues yesterday that with your way of writing you must despise us from the bottom of your heart. You refuse to write like everybody else. Even your rhythms are new. You would invent new modulations if such a thing were possible!"

As for Auber, who like Cherubini had voted for Berlioz, he warned Hector in a fatherly way that if he persisted "the public will not like it and the music sellers will not buy." Berlioz nodded sagely but discharged his retort into the friendly bosom of Ferrand: "If we are supposed to write music for pastrycooks and dressmakers, why do they give us a text involving the passions of the Queen of Egypt and her solemn meditations upon death?"

For the fifth and last time Dr. Berlioz used financial pressure to draw Hector home. This meant three weeks wasted to rehash the old story, not to mention the expense and weariness of the trip: those idle hours in a stagecoach, with one's nerves in knots, and under compulsion to exchange small talk with passengers for whom the few miles of their journey is the most exciting event of the decade. In spite of everything, Berlioz' first symphony was taking shape, and with or without an allowance, he was sure he could last another year. He now had a steady job teaching guitar in an "orthopedic" institution for young ladies, and though not prosperous he was no longer an unknown. All the more reason to act.

He could sense that the cultural movement of which he was a part was about to make its victorious assault on the academic Bastille. The theaters had already surrendered to the new playwrights—to Dumas's *Henry III* and to Victor Hugo's *Hernani,* scheduled for the following season. New names and new genres were gaining currency in pleasant profusion: among novelists, Balzac's *Les Chouans,* Vigny's *Cinq Mars,* and Mérimée's *Charles IX;* Sainte-Beuve's *Poetry of the 16th Century* was out in book form. The political historians, Thiers, Guizot, Sismondi, Barante, and Thierry were crowding the market with readable and revolutionary works, Michelet was translating Vico and reinterpreting the whole of Europe's past as a struggle for freedom. And the Salon was being invaded by the colorful enormities of Decamps, Huet, and Delacroix.

Nor did music lag behind: Rossini's new opera, *William Tell,* was a richer and more serious work than his usual "string of romances and cavatinas." Auber had just written his *Muette de Portici,* which would soon cause political riots, not by its form but by its subject—the struggle against tyrants.[13] Outside the operatic stage and the virtuoso platform, Berlioz stood alone, preaching the modern art of Beethoven. But neither Beethoven nor his prophet would be heard unless Berlioz gave a second concert at his own risk. This time Cherubini gave the hall, the players readily accepted, and Habeneck conducted. To his two overtures and the *Resurrexit* of the Mass (retouched again) Berlioz added the "Concert of Sylphs" from the *Eight Scenes of Faust.* He also induced his new friend Ferdinand Hiller, a young German who taught at the same girls' school, to play Beethoven's piano concerto in E flat—the first time in Paris. As window dressing, an Italian coloratura and two virtuoso instrumentists were added to the program. Despite the dangerous proximity of Beethoven's masterpiece, the musicians once again acclaimed Berlioz' overtures, and what is more, the box office netted a profit of one hundred and fifty francs. At this the government took notice and awarded Berlioz a bonus of one hundred francs, to offset the "nominal" charge made for the hall.

But the next day Hector was ill and deep in depression. He gave all these news to his father, deploring the absence of any member of the family, and adding: "Since yesterday I am depressed unto death; I should like to weep forever; . . . I wish I could die . . . I cannot connect one idea with another . . . I think I ought to sleep a great deal." The newspapers cordially acknowledged the success of the concert but scarcely analyzed the new music. Only Fétis in his austere *Revue* kept track of "the feverish young man, whose fever is not that of an ordinary being." In Berlioz' music, exclaimed the writer, "What accents from another world! What effects, varied in a thousand ways, sometimes felicitous, sometimes repellent, but almost always new and well found: they have shaken the souls of all the listeners."

One of the works, the Faustian "Concert of Sylphs," which was later rescored and transferred to the *Damnation of Faust,* had missed fire. In a passing reference to this fact, Berlioz who knew its worth, explains that he "had not had time to teach it to the performers nor to the public"—a remark of greater significance to his subsequent career and posthumous fame than he could possibly surmise.

CHAPTER 5

REVOLUTION IN JULY

Composed it on the spot—Mars by day, Apollo by night—bang the fieldpiece, twang the lyre.—Pickwick Papers

Eighteen-thirty, the year of revolutions, brought as much inner as outer upheaval in Berlioz' existence. In the career of one who began life so young, this twelvemonth seems in retrospect like the last act of a Shakespearean history in many parts: triumphs and reversals, endings and fresh beginnings crowd the short period to an accompaniment of cannon and trumpets. Not guessing its perfect symmetry, Berlioz opened the year with the musical subject that marked its close: "My working plans," he wrote to Humbert Ferrand on January 2, "are laid down for a good while ahead; I must compose for my concert a great instrumental work. . . ." Berlioz therefore declined a poem dealing with Faust's last night on earth which Ferrand had apparently begun. "If I had it in my hands," the musician argued, "I could not resist composing it." His own ideas about *Faust* were taking another form—that of a grand symphony whose outlines had "long been worked out."

The concert would have to take place before the Prize Competition in July, Berlioz' purpose being, as before—as always—to force the judges' hands or the Opera's doors by conquering the public. This necessity was both individual and cultural. In *The Red and the Black*, "a chronicle of 1830," Stendhal says that life must begin with a duel, and in Balzac's projection of himself, Rastignac looks down from the hills on Paris, saying "It's between you and me." Fiction mercifully reduces to one decisive battle what in many artists' lives is a Thirty Years'

War. And besides challenges and victories, war is made up of labors which are often sordid: Berlioz was still plagued by money troubles. He was again in debt to several of his close friends, and although his father sent him cash from time to time, remittance was usually followed by shopping orders, payable at once and likely to "disturb my whole economy." Two private pupils brought in forty-four francs a month in addition to the salary from Mme. Daubrée's school for young ladies. But the life of art, and particularly of music, is expensive. "I am as hard up as a painter," he reports, using the traditional comparison. Fortunately, as a musician and critic, Berlioz had his entrees at all the theaters and he need not disburse for this essential pleasure. Fortunately also, he managed to go on doing his own work in the mysterious oases of a calmed spirit and doing the world's work at the feverish pace that the world exacts.

Having enlisted the good will of the managers at the Nouveautés, the same theater where he had sung for a living not long before, Berlioz felt that his next concert had a fair chance of success. Though the chorus at his disposal was of only average quality, the orchestra was superior, and it was led by a devoted admirer named Bloc. With the addition of some of his other supporters in the Conservatoire and Opera orchestras, he would have a first-class instrument. A date toward the end of May would best fit in with the public's habits and with his own arrangements. Considering the amount of copying, correcting, and rehearsing to do for a work not yet written out, even this schedule would call for rapid composition. Hence the advantage of having ideas in one's head for a good while before committing them to paper.

Berlioz was also occupied during these same months in securing the acceptance of a new libretto at the Opera, not to mention keeping up his work as critic and as student at the Conservatoire. But these duties he could easily take in stride. Life was difficult rather on account of the unsatisfactory and unsatisfied state of his feelings. Harriet Smithson continued to come and go, and Berlioz' infatuation with her did likewise, though more fitfully. A promise she had apparently made through go-betweens, of putting her lover on probation, turned out to be an expedient on their part to get rid of him. When he discovered this, his ardor cooled. He enjoyed stretches of peace and freedom, whether she was in London or Paris. Then he suddenly fell again into "the anguish of endless and inextinguishable passion, without motive, without object. . . ." His pain was "useless, terrible."

To heartache was added a persistent toothache, which before the days of the dental drill Berlioz tried to cure by himself. As a student of medicine he was almost as patiently experimental as when he composed music, and he finally found a specific, which he communicated to Ferrand suffering from the same cause. The sort of remedy suggested the proper treatment for his own heart: "It can only be cured by a specific against life." He noticed that straining in so many directions paralyzed the will: "I was on the point of beginning my symphony . . . it was all in my head, but I cannot write a thing. We must wait."

This mixture of philosophy and irony was the sign of an inner revolution, indeed a revulsion of feeling. On returning one day from a long walk calculated to wear out his anguish and finding in Moore's poems the text of a Farewell Elegy to the Beloved, Berlioz was surprised to find himself able to compose the music on the spot. The experience shook him so that ever afterwards he declined to have the song performed, but as he himself noted, this was the only instance when he had been "able to render a feeling while still under its immediate and active influence." One may wonder whether this was not the exception that proves to be the rule in disguise:—one suspects that the feeling was dead or dying.

Another letter, this time to Ferdinand Hiller, the friendly young German who taught piano at Mme. Daubrée's, and who was further distinguished as having visited Beethoven thrice at his deathbed, marks the change in Berlioz' attachment to his inaccessible Ophelia: "Can you tell me what this power to feel, this faculty for suffering is, which is killing me? Ask your angel, the seraph who has opened to you the gates of heaven. . . . Still, let us not repine. . . ." For when he is tempted to this weakness, Berlioz imagines that "Beethoven looks upon me with severity; Spontini, who is far above ills like mine, regards me with an air of indulgent pity; and Weber, speaking in my ear like a familiar spirit, awaits me in a blessed country to console me. . . . All this is crazy," he adds, "utterly crazy, from the point of view of a domino player at the Café de la Régence or a member of the Institute. No! I mean to live yet awhile. Music is a heavenly art; nothing is above it save true love. The one may make me as unhappy as the other, but I shall at any rate have lived. . . .

"It is today exactly one year since I saw her for the last time. Unhappy woman, how I loved you! I write with a shudder that I do love you. . . . In fact, I am a very miserable man . . . an animal burdened with an exhausting imagination, eaten up with a boundless passion. . . . Yes! But I have known a few musical geniuses, I have been gladdened by their visions, and I grind my teeth only from unhappy memories."

Berlioz himself will soon be telling us more about this very palpable seraph of Hiller's. The tug of war in Hector's heart was finally decided by mid-April 1830. A kind friend told Berlioz either gossip or fabrications casting doubts on the nature of Harriet's relations with her manager. It was a blow in spite of the lover's natural return to reason. "My vessel," he told Ferrand, "strained at every seam but finally righted itself." He is on the way to a complete cure, or "as complete as my natural tenacity will allow."

Berlioz' natural tenacity had in any event allowed him to finish his symphony, of which he unfolded the dramatic plan to his friend. The title records the ending of the emotional strain in Berlioz far more than it describes the music itself:

" 'Episode in an Artist's Life' (grand fantastic symphony in five parts) *First Movement:* double, composed of a short adagio immediately followed by a developed allegro . . . *Second Movement:* Scenes in the Country (adagio . . .) *Third Movement:* A Ball (brilliant, headlong music) *Fourth Movement:* March to Execution (fierce, *pomposo*) *Fifth Movement:* Dream of a Witches' Sabbath.[1]

"And now, dear friend, here is how I've fashioned my novel, or rather my story, whose hero you will recognize . . ."

Then follows the first version of the famous "program" of the symphony. It was as secondary in the composer's mind as the place it occupies in this letter, or as its ostensible cause—the hero's love for Miss Smithson. The musical plan, described in musical terms, came first. The letter closed with thoughts of performance and friendship:

"I have just written the last note and I am afraid I shan't be able to have the parts copied in time [that is, by May 30]. For the moment, I feel stupid; the frightful stretch of thought to produce my piece has tired my imagination and I'd like to be able to sleep and rest continuously. But though my brain is drugged, my heart is awake and I feel most strongly that I miss you. When, dear friend, *shall* I see you?"

Humbert replied with such delicate sympathy to Hector's news about Harriet, and about the completion of the symphony, that the composer, who sometimes thought of himself as "almost isolated" and struggling amid universal indifference, was deeply moved. Berlioz replied in words that not only testify to his affectionate and remembering nature—his tenacity in feeling as well as in effort—but also confirm the impression that friendship in the Romantic period was a species of love affair: "It is so rare, my dear Humbert, to find a complete man, with a soul, a heart, and an imagination; so rare for characters as ardent and impatient as ours to meet and be matched together, that I hardly know how to tell you the happiness it gives me to know you." Berlioz values Humbert's "solicitude, anxiety, and advice" with regard to the Smithson "episode," and wishes it clearly understood that the symphony is not a deed of revenge. "It is certainly not in that spirit that I wrote the Witches' Sabbath. I pity and despise her. She is an ordinary woman, gifted with an instinctive genius for reproducing the wrackings of the human soul without ever having felt them, and incapable of conceiving a mighty and noble attachment such as that with which I honored her."

It is traditional for the unrequited lover to welcome like a reprieve the news that his idol is unworthy of him, so here again Berlioz is following tradition. Yet his judgment was not far from the truth in estimating the emotional make-up of the Shakespearean actress. Had he only been able to remember his own words when Harriet once more came within his ken, he might have spared himself much anguish. But she was now part of him and his "natural tenacity" would not let her memory go. The suffering and introspection undergone about her had certainly served him, for although his symphony was not in any literal sense about her, any more than his future works were about the accidents of his life, the power which creates music and the power which creates a beloved person are related if not identical. As Yeats says somewhere, "True love is a discipline. . . . Each divines the secret self of the other, and refusing to believe in the mere daily self, creates a mirror where the lover or the beloved sees an image to copy in daily life." Stendhal calls the process "crystallization," comparing the beloved to an ordinary twig which one dips into a saline spring and which comes out sparkling with a thousand jewels.

Whether Berlioz' next essay in loving has or has not artistic significance, it shows at any rate a pleasing variation from his first. At the institution where he and Hiller taught music to the crippled daughters of the rich, they had a third colleague, a pianist like Hiller, named Marie Moke, commonly called Camille. She was the daughter of an unpractical professor from Ghent, whose wife had left him in order to support herself and promote their child's musical career by keeping a linen shop in Paris. The shop had been given up when Camille—a pupil of Kalkbrenner's—had herself become a teacher. She shone by virtue of natural abilities and acquired graces. She was small and of a lively beauty—an oval face, dark hair and blue eyes, a bewitching figure and a light step, which led Berlioz to nickname her Ariel. But though gay and teasing she passed for a proper young lady, ostensibly chaperoned by her mother or a suitable substitute. Gifted and self-assured, she was determined to succeed.

She also liked masculine attentions, and as Hiller tells us in his long-subsequent memoirs, he and Camille found a way to exchange greetings first, then unsupervised visits, which were made possible by Mlle. Moke's having pupils at various points in the city. For some reason Hiller came to use Berlioz as his messenger, with predictable results. Berlioz' reserved manner, the story of his hopeless love for the illustrious actress, his maturer mien—he was twenty-six and Hiller hardly nineteen—aroused Camille's curiosity and she set about to break down his defenses. As Hiller is the first to admit, she finally told Berlioz outright that she loved him and that his reticence was foolish. Hers was the gift that makes artfulness assist and not replace nature: she was a siren as well as an extraordinarily good musician and vivacious companion. It was not long before she achieved her new conquest. By the end of April, Berlioz had done with Harriet. By the middle of May, he was completing his arrangements for the concert on the thirtieth; he was in touch with Haitzinger, the leading tenor of the German theater in Paris, for a production of his *Francs-Juges* opera at Carlsruhe, and hoping to go there himself in a few months. He was also pushing the same opera in the lesser Paris houses. By the beginning of July 1830, that is to say before the time set for the Rome Prize competition, Berlioz and Camille were thoroughly in love.

The letters which convey to Humbert Ferrand the progress of this affair doubtless sound foolish, like the earlier rhapsodies about Harriet, but the later ones display a superior brand of foolishness. "All that love offers that is most tender and delicate, I have from her. My enchanting sylph, my Ariel, my life, seems to love me more than ever. Her mother keeps saying that if she read about us in a novel, she would not credit it . . . I'm now locked up in the Institute *for the last time;* I must have that prize, on which our happiness so largely depends. Like Don Carlos in *Hernani,* I say: 'I *will* have it.' *She* is anxious about it too, and to reassure me in my prison, Mme. Moke sends me her maid every other day to give me news of them and take back news of me. God! How I shall reel when I see her again in ten or twelve days! We'll have many obstacles to overcome, perhaps, but *we will.* What do you think of all this? Is it conceivable? An angel like her, the finest talent in Europe . . . Oh, my dear fellow, if you heard her *think aloud* the sublime thoughts of Weber and Beethoven, you would lose your wits!"

This is love chatter of the sort that Molière approved when he said that the only reasonable way to love was to love madly. For the first time Berlioz' senses were awakened, and not merely his imagination: he was actually loved and kissed and doted over by an intelligent and beautiful creature. Camille must have been equally caught by his great capacity for passionate expression. "Delicate and tender" denote soothing qualities that are too readily ascribed by men to women in general, but that the son of Mme. Berlioz would probably not mistake, even though Camille had been the aggressor. She was so obviously a woman with whom conversation was possible, *the* woman fated by talent and inclination to be Berlioz' partner, comforter, lover—and wife, for Mme. Moke's privity to these love passages meant that Berlioz had made honorable proposals. A M. de Noailles, a friend of the Moke family, had spoken in Hector's favor as a match worth risking from the practical point of view. But this was not decisive. The rival without whom no comedy is complete was a man of fifty-eight, M. Pleyel, successor to the firm which Hector had approached about his first compositions when a boy of sixteen. Of course M. Pleyel's solid advantages outweighed those of the impetuous and impecunious young artist, and Mme. Moke's consent to the engagement between Camille and Hector may have been secretly provisional.

As for "Ariel," her coquetry and premeditation at the beginning, together with her greater experience of love-making, led to recurrences of that private double-intention which usually precedes faithlessness. The attentions of her devoted genius no doubt flattered her, his personal magnetism, which so many people were to feel and speak of, moved her, and his obvious innocence touched her. But his musical powers and artistic opinions made her feel an inferiority she sometimes rebelled against. To tease her fiancé and reassert her mastery, she would play him some trivial air, or some Italian cavatina with improvised embroideries that set his teeth on edge. When she declared that those fireworks were at any rate "prettier" and "more amusing" than his favorite Beethoven adagios, Berlioz would storm and preach and remonstrate, unwilling to hide from himself or from her that such a preference cut them asunder. He was head over heels in love, but music was his religion and just criticism a necessity of his nature. And at this she would laugh a shrill laugh. Not that she lacked a soulful side. She could play Beethoven magnificently and even feel or pretend that such playing sapped her strength, so that Hector would beg her to refrain from such musical indulgence. Clearly Camille was a two-sided creature, half Ariel, half coquette, and Berlioz' efforts to keep her at spiritual concert pitch may have sown doubts into her mind whether this orphic lover should enlarge into a husband.

The torments of the artist in love with a woman who by training and taste is conventional and worldly-wise have given rise to the maxim that any man with work to do should forego what is called romantic love; and to modern ears, full of echoes of science, the adjective suggests nothing precise or deserving respect. The truth, however, is more complex. The Romanticists themselves knew better than to be clinical or foolishly "romantic" about love. If they had to be given a label, they would have to be called "comprehensive realists," men who instinctively knew that there is more than one layer to experience and many mysteries encountered in exploring it.

Consider for example that "romantic" drama and historic event, Victor Hugo's play, *Hernani*. Berlioz was one of the squad of Hugo's defenders who on February 25, 1830, helped make the first night a success, but neither he nor a number of other partisans mistook Hugo's drama for a report on their own view of life, love, or historical truth. Although the play dealt with love in relation to social class, the rallying of an artistic generation to its support is not to be explained by "romantic" interest in this ordinary sense. The point of the battle was not philosophic but strategic. The victory meant a public recognition of certain technical liberties which had already been wrested in print, and supporting the play meant the public affirmation of freedom for all the arts.

This was something more than defiance and eccentricity, and in stressing the "revolt" we forget the high spirits. We hear of Théophile Gautier, aged eighteen, and of Gérard de Nerval—the translator of *Faust*—each leading his shock troops, whom Hugo had provided with a red card bearing the Spanish password *Hierro* (iron), but we must not miss the tone of self-mocking. We hear of Gautier's red waistcoat, which was in fact pink (on the reversed principle of the English hunting coat which is called pink and is in fact red), but we should recall his intense application as a student of poetry and painting. And at the same time we should think of the Gargantuan picnic held in the deserted theatre hours before the performance, the Rabelaisian traces being left, in the exuberance of youth, to discomfit later comers. Clearly the battle of Hernani was in part a collegiate "rag," in part a public demonstration of bright youth against bourgeois old age. The rebels wore their hair long and left their beards untrimmed in order to be conspicuous and because the academicians in the parterre were baldpates—whence their designation as *perruques* (wigs). There was a hint of flaunted sexual superiority in the manifestation, and its seriousness lay precisely in its refusal to be solemn.

To the playwright and his fellow romanticists, the virtue of this open cabal was that it was not bought support but testimony to principle. It was an artists' claque like the smaller one that Berlioz had himself organized for Gluck at the Opera. Hugo having passed the official barrier of the subsidized *Comédie Française* by getting *Hernani* accepted, it was essential for him and his friends to keep the work from being hissed off the stage. But the *perruques* were as determined as the innovators; for them the encounter was not only a defense of taste and tradition but of cash royalties. If the new school won, the old clichés would no longer be marketable. To preserve the sanctity of verse and dramatic seemliness, the *perruques* must shout down this "formless" work in which the scenes were laid in different places, in which the lines did not pause exactly in the middle, in which the meaning overran the riming edge of each verse, and in which such intolerable bluntness was reveled in as saying aloud "It is midnight."

Hugo's defenders won. The play ran on for an unusual

stretch of forty-five nights, enriching its author though exhausting his friends, for each night a new batch of Parisian bourgeois had to be outfought with lung power. What was finally vindicated, however, was not a new school of drama. Had *Hernani* been too unlike the older plays it would never have been accepted and produced by a company of actors brought up in the old tradition. What was won was the freedom to make verse varied and flexible, and the right of the artist to recreate reality by using the concrete, particular detail, and even the commonplace. The one scene that hushed both friends and enemies, the love scene between the brigand Hernani and the patrician Doña Sol, implied another lesson based on a natural fact—that love does not consult the Almanach de Gotha; but of equal importance was that it reintroduced lyric utterance into tragedy. These liberties, snatched in public before the habit-ridden Parisians had, for all the arts, the value of a successful revolution.

The new freedom did not of course commit every Romanticist to a complete acceptance of *Hernani.* Berlioz, in giving his sisters an account of the play, made reservations: "I find in it certain things, especially ideas, that are sublime, and other things and ideas that are ridiculous . . . as for the verse, which I dislike anyway in the theatre, these run-over lines and broken half-lines which enrage the classicists leave me quite indifferent. When spoken it all sounds like prose and for that reason alone I could prefer it. But since *Hernani* was meant to be in verse and since Hugo knows how to write regular verse when he wants, it would have been simpler to follow the taste of the crowd—it would have saved the breath of all the jackdaws of the pit. The innovation is one that leads nowhere. Still, Hugo has destroyed the unities of time and place and for that I take an interest in him as a daredevil who risks death to set a mine under an old barrier."

With the knowledge of what Shakespearean form could do for his own work, Berlioz supported Hugo on the unities, but curiously failed to see why the poet attacked the rigid, foursquare line and the stopping of sense with rime. Yet it was the same Berlioz whose melody and rhythm broke with rigidity and squareness, and who had written a little earlier: "When I think of this realm of chords which scholastic prejudice has kept untouched to this day, and which since my emancipation [from the Conservatoire] I regard as my own domain, I rush forward in a kind of frenzy to explore it." In effect, Berlioz was accomplishing reforms parallel to Hugo's; and so were Balzac and Stendhal, who sat apart from the rest on the famous night and later voiced strong dissent from Hugo's supposed principles. Delacroix, also present, soon grew to hate the label Romantic, and while indulging his distrust of both Hugo and Berlioz, dissociated himself from the movement which he none the less incarnates in the art of painting.

Thus in the aftermath of *Hernani* Berlioz and four of his peers, working in parallel ways for comparable ends, were kept by the fog of contemporariness from recognizing their intimate kinship. At best they sensed the common resistance and conceded one another a certain esteem. For a time they used, or they redefined for special use, the term "Romanticist." Berlioz, in an article of this very year 1830, discussed "classic and romantic music," but he was not attached to the word, and generally the new artists found the name embarrassing. In truth, all historic names are unsatisfactory—Renaissance, Gothic, Baroque, and Puritan, no less than Romantic. If the historian heeded individual disclaimers, every movement would be entirely emptied of participants. The names remain, for convenience and as a reminder of stylistic unity.

As for the Romantic temperament, enough of Berlioz' life has been shown to suggest that his nature was very complex, and not to be defined as simply "wild" or "rebellious," nor as the predominance of heart over intellect. In his first love affair the very opposite was true. His genuinely romantic love was precisely unlike what we think of as a storybook romance: it is the modern, fiction-fed public that boils down *Romeo and Juliet* to the balcony scene; the Romantic-realist Shakespeare required the feud and the murders, the coarse chitchat of the Nurse, the union of spirits and bodies, and even the preparation of Romeo by an earlier unrequited love.[2]

Berlioz' love for Camille Moke, or Victor Hugo's for Juliette Drouet, each following an attachment (like Romeo's) to a cool or distant goddess, fulfills this condition of completeness, of versatility, of eager exchange of selves, at the price of possible tragedy. The difference between this sort of romance and the ordinary sort is that the first is properly a piece of work, an energetic fusion of mind, sense, and knowledge into passion truly so called. Most people are as incapable, or as unwilling, to make this effort as they are to write a poem or compose a quartet. Convention sustains them in their laziness and so "romance" becomes a byword for trifling. Critics of manners can only conclude that in society a great emotion is as rare as a great idea, and thus on every point the man of thought is bound to conflict with the man of common experience. To the artist, idea and emotion are one, and love and art have a common root in the dedication of the person to a self-justifying activity. Hence Berlioz says that great music is only inferior to great love, and conversely that a passion for music is as complete a dedication of one's whole being as love or religious vows. On one side stands flirting or sensual sport; on the other, marriage for convenience; and beyond both, romantic love in the tradition of the troubadours, Dante, Heloïse, or Tristram.

Being simply affectionate as well as romantically passionate, Berlioz felt great misery in being at odds with his family over the very reason for his existence as he saw it—art. Until now he was still in their eyes a wayward son. Happily, in the midst of his preparations for the concert of May 1830, Hector received from his father a letter which made the son reply at once: "My excellent Father: How I thank you for your letter! What good it did me! You are then beginning to have a little confidence in me? I hope I may live to justify it. It is the first time you have written to me in this way, and I thank you a thousand times. It is such bliss to be able to bring honor and pleasure to those who are dear to us. Of course I should be delighted to have you hear me—*of course.* But for you to take a trip to Paris there must be more positive assurance of the concert, which in fact can be put off at the slightest whim of those in authority."

This prudent thought proved correct. The concert had to be postponed, each of the several parties to the arrangements waiting upon the others' authorization—the manager of the hall and of the orchestra, the Prefect of Police ("whose subordinates try to make an affair of state out of a mere formality"), and the Superintendent, "who could stop everything if he wishes, for in this free country the musicians are numbered among the slaves."

Other plans included the trip to Carlsruhe for launching the *Francs-Juges* and the winning of the prize—"If I can make myself small enough *to pass through the gates of the kingdom of heaven.*" These two objects would not be incompatible, provided the compulsory stay in Italy which went with the prize could be shortened and the optional sojourn in Germany lengthened. Failing Carlsruhe, there was Kassel, where Berlioz heard that Spohr "unlike the Paris composers" was favorable to new music.

About the same time a libretto based on Chateaubriand's novel *Atala* had been unanimously accepted by the Opera and orally promised to Berlioz for setting. The management had been strongly pressed by the influential composer Onslow, who had read the score of *Les Francs-Juges* and become an enthusiastic supporter of Berlioz. But the inevitable two-party system was developing around the newcomer. The opposition numbered some who had never heard his music but who had exercised a preventive caution by circulating the rumor that Berlioz was insane. The libretto moreover alarmed M. Lubbert, the Opera director. *Atala* was in a new genre—romantic, he thought—which "he did not want to introduce." He felt that "Auber and Rossini were enough novelty" and that "even if Beethoven and Weber came back to life, he would have nothing to do with them." The truth was that the director, being responsible to both the government and his financial backers, was looking for a sure draw. Rossini having broken the monopoly of the Gluckist school, the Opera had nothing left. Weber was too great a risk; Mozart always had to be patched up and failed anyhow. A new, adaptable, and money-making composer must be found; it was not likely that a revolutionary like Berlioz would turn into a darling of the public.

Berlioz could see through the director's irrelevant excuses; and writing of the general situation, the composer gives us the mood of 1830—the sense of a general apathy no longer bearable, especially after the victory of *Hernani*. There is a whiff of apprehension at the government's stubbornness and a hint of disaster, foreshadowing the barricades of July: "The Feydeau house is in the last stages of musical degradation . . . That odious monopoly must fall, and it will fall if the petition is presented to the Chamber of Deputies. Benjamin Constant [a famous liberal member] and two others were to sponsor it had the Chamber not been dismissed. Would anyone believe that any foreign troupe can set up an opera in Paris, while the French alone must submit to being skinned alive at Feydeau? . . . Apparently nothing must be done to give umbrage to that conservatory of routines and clichés; everything must be done to increase the prosperity of the rondo, the romance, and the duet. And despite the great power of these musical forms we must give subsidies out of the taxes (paid by provincials who never see a comic opera) in order to enable a new director to go bankrupt every other year." Through the voice of the exasperated Berlioz speaks the Liberal of 1830: "Why for heaven's sake not let them all play what they like—operas grand or little—give subsidies to none, and allow bankruptcy to take its course? It will cost the taxpayer less in the end, and some theatres will find a way to thrive."

Unrest was in the air and Berlioz was right to doubt whether his "instrumental drama would inspire sufficient interest to bring back to Paris" the public summering outside the capital. By the end of May, his concert was definitely postponed until autumn. But he had heard his new symphony at the first two rehearsals and he was fully reassured. "I apparently did not fool myself when I was writing it. Everything is as I conceived it. Only the March to Execution is fifty times more terrifying than I expected." The rehearsals were a strain, because the orchestra had to "blaze a trail through a virgin forest. Besides many things that are new to them, the greatest difficulty is that of expression, in the first movement especially. . . . It will take angelic patience on the part of the conductor to teach them all the nuances." In spite of contretemps, then, Berlioz' score—a revolutionary work if only in this elaboration of expressive nuances—actually resounded in Parisian air before the Rome Award and before the political revolution.[3]

It came into being also before a new piece by Berlioz, an overture-fantasia on Shakespeare's *Tempest,* whose public presentation happened to precede that of the symphony. The *Tempest* piece owes its double inspiration to Shakespeare and to Berlioz' feminine "Ariel," so it must have been taking shape in his mind in the late spring of 1830. These middle months of the year were in truth dramatically full. Berlioz' revulsion of feeling against Harriet Smithson coincided with her descent to a mute role in an inferior work, under the pressure of financial need. As the play opened, the *Figaro,* still counting on the performance of Berlioz' symphony, published the famous program which is supposed to retrace the development of the composer's love for the actress. The document attracted considerable attention in artistic circles at the time, though as is now clear its biographical worth is slight. Finally, during the early summer, Hector and Camille were making plans to be married as soon as he had won the prize.

He went *en loge* for the fourth time on July 15. Like other things, the cantata subject showed the influence of the stirrings of change: the poem on "The Death of Sardanapalus" was an almost prophetic choice. Harking back to Byron, it depicted a king refusing to abdicate and perishing in the fire set by his own hand—a drama which gained in vividness from the recollection of Delacroix's provocative masterpiece, exhibited at a previous Salon. Shut up in his little cell, Berlioz thought he had at last mastered the art of avoiding the evil consequences of his genius. He put all his skill into making a "regular" work, reserving his inspirations for a kind of appendix, which he would tack on afterwards, when the prize was safely in his pocket. For at the public performance in the autumn he could not afford to appear in the artistic undress of a routine score.

Things fell out as he had planned—or nearly. He won the First Prize by a unanimous vote, which was unheard of, and doubly remarkable because of the unusually large number of candidates. He was moreover the "first first" for the Institute having a prize left over from the previous year, was obliged to choose two firsts. Finally, at the public audition, after Berlioz' *Sardanapale,* that of his running mate, Montfort, suffered the indignity of a polite hissing. As "appendix" Berlioz had composed a "conflagration" in which the king with his treasures, slaves, women, and horses, dies amid the flaming ruins of his palace. All the melodies heard earlier in the scene—from the song of the bayaderes to the declamation of the stubborn despot, return together in altered form to create an expressive confusion. At the public rehearsal of the entire piece on October 29, the audience was uncommonly large and the numerous musicians present gave Berlioz' piece an extremely warm reception.

But the next day—Prize Day—Berlioz suffered a double disappointment. He had to attend alone, for Camille's mother had grown huffy at the failure of his parents to recognize the engagement and would not allow her daughter to appear with him at an official function; nor was Lesueur, ill in bed, able to applaud the public vindication of his pupil and of his own teaching. Worst of all, by accident or design, the performers missed their cue and the "conflagration" finale did not explode. The piece ended in a most *in*expressive confusion. And Spontini had come on purpose! Friends assured Berlioz that his entire work had been "deeply felt and appreciated," but his sense of reality denied him any comfort—"one can't feel and appreciate what one has never heard."

Meanwhile *The Death of Sardanapalus* had not been Paris's only excitement. Just as Berlioz was finishing his score *in camera,* the bullets and cannon balls of the July insurrection were crashing into the doors of the Institute. On Thursday July 29, after two days of fighting outside, Berlioz left—the earliest of the contestants—and spent hours seeking arms and ammunition in order to take part in the battle for liberty. He had first run to the Moke household to make sure the two women were safe, then accosted a patrol of National Guards, who sent him to the City Hall—in vain. Finally, strangers supplied him with a musket, a knife, powder, and balls, but by then the fighting had died down, and all Hector could do was to lead a street-corner crowd in the singing of the "Marseillaise."

The next day Berlioz went to St. Cloud with a great mob, then back to the gates of Paris at the Etoile. Nothing happened. The revolution was over. Even the guards posted in the Bois de Boulogne were returning to Paris. "The idea that so many good men have paid with their lives for the conquest of our liberties," wrote Berlioz to his father, "and that meanwhile I have been useless, upsets me a great deal. It's another anguishing thought added to the rest."

Surprising as it is to hear the unpolitical Berlioz utter such feelings and speak to the doctor about "our liberties," the reasons for the anomaly are not hard to find. The thirst for liberation, and especially for free expression, had come to affect all ranks. The King's ordinances seeking to muzzle all at once the press, the Chamber, and the electorate had set off the riots that destroyed the dynasty. Though violent, the outbreak deserved even an artist's admiration: "The splendid order that reigned during these magical three days," writes Berlioz, "is maintained and confirmed; no looting, no lawlessness of any kind. The people have been sublime." He regretted only "the dead who cannot be brought back to life . . . nor the poor trees on the boulevards, which are cut down too."

By its revolution the nation settled a quarrel of thirteen years' standing. The events that had made so vivid an impression on the boy Berlioz when his father became mayor in 1817 had been part of the royalist reaction seeking to annul the revolution of '89 and bring back the old regime. For ten years the "Ultras" made headway, exercising repression on the press and the schools, on beliefs and manners, and on the arts. They split their own party and angered the country by preventing Chateaubriand from carrying out a strong foreign policy. Then in 1827 the tide turned; Chateaubriand's group made common cause with liberals of every shade, their bond of union being the resolve to win individual and national self-expression. The young journalists—Guizot, Rémusat, Mignet, Carrel, Thiers—wanted intellectual scope and political careers. The artists wanted the *perruques* retired and the field opened to talent. During nine months of political imprisonment in 1828, Béranger wrote ballads that stirred the people, and when the moderate *Journal des Débats* attacked the Ministry and was prosecuted in August 1829, the alarm became general. Soon an organized refusal of taxes was under way, and too late Charles X planned a campaign in North Africa to secure prestige and divert men's minds. A liberal petition only roused him to issue the July Ordinances, and in three days all was over.

More than most revolutions, that of 1830 concerned the intellect. Precisely what is now felt to be its weakness—the precarious union of extremes that brought it about, its management by bankers and its prompt neglect of the masses—shows it to have been mainly permissive: every group wanted the Open Door, feeling that if only it were let alone it could do great things. It could, in Chateaubriand's words, "achieve reality by the way of dreams"—including the dream of high dividends. What the men of 1830 sought and accomplished was change under control, and the revolutionary leaders' appeal made much of their devotion to Order. But the more generous spirits among the young were moved by reforming zeal as well. The need for a more equitable society was preached by many (notably by the followers of Saint-Simon) and one of the most thoughtful among them, Charles Duveyrier, persuaded Berlioz that "the social question" was paramount. About the time that Carlyle and Mill across the Channel were feeling the Saint-Simonian influence, we find Berlioz writing that after much reading and reflection, he is eager to add his effort to the rest: "Tell me what I can do and I shall give you my ideas on the ways in which I can be musically useful to the great work when I return to Paris." [4]

For the nation at large, the issue had been Old regime versus New, and the new order should have meant, in Berlioz' words, "the betterment of the most numerous and poorest class, the natural ranking of talent, and the abolition of privileges of every kind." The hope was to carry forward the early work of the Great Revolution, which implied, besides social justice, the individualism of the educated and the articulate. It was precisely this double goal that nullified the Three Days' work: the workmen who had held the barricades were cheated out of their claims by the businessmen and lawyers. While the aged Lafayette played to the gallery and a bourgeois king was handed a scepter in the shape of a green umbrella, the common people were hoodwinked.

They showed that they knew it in the further outbreaks of 1831-1832 and succeeding years. But they were put down because the demand for "the natural ranking of talents" conflicted with ameliorating the lot of the poor. Those who had engineered the revolution knew what they wanted, and they wanted it for themselves. Like the young artists, the young journalists and politicians had knowledge behind them and purposes ahead. They seized the facilities they needed with the least show of force because they knew that "perpetual revolution" can be an ideal only for people who have nothing to do. This is what imparts to this historic year the character of a skillful, conscious, and high emancipation, even though the postponement of the social question prepared the next revolution: to stay in power the statesmen of 1830 were driven to destroy the hopes they had aroused. And yet, for a brief time, the workaday world seemed to welcome liberty and to emulate the artist in his love of ordered freedom. Great things might indeed be about to begin.

CHAPTER 6

REVERIE AND PASSION

Is not this something more than fantasy?—SHAKESPEARE

Though Paris and Berlioz were impressed by the moderation of the people in their uprising, the rest of Europe, beginning with the French provinces, continued apprehensive. Insurrections of varying success filled the remaining months of 1830. Belgium shook herself free from Holland, and music signalized the event: the singing by the young Frenchman, Adolphe Nourrit, of Auber's *Masaniello* at Brussels in August 1830 precipitated a riot.[1] Elsewhere—in Spain, Italy, Poland, the Rhineland, and Prussia—students and professional men joined with the bourgeoisie and common people in attempts to secure charters granting constitutional government.

But several of Berlioz' friends, having no artistic stake in the revolution, were aghast at the turn of events and at his sympathy with their outcome. Du Boys, the part-time versifier who had written the text for a minor Berlioz work, the "Ballet of Shades," gave up his judgeship so as not to take the oath of allegiance to Louis Philippe. As for Hector's bosom friend, Humbert Ferrand, religious fervor made him a fanatical enemy of the liberal regime and Berlioz had to beg: "Let us not talk politics." Meanwhile at La Côte, Mme. Berlioz was made ill by the July Days and her son's exultation about them.

Even from the composer's point of view, a time of revolution had its drawbacks. Although the people had quickly accepted as their Citizen-King the cousin of the deposed monarch, they had had a second spasm of fury. The hungry paraded and broke windows; shops closed down and the new government, run by bankers behind the scenes, had to strengthen as quickly as they could their National Guard of solid citizens. Berlioz did not join it at this time, but later, when membership became compulsory. He contented himself with orchestrating the revolutionary "Marseillaise," for music seemed to be imperiled by the upsurge of the masses. Not only were concerts suspended and theaters empty, but the new patriotic songs were abject. The mediocre poet Casimir Delavigne had written a "Parisienne," which the sublime people "bellowed to an ignoble tune." Meantime nothing was being done for art by the new Minister of Interior. "He has other things to think of: so much agitation everywhere means that politics is the only business."

The recovery of the "Marseillaise" was a clear gain, for music and for the public good. Berlioz arranged it for double chorus and orchestra, assigning the vocal part to "all who have voices, a heart, and blood in their veins." The orchestration was—as one might expect from Berlioz—a dramatization: the first four stanzas are sung in unison, with the band supplying a fanfare. The fifth stanza offers the contrast of softness to underline the words "magnanimous warriors of France" and the final stanza, opening for three unaccompanied voices leads to a tremendous crescendo for the call "To arms, O citizens!" followed by a magnificent chromatic scale beneath the descending fanfare of the *Marchons!*

The young lieutenant of the first revolution, Rouget de Lisle, who had composed the tune in a state of slight inebriation in 1792, was now an old man, obscure and nearly destitute. The revival of his most inspired work drew attention to him. A benefit was held in his honor, and the government which adopted his song as a national anthem gave him a pension. The proceeds of the benefit he gave to aid the victims of the July Days. As for Berlioz' orchestration of his masterpiece, it had the effect of reawakening Rouget's dormant ambitions. In thanking the young composer, he proposed collaboration in a letter of which one sentence is often quoted by itself, with somewhat misleading effect: "Your brain seems to be a volcano in constant eruption. Mine never harbored anything but a straw fire which is petering out with only a bit of smoke to show for it. But perhaps if we combined the resources of your volcano with the remains of my bonfire. . . ." Rouget had two opera librettos to contribute. But by this time, the last months of 1830, Berlioz had to excuse himself. Much was happening to him that engaged all his attention, and moreover he had to leave for Rome.

The prize had finally removed all paternal objections to Berlioz' career. In a letter to Lesueur, the doctor had made amends for his earlier brusqueness: "If my son is already on the threshold of the Temple of Fame and Fortune, it is to your affectionate counsels, to your learned lessons, to you as friend and master, that he owes the fact." This eighteenth-century *billet* is touchingly sanguine as to Fortune, though one effect of this optimism was the willingness of the Berlioz family to consider Hector engaged to Camille Moke. She was a "player," but not in the same sense as the dreadful Harriet Smithson.

About Harriet, at this time, Hector entertained curious feelings. Believing what he had heard, he "despised and pitied her" and occasionally alluded to her as "the Smithson wench." But other references, colored by Shakespearean associations, show that his "tenacious nature" clung to the idea, if not of Harriet, at least of the Ophelia she had incarnated—a sad beloved, remote but poetic. The thought plunged him into Hamlet-like reveries mingled with tempestuous passion. He was, to be sure, genuinely in love with Camille, whose person, endearments, coquetries, and musicianship set him on fire. Yet he could not sustain the image of her as a poetic heroine. Ariel was an elusive sprite who would not pledge herself wholly and who used her mother's preference for M. Pleyel to keep Hector on tenterhooks. Camille teased him too much about his musical convictions and his one-sided romance with Harriet, and thereby showed a hardness which boded ill for domestic life with the sensitive but masterful Hector.

"Ophelia" was in truth more than ever a proper object of pity. The troupe of which she was leading lady had gone bankrupt in England, and in order to support her mother and sister she was reduced to walk-on parts at the Opéra-Comique. Instead of the former adulation she now evoked only brief sarcasm in notes "of local origin." Berlioz, who could always endure his own misery better than the sight or the imagining of another's, brooded over these reverses. He had had no claim upon her and could certainly not gloat; on the contrary, her misfortunes as an artist established a claim on him because he understood.

Glimpses of his state of mind show through his account of musical affairs during the last months of 1830: between October 20 and December 5—six weeks—Berlioz had three concerts to attend to. The first was the public audition of his prize piece *Sardanapalus,* with its added conflagration. At the Opera, his overture-fantasia to *The Tempest* was to be performed in early November. It was the "newest thing" he had done, and he meant it as a sort of betrothal celebration of and for Camille, who had never heard any of his works. She had obtained her mother's permission to go. In addition, the concert was in the nature of a musical manifesto, the date having been originally set to come immediately after the publication of Berlioz' article on "Classic and Romantic Music." In short, the event was to combine all the meanings, public and private, that it could stand for: the composer, theorist, prizeman, and affianced lover should triumph within the walls of the Opera where nine years earlier he had recognized his vocation. Politics interfered: on the chosen day, the new regime scheduled a parade of National Guards, and Berlioz himself, whose experience as his own manager was increasing, preferred to postpone the concert. No one would go to the Opera after a weary day of cheering brass bands. The second date, November 7, was no luckier. This time the elements played Berlioz false. Fire had failed him in *Sardanapalus,* now the heavens opened for his *Tempest* and deluged Paris. The streets ran ankle-deep with muddy water and the house was practically empty.

It is doubtful whether even a dry night would have brought out the aristocratic connoisseurs so soon after the political upheavals. They kept out of sight and sought to undermine the new government by provoking disturbances and boycotting the fashionable places: nothing was quite safe or settled. Berlioz' *Tempest,* for chorus, orchestra, and two pianos—a tone poem in four parts rather than an overture—nevertheless echoed within the vaults of the rue Le Pelletier and impressed its author as worth saving.

December 5, the date of Berlioz' third and last concert of 1830, marks the official appearance of the *Symphonie Fantastique* and a milestone in the composer's career. Berlioz was closing one epoch in his life—the years of apprenticeship—and opening to others a new era in music. From this score one can date Berlioz' unremitting influence on nineteenth-century composers. A capital fact emphasizes the relation: Franz Liszt was in the audience.

The concert public, less fashionable and more professional than that of the Opera, turned out in large numbers and responded with as much enthusiasm as Liszt himself. Protracted applause greeted the end of the symphony, and the next days' reviews expressed the shock and pleasure it had given. In his novelistic "program" Berlioz had accurately struck the mood of the moment. By Berlioz' day program writing had become a custom—undoubtedly educational at a time when instrumental music was expanding its forms and purpose. In writing his Berlioz was following a tradition in which Lesueur, Knecht, Schubart, Spohr, Weber and Beethoven had preceded him. Since Berlioz never wrote another, he ranks among the first to break with a practice he was far from having originated. And since this goes counter to a still current belief that he never composed without a program, a word more on his first and only one is necessary.

In the document itself he tells us its function: it was to "furnish an occasion for characteristic pieces of music." Berlioz "supposes a young musician in love," who never thinks of the beloved except "as associated with a musical thought," the two forming "a *double* idée fixe" [*italics added*]. The artist-hero, after experiencing the longings of love, goes to a ball, to country scenes, to execution, and to a posthumous revel of witches. This scenario is anything but literal and exact. Action and musical ideas are interwoven quite carelessly; we find, for example, under the heading "A Ball" a reference to Nature. Further on, the phrase about the shepherds' making dialogue out of a *ranz des vaches* clearly states that no representation is intended. The music *is* the dialogue, just as for the last movement the text draws attention, with not a word of programmatic significance, to the superposition of the witches' dance and *Dies Irae.*

In short, Berlioz' opening remark is nowhere contradicted: "The composer," he says, "has aimed at developing from certain scenes what they contain that is musical." This is not to duplicate literature, nor to imitate real life but to develop in sounds certain unnamable elements which life and music hold in common. This remained Berlioz' esthetic principle to the end. Though he did not give perfect theoretical expression to his view of music drama until 1847, when he published his *Romeo and Juliet* symphony, the form itself had been developing steadily since his cantata days: it was, in a word, the organization of musical moments around a single subject, at once musical and dramatic. The idea of a unifying device in the music itself was of that same early date. In the *Symphonie Fantastique,* he named this device *idée fixe* and made up a set of incidents to fit. But the music came first and its intelligibility by itself is by now acknowledged. Berlioz was indirectly proving it when he gave instructions to omit the program altogether and give the concert audience merely the titles of the five movements. These could even be reduced still further, to read: 1. Appassionata; 2. Waltz; 3. Pastoral; 4. Death March; and 5. Witches' Dance.

This would leave to the program-ridden subscriber but one question: is the *Symphonie Fantastique* autobiography? Now or never is the time to be literal in order to judge the commonplace that Berlioz wrote the work about himself and Harriet Smithson. The striking thing is the total lack of connection between Berlioz' relations with the actress and the scenes he chose for his story: he had never taken her to a ball, never been with her in the country—much less at a public execution: he hardly knew her except across the footlights. Even the "revenge" of introducing the love theme into the witches' revel answered far more to the need of using the *idée fixe* in different contexts than to any symbolic significance: this part of the program suggests *Faust* and a then recent version of De Quincey's *Opium-Eater,* rather than life. What is to be said about the general significance of the symphony has been said by a critic of our own day. It is: "the only musical work which can compare in sincerity and truth of expression with the literary masterpieces portraying the awakening of the mind under the spell of passion—Shakespeare's *Sonnets* and Dante's *Vita Nuova.*" [2]

As for "the story" in the program, we need pay no more attention to it than Berlioz did himself. People in 1830 liked it, grateful (no doubt) that it filled the gaps between the five highly diversified movements. They accepted the strangeness of the music more readily when aided by the description of a setting. The character of the last two movements—the only ones to justify the title "fantastic"—was unmistakable, and it was praise when the *Figaro* termed the entire work "bizarre" and "monstrous," for these were qualities in demand after a long course of pallid operatic conventions. If to this day the Witches' Dance finale still seems modern and aptly monstrous, one can gauge its effect on eardrums unaccustomed to dissonance, clashing rhythms, and polytonality. Fétis, as usual, tempered praise with good advice. He found the second and fourth movements ("A Ball" and "March to Execution") "indicative of a vast imagination." Everywhere else he discerned "a strong individual character expressing itself outside the usual forms of art," but yearned for a greater dose of sensuous pleasure. He urged Berlioz to "charm the ear." Spontini, on the contrary, was moved to wholehearted admiration, in token of which he presented Hector with one of his own scores autographed. In a letter of introduction to his brother (who was a monk in Rome) he wrote of Berlioz as "a French composer of the most unmistakable merit."

By a coincidence that Berlioz must have found ironic, the night of the concert (set, as usual, for two in the afternoon) a benefit was held at the Opera for Harriet Smithson. Knowing no French and lacking a singing voice, she was hard to cast, but good will had secured for her the role of Fenella, the deaf-mute in the now popular *Masaniello.* The critics, however, did not find her pantomime equal to her predecessor's and the success was slight, both financially and artistically. Berlioz of course stayed away. Even had he wished to go, his presence would have given rise to malicious gossip after the rumors connecting the "beloved" of the *Symphonie Fantastique* with Miss Smithson. He did not even rejoin Camille at her mother's but gave in to Liszt's passionate entreaties that they dine together and cement their musical friendship in tête-à-tête.

A few days later Mme. Moke once again gave her formal consent to the engagement of her daughter to Hector. But the prudent lady insisted on his going at once to Rome so as not to forfeit his stipend, and she cheerfully named the wedding time as Easter 1832—eighteen months away. Hector had other reasons besides the impatience of love for not wishing to go into "an exile enforced by the despotism of custom." He would have preferred a trip to Germany, where new music was thriving, feeling that the antiquities and pictorial art of Rome had nothing to teach him. He gave his gold medal to Camille in exchange for a plain ring which was the pledge of their betrothal, and set out for his Italian journey, planning a few days' stopover at La Côte.

CHAPTER 7

ROMAN HOLIDAY

The perfection of life is to carry out in maturity the dreams of one's youth.—VIGNY

On December 29, 1830, Berlioz had written to the author of the "Marseillaise," "I am leaving Paris in a few hours" (to comply with the rules of the Institute) "at a time when my presence here would be most advantageous." An acclaimed musician at twenty-seven, a leader, as we should say now, of the *avant-garde,* Berlioz was reluctant to leave the Parisian battlefield. Being moreover betrothed to a volatile pianist, Hector could hardly act the gay prize winner eager for freedom and adventure.

On his way to Rome he stopped at La Côte, where his parents gave him an affectionate welcome intended to wipe out the memory of ten years of misunderstanding. He responded but was not distracted from his anxiety over a separation of eighteen months from Camille. His sisters were sympathetic; young Prosper, aged ten, was entertaining; and the neighbors were full of compliments for the doctor's son who was making a name in the capital. Still, to Hector the little village now charged with grim memories was oppressive. Reduced to inactivity, his will fed riotous visions to his mind. Current political news encouraged the thought of a European struggle between the liberal revolution and its enemies. From this uninviting prospect Hector could only hope to snatch the bliss of dying with *her* in his arms.[1] But music held an equal place with love: "Is there still no music in Paris? Have you finished your trios, and is Meyerbeer's new opera in rehearsal? Please greet him for me when you see him." [2]

Meantime, though Berlioz reproved himself ("a truce to this gnashing teeth"), he was alarmed at receiving no word from his fiancée. Instead, he received malicious hints from Hiller, Berlioz' predecessor in Camille's favor. Hiller had taken his superseding in good part knowing perfectly well who had engineered the change. Now Ferdinand enjoyed a mild revenge by intimating that Camille did not miss her lover in the least, and that the absent one ought to find consolation wherever he was: "No one was in despair on his account, nor felt any gratitude for *his* despair." Hiller described the physical charms of some other nymph, to which Hector replied testily that he wanted no Epicurean counsels. In an energetic play on words, he repudiated the proffered means for reaching a minor happiness [*arriver au petit bonheur*—"getting there somehow"], and declared for major happiness or death. He was in fact ill. The weather was extremely cold, he had been taken on visits that reminded him of his Estelle, and he felt he was deceiving himself about Camille. He had to take to his bed, while his sister Nanci wrote to Camille and privately pitied her for being involved with a man of persistent ideas and moody as well. When Camille's reply came, Hector had left and his sister's sympathies shifted: in Camille's letter, she thought "not a word was written from the heart."

Hector had also had to give up hope of seeing Humbert Ferrand, who was incapable of acting or writing promptly, and he had pushed on to Marseille. There he found several friends from the Conservatoire, went with them to the theater, and was treated by other musicians as a man of rising fame. "The town is superb, and were it not for the turmoil in my thoughts I would have enjoyed it." More important than the town was Berlioz' first sight of the sea. The one available vessel for Leghorn would sail when the skipper chose, so Hector went out for a trial trip in a fishing smack. "Your sea is a sublime monster," he wrote Adèle, "I like to see it swishing around my feet on the beach, covering them with foam and roaring like an angry beast. It should be magnificent out in the open sea."

He finally embarked for the five-day crossing, which took eleven. While becalmed, one of the old sea dogs related tales from the time when he was skipper to Lord Byron. Then contrary winds came up. Near the Gulf of Genoa the ship struck a gale, which besides being icy cold threatened to capsize them. The captain would not or could not shorten sail and for two days tacked and wore in stormy waters. A young Venetian corsair on board predicted disaster. The waves broke on the pitching deck, the passengers staggered about in agonies of fear and seasickness, even the sailors were losing hope, when the corsair, encouraged by some of the passengers, undertook to give orders and take in reefs. The pumps meanwhile had to be manned and a fire, set by the vessel's rolling, had to be put out: activity helped to curb the growing panic. Berlioz, though not seasick, had gone through all the stages of apprehension from the fear of drowning to the fear of not drowning fast enough. To keep himself from swimming he planned to pinion his arms in his own greatcoat, ready to welcome "the white spumed waves . . . that would rock him to sleep without pain."

On land, other troubles awaited him. Although the new French government had decided on peace, revolution was still active on Italian soil, and so were the police. Two of Berlioz' shipmates were arrested while the rest fled to join "the brave and unfortunate Menotti." [3] Berlioz' baggage was repeatedly searched; all foreigners were suspect. "There are fifty formalities to go through before one can stop in a city." Berlioz might have thought himself in the blissful twentieth century except that the inefficient police were more of a nuisance than a threat. Still the Papal Nuncio would not grant him a visa to Rome. At Florence, Berlioz received his first remittance from the Director of the Academy toward which he was bound, and at the same time heard the news that revolution was driving the foreign residents from Rome. "And I must go into that hornet's nest because forty old dotards, high priests of Routine, have decided that I shall be competent only after a stay in that musical sink."

Berlioz' obviously bad mood was not soothed by Italian music. He went to the first night of Bellini's *Romeo and Juliet* and exploded to his father: "Disgusting, ridiculous, impotent. That little fool has apparently not been afraid that Shakespeare's shade might come and haunt him in his sleep. . . . I ran here into a young Danish architect whom I knew in Paris. Danish! That also brings up Shakespeare. We spoke of Elsinore and *Hamlet.* . . . I may be in Italy but my sky is overcast. My life is in Paris and what I suffer cannot be put into words. . . . No letter from Camille. . . . I regret the watery grave."

It was mid-March, almost three months after the arrival of his fellow-pensioners, when Berlioz reached Rome. As a visible presence, the "musical sink" made a great impression on him: its situation in the flat Romagna, its austerity, the majesty of the Piazza del Popolo, aroused in him a host of esthetic feelings whose roots went back to the words of Virgil and Chateaubriand. The spacious elegance of the Villa Medici—the seat of the French Academy in Rome—completed his conversion. He entered the place just in time for drama. The French being suspected of revolutionary leanings, were assailed on the streets by partisans of the Pope; they broke into the Academy grounds at night and sent threatening letters by day. Horace Vernet, the director, having made futile representations to the Vatican, decided to arm his young artists. He himself put to flight an Italian whom Mme. Vernet found "armed with a knife and hiding in the shrubbery." If these fanatics, scoffed Berlioz, "had only set fire to the Academy, who knows?—I might have helped them!"

Apart from the risk of murder, the atmosphere of the Villa was anything but solemn. Horace Vernet, then aged forty-two, an historical painter descended from a long line of painters, was a charming, sociable, lighthearted character, for whom noise, masquerades, and parties of all kinds were a tonic rather than an interference. The small, thin, grayhaired artist had come to Rome in 1828 after a rise to eminence packed with incidents: decorated for his early work by Napoleon himself, he had fought on the barricades in 1814 for the Emperor's return, side by side with Géricault; five years later the two had come out in the same Salon, which included Géricault's epoch-making "Raft of the Medusa" and the "Odalisque" of Ingres. Befriended by Guizot and the Duke of Orleans, Vernet had striven for liberty in a Bonapartist spirit and hailed the victory of July 1830. "Now," he had said, "I can paint anything . . . any part of our glory, in any color, without fear of censorship. . . ." Nor did he harden into an administrator: though he had to act as ambassador to the Vatican during the French interregnum, he remained boyish and buoyant, unafraid to give Thiers or the Paris Academy a piece of his mind when they tried to dictate.[4] And for all his ebullience, visible in the disorder of his studio, which was a litter of books, guns, musical instruments, dogs, and official dispatches, he was a great worker.

It was both good and bad luck that Berlioz came into such a household, where everyone was or acted young—the director, his charges, his young wife and daughter, and his father also, Carle Vernet, who was mad about music and went dancing in spite of his eighty years. It was unfortunate because Berlioz' black mood of lovesickness was intensified by the attention it received. Whether laughed at or taken to heart, his Werther-like sorrows tended for a time to become institutionalized, as they would not have been in a more sober or preoccupied milieu. The instant camaraderie and general Bohemianism of the place only heightened Berlioz' sense of isolation. Yet it was a piece of good luck that Vernet was a *bon vivant* who had married for love, thrown away his chance of a Rome Prize, and made his way by being jovially unbusinesslike. Another man, more impressed with his own official dignity, might have made Hector suffer in the days of his folly just at hand.

Since leaving France two months before, Berlioz had not heard from Camille or her entourage. Waiting was intolerable, uncertainty was a torture. Being a man of strong and explicit feelings, he could not stoop to assuage his pain with cynicism or foolish hope. He had not left Paris with vague promises: Mme. Moke had publicly acknowledged him as "my son-in-law" and Camille had not withdrawn her plighted word. Hence some plot must be brewing. Vernet had to hold him back from making a flying trip to Paris in order to learn the true state of his marital prospects: if he left the Villa Medici, he would lose the very status upon which his engagement to Camille had been ratified by her mother. After a week of conflict, on April 1, Berlioz left none the less. He went as far as Florence, where fever and sore throat held him in bed. He wrote to a friend in Paris asking for news, and in a few days recovered, but the internal debate continued. The countryside being tempting, he tramped into the hills and there read *King Lear* for the first time. Artistic excitement acted as a safety valve for overwrought feelings as he seized on the proper expression of his troubles: "As flies to wanton boys are we to the gods; they kill us for their sport."

Having brought his manuscripts with him, Berlioz resumed work. He corrected the score of the *Symphonie Fantastique,* and jotted down ideas for several new works, including in all probability the *King Lear* overture. But there were also long idle hours waiting for an answer from Paris. Going one night to the cathedral, he witnessed the services for a young woman dead in childbirth, with her infant in her arms. The sight of death aroused his sense of life and even reawakened dormant medical knowledge. For lack of anything better to do, he followed the funeral procession and at the cemetery, seeing the corpse nearer to, hazarded a diagnosis, while revolving morbid thoughts.

Still waiting, twelve days after leaving Rome, Berlioz could not help seeing and brooding over another funeral. Young Napoleon-Louis Bonaparte, son of the great Napoleon's brother Louis, was dead at twenty-six. Though succumbing ingloriously to measles, the heir to the name had been leading insurrection in the Romagna; his death left at the head of the clan his younger brother, Louis Napoleon, with whom Berlioz was later to have dealings. Already in 1831 Berlioz noted with bitterness the kind of music chosen to celebrate these great and unhappy memories: "The organist pulled the piccolo stop and disported himself in the treble, playing gay little tunes akin to the warbling of wrens. . . ."

Staying in Florence was a compromise between giving up his stipend and wearing out his patience under the eyes of the whole Academy; but the protracted silence of the Moke family and of his Paris friends was daily increasing his helpless indignation. His thoughts swung from the desire to join the Calabrian banditti to the planning of an oratorio on the Day of Judgment. Since music was life transmuted, and he was unable to lay violent hands on the Moke family in the style of Gil Blas or Rob Roy, he could at least blow up the world musically in the name of Jehovah. For a start, there was the *Resurrexit* of the Mass of 1825, not to speak of local inspiration from the hand of a kindred world-builder and world-destroyer, Michelangelo.

Finally, on the fourteenth day, the Paris letter came. Camille, said Mme. Moke, was about to marry M. Pleyel, the piano manufacturer. Hector's blood instantly reached the boiling point. At last he could act, but his passion was modified as always by amazing (in this case ludicrous) forethought. Mme. Moke's letter was "a model of impudence," in which she "strongly urged me not to kill myself—the good soul!" He decided to exterminate the two faithless women first. But reflecting that if he turned up in Paris the old lady would not receive him, he bought a chambermaid's outfit as a disguise. In addition to loaded pistols, he took vials of laudanum and strychnine for his own quietus, and in a final act of foresight he dispatched his clothes to his father and his scores to Habeneck with directions for carrying out changes recently made in the Symphony.

On the first leg of the trip home, the suitcase containing the disguise was lost. Berlioz bought duplicates at Genoa, but failed to obtain a visa for Turin. His impulse momentarily deflected, it turned on himself and he clumsily attempted suicide by jumping into the sea. Rescued, he returned to his original idea and headed for Nice. On the long road which unrolls the superb panorama of the Riviera, Berlioz came to his senses and in the dusk gave up the whole plan. Sea and mountain on either hand dwarfed the importance of the unworthy pair who had injured him. With a sigh of relief he turned his mind to the question of reinstating himself at the Academy. He gave Vernet a straightforward account: "A shameful misdeed, an abuse of confidence of which I have been the victim, has put me in a delirium of rage ever since I left Florence. I was flying back to France to exact a just and dreadful revenge when at Genoa, in a moment of giddiness I gave in to childish despair. An inconceivable weakness got the better of my will. But my sole punishment was to swallow a lot of salt water and be yanked out like a fish . . . People thought I had fallen in by accident while walking along the ramparts . . . Now I'm alive; I *must* live—for my two sisters whose lives would have been broken by my death, and also for my art . . . I am therefore returning to pledge on my honor not to leave Italy. . . ." [5]

Berlioz came to regard this series of events as "an offprint of a Byronic tale." For Byron's tales of love, jealousy, and revenge then furnished words and attitudes to fit the eternal flux of human passions. Berlioz would have agreed with Henry James that "art is our flounderings shown," and that "passion can mean only one thing—the enemy to behavior." Having purged his soul in verbal outbursts and calmed his body by exertion while Vernet was taking thought, Hector enjoyed three weeks of springtime convalescence at Nice. As he looked back on them they were the "twenty happiest days of my existence"—in part because pleasure unanticipated is doubled, in part because it was a relief to accept the truth about Camille and her mercenary mother. He wrote very fully to his family, who responded with affectionate consolations, and he told the tale to his Paris friends, asking musical news in return.[6]

He also composed. The *King Lear* overture was all but orchestrated, and the other overture, "The Tower of Nice"—so called from the ruins of an old tower in which Berlioz sat and worked facing the sea—was well under way. Hearing, moreover, that his old collaborator Victor Bohain was adapting Scott's *Rob Roy* for the stage, Berlioz sketched a third overture to be named after the novel. In between bouts of composition, he soaked in the myriad impressions of the sounding sea (still a novelty to the mountaineer) under the infinite blue sky.

At last a letter came from "M. Horace" as Vernet was familiarly known, saying that no official notice had been taken of Berlioz' escapade. Hector was still on the list of state pensioners and could return to the Academy without further apologia. The whole Vernet family sent sympathy, and Berlioz himself felt that he was "being born again, a better man than before." He might well have said that the Sappho who cast herself into the sea and the Sappho who wrote poems were not the same person. On the slow journey to Rome he was full of musical ideas and he plotted a sequence of "occasions" which might unite earlier pieces that he wanted to work over. A note in Thomas Moore's poems gave him the idea of a "melologue" which he christened *The Return to Life,* and thought of as a sequel to the *Symphonie Fantastique*. "I hardly know what it's worth," he wrote to Gounet, the translator of Moore, "but I'll tell you this anyhow: my run to Nice cost me a thousand and fifty francs. I'm so glad not to have carried out my original plan that I don't begrudge the money."

The Villa Medici was no longer besieged but its atmosphere was rather stifling nevertheless—like the narrow, ill-furnished rooms upstairs, or the contents of the library, which had scarcely any new books. The twenty-two pensioners representing five of the fine arts were for the most part "good students" with an assured future in official art. "Two or three," thought Hector, "are mildly exceptional, but no more." It is true, they made up in boisterousness for their lack of genius and frequent low spirits, and a surprisingly large number liked music. After a dinner in town they would make the climb back to the Monte Pincio while singing in chorus as many different tunes in as many different keys as possible. All the dogs of Rome joined in this "English concert," as the band called it, knowing that the tradesmen on their doorsills were sure it was *musica francese*. Among this inner group—Montfort the musician,

Dantan and Etex the sculptors, Garrez and Duc the architects —the last-named alone formed a real friendship with Berlioz: he had both music and sensibility in him.

Fortunately for Berlioz, Felix Mendelssohn was at this time in Rome, and despite angularities of character in both the young musicians, their talents and common love of music brought them together. Mendelssohn was prim, pious, and a former infant prodigy. Berlioz, as he was the first to admit, was often intolerant and intolerable. He teased the German about his devout Lutheranism, he played the trick of putting an Italian aria of Gluck's on the piano, so that Mendelssohn ridiculed it before discovering it was by a master they both admired. In short, Berlioz worked off a good deal of ill humor on the person he had most affection for, all the while expressing about Mendelssohn's gifts an unmixed admiration that lasted through life. Writing to Paris friends in May 1831, Berlioz says of his new companion.

"He is a wonderful fellow. His performing talent is as great as his musical genius, which is saying a great deal. Everything I have heard by him has always delighted me. I am convinced he is one of the highest musical talents of the age. He has been my cicerone. Every morning I would go to his house. He would play me a Beethoven sonata; we would sing from Gluck's *Armide;* then he would take me to see all the famous ruins which, I confess, did not move me very much." Toward the end of the year, Berlioz tells Hiller by way of introduction: "He has an enormous talent, extraordinary, superb, prodigious. And I can't be suspected of comradely partiality in speaking like this, since he has frankly told me that he understood nothing of my music."

On his side, Mendelssohn was just as confident in writing to his mother about Berlioz: "Without a spark of talent, he gropes in the dark while he thinks he is the creator of a new world. He writes detestable things and thinks only of Beethoven, Goethe and Schiller . . . Full of vanity besides, he lords it over Mozart and Haydn, so that his enthusiasm seems to me suspect . . ." Mendelssohn's mother apparently tried to moderate her son's judgment of Berlioz, for Felix having written that he would "be only too glad to strangle Berlioz —until he chances to praise Gluck," he goes on to concede that his two French friends are "most agreeable and charming . . ." but . . . "you say, dear Mother, that Berlioz must have some real artistic purpose and there I don't agree with you. I think what he wants is to get married, and I think him the most affected of the lot, because I cannot stand this wholly external enthusiasm, this affectation of despair . . . and genius; and if they were not French, that is, people with whom one always has pleasant relations, and who always have something interesting to say, it would be unbearable."

It *was* bewildering: the relationship was pleasant, but if it hadn't been it would have been unbearable. Cultural differences account in part for his dislike: it is a conventional vanity that he takes for affectation, for he found it again in Mickiewicz and again imputed it to character. Only a still provincial mind would have taken its occasional manifestations seriously. Reared in a different musical tradition, Mendelssohn never lived to see what Berlioz' scores signified. He did like some of his friend's melodies, but could not understand his dramatic structure or unpianistic orchestration. History supplies few such instances, of the mutual liking of two geniuses, of whom the narrower cannot take in the broader, but who despite this sufficient cause for enmity remain actively devoted friends.

Apart from Mendelssohn, Rome afforded little or nothing satisfying to Berlioz' musical passion. Gounet had asked if Berlioz had found some new beloved, he himself having broken off an irksome liaison. Berlioz replied "No . . . but what is worse is that I cannot live without music. I cannot get used to it, it's impossible." During the winter months the famous *Café Greco* which survived until a year or so ago, was the meeting place of foreign artists. There Berlioz met Michael Glinka, later to become "the father of Russian music," and now studying under Basili. Despite this connection with the Italian opera, he and Berlioz quickly established sympathetic relations. But it was all talk, not music. At the same *café* Berlioz met two French poets, followers of the English "Lake" school, Auguste Barbier and Auguste Brizeux, and a Paris acquaintance, the singer Duprez, all of whom were to have important dealings with Berlioz in the sequel.

Italian antiquities, Italian religion, Italian music—none of these things fed Berlioz' spirit. He was impressed by the scale of Saint Peter's and the Coliseum, but the best use he could find for the amphitheater was to read Byron there. Church processions, unlike the rural ones he knew, struck him as cheap and mesquin, and the Carnival as gross without gaiety. As for music, "My hatred for what they have the impudence to adorn with that name in Italy is stronger than ever. Their music is a whore: from a distance its appearance spells shamelessness: from nearby, its dull speech proves it a silly fool."

But one prejudice that he had brought with him he quickly overcame: "I find the Italians just as good fellows as anybody else, especially those in the mountains whom I know best of all." This remark alludes to a use of his pensioned time which supplied Berlioz with the most vivid as well as fruitful impressions of his Italian journey—his excursions into the countryside. Here was his real reward for ten years of arduous career-building, the real holiday during which the two halves of the youth's character joined to make the balanced man. In communings with nature, with simple souls, and with himself, Berlioz experienced his "Italian Journey" in the Goethean sense. During the twelvemonth from May 1831 to May 1832, he stored up impressions or felt renewed inspiration from sources congenial to his temper and lasting in their effect. One thinks not only of Goethe but of Scott's great tour of Scotland at the age of twenty-three. Without premeditation he was living out the maxims of Schiller, Wordsworth, and Vigny about dreaming dreams in youth for the mature man to turn into realities.

Berlioz of course thought of himself as idle, waiting out his time in pure waste. Too often he suffered from the malady then known as spleen—boredom—and it was this which drove him to the mountains. "As soon as I find myself more tormented than usual, I put on my hunting coat, I take my gun, and I make tracks for Subiaco, no matter what the weather. A week ago I went from Tivoli to Subiaco under a driving rain which lasted all day. Last month I made my way from Naples on foot, through hills and woods and high pastures, having to take a guide only once. You have no idea how delightful such a trip can be. Fatigue, discomfort, the possibilities of danger—I was enchanted with everything. I spent nine days that I shall long remember. As for my innumerable impressions, I have no room to detail them—only, I still think nothing equals the sea."

While there were rumors of a fresh revolution in France, and Horace Vernet rushed to Paris to gauge the political situation, Berlioz was making friends with the peasants and bandits of the Abruzzi. If he took his gun he shot indifferently at a few wildfowl—a bloodless pastime he soon abandoned altogether. When he came to know the villagers he left the gun at home and took his guitar. At nightfall the girls would come out and dance to Berlioz' improvised accompaniments while the old folks watched. Having been content with a meager tambourine, they gave the welcome of a virtuoso (which he was) to the player of the *chitarra francese*. From them, in return, he received hospitality, warmth of feeling, and the delight of real folk music. He jotted down a few of their tunes but remembered even more vividly the mood and pathos of the occasion, which he would recapture in his own works to be. Listening one night to a lover's serenade he found himself transported out of his self-preoccupation. But the singer stopped abruptly; "It then seemed to me that all of a sudden I was deprived of something essential . . . I spent the rest of the night without sleep, without dreams, without thoughts."

Sometimes Berlioz set out with a companion from the Academy, usually a painter in search of scenery. Hector would sing in his natural tenor voice appropriate woodland songs—Lesueur's "Bardic Hunt" or his own "Irish" melody "Hélène." [7] Antoine Etex, now known for his bas-reliefs of the Arc de Triomphe, was one of the walking companions who long remembered these expeditions. "Berlioz, who was as sad and discouraged as I, went with me to the Dominican Fathers with a view to a retreat, but a thousand circumstances plunged us back into our low spirits. One day after walking in the hot sun to Tivoli and ordering our dinner at the inn, we could not resist the temptation of swimming in the limpid blue waters of the lake. This we did, and as we swam we sang the famous duet from *William Tell,* 'O Mathilda whom my soul adores.' But in those icy waters we suddenly turned blue, our teeth chattering and our gaiety all spent. We got out as quickly as we could and went to our dinner. An hour later we were both asleep. The next day at five, we set out for the mountains in hopes of meeting brigands and taking up our abode with them, but we had no luck."

The intoxication of the senses by nature, the absence of social restraints, and the thronging reminiscences of the historic past repeatedly brought Berlioz in touch with his true inner self. He felt the tragic commingle with a furious *joie de vivre,* and as he tells us, the bout might end in a flood of tears. The thought of death was no longer morbid or sought after as in Florence: when his Italian friends' boy Tonio languished and died, Berlioz was shaken. Another time, having drunk more than usual and lost his way, he found that a canto of the *Aeneid,* forgotten since childhood, came back entire to his memory. This led him to improvise "a wild recitative to still wilder harmonies, on the death of Pallas, the despair of good Evander, the youth's funeral—at which his own horse wept—the dread of King Latinus, the siege of Latium—whose soil I was treading—the sad death of Amata and the cruel death of Lavinia's betrothed. Under the combined influence of memory, poetry and music I reached the highest pitch of exaltation . . . ending in convulsive sobs. What is most singular is that I could pass judgment on my own weeping."

In contrast with natural life, there was the duty of attending some of Mme. Vernet's weekly soirees. "It's always the same story: there is dancing, talking about nothing, looking at engravings. . . . You drink weak tea and saunter to the balcony overlooking Rome. In the moonlight you can make some well-worn remarks, quite academic and stupid. You refer to cholera morbus, the Paris riots, the Poles' defeat, the defeat of the French in Algiers, the illumination of St. Peter's and the way Mlle. Horace dances." At one of these evenings, however, he saw Countess Guiccioli, Byron's great love, with her sad face and rich golden hair.

Nor could he get used to the abundance of clerics in the Church's capital: "These abbes, monks, priests are everywhere, right and left, above, below, within, without, with the poor and the rich in church, at dances and cafes, in the theatres, with the ladies in cabriolets, on foot with the men, at M. Horace's evenings, in his studio, in our gardens—Everywhere."

This anticlericalism was not antireligious. On the contrary, Hector's mind was full of musical ideas for sacred subjects. He sketched or composed half a dozen first drafts and finished a "Religious Meditation" on a text from Moore, "This world is all a fleeting show." In the untended gardens of the Villa Borghese not far from the Academy (where Goethe had worked at *Faust* forty years before) Berlioz hid away to revise his pastoral movement of the *Fantastique*. He also added to the first movement the twenty-four bars of the present *religioso* ending; and being obliged to send the Institute a sample of work done at Rome, he dispatched a Chorus and Quartet of Magi, based on an earlier (Paris) draft, and joined to it the *Resurrexit* of his early Mass, once again revised. But on seeing a peasant kiss the toe of a statue of Saint Peter, Berlioz envied the "happy biped" who had "faith and hope," for to the educated mind historical criticism stood in the way of literal belief: "This bronze that you worship and whose right hand holds the keys of heaven was once a *Jupiter tonans* holding lightning. But you know it not, lucky biped!"

News from Paris was not encouraging. Plots and riots succeeded each other rapidly. The European cholera (of which Hegel had just died) was carrying off its hundreds, among them the ablest statesman of the new regime as well as a compatriot of Berlioz, Casimir-Périer. And Berlioz' circle of musical friends—Hiller, Richard, Du Boys, Prévost, Turbry, De Pons, Girard, Desmarest, and Stephen de la Madelaine—were dilatory correspondents.[8] Only Gounet, to whom Berlioz felt very close, took pains to keep him posted. Everyone, it seemed, was getting married: Humbert Ferrand, in his province, had obtained the hand of his great love, but in his usual indolence had not written. Berlioz' cousin Auguste was planning to marry, and so was Hector's sister Nanci: Berlioz knew that he would find marked changes in the world of his contemporaries. This made him all the more impatient to leave his "barracks," possibly extending by some months his third statutory year in Germany.

Trouble was still brewing there, as well as in England, where the struggle to pass a Reform Bill brought the realm to the verge of revolution. Sir Walter Scott, dying and in despair, was by doctor's advice taking a Mediterranean cruise. He did not know how near it brought him to his admiring fellow artists, Stendhal and Berlioz—the one in Rome, the other Acting Consul in Civita Vecchia. Stendhal came to Rome and the Villa from time to time, but we do not know whether he and Berlioz met. We know only that during the carnival of 1832 Berlioz caught a glimpse of the elder Dauphinois driving through the streets with "a mischievous look that he vainly sought to render solemn." Hector knew that the novelist had also written about music, in particular an admiring and provocative *Life of Rossini.* This would not endear him to Berlioz, although in reality the two shared many opinions about the state and the purpose of the arts, felt the same way about the average culture of their own country, and even expressed themselves in the same tone of intelligent mockery. But as often happens, this was not evident to them as it is to us. The musician was irritated by a manner and dismissed the other as a littérateur, and there is no reason to believe that Stendhal ever heard any of Berlioz' music. And yet they stand to each other as prophet and messiah, for Stendhal long before 1830 had predicted, or rather demanded, the Romanticist revolution in music, painting, and drama.

Toward the end of 1831, it seemed as if the cultural renovation desired by Stendhal had been carried to a point far beyond Rossini: the newspapers were full of a great new work which was said to combine music, painting, and drama, and to express to perfection the modern spirit through its *Faust*-like subject matter. Impressive scenic effects employing new machinery, a fresh style of directing and dramatic composition, and above all an expanded use of the orchestra, made Meyerbeer's *Robert le Diable* the model of a new genre—French grand opera. Berlioz read the comments and could hardly sleep. To "rot in Rome" while a renovated dramatic art was making headway in Paris against the old Italian monopoly; to miss the first performance of Beethoven's Ninth—even though given in two halves—was maddening. The critics' references to Weber, Beethoven, and modern instrumentation might mean that the mood of Paris was changing. The title of Houssaye's new periodical, *L'Artiste,* was significant: it implied that the political revolution had vindicated the earlier, cultural reform—in a word, that Berlioz being no longer alone might find his hour about to strike. He asked Hiller to present his sincere compliments to Meyerbeer, who had always shown kindly interest in him and his works, and indeed had already begun to learn from his junior.

Having meantime read Victor Hugo's extraordinary new book, *Notre Dame de Paris,* Berlioz indited a rhapsodic letter to relieve his feelings and cheat impatience by taking a sideswipe at Rossini: "It is said that you have made a libretto out of your *Notre Dame* and that the 'gay fat man' is doing the music. He is *such* a gay fat man—naturally, Weber being dead. . . . There, my broadside is discharged. I feel better. . . . *Viva l'ingenio tuo!"* [9] Sensing progress in the French capital Berlioz, whose last published article had dealt with a possible revitalizing of lyric drama by means of the Beethovenian orchestra, was now moved to write a "Letter on Italian music, by an Enthusiast"—an ironic name for himself. In it he points out that the belief in Italy's supremacy in every art is no longer justified. The orchestras are beneath notice; people do not listen but talk,[10] the overtures are strings of platitudes which the organ grinders themselves disdain, and church services consist of operatic airs badly played on the organ or poorly sung by minuscule choirs. In substance, Italian music aims only at "sensory effect and external form," it is "perpetually laughing" (hence Berlioz' nickname for Rossini) and its undeniable melodic exuberance is rendered monotonous by habitual garnishing with *fioriture*.

Real music exists only among the folk—the serenade of a mountaineer to his *ragazza,* or the plaints of the *pifferari* to the Madonna. Berlioz admits that being out of Rome he did not hear the special music of Holy Week, but he wonders with what musicians, hidden for the remainder of the year, it could have been adequately performed. Saint Peter's was a challenge and an opportunity: "It is huge, sublime, overwhelming . . . These paintings, statues, and columns, this grand architecture are the body of the monument; music is its soul, but where is it? Where is the organ?" On searching, Berlioz found a harmonium on wheels, "a kind of accordion behind a pillar." As for the choristers, who should number thousands in order to sound in scale, they were eighteen on ordinary days and thirty-two on special occasions. "Rome," concludes Berlioz, "is no longer in Rome. It is in Paris, Berlin, Vienna, London even . . . , so that the Institute is quite right, its aim being to make young composers waste time, to halt the first steps of their career, and extinguish their fire by keeping them from the great centers of art . . . Theirs is the motto of Molière's doctors—though the patient die, 'we shall not depart one iota from the prescription of the ancients.' "

Berlioz screwed up his courage and asked Vernet for permission to leave early. With a view to giving a concert as soon as possible, he copied out parts of the revised *Fantastique,* of its sequel, *The Return to Life,* of the two new overtures, and of the *Religious Meditation*. Reading Hugo's *Orientales* had moreover put into his head a new song which, yielding to the demands of sociability, he arranged for Mlle. Vernet. *La Captive* was a catchy melody, and soon the whole Villa was humming it. It spread throughout artistic circles in Rome and was whistled wherever Berlioz went. "They want to make me rue it." He deemed it a trifle, but happily the trifle proved to be the germ of one of his finest orchestral songs, which he himself grew fond of.

On Palm Sunday of 1832, Berlioz climbed for the last time the sugar-loaf hill around which spreads Subiaco. He went to church with the village population, sang with them, and on leaving felt a pang of homesickness. Vernet had consented to Berlioz' leaving on May first, thus reducing the required two years in Italy to fourteen months. Berlioz spent the remainder of April at the Villa, making himself agreeable to the ladies, his fellows, and their guests. When he put his mind to it he could be most entertaining, and though only twenty-eight could act the accomplished man of the world. He told stories and historical anecdotes, he made up musical extravaganzas or sang Gluck in the moonlit gardens so that old Carle Vernet—who had known both Gluck and Piccinni—wept with emotion. Near the time of leaving, Berlioz had to sit for his portrait. His housemate Signol did the half-caricature which may still be seen in the Director's office at the Villa. One sees, in the becoming costume of a Jeune-France (tight coat, high pointed collar and neckband) a pale face under a glowing mass of hair and deep-sunken eyes of a soft blue, which look out with the candor and inward thoughtfulness of a child.

As if reluctant despite his eagerness to leave, Berlioz took the whole month of May for the trip home. He drove by way of Spoleto, Foligno, Perugia, and Lake Trasimene—the scene of Hannibal's great victory—reaching Florence for his fourth stay, each time "with a more loving love." He read Dante and Shakespeare and filled notebooks; then pushed on to Milan by way of Lodi which, acting on childhood memories, made him dream of Napoleon's glory, "fled like a mirage." It was already more than a year since young Napoleon-Louis had died on this same spot. Music had not improved. He heard Bellini's *La Sonnambula* which he found pitiful, and in Milan tried to overhear Donizetti's *L'Elisir d'amore* but could make out nothing: "The people talk, gamble, sup, and manage to drown out the orchestra. It's impossible to follow anything but the bass drum."

From Milan to Turin the impressions gathered on the Bridge of Lodi began to take shape as music, and he sketched the plan of a choral symphony, for which he thought that a Napoleonic Ode of Victor Hugo's might furnish the text. But having recently worked on the words of his "melologue," and knowing that the meters of French verse are ill-suited to melody, he began jotting down words of his own—cadenced prose would do as well as rime. The "occasions" for two movements of this symphony suggested themselves as Berlioz followed the conqueror's footsteps: "Farewell to the Fallen Heroes from the Crest of the Alps" and "Entrance of the Victorious Army into Paris." Never composed in this form, the work quite naturally evolved into the Funeral and Triumphal Symphony of 1840.

Coming down into his valley by the Mont Cenis pass and the Isère, Hector felt the shock of familiar beauty and reawakened emotions. He gazed at the St. Eynard and went up it to Meylan for a visit to his maternal grandfather, old Marmion. Here was Hector's chief link with prerevolutionary France; here was Estelle's home; here too, by a contrast suddenly felt, the imagined roar of Paris. The thought was like a stab of pain, quickly forgotten in festivities: Nanci had just been married to a Grenoble judge, Camille Pal, and the family reunion was full of excitement. At La Côte, the house seemed empty without her. Nanci had had a soothing effect on her mother whose ill temper, now chronic, was aggravated by the behavior of young Prosper. The boy, it is clear, was also endowed with unusual musical talent. Though never taught, he could remember and reproduce on the piano anything he heard. But he had other traits which we can easily recognize as the result of his unhappy upbringing. Besides tantrums and obstinacy, he had compulsions to arrange his clothes in a certain order, only to pretend the next day that he had forgotten how to dress himself. Hector was much concerned. He could relax only with Adèle and with his kindly father who, under the pressure of domestic and political turmoil, was becoming philosophical to the point of solipsism. The doctor nonetheless took pains to bring his son up to date on what was actually happening in France, for in Rome the newspapers ignored French affairs as seditious, and the police, as Stendhal loved to prove, would censor the most trifling remarks in letters as politically sinister.

Hector heard for the first time of the riots in Lyon and Grenoble and the dubious colonial enterprises in North Africa. But his readiness to fight tyranny as in the July days did not make him believe in the "principles" of subsequent French politics. His indifferentism returned when he noticed that there were in fact no principles. He had written to Gounet from Rome: "What are you up to in the midst of all these plots, conspiracies, and factions, which are the desolation of common sense, of the arts, and of peaceable folk? . . . I wish for the sake of your peace of mind that you were no more concerned with them than I." Now he could see how "the traitors of yesterday become the heroes of tomorrow" and how force "blurs right and wrong under the name of legality."

He did not want in any case to argue politics with the neighbors, nor with his new brother-in-law, Judge Pal, whose loquacity thereupon switched to matters of high art in a fashion that "wrecked" Berlioz. Even less did he want people to discuss music. He was willing enough to talk of his travels and to learn of local marriages and deaths,[11] but he found the old circle of acquaintances more bourgeois than ever. So many of his friends were now leading the dull existence of married provincials: Charbonnel, Edouard Rocher, Albert Du Boys, Auguste Berlioz, as well as the timid and ill-favored Humbert Ferrand, whom Berlioz went to visit after an absence of more than six years.

A certain constraint at first spoiled the reunion, even though Mme. Ferrand was away, because Ferrand had quite sunk his youthful ideals in domestic comfort and routine. Poetry, heroism, and love seemed far away, but Hector managed to galvanize him a last time. Giving Humbert a glimpse of his own freedom on the Italian hills, Berlioz urged him to write the verses for his projected oratorio on the Day of Judgment. He sketched an outline, a "carcass," on which his friend was to put "muscles." He begged him to follow inspiration freely, "to do without rime whenever it seems needless—which is often the case" and to drop whatever "dusty conventions" belong to "the infancy of art." Ferrand promised to do his best. Later at Aix les Bains, Hector met his friend's wife, whom he found charming, though he still could not conceive how she had weaned Ferrand from artistic ambition. In the end, Ferrand did no writing. When fall came, the return visit to La Côte which they had planned did not take place.

Meanwhile Berlioz was marking time. That is, he corrected scores and copied parts. In his father's library he also reread his old medical books, studied Gall and Cabanis and found them philosophically empty.

In the round of dinners and *politesses,* where, to please him, acquaintances broached musical subjects "as if they were talking of wine, women, riots, or other filthiness," Hector found time to make friends with young Prosper. They went on walks, played bowls, or hunted birds' eggs; Hector gave the child the understanding and companionship of an affectionate equal. But Berlioz must think of Paris. If he was to catch up with the current of artistic life and give a concert before his trip to Germany (scheduled for the beginning of the New Year) he dare not linger at La Côte. With ripened mind and heart, he felt his mission more clearly than ever. "You see how patient I am," he wrote at this juncture; "one needs patience not solely in order to bear evils with doggedness, but in order to act." Accordingly, on October 28, 1832, aged not quite twenty-nine, Berlioz set out for his second conquest of Paris.

CHAPTER 8

RECOLLECTED IN TRANQUILLITY

. . . and thus subdue
Imperious passion in a heart set free.
WORDSWORTH, Tour in Italy (1831–1837)

"I have been in Paris only since yesterday," wrote Berlioz to his sister on November 8, 1832, "and already my musical affairs are under way . . . Everyone here received me with the warmest affection. I dined with M. Lesueur. I am going to see Alphonse,[1] but it's quite a trip because I lodge miles away from him, at No. 1 rue Neuve-St.-Marc." This address, and in fact the rooms that Berlioz occupied, were those formerly inhabited by Harriet Smithson. There is no evidence to show that anything but convenience—with a dash of curiosity—dictated the choice. He was in his old quarter—near the Opera and the *Café Feydeau,* near Lesueur and his own publisher—a central position from which to carry on his work.

Berlioz' first object was his concert. His strategy, the same as before, the same for the rest of his life, was dictated by the facts of Parisian life: concerts created a public, public pressure would force one of the official houses to commission an opera, and if it succeeded an opera brought income and further commissions. No other career was open to a musician except as a virtuoso. Pending this single salvation, the composer had to support himself by journalism and pay his way. So it was and so it remained until the end of the century, after which things did not improve but grew worse. Fortunately, in December 1832 Berlioz could not foresee his long life of quasi-unrewarded artistic work. His energy was at its peak;

he had grown in self-assurance in the two years since the *Fantastique,* and he meant to win a place for himself in spite of the competition of the prolific Auber, the adroit and complacent Adolphe Adam, and the man who was skillfully adapting to the stage a secondhand romanticism together with the showy side of symphonic music—Giacomo Meyerbeer. The Opera was run by a new director, a Dr. Véron, whose wealth came from patent medicine and the periodical press, and who therefore had an instinct for what the public wanted. He dabbled in the arts with a master hand, founding reviews and attaching to himself the purchasable talents of a certain kind. His reign of five years at the Opera was the only profitable one in its history since Lully's.[2]

It goes without saying that Berlioz' proposal of an opera on the Day of Judgment met with no favor. The last months of 1832 were disturbed by political violence—the arrest of the Duchess of Berry in connection with plots against Louis Philippe, and universal recrimination about these events. The Day of Judgment seemed near enough without paying for a preview at the Opera. None the less, Berlioz prepared his concert. He obtained the hall at the Conservatoire (seating twelve hundred) for the afternoon of December 9, and secured the aid of the popular actor, Bocage, for the speaking role in his "melologue," *The Return to Life,* which Berlioz had put together in Rome and copied out at La Côte.

This is the work that established him—much more than his first symphony—with the novelty-seeking public of the capital. Berlioz was now by official title an accredited composer, and the score that he brought back from Italy was cast in a form that seemed at once original, entertaining, and easily understood. None of the music was new, it had merely been revised; but virtually no one had heard it in its earlier forms. Of the six parts, the ballad on Goethe's "Fisherman" dated from 1827, the next three numbers came from the prize cantatas of 1827 and 1829, and the Brigand's Song had probably been composed in 1828. As for the finale, it was none other than the *Tempest* fantasia which had been played to a scattering of courageous operagoers during the political and other storms of November 1830.

As Berlioz started rehearsing his orchestra, the cohorts of Romanticism were with him, ardent, curious, sympathetic, and outspoken. Despite dark omens, it still seemed possible to accomplish the great things to which July 1830 had been a prelude. At the rehearsals and the concert itself were to be seen Liszt, Chopin, and Hiller; Hugo and the brothers Deschamps, Heine (who had recently settled as an exile in Paris), Eugène Sue, George Sand, Legouvé, Vigny, Dumas, Gautier, and scores of journalists headed by Jules Janin and Joseph d'Ortigue. They prepared the wider public who thronged the hall on the day of performance. The program handed to them consisted of a revised text for the *Symphonie Fantastique,* together with the new libretto of the melologue, its sequel. Rumor had it that the second part of the musical drama contained things both touching and satirical, and that the satire was aimed at the well-known music critic, F. J. Fétis, representing the clan who "improve" masterpieces and who, "like the vulgar birds that people our public gardens . . . , when they have stained the brow of Jupiter or the breast of Venus, preen themselves as if they had laid a golden egg."

Fétis, who was in the hall, heard his manner of speech being mimicked by the actor, and naturally wrote an unforgiving review, but Paris had relished on that day one of the many "artistic manifestations" (as they are traditionally called) which enliven its history. Strange to us, these challenges show that aristocratic honor was still in vogue and blows were dealt in front of witnesses.

Nor was the declamation purely an aggressive act. Like Hugo's *Hernani,* Dumas's *Antony* (playing at that very time), or Vigny's *Chatterton,* the melologue of Berlioz was in part didactic. The Romantic artist had to explain himself or, as De Quincey put it about Wordsworth, had to create the taste by which he is to be appreciated. We are now inclined to be impatient with the textbook, but in 1832 it was by no means pointless for Berlioz to expound the quality of his emotion, the character of his successive pieces, and the attitude he took towards his art. That he was right is shown by the delight of his fellow artists and the public's response. There was a spontaneous demand for a repeat performance of the whole *Episode from an Artist's Life.*

At the *première* of the work one undesigned dramatic scene had been witnessed and, thanks to gossip, understood by the public: in a box, not ten feet from Berlioz, sat Harriet Smithson, the other supposed protagonist in the "plot" that occupied the stage. Berlioz had certainly not invited her, but the next day he was introduced and they spoke face to face for the first time. No record exists of their conversation; in his letter home after the concert, Berlioz speaks only of its success, of the congratulations of Paganini, Victor Hugo, and Adolphe Nourrit, as well as of the snobbish curiosity of *Tout-Paris.* Newspaper reviews bore out this report. In the *Journal des Débats,* more than ever powerful owing to its association with the reigning house of Orleans, Janin wrote: "This young man has from this day forward an audience at his feet."

Since Berlioz had to leave for Germany by January first, he would consolidate his position—and possibly recoup his expenses—at the second performance set for December 30. It netted no profit but spread his name still farther: he and Liszt were the twin wonders of the season. The musically reliable d'Ortigue pointed out that Berlioz was the first French composer to "produce in the symphonic genre those picturesque effects, those lively and strong colors, that elegiac and mystical utterance which the great works of Weber and Beethoven first made known to us. What distinguishes Berlioz is vigor, brilliance, daring, and an almost exuberant power of dramatic expression." The critic warned the authorities: "Do not let this burning gift cool down. . . . Spare him the disgust and mortification which arrest talents on the verge of creation. Take him in his vigorous youth, in the strength of his noble self-confidence."

This advice might well have been heeded by others than musical officials—by Harriet Smithson, for instance. For Berlioz' interview with her had had its sequel too. The actress was in difficult circumstances: the vogue of English plays was declining; her manager was in America, and she lacked business ability. Whether this predicament rekindled warmth of feeling in Berlioz, whether she made an appeal to him in her distress, mistaking one sentiment for another, the fact remains that by mid-December the pair were deeply involved. She had declared herself to Berlioz, who was soon writing to Franz Liszt: "Yes, I love her. I love her and am loved in return." And to another friend: "What an improbable romance life is!" He and Harriet corresponded, each in his own language, and Berlioz, always able to observe himself, could but be amused by the pace of the affair: "What love, . . . what idolatry, *quanti palpiti!*"

Complications soon arose. Harriet having a mother and sister to support was beset by money worries, and the sister, being a jealous and censorious cripple, made as much trouble as she could. It would have been difficult enough without this for both the lovers to overcome their previous qualms about each other. Harriet had been represented to Hector as a woman of easy virtue, and he to her as irresponsible and even epileptic. Berlioz, moreover, was a man of quick decision, whom others' delay and shifting thoughts rendered impatient. Insight did not lessen his torture: "She has a true and deep sensibility which I did not suspect. I love her as upon the first day and I think I am sure of being loved by her. But she is timid, hesitant and cannot come to a resolve: how will it all end?"

He naturally gave up all thought of going to Germany. Leaving a *second* beloved a prey to alien influences would have been idiocy. The success of *The Return to Life* taught a similar lesson. A year's absence abroad would require still another effort to reproduce the present favorable conditions. To entrench himself with the new authorities and help put Romanticism in power, he must stay active and on the spot. In the midst of a bad moment with Harriet, the Italian Theater asked him for a comic opera. Berlioz chose *Much Ado about Nothing* and sketched the libretto with a speed which argues previous thought. But musical politics are treacherous: thirty years elapsed before he was enabled to carry out this project.

By the next month, February 1833, Hector had decided to end Harriet's vacillations and risk alienating his family by offering her immediate marriage. She accepted his reckless proposal; given her plight and his situation, his offer could only mean absolute devotion. His "tenacity"—loyalty to an idea, rather—was his undoing, for he was conscious of the nature of his passion: "It is no love of the senses; the heart alone and the head are impregnated with this sublime sentiment." It seemed like a fated choice; as before towards music, now towards her he was "voluntarily driven": "I shall never leave her; she is my star; she understood me. If this be error, I must be left in the grip of it." And again: "I am immensely happy—until further notice." This refers to the "persecutions" which both their families had begun in order to break the engagement. Dr. Berlioz had uttered an uncompromising "No," but Hector was sure of his own fortitude and "she promises that she will be courageous and firm . . . we shall soon, I hope, overcome these difficulties."

"Soon" turned out to be eight months, during which impediments were aggravated by catastrophes and led to misery in common. By refusing his consent, Dr. Berlioz forced Hector to take laborious legal steps—the so-called *sommations respectueuses*—by which under the Code a son enjoins his father not to cut him off despite the action he is about to take. On Harriet's side, the preparations for two benefit performances were nipped in the bud by her breaking her leg as she stepped from a cab. Financial preoccupations would be enough to explain her misstep, but it is clear that her anxiety was increased by a sense of inadequacy. Under the badgering of her family she grew apathetic, and then distraught by her lover's demands for certitude and action: "A trifle frightens her; she is afraid of my exasperation . . . we mutually torment each other. . . . But the worse her position becomes, the more devoted I shall be. . . ."

In the interstices of this deplorable drama, there were articles to write and musical proofs to correct. The publisher Maurice Schlesinger was bringing out three pieces from the Melologue and Berlioz saw to it that they were circulated. By the end of May, Harriet was beginning to walk on crutches, but her sister still hoped to discourage the devoted Hector. The "devilish little hunchback" told him to his face that if she were strong enough she would pitch him out of the window. He kept his temper but agonized over the effect of this nagging on Harriet. His own family, except the faithful Adèle, "treated him like a pariah," and he had to inquire of Paris friends in order to find out how Nanci had fared through her first childbirth.

By mid-June the strain had nearly worn him down. He was anesthetized by the effort toward a seemingly unattainable object. He broke with Harriet, which had the effect of rousing her, but he withstood her entreaties. He ended by giving in: had she not done as much earlier for him? Still his practical sense was revolted. Refusing to accept money from him, she had struggled to obtain from the Ministry of Fine Arts a "gratuity" of a thousand francs, whereas she should have been ready to marry him and help him start rebuilding their finances. But she was still "timid, irresolute, incapable of making a decision." He finally persuaded her to take the step. Her sister tore up the preliminary license. Caught between two strong wills, Harriet reproached Hector with not loving her. Whereupon by way of enraged testimony he swallowed in front of her an overdose of laudanum. Her tears and supplications induced him to take an emetic—a second return to life.

Even then the tragic farce was not over. She wanted to "wait a few months." Berlioz determined to leave her, to leave the country and settle in Germany—if need be with a waif of eighteen, whom some friends had rescued from bondage to an exploiter and were trying to distract him with. His father meanwhile having written him a "dreadful letter," he no longer cared about his own happiness, and was ready to accept anything as part of his "absurd story."

Four days later Harriet came to plead with him again, and in return for an ultimate change of his plans, consented to have their banns put up. The waif was taken care of by a collection among friends, and Janin undertook to see her out of harm's way. On October 3, 1833, the marriage of Harriet and Hector was solemnized at the British Embassy with Franz Liszt as principal witness.

Aided by Liszt, d'Ortigue, Berlioz, and other musical friends, the Romantics in the several arts had meanwhile joined hands to promote their views and fulfill designs long matured. They enlisted the aid of men high in government places and founded a magazine, *L'Europe Littéraire*, which was to publish their views and, by a foreign as well as native catholicity, help modern art to overcome the usual obstacles of ignorance, Philistinism, and national prejudice. "Art," said the prospectus, "has always been a social and general concern. This concern is reflected and made visible through journalism. But hitherto this mirror of the times has only cast back the image of past epochs, and contemporaries have perforce ignored one another." The new organ meant to "focus the rays of all living genius" and raise a "temple to the universality of all the arts." Under Victor Bohain's editorship, men of letters formed the majority of the contributors, but the magazine undertook to sponsor concerts, and this naturally meant featuring the work of the outstanding modern musician, Hector Berlioz.

At the first of these concerts, on May 2, 1833, six of the eight works were by Berlioz—two overtures, three movements from the *Symphonie Fantastique,* and the fisherman's song from the melologue. It was a successful as well as fashionable occasion. One could count peers of the realm, great ladies, artists, and critics. Berlioz' friend Girard led the orchestra, even though at another concert two months before he had made a hash of the *Francs-Juges* overture. Habeneck and the

Conservatoire Society likewise vied in willingness to tackle the unfamiliar difficulties of Berlioz' scores. On April 14, 1833 they gave his new overture *Rob Roy,* but the work had no success, for the sufficient reason, Berlioz felt, that it was "long and diffuse." He destroyed it, though keeping in mind some of its melodic material.[3]

Although the Conservatoire was soon to turn against Berlioz by a natural conspiracy and made use of this lack of success, other official bodies seemed at this time fairly well disposed toward the new generation. The Institute, according to its custom, publicly reported on the works sent by its Rome pensioners. Montfort's little pieces received vague compliments but Berlioz was assured with some warmth that he had greatly improved. He had profited from experience and was now "original without eccentricity." This opinion unknowingly bore on music that Berlioz had written before winning the prize, and he enjoyed the irony while noting the Institute's kindly frame of mind. At the same time, the Ministry refused his request for a grant-in-aid and reminded him of his obligation to go to Germany. Subsequently this requirement was waived and Berlioz received fitfully but in full the stipend to which the award entitled him. State involvement in art means politics, it works by favor and exception, and responds only to the pull of power. This being known to all Parisian artists—Delacroix was at that moment being pushed by Thiers who fancied himself as a connoisseur, and Rude had finally made his mark with his "Neapolitan Fisher-Boy"—Berlioz could "arrive" and be given the leisure to write music only if he forced his way by an alliance with some faction or other. He must also acquire a public personality and become one of those whom the government dare not turn down. In short, he must coerce and cajole like any vulgar politician, whatever the risk to him as an artist in this struggle for power.

This compulsion was the inevitable counterpart of the process by which art had become public and social instead of private and domestic. This change is the clue to understanding the fate that overtook Berlioz and his generation, the first under the modern system. So far from being "divorced from society," they were violently thrown into society to sink or swim in competition with other manufacturers and promoters. As individuals, their sole defense was the power of the press. Now the newspaper closest to the government in the 30's was the *Journal des Débats,* where Jules Janin—the Lousteau of Balzac's *Lost Illusions*—favored Berlioz, originally because the musician was "good copy." In a column of literary gossip he could be represented as an uncommon specimen. Soon Janin put him forward as the only living composer likely to bring world renown to the French School. This was sound prophecy, but the need persisted to turn Berlioz' life and character into reading matter, and from this grew the Berlioz legend, itself part of the Romanticist legend.

Because Berlioz himself contributed to this publicity—giving notes to d'Ortigue or Gautier—it has been inferred that he was unusually avid of newspaper notice. In reality he had little choice. If experts in public relations had been available in 1833, and if he had been able to pay them, he would undoubtedly have hired someone to relieve him of the job. Meyerbeer was soon to assemble a corps of secretaries for just this purpose. But Berlioz, like Weber before him and Hugo and others in his own time, had to create his legend single-handed. Unlike Hugo, however, he did not play up to it in private life: he was never the maestro, and always hated pose. Of Berlioz' ways among friends at this time, we have an account by d'Ortigue: "His conversation is . . . uneven, abrupt, interrupted . . . sometimes also expansive, but more often reserved and formal, always frank and worthy of respect."

"Sometimes expansive, but more often reserved" is the real Berlioz, and one regrets that the legend had to exhibit a creature always flamboyant, volcanic, and indifferent to privacy. Propaganda has to fit the minds of the recipients, and the artist's new patron—at once snob and mob—required its heroes to be patently demonic and self-assertive. In the smaller Paris of those days, of course, legends found their own corrective; they were reinterpreted in the light of common knowledge. Looking back in the 1860's, Sainte-Beuve tells us how incredible it seemed that thirty years before one used to carry on one's life through the columns of the newspapers: "A sheet with five thousand subscribers was practically a family of intimates."

Style in these matters changes quickly. In Berlioz' own reviews and autobiographical fragments one can follow the shifts in tone and substance which each decade brought about from 1830 to 1870; the series amounts to a miniature history of journalism and of class emancipation through widened literacy. In these middle thirties, his music criticism shows the clear intention of establishing himself as a Personality. Around a musical subject, and sometimes with the addition of a short-story plot, he wove fantasies based on his Italian experiences. He had the storyteller's gift and could imbue, for example, an account of the way the Rome Prizes are awarded, with a humorous lifelikeness which secured for him and for music criticism readers hitherto untouched. But here again power created resistance. To take the public as witnesses of musical affairs was to declare war on the Institute and bring on reprisals. In a solemn sitting on October 12, 1833 the secretary read a report in which Berlioz was admonished like a schoolboy. His views on modern music were indirectly assailed and a malicious reference was made to the unapplauded *Rob Roy* overture. Reversing themselves like a supreme court, the judges discovered that Montfort's work was "clear, lively, spirited throughout," in fact remarkable for "elegant melodies and brilliant orchestration."

Except for these skirmishes, his marriage to Harriet, and the concerts previously mentioned, the second half of 1833 brought Berlioz nothing but dull disappointment. He continued to be on distant terms with his family—all but the loving Adèle, to whom he poured out his hopes and his gratitude. With Harriet's debts weighing on him, he had little time or strength to compose. Instead, he struggled to arrange for November a benefit recital for her and himself together. By midsummer he had worked himself to exhaustion in the preliminaries, meanwhile revising and rehearsing his "Heroic Scene" for another ceremony. Napoleon's statue was to be put back on the column, Place Vendôme, and Berlioz' choral work, though first associated with the Greek Revolution, was perfectly suitable.

For the first time since the July Days a popular celebration was to include music on the large scale. Huge stands were built opposite the Tuileries for the three hundred singers and two hundred and fifty instrumentists who were to follow the solemn beating of three or four hundred drums. The official program comprised Rossini's *William Tell* and *Gazza Ladra* overtures, Auber's *Masaniello* overture, a battle piece by the choral composer and conductor Schneitzhöffer, and four other choruses. It was only at the last minute that Berlioz had managed to have his own work added, certainly the most fitting item on the program. The rehearsals (indoors) under Habeneck created a stir. That hardened conductor wept at the mere richness of sound, and Berlioz, alert to his opportunity, was able for the first time to study the properties of large ensembles.[4] But by the appointed day, Berlioz' piece had been surreptitiously worked off the program. Then the musical part of the festival was drowned out by incessant political demonstrations. The troops were armed and the mob angry. They did not return their King's greeting but shouted *vivas* when the Emperor's statue was raised. The Opera announced that the concert would be given again on its stage. More work for Berlioz to reinstate his "Scene": the concert was canceled.

As for the joint "benefit" for Hector and his wife, it was a fiasco of another sort. It began late and Marie Dorval (Vigny's great love) stole the show. Coming after, Harriet Smithson found little favor with her pantomime from the fourth act of *Hamlet*. Berlioz and his music did not get under way until 11:30 in front of a politically excited audience. They listened to Liszt, who played superbly; but in conducting his *Sardanapalus* cantata Berlioz miscued his orchestra and the crowd began to demand the *Symphonie Fantastique*. At this point the orchestra had had enough and started to leave. Berlioz had to make a speech of apology to the audience, despite the fact that it was long past midnight and they kept demanding the March from the *Fantastique*. The humiliation of Berlioz and his wife was complete.

This failure, however, netted two thousand francs, which was swallowed up by Harriet's debts and the support of her family. No help was forthcoming from his; so he accepted the post of music critic on *Le Rénovateur*—an offshoot of the *Correspondant,* that is to say ultra-royalist, ultra-religious in tone. But as Berlioz wrote to Adèle: "Since I have no use for politics, their shade of opinion does not bother me in the least." In short order, Berlioz wrote two excellent articles—a diplomatic one on the dancer Taglioni and the new Opera management (Dr. Vèron and Ciceri) which featured her work, and a delicate and penetrating study of Chopin as pianist and composer.

Berlioz did not consider this enough to fill the remainder of the year. A whole month was left in which to turn the defeat of his last concert into a victory. Aware that he lacked experience as a conductor, he did not dare risk a fresh disaster. Only one man in Paris could really give Berlioz' music properly, François Habeneck; but he abruptly refused. Girard was once again called on, the lesser of two risks. Liszt readily agreed to play some Weber, and Paganini's protégé, Haumann, offered a piece of his own composition. The rest was all by Berlioz: two new songs—*"La Romance de Mary Tudor"* and *"Le Jeune Pâtre Breton,"* the *King Lear* overture, and the *Symphonie Fantastique*. The effort was worth it; expenses were met, and both public and critical acclaim were considerable. Only Fétis's *Revue Musicale* complained that M. Berlioz did not produce many new works.

Berlioz was by now just turned thirty. He was married, had begun to pay off some fifteen thousand francs on his wife's account, was supplying money to her mother, and was about to become a father. His sole means of support being his pen (plus the uncertain remainder of his prize) he could not afford the time to compose, even though he had a new symphony in his head. Two occurrences came to his aid. His publisher and friend, Maurice Schlesinger, sensing that the new young men would turn out to be the great men of tomorrow, founded a periodical, *La Gazette Musicale,* which was to unite French and German musical thought against the frivolity of the Italians. Since the Paris Schlesinger was the brother and partner of the Berlin Schlesinger, and their firms published music on both sides of the Rhine, the new periodical would aid their business as well as promote the works of a very productive group of performers and composers. Berlioz was at once among the leaders of this enterprise, to which he contributed articles, editorial advice and practical work.[5]

The second piece of luck was a request from Paganini for a composition in which he might play his newly acquired Stradivarius viola—a concerto for viola and orchestra. To make the most of this request, the *Gazette* announced a new work by Berlioz for viola, chorus, and orchestra, with the improvised title, *The Last Moments of Mary Stuart*.[6] Within the next six months Berlioz finished the work—not a concerto, not for voices, and never again called "Mary Stuart," but during its gestation simply called "the symphony" or "my symphony with viola." It grew from two movements to three, then to four, until on May 31, he wrote to d'Ortigue: "It is nearly finished and will soon be born and baptized." The nameless symphony was associated by the author with some of the musical experiences he had brought back from Italy, so that after casting about for the proper allusive tag he finally called it *Harold in Italy*.

The speed and joy with which he composed this sizable score show how ripe it was in Berlioz mind. The "inexplicable mechanism" within him worked just as soon as he could enjoy a little of the "time and tranquillity" which he said were his sole requirements. Though there were still duns, and some apprehension, both medical and financial, at the forthcoming addition to the family, Hector was in love and happy with Harriet. His need to give and receive affection was satisfied for the first time in his adult life. As Harriet's time approached, the pair moved to a quiet cottage and garden on the hill Montmartre, overlooking a plain as yet free of all industry, whose greenery reminded Berlioz of home and Italy.[7] His good friends Liszt, Chopin, Hiller and others came out to the countrified suburb for the day. At other times there were quartets and piano sonatas at Schlesinger's, readings at Victor Hugo's, dinners where one met other young celebrities such as the ardent Liberal Catholic Lamennais ("What a man! Genius burns him, eats him away, dessicates him. He made me tingle with admiration.") Lamennais was an excellent pianist, he held congenial views about the social role of art, and in fact Berlioz' two closest friends, Liszt and d'Ortigue, were the Abbé's disciples. Of the salons, that of Marie, Comtesse d'Agoult, was at once the least showy and the most lively. It was intellectual and cosmopolitan. Sainte-Beuve, Heine, Mickiewicz, the Princess Belgiojoso, Balzac, George Sand and Berlioz could be found there. Berlioz took Liszt, with the famous result that the pianist and the countess fell in love and eloped. But until this event, there was music, brilliant talk, and friendship among men who could love and admire one another without envy or reserve.

Unfortunately, there was also "an avalanche, a cataract of concerts" to be reviewed. Between *Le Rénovateur,* and *La Gazette Musicale,* Berlioz had to sweat out copy on all conceivable subjects, good and bad, real and imaginary. And the most real were by no means those which induced him to put himself in the limelight as artist-hero of significant adventures. For he had taken on the mission of enlightener to the French in musical matters—an enterprise requiring equal parts of knowledge, tact, firmness, and ability to entertain. Berlioz preached Beethoven, analyzed his symphonies (beginning with the Third, Sixth and Ninth) and dissected the prejudices of those who, in any age, use famous names to damn the moderns without caring about the works of either. By dramatic parallels and allusions designed to rouse the imagination of his readers, and technical arguments designed to quiet their scruples, Berlioz acted as mediator between academic or fashionable conservatism and the boldness of the late symphonies and quartets. "Art being always a social and general concern," as the romanticists had said, these half-technical, half-poetic sermons wound up with a broadside against the impercipience of the public. "The Greeks made of Homer a god. So long as Beethoven has not a temple in our midst we shall deserve the name of Barbarian."

Berlioz also took the opportunity offered by a feeble revival of Mozart's *Don Giovanni* to demonstrate the difference between musical drama and commonplace opera. To the poet Deschamps he wrote in confidence: "I'd like to talk to you about Mozart. We must absolutely lather up the masterpiece in such a way as to bring on a fever in the lovers of the big bass drum," that is, the Italians.

In a society which freely admitted that musicales were held in order to start conversation, and which required tunes (as Berlioz put it) "so written that the ladies and gentlemen who sell ribbon can remember them easily the next morning," the standards that Berlioz tried to establish were exacting but would not seem to us impossibly high. Since it was agreed that "music-desk music" is boring and always too long, Berlioz affirms without mincing words that a nation which is sunk in such Philistinism cannot lay claim to high culture. By witty asides, calculated effrontery, or adroit storytelling he compels the reader to go on and be indoctrinated against his will; he communicates his contempt, his enthusiasm, and even his subtlety.

This effort took its toll. In a man of artistic faith, the constant dissent of mankind engenders at last a spiritual weariness. Though not strengthened, faith is made at any rate more cheerful by agreement. In early May 1834, within a month of completing his symphony, Berlioz shared some of his spleen with Liszt, urging him to come out, with Chopin and others, to Montmartre:

> I cannot tell you how much this springtime scene moves and saddens me. Besides, yesterday I suffered several *wounds in my artistic affections,* which make me miserable to the point of tears, and which all my reason (for I have a good deal more reason than you might think) or that of my poor Harriet cannot make me forget or overcome.

Is Vigny coming with you? There is something gentle and affectionate about his mind which always charms me and which today I find I almost need. Why aren't you both here now? Perhaps tomorrow I shall feel differently. Are we really playthings of the air? . . . And is Moore right when he says: "And false the light on glory's plume, As fading hues of even; . . . There's nothing bright but Heaven!" [8]

But I do not believe in heaven. It is horrible to confess it. My heaven is the poetic world and there is a slug on each blossom. Look here, come and bring Vigny with you. I need you both. Why can I not keep myself from admiring with tenacious passion certain works which are, after all, so fragile —like ourselves, like everything that is?

Berlioz then quotes from memory (that is, with some inaccuracy) fourteen bars from Spontini evocative of anxious longing.

The visitors did come and Berlioz could report to Adèle: "We discussed art, poetry, philosophy, music and drama—in a word all that constitutes life—in the presence of this beauty of nature and Italian sunshine which has favored us these few days past." Then in an upsurge of anguish: "My father is well, I gather from the Rocher ladies. Is everyone else well? They tell me you are losing weight. Why? What is wrong? You are so alone, so sad. We shall meet again, I tell you, sooner or later. It is impossible otherwise. Farewell, these thoughts sadden me. Farewell, I embrace you with my whole affection and that which my good and sweet Harriet bears you."

By the middle of May 1834, three parts of *Harold in Italy* were finished and the composer was offering his old friend Humbert Ferrand the dedication of the work. Practical affairs were once more crowding the desk where only score paper should have been. "I am dead tired and bored from scribbling at so much a column for those rascally papers. My opera plans are in the hands of the Bertin family"—owners of the *Journal des Débats* and influential at court. The scheme—most appropriate to Berlioz—was to offer him "a superior libretto" on Hamlet. "Meantime," he adds (for he was inured to delays and never waited for a hare to be caught before starting another) "I have chosen as subject for a two-act comic opera, *Benvenuto Cellini.*" By May 31, Berlioz, working day and night, was in sight of the end as regards the symphony: it was soon finished, and "baptized" not long after. The autograph bears the date June 22, 1834.

CHAPTER 9

THE GOTHIC TRADITION

With all his faults, and with all the irregularity of his drama, one may look upon his works as upon an ancient majestic piece of Gothic architecture, compared with a neat modern building. The latter is more elegant and glaring, but the former is more strong and more solemn.—POPE on Shakespeare, 1728

The *Harold* symphony once finished, it had to be played—if only because Berlioz wanted to hear and revise it. He must accordingly give one or more concerts at his own risk in the coming winter season. The preparation went on amid expected chores and fresh difficulties. On August 14, 1834, Harriet Berlioz gave birth, after a painful labor of forty hours, to a son, Louis.[1] A few days later, the Opéra-Comique turned down the libretto that Berlioz and Auguste Barbier (the well-known poet met in Italy) had fashioned around the figure of Benvenuto Cellini. Meanwhile, Paganini had found the viola part in Berlioz' new work too slight for him, and Urhan, a classmate of Berlioz' at the Conservatoire and a pious Beethovenian, was entrusted with it.

As Harriet slowly recovered, Berlioz breathed easier—on two counts: relief and the fact that his family took this occasion to relent, sending congratulations and gifts. Possessed of strong family feeling, the young husband felt as if reunited after a gnawing separation. By further good fortune, the *Journal des Débats,* seeking a new music critic, tried out Berlioz on its readers by reprinting one of his *feuilletons.* Early in November a first concert, still lacking the symphony, brought forth two new choral works—both slight but charming idylls—that Berlioz had somehow found the tranquillity to compose: *La Belle Voyageuse* and *Sara la Baigneuse*. Even this modest program had cost much effort. For a musician without power in the regular theaters "nothing is scarcer than passable singers. I cannot find any for my concerts, and twice I have had to postpone a trio to which I attach some importance, for lack of a moderately decent bass. The managers refuse to lend their people."

On the twenty-second, Harriet made her debut at the Théâtre Nautique in an appalling pantomime entitled "The Last Hour of the Condemned." She acted well enough but the piece failed, together with the manager. The theater shut its doors without paying its debts. But the next day, *Harold in Italy* was played with resounding success before a picked audience. Fashion, journalism, and art were represented by Jules Janin, Liszt, d'Ortigue, Heine, Eugène Sue, Legouvé, Barbier, Léon de Wailly, Victor Hugo, Gounet, Sainte-Beuve, Lesueur, Chopin, the brothers Deschamps, Vigny, Gérard de Nerval, Dumas, plus the publishers and patrons of art, Schlesinger and Renduel. The second movement (Pilgrims' March) was wildly applauded and called for twice, but Girard mixed up his cues and ruined the encore. From this moment Berlioz determined to master the art of conducting and lead his own works.

The last movement of the symphony is the well-known "Orgy of Brigands," whose significance deserves a word, for it is a cultural symptom as well as a rousing allegro. The brigand of Berlioz' time is the avenger of social injustice, the rebel against the City, who resorts to nature for healing the wounds of social man. Berlioz had already given vent to the feeling in an extravagant passage of the melologue which introduces the brigands' song and chorus. In *Harold* he purged himself more thoroughly, the release of violence and vulgarity acting as a needful antidote to the repressions of conventional life.

This flirting with the idea of brigandage hinted of the nascent democracy already undermining the bourgeois monarchy of Louis Philippe. By 1834, the King's green cotton umbrella had figuratively extinguished the first high hopes of the culture-makers. What in England would later be known as the Victorian Compromise was beginning to solidify in France. Moralism invaded daily-life; masculine clothes lost their superfluities and grew darker until they reached the uniform "decent black" of the mid-century. With moralism came its twin, literalism: at the new "nautical theater" where Harriet Smithson had hoped to be permanently engaged, the great lure was an actual positive lake, made of water, on which genuine boats could be seen to float.

The so-called practical intellect was in the ascendant. Among the newly emancipated men of affairs, the men of art were looked at askance and forced into the opposition, for when Louis Philippe's son-in-law tried to gather around him a salon of the best talents in France, his efforts were vetoed by "Papa." In order to survive, genius could only pursue an anti-bourgeois policy. In a year when young Gautier was being prosecuted for the boldness of *Mademoiselle de Maupin* and was retorting in a pyrotechnic preface; when Rabelais and Villon were attacked in the public prints as being "in exceedingly bad taste," when Berlioz was attacking the Institute and defending Chopin, he privately cheered himself by reading the newly translated *Memoirs* of Benvenuto Cellini, discovering in this "bandit of genius" a perfect subject for another dramatic parable on genius itself.

Meanwhile he was playing *Harold* again. The second performance of the *Harold* symphony three weeks later, with Chopin playing one movement of his new concerto in F Minor, brought little into the box office, but the third performance on December 28 netted Berlioz two thousand francs. The toil, the excitement, and the indecisiveness of such artistic victories left Berlioz exhausted. To his previous obligations and the expenses for the newborn child, he found he must add the cost of moving the family back within city limits; his goings and comings were otherwise too tiring. So the year 1835 opened in an atmosphere of worry and strain. He cautioned d'Ortigue: "Please don't stress in your articles my present financial situation. It's useless to dwell on it." The band of Berlioz' admirers was bent on rousing the nineteenth-century goddess Public Opinion so as to "force the doors of the Opera." They wanted a great public success not only for him but for the satisfaction of their faith. Berlioz must naturally live up to the view they entertained of him as a potential master in the opera, and on the strength of the esteem shown him by the brothers Bertin and the staff of the *Débats*, Berlioz made new overtures to Dr. Véron. Perhaps a revision of the Cellini scenario into a grand opera might suit. Nothing came of it. Instead, for its customary New Year's masked ball, the Opera produced on January 10 a skit parodying Berlioz and his friends.

It was a sign of celebrity and the parody (greatly enjoyed by the audience) testified to the impact made by the composer's works and ideas upon the public. Berlioz' colleague and rather envious rival, Adolphe Adam, had had a hand in the skit, and the actor Arnal—who later apologized very contritely—played the speaking role. This aped both Berlioz and his projection of himself in the melologue. The mimic told his audience: "You will hear a grand Symphony . . . 'An Episode in a Gambler's Life.' To make my dramatic thoughts understood I have no need of words, singers, or scenery. All this, gentlemen, is in my orchestra. You will hear my hero speak. You will see him portrayed from head to foot, and at the second reprise of the first allegro, I will show you how he puts on his necktie. Ah, the wonders of instrumental music!"

Berlioz was present and laughed good-naturedly. "I sincerely hope," he wrote, "that before next year I can write and perform another *similar* composition to add to the gaiety of the Opera's buffooneries." A touch of bitterness may be supposed to enter here, for on second thoughts, what would be the effect on the unthinking public of the ridicule heaped upon a new and serious esthetic creed—that of drama through music alone? And was it not a bitter thought in itself that the Opera should be so easy of access for "buffoons" and so tightly shut against serious composers?

What Berlioz and his friends did not take into account was that to ingratiate himself with the Opera management he would have had to be not merely a different kind of artist but a different kind of man. Under Véron, the house was more than ever a fashionable resort for those bent on self-indulgence: part night club, part house of assignation. The pageantry which Meyerbeer knew how to provide, and which he reinforced with substantial favors and flattery, made that composer *persona grata* on the business side, while setting at rest the susceptibilities of the lubricious Doctor and his ostentatious protégé Loève-Veimars.[2] A man of aristocratic reserve and probity like Berlioz was on the contrary a living reproach to their ways and outlook on life. He was, to be sure, courteously treated by Véron, who would even "lend" him Mademoiselle Falcon for a concert appearance, but he would have been more popular with that crowd had he wished to borrow a ballerina for another purpose.

The Duke of Orleans, with his flair for men of artistic integrity, aided the Bertins to decide on retaining Berlioz for the

Débats. The latter began his well-paid duties on January 25, 1835, and left the paper only on his resignation twenty-eight years later. Were it not for debts and concerts, his financial situation was now assured.[3] But the expense of furnishing his apartment in town, and providing servants for Harriet and the baby, was aggravated by her want of management and kept him financially harassed. In his student days he had acquired the habit of keeping accounts, preferring to live within his means. His debts then were only for musical purposes—playing or publishing his works—and he could feel personally solvent while using credit as a capital investment in his career. Now the steadily increasing arrears added to the strain of journalism and *non*-composition. Though he complained merely of excess of work, Hector's letters to Ferrand and Adèle show that his mind spent itself in writing several reviews a month for each of three papers, expanding earlier articles for serial republication, and keeping in touch with the authorities in hopes of some musical commission—state festival or grand opera.

Family life, it is true, had its rewards. He was passionately devoted to his wife and child. "Our little boy," he confided to Adèle, "continues charming; you have no idea how beautiful he is. He never cries but laughs aloud as soon as one is willing to play with him. Harriet grows prouder of him every day. . . . Incidentally, you miscalculated the size of the kid's head: your bonnet just fits, but a little more width wouldn't have hurt." Then in the margin: *"Important note:* it's not the bonnet, it's the tape that isn't long enough. You are vindicated and I am an ignoramus."

Being concert critic for the most influential newspaper in Paris, Berlioz could choose what to review, which usually meant the programs of the Société des Concerts du Conservatoire. This gave him the chance to expound the principles of modern instrumental music to a wider public. The fifteen to twenty thousand subscribers of the *Journal des Débats* were treated to a virtual course, an orthodoxy, in the principles of Gluck, Weber, and Beethoven. The music reviews of those days were sizable affairs, six to nine columns long, of a format resembling that of the London *Times,* and in them Berlioz repeatedly analyzed Beethoven's symphonies, which he regarded as the fountainhead of the expressive genre. It was his own stake in creation that Berlioz was one-sidedly defending, sometimes at the expense of the eighteenth-century masters—just as Shaw later defended Ibsen at the expense of Shakespeare. The

Parisians, then brought up on the earlier works of Haydn and Mozart, were still one step behind: they could not even keep *Don Giovanni* in the operatic repertoire. Berlioz' defense of that score shows perhaps the exact line separating the eighteenth from the nineteenth century in music, as well as that marking off the public taste of 1835 from "modern" art. What the paying public meant by dramatic music was opera, and opera meant Rossini, Adam, Auber, and Meyerbeer. Beethoven was still caviar, except to a small band of intellectuals.

And they, the intellectuals, while defending their chosen masters were also fighting to secure for art a recognized status and function. "That is the question," wrote Vigny in the preface to his play *Chatterton,* "the perpetual martyrdom and immolation of the poet. Our concern is the right he is entitled to, of staying alive . . . the bread that is denied him, the suicide he is compelled to commit." [4]

So far the complaint is familiar, though Vigny was above the need to make it on his own behalf. The significant part is the description of what results from a general neglect of art:

Three kinds of men, who must not be mistaken one for the other, act on society through the workings of their minds. . . . The man with an aptitude for savoir faire, and who is therefore much valued, is everywhere to be seen. Void of real emotions, he writes of business as if it were literature and of literature as if it were business . . . He is a Man of Letters. Above him is a man of stronger and finer nature. His genius consists of attention brought to its highest pitch. He seeks especially order and clarity, having always in his eye the people whom he addresses. He is the true Great Writer. He is fought, but with courteous weapons. He needs no compassion.

But there is another kind of being, more passionate, purer and rarer. He who belongs to that kind is incompetent for whatever is not the work of divinity. Emotion with him is so deep, so intimate that it has plunged him from childhood in involuntary ecstasies, in endless reveries, in infinite discoveries. Imagination possesses him exclusively. His powerful soul judges and retains everything with a sure instinct and a strong memory. Disgust, vexations and the resistance of human society throw him into deep depression and black indignation. Still, on the day when he bursts forth one would say that he observes as a stranger what takes place within him. He should do nothing useful or workaday so that he may have the time to listen to the chords slowly shaping in his soul. He is the Poet. . . .

It is in his first youth that he feels his strength and foresees the future of his genius, that with love he embraces life and nature, that he arouses mistrust and suffers rebuff. He cries to the people: "It is to you that I speak" and the multitude answer justly enough: "We do not understand." He cries to the state: "Heed me and help me live." But the state replies that it is set up to protect positive interests. "Of what use are you?" Everybody against him is in the right. Is he then in the wrong? What can he do?

If he has bodily strength, he can become a soldier . . . Physical activity will deaden the spiritual. He can become a Man of Letters or even a Great Writer . . . Judgment will kill Imagination . . . but in any case he will kill a part of himself . . . as Chatterton killed himself altogether.

Though the language is strained, the psychological and sociological report is accurate; and though the biography of Chatterton may not support Vigny's case, the interpretation will still serve to explain what happens to our Van Goghs and Hart Cranes, as well as to understand what stronger natures—like Vigny and Berlioz—felt they were up against. Vigny's bitterness was partly congenital, but in this document it fits a contemporary mood. The observant now knew that the honeymoon between Liberty and the Orleans regime was over. This was the trough of the first wave of disillusion after the liberal revolution. The buoyant and irresistible Hugo himself underwent a period of black depression; he spoke of Darkness advancing, and entitled the poems of this period *Chants du Crépuscule* (Songs at Twilight).

Meanwhile social critics brooded upon the seemingly unquenchable unrest. The merciless shooting of strikers at Lyon in April 1834 was the bloodiest yet of Louis Philippe's efforts to establish himself. Repression was failing, and its opposite no one dared conceive. In a word, 1830 had not closed the era of revolutions, and by 1835 it was evident that the compromise had created no order: from the culture-makers to the textile workers every interest must not merely plead but fight for the recognition of what seemed to each its elementary rights.

For Berlioz, we gather from a note, the *première* of Vigny's play on February 12, 1835 was a doubly poignant spectacle: "My wife did for a moment think of accepting your gracious offer [of a box] but all things considered, the thought of the eclipse in which her talents stand for the time being is too painful to permit her to attend a notable occasion such as that to which you have kindly invited us. I shall therefore go alone to applaud *Chatterton* with all the warmth of affection and enthusiasm which I feel for its author, and for the cause he pleads so well." On her side Harriet, who had become passionately devoted to her husband, was full of self-reproach at seeing him carrying his heavy burden alone. She, who had supported her whole family since her adolescence, was now helpless. She wanted to act again, but her imperfect knowledge of French prevented. Hugo was approached for a play in which this drawback could fit, but all the plots involving mutes and foreigners seemed to have been used up. He none the less promised to try.

Not stopping to consider whether he was a musical Poet or merely a Great Artist, Berlioz had begun composing *Benvenuto Cellini*. Obviously, he still believed in the power of example and the force of integrity. If the Opera would once let him in, he could make its frivolous, overfed, finical, and convention-ridden habitués swallow serious music. "I may have to compose for a few years more outside the theatre before I can step on the neck of these stupid manufacturers. What wretchedness to see the best years of my life lost for dramatic music simply because three rascals have the misfortune of being idiots as well. Véron, for example, whom Meyerbeer had to compel by law to produce *Robert le Diable* and thus to make his fortune in spite of himself, has since then staged only platitudes of which *La Juive* is the culmination . . . Patience is in order. Everything will come in its time." Ideas for scores kept bubbling up, although Berlioz' conception of dramatic music, which required the musical personnel of the Opera, actually went beyond stage work. As he had written to Ferrand when *Benvenuto* first came into being, he was dreaming of other and greater things than operas: "Music has wings that the walls of a theatre will not allow to unfold." Dramatic music was a generic term under which opera was but a subclass, so in January 1835 he writes again: "If I had time, I would be making progress on the work I am mulling over . . ."—a symphony —"on a new and enlarged plan."

Outwardly Berlioz seemed to prosper. In April, Liszt played a *Fantasia on two themes by Berlioz* ("The Fisherman" and "Brigand's Song" from the melologue, and added to the pianistic program "The Pilgrims' March" from *Harold in Italy*. The press hailed the "Paganini of the piano" and Berlioz writing very discreetly of his own share in the concert, was happy to declare that "our views on music, [Liszt's] and mine, are exactly the same . . ." that is to say in accord "with the exigencies of the times."

The next month, Berlioz gave another concert, consisting of *The Return to Life* entire, no doubt as a reply to the New Year parody. Though the box-office receipts were fair and the royal family were present, Berlioz regretted the "detestable performance": for economy's sake, he had scheduled only one rehearsal. Moreover, on that bright day of May the fountains of Versailles were also playing, which somewhat reduced attendance at the concert. Shortly thereafter, on May 28, 1835, the Gymnase Musical opened its doors and offered Berlioz another chance to draw the crowd. Unfortunately its musical resources were feeble, and when the Berlioz program took place on June 4 (the *King Lear* overture, *Harold in Italy,* and songs by Gluck and Berlioz) the playing and acoustics were a disgrace. To indemnify Berlioz the management weeded out the poorest performers and a second concert was announced. But the fact that it was to take place at night put it under the jurisdiction of the prefect of police.[5] This official, acting from political prudence and also to safeguard the monopoly of the Opéra-Comique, forbade singing. So the program was whittled down to overtures and solos on violin and piano—no vocal numbers "which the public must have." Berlioz wondered how a motet by Palestrina would "compete" with the usual ariettas of the Opéra-Comique. But a rule was a rule, especially when politics and money interests backed it against a mere artist.

The summer did not see the writing of the projected third symphony. There was little time and less tranquillity. The plan nevertheless haunted Berlioz. First conceived in Italy, this Heroic and Funeral Symphony in seven movements would celebrate the great men of France. Popular in character, like the finale of Beethoven's Ninth, it would be scored for a large body of players and singers, like the festivals of the revolution. The idea did not die; its elements found a place in several later works, notably the *Te Deum, Les Troyens,* and especially the *Funeral and Triumphal* symphony of 1840.

Meantime, with an obsessed spirit bent on not giving up its obsession, Berlioz finished the setting of Béranger's mediocre Ode on the Death of Napoleon, "The Fifth of May." Berlioz' score is not a great work, though genius and craft are visible on every page. The something lacking might be called by a metaphor the "heat of fusion of art," and its absence suggests that in classifying the works of any artist we should perhaps distinguish three kinds—the successes, the failures and the *characteristic* failures. That is, we find in Berlioz: good Berlioz, bad Berlioz, and bad *music;* just as there is good Beethoven, bad Beethoven and bad music which happens to have been written by Beethoven. Only from the first two categories can one learn anything about the significant processes that fail or succeed in an artist's mind. From the evidence of *Le Cinq Mai,* Berlioz' technique at thirty-two had reached the fullness of a "second manner," but the inner fire was temporarily banked, smothered under too much irrelevant work. Those who have been hacks as well as conscious craftsmen will here salute a brother in sorrow.

Berlioz' next preoccupation had to do with the selection of a new director at the Opera. After five years of prevailing success Véron judged that his luck could not last and withdrew before it was too late. The Bertin brothers, the politicians, and Berlioz' friends now engaged in the usual intrigues and parleys. Véron wanted his friend Loève-Veimars, to succeed him. His scheme failed, and the unedifying architect Duponchel, who was already in league with Meyerbeer and who had dabbled in several trades, was chosen as a compromise candidate.[6] He would be committed to the *Débats* party, which meant his accepting not only the works of Berlioz, but also those of Mlle. Louise Bertin (the crippled sister of Edouard) whose moderately successful *Faust* gave color to her pretensions as a composer. For his disappointed hopes and wounded feelings, Loève-Veimars received 100,000 francs, besides the Legion of Honor, a baronetcy, and a mission to Russia: in Vigny's classification he should rank as the Man of Letters par excellence.

All was settled when, on the anniversary of the July Days, as the King was reviewing troops, a barrage laid down by one Fieschi felled forty persons. Louis-Philippe miraculously escaped, but Duponchel's appointment was delayed a month. This enabled him to shift alliances and once in office he tried to repudiate his campaign pledges. Further battle led to an agreement that Mlle. Bertin's *Esmeralda* (based on Victor Hugo's own adaptation of *Notre Dame*) would be accepted and that Berlioz' *Benvenuto* would be "submitted to a committee." Matters stood thus by the fall of 1835. To keep public interest in him alive, Berlioz gave a concert on November 22, in which he presented "The Fifth of May" together with a song by Meyerbeer—the great power behind the scenes. At a second concert on December 13, Berlioz conducted, not indeed for the first time, but for the first time by deliberate preference: he was adding a weapon to his armory of defenses.

Throughout this period Berlioz could hardly feel that his family, immediate or remote, was giving him much comfort. Since their son's birth, Harriet had insensibly grown restless, vaguely resentful, unhappy at the ending of her career. It was slight comfort, or none at all, to read in the papers that Hector's former fiancée, Camille Moke, had just been repudiated by her husband Pleyel, on grounds of repeated adultery and disorderly conduct. As for Berlioz' relations with La Côte, carried on mainly through Adèle, one senses that the father and mother were again waiting for their son to make a success that they could understand—after the Rome Prize, an opera at the Opera. They had recognized their daughter-in-law and sent gifts for the baby, but they had not supplied what every young couple needs—money. When Adèle, with kind intent, tried to explain the local "prejudices that time would efface" Hector had had to keep the letter from his wife to forestall one of her long bouts of weeping. The elder sister Nanci and her husband were still holding aloof, Berlioz ironically sending his compliments through Adèle to "Their Royal Highnesses." At the same time he was worried about his father's health, concerning which he was not given enough news. His own constitution was just then suffering from the strain he put upon it. Nervous tension brought on sore throats and headaches. He felt he ought to sleep long restorative hours, as in youth when he had passed a crisis or a concert; now the very need made for insomnia.

The beginning of 1836 brought reconciliation with Nanci, one word from her being enough to elicit from Hector a quick and warm response. But the New Year also brought the news that the Ministry had canceled Duponchel's private agreement, and that Berlioz' opera was as uncommissioned as on the first day of negotiations. The composer determined to finish it nevertheless. He was in love with the subject and his inner mind worked at it regardless of his will. Besides, the chatter of the press over the whole affair had led someone to announce another "Benvenuto" for one of the lesser theaters. To keep his priority Berlioz made a counter-announcement that he was "just completing the score." This exaggeration was soon dangerously tested by the merger of *Le Rénovateur* with another periodical. This cut into Berlioz' income, and all other posts being occupied, his situation was extremely difficult. If he tried to make up his loss by free-lance writing, what would happen to the score of *Benvenuto?* In this quandary Berlioz applied to his friend Legouvé who readily advanced two thousand francs.[7]

Meantime Berlioz had a debt of another kind to pay. Mlle. Bertin's *Esmeralda* needed revising and it was as natural that she should apply to him as that he should show his gratitude to her family by giving help. Being half-paralyzed from birth, she also needed a trusted deputy to run the errands incidental to rehearsing an opera in manuscript. Berlioz was this deputy and three quarters of each day for more than a month went into *La Esmeralda*—as many hours taken away from *Benvenuto.* Nevertheless, by sheer application, the writing of his own score was progressing: "I have done about half. It's a long job to write out, but I must say that compared with the problems of symphonic composition it's relatively easy."

The success of *La Esmeralda* would have been of considerable indirect advantage to Berlioz: it could not seriously compete with his work, it would have set a perceptible value on his help—for this fact was generally known—and it would have further heightened the prestige of the Bertin family or at least neutralized the opposition. As things fell out, the opera reached the stage on November 14 and was hissed off it without reprieve. During the rehearsals Berlioz had written to his sister: "There are charming choruses which rumor does me the honor of attributing to me, though I have had no hand in them. Unfortunately, the single roles are by no means so good, not by a long shot, and the actors make awful faces."

At the first performance, political feeling burst in a rhythmic chant of "Down with the Bertins, down with the *Débats!*" The curtain had to be lowered to enable the actors to regain composure. When Quasimodo's aria on the bells of Notre Dame rang out and won applause, Alexandre Dumas, who disliked the Bertins, shouted in his stevedore's voice: "That's Berlioz . . . that's Berlioz!" It was not by Berlioz: "If I had anything to do with its success," he wrote to Adèle, "it's in a trifling way. The air is really by Mlle. Bertin, but (between ourselves) it ended lamely. . . . My help was limited to suggesting a peroration more worthy of the exordium. That's all. . . . As for my own opera, here is how it stands. I have finished it. I have only to write out the denouement and orchestrate the score. According to my arrangement with Duponchel, I am fourth on the list . . . They are now putting on Niedermeyer's *Stradella* . . . Then I should go on next, if nothing else is ready; but Halévy . . . is straining every nerve and writing his new score at a gallop so as not to lose his turn . . . Anyhow, I'm ready to go into rehearsal, and I'd have been ready with all the music long before if, like my hero Cellini, I had had *the metal* with which to cast my statue." The allusion was to the last scene of the opera, based on fact, in which Benvenuto runs short of metal in the casting of his masterpiece, the bronze Perseus.

Just lately, "metal" had not been wanting. Besides Legouvé's loan of two thousand francs, Berlioz had received increased honorariums from the Bertins—a tactful acknowledgment of his services to Mlle. Louise—and he had had the pleasant surprise of a gift from his father. He was deeply moved: "I am afraid my excellent father inconvenienced himself to send me this sum, which I was far from expecting, and this thought bothers me more than I can say. Kiss him and Mamma for me."

Moreover, in a cabinet reorganization of September 1836, a new Minister of Fine Arts had taken office whose influence was altogether favorable to Berlioz. Devotees of music should keep a place in their memory for the Comte de Gasparin, who besides becoming Minister became the efficient cause of Berlioz' great *Requiem*. The political basis of this double merit is again quite clear: M. de Gasparin had been prefect in Berlioz' county and doubtless knew the excellent standing of the composer's family. In addition, Gasparin's son acted as his private secretary and had a close friend in common with Berlioz. Politically allied with the *Débats* and personally interested in music, the count was an ideal patron for one in Berlioz' position. His utility was shortly to be seen.

Berlioz' reputation was in fact just on the point of passing from a fighting opinion to an accepted truth.[8] Throughout 1836 he received requests from abroad for copies of his scores —Vienna, Milan, and New Orleans wanted to play him; Schumann had him performed in Leipzig. Local societies at Douai and Dijon gave him a try—all, of course, without royalties. The idea of a trip to the United States even crossed Berlioz' mind, for the artistic exodus in search of American dollars had begun, and the new world seemed to offer opportunities for Harriet's comeback. "All the English actors fly to America. Politics, Puritanism, and the senility of our civilization have killed the drama." London, too, had tried Berlioz, but the performers had been unable to get through a rehearsal of the *Francs-Juges.* That same overture had been "arranged" for piano in Germany and published as wholly his own work, but it was so "monstrously mutilated" that Berlioz wrote a protest and decided never to let copies out of his hands nor to sanction any performances until he had gone to Germany and established his tradition in person.

This resolve shows to what extent music was still considered in 1836 a commodity to be sliced and sold at will. Copyright did not protect the author, only the publisher, and musical customs outside a few centers were extremely primitive. On a similar occasion, he summed up the state of things: "Music . . . is now flooding in everywhere; but it is like the fury of a child, who lunges at everything that shines, without any idea of its use." In six or seven years, he thought, there might be a public in France for serious instrumental music. This was too sanguine. Had there been such a public, Berlioz would certainly have been its singlehanded creator, for even when his friends showed their enthusiasm for his works, they always thought of him as a champion who would be crowned by acceptance at the Opera. The post-Beethovenian symphony did not exist. "It is at the theatre," exclaimed d'Ortigue, "that we must give Berlioz a rendez-vous." Liszt publicly railed at the Opera directors for excluding Berlioz. And the circumspect Guéroult in *Le Temps* in reproaching officialdom made the same assumption: "No one gives promise of a more brilliant future than Berlioz. It would be at once cruel and ridiculous to affect any further hesitation about him."

The seal of celebrity was put on him by Dantan the younger —the Max Beerbohm of the period—whose series of caricatured busts formed a representative hall of fame: Paganini, Balzac, Victor Hugo, Alexandre Dumas, Adolphe Adam, and Berlioz among the moderns were adjoined to Horace Vernet and others of the older generation. Reproduced in lithograph, Berlioz with his mop of hair was described as a "musical O'Connell," [9] a pioneer who would reform and galvanize French opera. But Duponchel, with his haughty manners and his monocle, was still dissembling about *Benvenuto Cellini;* for operas are a heavy investment, and like all managerial powers he could form no judgment of his own. "He fancies he likes my music, though he knows as much about it as did M. Véron." Still, in October 1836, he had given Berlioz a written understanding.

Since August, Berlioz had been editing the *Gazette Musicale* as temporary substitute. Two concerts, one with Urhan, the other with Liszt, both directed by Berlioz, closed a busy year. Besides his Fantasia on themes by Berlioz, Liszt played his own transcription of the Waltz and the March from the *Symphonie Fantastique:* the effect was extraordinary, pyrotechnic. No one could approach such dexterity and force, and the lady who later complained that it was a shame to put such a fine-looking man at a keyboard would have been answered. As for Berlioz' conducting, it gave him increasing satisfaction: "Apropos of artistic success, I have never had one to equal it, by reason of the superior performance due to my conducting the orchestra." The net return of the two concerts was sixteen hundred francs.

During December also, Harriet Smithson appeared on the boards for the last time. She gave her Ophelia scene, in the midst of a benefit for the great comedian Frédérick Lemaitre, and the conjunction of genres was disastrous. No one wanted to see the mad scene sandwiched in between farcical skits. Berlioz' friend and colleague Janin counseled her, for Shakespeare's sake, not to appear in anything but a full-length play enabling her to create a distinct atmosphere.

The turn of the New Year was marked by three important events: Niedermeyer's opera failed, *Benvenuto Cellini* was officially announced, and the new Minister of Fine Arts definitely commissioned from Berlioz a Requiem Mass. The intention was to celebrate on its seventh anniversary the death of the heroes of July 28, 1830. This project was of course hedged in by bureaucratic rules: the commission must go to a prize winner of the Institute who had not yet written for the official theaters. Could Berlioz, with his *Benvenuto Cellini* accepted but not staged, be considered eligible? Such a plum could not be handed to anyone without a struggle, several struggles, part of the great struggle for power. The Minister must wrangle for an appropriation, underlings must assert their authority, rival composers must fight for their prestige. Cherubini held office and had to be reckoned with. He disliked Berlioz intensely, and more important, he had a new *Requiem* of his own just asking to be played. Delaying tactics would be to everyone's interest except Berlioz', for Ministries fall, and in statecraft delay is always the simplest thing to achieve. The comings and goings of all the actors in this veritable Florentine history form an inextricable melee, in which certitude as to the order of events is illusory. What seems clear is that by the end of March 1837, Berlioz had in his pocket the signed ministerial decree. The sum allotted was fourteen thousand francs and the time a little over three months.

In accepting these terms Berlioz was taking a great risk—his position was exactly that of Michelangelo when forced by his enemies to undertake the Sistine Ceiling—but his was a philosophy of risk, and unlike Michelangelo, Berlioz had in fact long been preparing for precisely this chance. From his Mass of 1825 he had saved and worked over the *Resurrexit;* in Italy, under the impact of Saint Peter's, he had gathered ideas for a Judgment Day oratorio; more recently, the ceremonies for the victims of Fieschi's attempt on the King's life had reawakened these same thoughts and had inwardly advanced the project of a Funeral Symphony. For the great crowd scene of the *Cellini* opera he had adapted another section from his early mass. Although all but one of these ideas were pre-empted and therefore useless for the *Requiem,* they had a spiritual kinship which was a stimulant. He felt in the mood for "architectural" constructions and mass effects.

So much so that when the signed commission came Berlioz felt no qualms. The sublimity of the subject intoxicated him. "At first my brains boiled over," he writes to Adèle, "I was dizzy. Today the eruption has been regulated. The lava has made its bed and God willing everything will go well." It went so well that he had to devise a musical shorthand for fear of losing the thronging ideas. Once before, in composing the *Harold* symphony, he had had to capture fleeting inspiration in a kind of shorthand still visible in the manuscript, to be expanded at leisure. For the *Requiem* all this had to be done at breakneck speed, since in the twelve weeks at his disposal time must also be found for reviewing concerts and writing an encyclopedia article he had contracted to do. This is the definition of music which now heads *A Travers Chants,* and although the statement was not a new one with him, its reassertion at a time when his oldest musical project—the Mass of 1825—was being similarly reworked is a symbol of his consistency: "Music is at once a science and a sentiment . . . It must not solely satisfy the ear by correct and artistic combinations of sounds, but must also speak to the heart and the imagination . . . Many persons are not made for music and consequently music is not made for them . . . the musical sense can be trained and exercised, but the motions of the spirit, which are very active in certain people are but slight in others. . . . As for the perceptions that the writer himself owes to the hearing of music, nothing can convey their exact character to one who has never experienced them."

This sense of being apart yet in the melee was not Berlioz' portion alone. An incident with a tragic sequel occurred just then which discloses as in a fictional plot the emotional temperature of musical Paris in the spring of 1837. A new tenor named Gilbert Duprez made his debut in grand opera on April 17. Berlioz knew him since the days of Choron's concerts of sacred music; they met later in Rome; and now the critic praised the newcomer, with only a few reservations: Duprez had a magnificent voice but was a poor actor. He gesticulated too much and overused the *notes sombrées* (veiled tones) for which he had a knack. But the Paris public went wild and with no reservations worshiped a new idol.

The immediate result was that Adolphe Nourrit, after fifteen years of superior craftsmanship, felt cast out overnight. Being short and stout, he was not a theatrically commanding figure, but he was a greater and finer artist, both as singer and composer. It was he who in his very first role had moved the young Berlioz at *his* first hearing of Gluck; it was he who had roused the Belgians to revolt with his Masaniello in 1830; it was he who had fashioned the librettos of *La Sylphide* and other ballets danced by the airy Romantic dancers, Taglioni and Fanny Elssler. It may even be conjectured that it was Nourrit's uncommon gifts that inspired Berlioz when he wrote the role of the actor-singer in his melologue. Nourrit was a musical institution, suddenly overthrown by Duprez' powerful organ.

Very soon after the latter's debut, being momentarily voiceless, Nourrit had what we should now call a nervous breakdown. It was not artistic egotism but artistic sensibility that was wounded. He felt not only dethroned but outraged. Berlioz could readily sympathize, and with his friend the Irishman George Osborne they walked Nourrit up and down the boulevards until a late hour, reassuring him and dispelling a hundred rash resolutions.

Nourrit gave up his first violent projects, but felt he could not stay in Paris nor continue in opera. He applied to Berlioz' other friend, the dramatic poet Legouvé, for a "monodrama" precisely of the type that Berlioz had previously produced.

When Legouvé had cast in this form the woes of the Italian liberal Silvio Pellico, Lesueur's last pupil, Ambroise Thomas, set the text, and with this work Nourrit toured Italy successfully for two years. But his self-confidence was irreparably shattered, and after an admirable concert at Naples in 1839, he ended the struggle by leaping out of a window, aged thirty-seven.

By the end of May 1837, portions of Berlioz' *Requiem* were in the copyist's hands, but the Ministry, which had not scrupled to delay for its own red tape, was now worried about rehearsals and begging for speed. By dint of exertion, Berlioz finished the last page on June 29. This left him less than a month in which to have the parts completed and proofread, and to rehearse a chorus and orchestra of four hundred.

The voices were going smoothly when without warning and indeed without notifying Berlioz, the "bureaus" countermanded the entire ceremony. "Ten thousand plagues on their heads!" he wrote to his intimates. "The devil must be in it . . . The scoundrels choose to stop me *now*. It's outrageous!"

Still, as he himself remarked, the work was *there*. "The *Requiem* exists and I swear to you, Father, that it is a piece which will count; sooner or later I'll get it performed." And to his friend, the Librarian of the Conservatoire, Bottée de Toulmon: "I defy them to wear me down." The musical injury was bad enough; there was, besides, the question of who would pay, not the piper merely, but the copyist, singers, and so on—some five thousand francs Berlioz had already spent, exclusive of his fee. The government not being a person, its morality is often dubious and its memory frail. "M. de Montalivet, Minister of the Interior, asked me how I could be indemnified for this contretemps, which he says has been caused by politics alone; I replied that no indemnity was possible except the performance of the work."

The affair was not calculated to make Berlioz take a more lenient view of politics; rather it reminded him of the very different treatment which Lesueur spoke of receiving from a responsible "tryant." Berlioz drew hasty inferences. "Oh these representative governments—and cheap ones at that—what a stupid farce! . . . Under the Empire a minister would not have dared act in this manner . . . Napoleon would have attended to him; for I say again, the thing is a swindle. . . ." The minister hinted that Berlioz would at the next opportunity be given the Legion of Honor—that emergency coinage for settling bad debts. He might even be appointed Inspector General of Music for primary schools—an anticipation of Matthew Arnold. In response to all this Berlioz deliberately acted the monomaniac. He had one idea in mind—performance—and he dinned it into the head of every bureaucrat he could reach in the offices of three ministries—Fine Arts, Interior, and War.

It was war, actual war, that finally brought him victory after three months of relentless hounding. On October 23, 1837 the news of the taking of Constantine, in Algeria, was relayed by (visual) telegraph from the south of France, and with it the intelligence that General Damrémont, commanding, had been killed in the assault. The government would specially honor his memory, since the feat of arms lent needful prestige to the regime.

At once the unpolitical but not impolitic Berlioz asked Dumas to put in a word in his favor with the Duke of Orleans, to whom Dumas was secretary. The ceremony was soon set for December; a few more letters were exchanged, Berlioz had a cordial interview with General Bernard, the Minister of War, and he finally received the second commission for his one *Requiem*. The terms again provided 14,000 francs for all expenses, plus a bonus of 1500. Berlioz was moreover accorded a sort of public accolade by the Comte de Montalivet who spoke at the Conservatoire graduation on November 19: "Music is the handmaiden of all national ceremonies. Without it there can be neither pomp nor grandeur. . . . It is music we look to for uttering the grief of France on the day when the church of the Invalides . . . will receive the body of an illustrious general. On that occasion the students of the Conservatoire will perform music composed by a former student of the Conservatoire."

On December 4, the day of the dress rehearsal, all of artistic Paris was present at the Invalides. The impression was overwhelming. Vigny wrote in his Journal: "The music was beautiful and strange, wild, convulsed, and dolorous. . . ." [10] In composing his *Requiem* or Grand Mass for the Dead, Berlioz had had other things to take into account than his need to release the music within him. He faced a very definite practical problem. The Chapel of Saint Louis at the Invalides is a vast domed building which on the day of the funeral would be filled by many hundreds of people. The windows were to be blocked and the walls draped in black. On December 5 at noon the service took place before the royal family, the diplomatic corps, and all the fashion, power, and frivolity of Paris. Around the coffin flickered six hundred candles and incense boats. Four thousand other pinpoints of light dotted the gloomy shell. Major Lehoux headed the cortege with twenty-four muffled drums beating in the name of the twelve Paris legions, and Séjean played the organ for the service. When all this had been seen and felt and heard came the *Requiem* music, not consecutively but with interruptions for intonings and responses.

Now Berlioz had heard Mozart's *Requiem* at the Madeleine and one of Cherubini's at the Invalides. Comparing their effect in those large churches with that in the acoustic hall of the Conservatoire, he could see that the volume of sound must be brought into scale with the place, and that sharp contrasts must be established between successive numbers to sustain attention during the rites. For his purposes Berlioz found he needed 190 instruments and 210 voices, with additional timpani and brass choirs to be used in the *Tuba mirum*. This enumeration is striking, but it is not the chief point of interest in Berlioz' *Requiem*. Even the full deployment of these forces in the Vision—or rather audition—of Judgment is not characteristic of the work as a whole. In dealing with Berlioz it is always a mistake to remain under the spell of the immediately obvious facts and to suppose his mind moving on a single plane or aiming at a single effect. True, he wished to use again in perfected form his *Resurrexit* of 1825 with its admirable fanfare and timpani chords. But he also paid heed to the liturgy, the religious habits of his compatriots, and the special occasion. Through his teachers, Lesueur and Reicha, Berlioz was in touch with the revolutionary tradition of music for mass gatherings. He knew in detail how under the Empire Marshal Lannes had been buried, and as far back as 1825 he had asked the use of the Pantheon for his music. Thus one national tradition made him take for granted the union of religion with daily life; another, more recent, used music to suit the needs of a people assembled. The original assembly, it will be recalled, was to celebrate the revolution of 1830, the prevailing mood being sad, solemn, and martial. Hence this *Requiem* must combine massiveness, dramatic intensity, and religious awe; it must be vivid and contemporary as well as lead the spirit to serenity—a work of Gothic art.

It had passed the test of judgment by artists at the dress

rehearsal; now it must face the public. Habeneck, who had been forced on Berlioz by the opposition, conducted his four hundred musicians grouped left and right in the transept. During the first number, *Requiem and Kyrie,* things went well in spite of the usual mistakes by nervous performers. Habeneck thereupon relaxed so fully that he nearly spoiled the effect of the fanfare in the ensuing *Tuba mirum* by failing to cue the small brass ensembles at the four corners of the orchestra. According to his habit, after setting the tempo, he laid down his baton preparatory to taking a pinch of snuff—as Berlioz tells in his *Memoirs*—and the composer himself had to give the signal.[11] The rest proceeded without a hitch.

Whether the audience was moved or bored or bewildered by Berlioz' music it is impossible to say, since there could be no applause, but the critics were with few exceptions favorable. Nothing like the *Requiem* had ever been heard by human ears, and the impression of sustained power could not be gainsaid. It suggested to Heine the famous hyperbole to the effect that as a maker of music Berlioz was like "an antediluvian bird, a colossal nightingale or a lark the size of an eagle." [12] General Bernard sent Berlioz a well-turned note of congratulation which the papers reprinted, and Schlesinger, scenting a first paying success for one of his authors, opened a public subscription for the immediate engraving of the score. Unhappily, Berlioz' devoted sponsor, Lesueur, was not there to rejoice: he had died on October 6.

For Berlioz at thirty-four, it had taken only seven years from the Rome Prize to the nation's highest artistic trust—but what an obstacle race it had been!

CHAPTER 10

THE HERO AS ARTIST

Come, cheer me up with an account of the Roman Carnival!
—SCOTT, on the news of his financial disaster

The *Requiem* had been an artistic success. No one in Paris who was capable of exercising judgment could doubt that this new music was something to reckon with. The leaders of the Romantic generation never forgot it, and thirty-five years later, after Berlioz' death, Liszt was still pondering the powerful, inscrutable score.[1] No less important was the composer's own opinion of the work, for like the playwright, the musician can never be entirely certain that he has hit his mark. And Berlioz, who had canceled an edition of his Opus 1, and destroyed a good many other works, was hard to please. For the *Requiem* he always felt a special regard, in spite of the fact that he had never submitted it to painstaking revision. It enshrined some of his earliest musical inspirations and its subject had enabled him to express at once his humility and his pride. Two years before his death he declared that if all his works were to be ordered burned, he would ask a reprieve for the *Requiem*.

But in February, 1838, he was thinking of the present, not of the past or future, and the present signified another large work, virtually finished. *Benvenuto Cellini* "existed" also, its orchestration all but complete. Yet unlike the *Requiem* it would have to be produced soon if the publicity it had already received were not to spoil its chances by becoming an old story. Now the Opera in March 1838 had on the boards a reasonably good commercial success, also on an Italian theme—Halévy's *Guido and Ginevra, or the Florentine Plague.* Nevertheless the agreement with Berlioz and the Bertins was fulfilled and *Benvenuto* went into rehearsal, though not in a way to make the composer's life easier. All Berlioz knew of "the house" was from outside—the political intrigues and chicanery of its managers and its relations with press and public. He now entered its arcana and discovered how it functions as a curb market of artistic personalities: the lion will sooner lie down with the lamb than the prima donna with the bass—though exceptions have been known; each singer believes that the other's bark is far worse than his bite, for they all know how to bite; and while every department acts as if the rest were a superfluous nuisance, all agree that the most needless and nettlesome is the author. Throughout the personnel, actor's vanity perpetuates a hundred treasured jealousies and teamwork is not a habit but a concession; as in politics, self-seeking cannot be distinguished from devotion to the cause; while beneath everything the hum of petty gossip plays a discordant counterpoint to the genuinely hard work done under pressure and fraught with risk.

Nor is the institution self-contained. The ballet draws into the wings a host of interfering gentry from the world of finance, politics, and letters; and in a state-run opera the bureaucracy, the trades, and the blackmailing press are grafted on to the main trunk and live on it like parasites. How happy must a nation be which has no official theaters! Yes, some maddening plant grows in the very heart of opera, for to this day history records no instance of an operatic house of peace and harmony. A century ago in France, Berlioz could only keep his courage bright: "Intrigues have been weaving around me since the first two rehearsals, so that my head swims. But one must go on, keep an eye on everything and be afraid of nothing."

What made his position worse was that he was at the same time embarked on a complex enterprise designed to make him Director of the Italian Theater. The building itself had recently been destroyed by fire, the manager had been killed while trying to escape the flames, and Berlioz was being put forward for the vacant post. The inducement was purely monetary, for according to the instructions drawn up by the Ministry only Italian works could be performed. He himself would not be allowed to compose for his own theater and he would have no chance to run a choir school such as he wanted to develop in the tradition of Choron's. But the income would mean affluence; it would release time and remove journalistic pressure: he could compose. Perhaps too, if he became one of the potentates of the inner theatrical ring he could enforce and open-door policy in other musical establishments: in short, having favors to dispense, he would have power.

The ups and downs of this project, in which the Bertins and members of the cabinet were concerned, lasted three months. Part of the delay and difficulty was due to the fact that the concessionaires, whoever they might be, would be responsible for rebuilding the gutted theater. At last the bill naming Berlioz Director and enacting the conditions of tenure was brought up with an unfavorable report by the parliamentary committee, and the Chamber turned it down 196 to 32. Before and after this blessing in disguise—for it spared Berlioz endless worries of an alien kind—the press argued the case with its usual knowingness and concluded that Berlioz had been turned down because the Bertins were behind him. They were theoretically "in power" but the opposition was just strong enough to beat them on secondary issues, and as an *avant-garde* artist Berlioz constituted their vulnerable side. He was the buffer state which is the first to be overrun in the war of big powers.

Unfortunately this defeat in the national legislature and the press would probably encourage a cabal against *Benvenuto,* for its success would give too much comfort to its backers. The dilemma for a composer without private means was complete: no possibility of succeeding without pull, no possibility of succeeding with it. Berlioz was too far involved to withdraw, even had he been willing to condemn his family to penury, and he felt within him dramatic and organizing talents that should not be buried. Even when he was fully within his rights, the situation was still one of catch-as-catch can: he had had to make a scene in "the bureaus" in order to obtain full payment for his *Requiem.* Now he was gambling his time, effort, and reputation on the most chancy of political platforms —the stage of the Paris Grand Opera.

In his private life, Berlioz received equally mixed blessings during this first half of 1838. In January he experienced considerable alarm at reports of his mother's ill health, which made him hope to get away for a visit at La Côte. He wrote:

"I long for you tenderly." She died the next month, aged fifty-three. A little earlier, the deaths of a good friend and of a near relative, both young, had already cast gloom over Berlioz' ceaseless activity. All his unhappy beginnings as a musician came back to him at the thought of his mother. More cheerful news came from Liszt, successful at Milan and joyfully sojourning on the Italian lakes with Marie d'Agoult. Reliving in his mind the pleasures of his own *Wanderjahr,* Berlioz sought to express his affection and sympathy with his fortunate friends by composing some trifle for Liszt's beloved. But nothing came to his pen. He had verses on hand that Brizeux had written at his request, and he sketched portions of a setting for the *Erigone* of Ballanche, but neither composition seemed to take shape. "If I can find the time to work . . ."

At least the fact of Adéle's engagement to Marc Suat, a solicitor from Vienne, near La Côte, was wholly good. Berlioz knew him well and esteemed him highly: "Your letter," Berlioz writes to his future brother-in-law, "made me very happy, and if I haven't answered sooner it's because my present work makes me lose both sleep and sense of reality. I snatch a moment to tell you how enchanted I am to hear of the lively affection you bear my sister. She is an excellent child, who will make you most happy, I know. As for you, I know the goodness of your disposition and my sister's future strikes me as secure—I may have misread your notes but are you thinking of coming with Adèle to Paris . . . can you? will you? It would be such happiness for me. . . ."

His chief worry was now Doctor Berlioz' solitude and ill health. Hector wrote to his father: "Adèle tells me of testamentary dispositions which our dear mother made in her special favor, and she seems to fear the effect of this on the mind of her brothers and sister. And now it is you who tell me of your own intentions . . . which suggest the deep depression with which you face the future. . . . We'll talk later, much later, of all these money matters that you propose to me in such cold blood. In any case, as regards me, whatever you do will always be right. . . . Farewell, dear Father, don't worry about my future and think more about yourself. The best proof you can give of your affection for your children is to take care of your health and peace of mind . . ."

In his own home, Harriet and the child continued to thrive (Louis, in his fourth year, is growing fast but cannot yet read) but the arduous repayment of debts kept the exchequer drained. At last the combination of business, intrigues, rehearsals, and journalism wore Berlioz down. He took to his bed with his ordinary symptoms—sore throat, fever, and headaches—getting up only to supervise the Opera rehearsals. He was later to describe this ordeal with humor, and sympathy for a fellow composer: "I could imagine the cruel slowness of these 'studies' in which everyone wastes time on trifles . . . , the witticisms of the tenor and prima donna, at which the unhappy author thinks he is obliged to laugh heartily. . . . I could hear the voice of the Director treating him with condescension mixed with blame in order to remind him of the great honor being done to his work by such sustained attention. . . . Then someone would come in to announce that the mezzo-soprano was going on vacation and the bass on sick-leave, whereupon it was proposed to replace the singer by an apprentice and give the leading part to a chorister. And so the composer felt himself being assassinated, yet took great care not to cry out."

By the end of June, the voice parts had been pretty well learned, except that of Cellini—assigned to his old acquaintance Duprez who was vacationing. There remained the orchestra, some of whom were inclined to make trouble. The old-timers who took their cue from Habeneck declared they had never seen such difficult music. Yet at the same moment Habeneck himself was conducting five hundred musicians at Lille in the *Lacrymosa* of Berlioz' *Requiem,* and receiving great applause for it. In Paris, in the pit where *Benvenuto* was struggling to come to life, there were "millions of wrong notes, wrong tempi, and especially wrong rhythms. . . . This causes me so much irritation, so much torture of the nerves" (Berlioz confided to Legouvé) "that it is the sole cause of my present indisposition. I am not yet over it. But patience! We'll be ready for the first night by August 21st or 25th. . . . The overture, by the way, I think you'll be pleased with. I don't want to count my chickens before they're hatched, but if my score is published, you'll give me the pleasure of accepting the dedication, won't you? For after all it's you who gave the *metal* for casting the Perseus and it is to you that poor Benvenuto owes his work of art, such as it is." [2]

Though Duprez was inferior as an actor, he practised his role to Berlioz' moderate satisfaction and by mid-July everything was nearly ready. The censorship, it is true, "took away the Pope" from the cast and forced the substitution of a Cardinal, which somewhat spoiled the conflict of wills between the "bandit-genius" Cellini and Clement VII. The revolt in the orchestra had been more or less tamed, after which there was only "one more barrage, that of the newspapers and of one's intimate foes hidden in the four corners of the house." What Berlioz was thinking of occurred even before the opening. An erstwhile friend, the German ex-priest and music critic, Joseph Mainzer, published a pamphlet elaborately seeking to discredit the composer, his writings, and his opera as yet unknown to the public.

Benvenuto Cellini did not open on August twenty-first, nor on the twenty-fifth. There were unaccountable delays, conflicting announcements and denials, all matched by a steady crossfire of questions in newspapers friendly to Berlioz. The dress rehearsal took place on September 1, before a house of colleagues and critics, who kept distinctly cool. Two days later was the scheduled *première:* postponed again. Duprez had caught cold and none of the roles had been understudied. "Cellini" was given a week to cure his cold. This brought the opening to the tenth of September and everyone knew that on the fifteenth Mme. Dorus-Gras, the leading lady, was quitting the Opera. By accident or design, a *short* run had been assured.

The first public audience that heard the already maltreated score was most whimsical: it applauded the overture with great vigor, expressed its disapproval of the rather cheap scenery, then picked and chose, seemingly at random, from the rest of the offering. Mme. Dorus-Gras's roulades went well, but certain words of the libretto afforded great opportunities for ridicule. In an air of Cellini's it was said that "in early morn *the roosters crowed.*" Laughter swept the stalls. What Parisian could lend credence to such crude Romanticist realism? The parterre hissed and the gallery's barnyard noises managed to disconcert the actors. No such fun had been had in the City of Light since the first English actors had put on Shakespeare. The cabal deliberately killed the opera. The music was hardly attended to.[3] Duprez-Cellini kept on singing as if he were in on the joke, though the two women in the roles of Teresa and Ascanio did their utmost and were warmly applauded by Berlioz' admirers.

The faithful cohort called for him at the end, but his name was drowned in the tumult. He barely escaped the humiliation inflicted on Henry James after *Guy Domville,* of coming forward to be jeered at. The press behaved in the usual way, strong on politics and on the faults of the libretto, weak or irrelevant about everything else.

The very next day Berlioz set to work altering words and making cuts. On the twelfth a second performance half filled the house. There was no more laughter, but not enough applause. On the fourteenth a fuller house witnessed a performance which, despite Duprez' cynical carelessness, aroused the public to genuine enthusiasm. But the box office is inexorable: three thousand francs amounted only to one third of what Meyerbeer could "do."

At this point the press temporarily abandoned jokes and recrimination and suggested that an injustice was perhaps being committed. They urged Berlioz not to be discouraged, acknowledged the power of his music, the abundance of his ideas, and concluded that "such an opera is entitled to ten first performances." One critic roundly asserted that Berlioz "opens up to us a new continent." Another, putting his finger on the difference between Berlioz and Meyerbeer, explained the conflict of tastes: "However useful and even glorious M. Meyerbeer's works may be, they are only transitional and . . . eclectic, which is a very different matter from creative . . . At certain times eclecticism is serviceable, for it sums up and prepares us for what is to come, but in order to last, a work of art must carry reality within its flanks. It must be a creation. *Benvenuto* is such a work. *Benvenuto* is a masterpiece."

A private letter from a contemporary to Desmarest, the virtuoso violoncellist, shows how a witness who was free from party allegiance viewed the facts, and to what extent Berlioz could hope for understanding from the thoughtful minority:

I thank heaven that an unforeseen obstacle put off the opening of *Benvenuto.* Its inexplicable failure would have caused me too much pain to look on directly, and I would rather take it in from a distance than be close to all the dirty business you tell me about. Whether as is said, poor Barbier's poem is no good, I hardly know; I paid no attention. But after all, what difference does the canvas make when a masterpiece has been embroidered on it? One thing especially is beyond me and that is the reception given to the finale of the first act. I can hardly believe it. That the public should have failed to grasp at once all that is subtle, delicate, witty, and touching in this opera, I can perhaps understand. But this sublime finale, this magnificent conception which struck me like the fusion of a hundred thousand voices, distinct and single at first, then mingling and blending in a magnificent harmony, is fit to move the most vulgar clods, the most ungifted individuals. I am no artist . . . but at the dress rehearsal, while listening to that finale I was sweating with excitement, I was shaking in my seat with wonder and enthusiasm. No one will persuade me that something which could move me so, ignorant as I am, is insignificant or dull music. Neither the public's opinions nor the hissing of a whole theatre will convince me that I was wrong.

But something which surprises even more, perhaps, and infuriates me, is the behavior of Duprez. . . . Duprez has forgotten that scarcely a year ago he too was making his debut, nervously trembling before the public; he has forgotten that he would then have begged on his knees for the handsome support that Berlioz so generously accorded him. He forgot it, God help him!

The protracted dispute over the merits of the opera led to the challenging of a stubborn critic by an enthusiastic Vicomte. The duel did not take place, but it gave Berlioz an opportunity to defend Mme. Dorus-Gras, who had been accused of sabotaging her role. In an open letter defending the cast, he said: "She gave me her fullest support with a fervor I should be sorry to see misrepresented." At the same time he stood by his librettists. The few words that had offended delicate tastes he felt were a trifle compared to the genuine dramatic interest of the whole. Later, with more experience of the theater, Berlioz further recast the scenes, making of the two acts an excellent text in three.

Throughout this voluble post-mortem, after the first shock of disappointment, Berlioz seemed the calmest and most confident. He had heard his score and knew what it was worth. Reviewing his score after fifteen years, he confided to his sister, "I like better than ever that dear old *Benvenuto,* which is more vivid, more fresh, more *new*—that is its greatest disadvantage—than any of my works." This is no more than was to be said a hundred years later by the British critic who heard the radio version and studied the score: "Listening, it seemed strange that a work so rich in ideas and of such beauty, should have been for so long completely ignored. . . . This admittedly flawed masterpiece surely deserves as much popularity as, shall we say, *Boris Godunov,* which, incidentally, it resembles in form. One is no less a masterpiece—and no more flawed—than the other." [4]

It is true of Berlioz' great works that the assimilation of

their substance, the recognition of their form, and the enjoyment of their varied kinds of beauty is a bigger task than seems required by other works of the same sort. We may therefore sympathize with the Paris audiences of 1838 insofar as they were sincerely bewildered, and we need not be as surprised as modern critics at the neglect of the score. It is no bagatelle which may be casually taken up, produced, or received. Berlioz knew this even while he hoped that the Opera would continue to din his music into the public's ears by additional performances. He was sure that no amount of journalistic drum-beating was going to increase the size of his public. Art is a serious addiction which newspaper reports and common opinion mistake for a gastronomic exercise. But Berlioz had learned like the hero of his opera that the great artist having lost his religious function in modern secular society, he is at the mercy of the casual passions of men. He can succeed only slowly, by building up, inch by inch, the canons of judgment appropriate to his unique creations.

CHAPTER 11

THE DRAMATIC SYMPHONY

. . . Let music's rich tongue
Unfold the imagined happiness. . . .
SHAKESPEARE, Romeo and Juliet

A "fallen author" at thirty-five, Berlioz could look back on seventeen years of unremitting struggle. Though unlike Benvenuto he had not had to murder anyone, his beloved had been won and his statues fashioned by sheer Cellinesque energy. As he tried to keep his opera afloat through the autumn of 1838, the score of the *Requiem* was published—the first large work for which he had not had to pay. But the engraved notes had value only for other musicians, and only for the most gifted at that. Knowing that for his music to create a public, "it must be heard and heard frequently," Berlioz managed to obtain no fewer than eleven announcements on the official billboard that *Benvenuto* was to be played "any day soon."

By mid-October the words regularly put beneath the mention of other works were: "This is being played while awaiting the fourth performance of *Benvenuto Cellini*." Owing to the departure of Duprez and Mme. Dorus-Gras, two new singers had to be rehearsed and the beginning of November 1838 found Berlioz exhausted. Once again he took to his bed, despite other pressing cares: his brother Prosper had been sent to boarding school in Paris and depended on Hector's attentions.

On the uncommon mind of the boy of eighteen, the capital had the same effect as it had exerted on his elder brother in the now remote 1820's. A new world was opening out to the sensitive, nervous young provincial; his faculties were intensely aroused, and by a singular recurrence these were also musical faculties. Prosper went to the performances of *Benvenuto* and was later able to reproduce from memory at the piano large portions of this complex score. Sainte-Beuve, who made a point of searching biographies for indications of talent in the brothers and sisters of great men, would have found here a Mendelian proof that the Berlioz males of the seventh recorded generation were born musicians.

Prosper was even something more. Matching Hector's literary facility, Prosper began to develop a supernormal mathematical gift which astonished his new teachers. Though the school building was far from Berlioz' house, Hector went there often and tried to lessen the boy's homesickness, to dull the pangs of their mother's recent death, to give and to receive the affection which their upbringing had made either scant or stormy. There is something heartrending about Berlioz in this brief period—sick, fighting, harassed, and showering a fruitless maternal care on Prosper. For the boy died suddenly, three months after his arrival, on January 15, 1839.

The fourth performance of *Cellini* had not yet been given when the New Year began, though everything had been in readiness by November 21. Berlioz was then in bed, feverish yet satisfied, when just a few moments ahead of curtain time, notice of one of the singers' illness postponed the work. The same thing happened on December 2, despite a formal listing, and without any illness to account for the new delay. Three days before, a concert of his works at which Berlioz could not be present was extremely well received. Public indignation at the treatment of the opera added to the warmth of the notices. A second concert was scheduled for December 16, but Berlioz did not know whether he could rouse himself to direct it.

He was played out by a series of events comparable to the most intricate plot of Dumas, and in which he was almost the only one aware of all ramifications: "My sisters," he told his father, "wrote to Prosper asking him for details of the . . . multiple machinations that surround the production of my opera. The poor boy is far from being in a position to answer, and even I can hardly do it by letter. But d'Ortigue has just published a book in which everything is quite clearly set forth. When I say 'everything,' I mean 'almost everything' because there is many a detail which I asked him to suppress.

I haven't yet broken with the administration at the Opera . . . [which] is a world of intrigue as complex as any that goes on at court."

As for the causes of the present imbroglio, Berlioz had sketched them two months before: "To tell you all the goings and comings, cabals, disputes, and insults to which my work has given rise is impossible. It is a miracle to have stayed in the saddle. The fury of certain newspapers against what they call "my system" gives you only a dim notion of their fighting madness. Pamphlets are being written. It is a mêlée in which my defenders utter almost as much nonsense as my detractors. It must all be borne; it will all dissipate in time. The French have a mania for arguing about music without possessing either the rudiments of the art or any feeling for it. It was so in the last century; it is so, and will be so. . . . I count on my music . . . far more than on anything that can be said in its favor. But there have been so many changes to make because of the alteration of the text that I am stupid with fatigue."

D'Ortigue's three hundred and fifty-page book on "The Italian School and the Royal Opera, apropos of M. Berlioz' new work" was a full vindication as well as a very sound critique, for d'Ortigue not only knew music but had "the feeling for it" and he could assess Berlioz' "musical revolution" in every department of the art even when he himself disliked some of the results. D'Ortigue's thesis was simple: Gluck had fought the Italian school of his day in order to reform opera in the direction of dramatic force and extended musical means. In fighting the modern Italian opera, still ridden by convention, routine, and misplaced virtuosity, Berlioz was carrying on Gluck's work. Had Berlioz not been ill, as well as worried by illness in his family near and far, he could have felt that his achievement in *Benvenuto* was very precisely measured by official opposition and admirably consecrated by d'Ortigue's essay.

On December 16, he was able to get up and conduct. The program included selections from Gluck and Berlioz' symphonies 1 and 2. In the hall of the Conservatoire which was filled to capacity, Berlioz had a roof-raising success. In 1838 in Paris, one concludes, there was a phalanx of some twelve hundred people who understood and admired Berlioz' music. They were not numerous enough to uphold an opera, but they justified the existence of an orchestral composer even though his financial reward was inadequate. Certainly the moral support was immeasurably greater than anything our own century has been able to do for comparable innovators, for a Varèse or a Van Dieren. Nor has our collective practical faith in the arts been able to match the individual largesse of a Paganini. For it was at this very concert that the thin cadaverous figure of the virtuoso came to the front of the stage and declaring in his hoarse whisper that "Beethoven had at last a successor" knelt at Berlioz' feet in full view of the circle of friends and handshakers.

Two days later, Berlioz—who had caught more cold on coming out into the damp fog—received the often quoted message:

Beethoven being dead, only a Berlioz could reincarnate him. I who have fed on your divine compositions, worthy of a genius such as yours, feel it my duty to ask you to accept in homage the sum of 20,000 francs, which the Baron Rothschild will remit on sight of the accompanying note.

Believe me always your affectionate friend

NICOLO PAGANINI

Berlioz replied:

How can I express my gratitude? Though I am anything but rich, I feel bound to say that the approval of a man of genius touches me more nearly than the kingly generosity of your gift. Words fail me. I will go and embrace you as soon as I can leave my bed.

The newspapers having reproduced the letter and told of the act of homage on bended knee, Paris was as excited as if a new revolution had broken out. The scene was re-enacted on the stage by impersonators of the principals; and Paris naturally had to "explain" what it could scarcely grasp—*giving* away twenty thousand francs, and to a composer! Paganini moreover had the reputation of being a miser, which in reality was but the desire not to be fleeced by plausible beggars, and not to be swamped by requests for charity concerts. Stories were soon made up to accommodate old rumors and new facts. The first inspiration of the crowd was that with twenty thousand francs Berlioz would surely buy a house. Then it sought to incriminate Paganini's motives: by his gift to Berlioz, he was purchasing public esteem; or else Paganini had not given the money, but only lent his name to cover a present from the Bertins to their protégé and newspaper critic.

When these tales reappeared in books in the fifties, Paganini's son utterly denied them, and modern students of the violinist's career sustain the good faith of the man and the deed. Human motives are mixed, no doubt, and Paganini may have enjoyed the histrionic side of the adventure, but he chose in accordance with his instinct and reason: there were dozens of others to be a patron to—more popular than Berlioz or less popular, richer or poorer. Paganini could buy himself whatever magnanimous role he wished, and he chose unerringly an artist who would use the gift to create music, not to set up housekeeping. In Paganini's own words, "I saw a young man full of genius whose strength and courage might have ultimately broken down under the strain. . . . I said to myself, 'It is my duty to help him.' . . . When my claims to musical renown are reckoned up, it will not be the least that I was the first to recognize a genius and draw public attention to him. . . ."

Besides this "metal" which spelled for him the leisure to compose, Berlioz had two other pieces of good fortune by way of Christmas gifts: d'Ortigue's book appeared and caused considerable stir, and he was named curator of the Conservatoire library at an annual salary of fifteen hundred francs. Though there were delays, the appointment was ratified in February and made retroactive to January 1. Berlioz' immediate superior, the librarian, was Bottée de Toulmon, a scholar who was also an admirer and who had written judiciously of Berlioz' works, especially of the *Requiem*. Under him, short of earthquake or revolution, Berlioz would have a lifelong post whose duties were extremely light.

Berlioz paid his visit of gratitude to Paganini and in telling all his good news to Adèle gives us a glimpse of the virtuoso as he was and as he was thought to be: "You know he has lost the use of his voice [from tuberculosis of the throat.] . . . When he saw me, tears came into his eyes. I confess my own were not far behind my lids. He wept, this man-eater, this murderer of women, this ex-convict—as he has so often been called. . . . Then, wiping his eyes and striking the table in a loud burst of laughter, he started to address me volubly; but as I could not clearly follow his words, he went to fetch his little son to serve as interpreter . . . I gathered that he was 'very happy . . . because the insects who write and speak against me would be rather abashed. . . .' What a rumpus the news [of his gift] will make in Germany and England. Such a gesture—and from an Italian . . . but one must add that he does not compose Italian music."

Then, unaware of the significant and touching jump in his

thought: "I hope my father will be satisfied. . . . Now I shall be able to make my trip to Germany. It so happens that many German artists are in Paris this winter, and they exhibit towards my music a most encouraging fanaticism."

A few days later, on January 11, 1839, the fourth and last performance of the original version of *Cellini* took place. It was precisely at this time that Prosper took sick, recovered momentarily, then died. Berlioz wrote on the same day to Jules Janin, "I am very sad today. I have just lost my brother, a poor boy of nineteen whom I loved." Hector could only do what he had always done with grief: repress and bury it. But the effort brought on the usual nervous reaction, visible in his next letter to Liszt; to be affectionate and talk of music and recall Italian days was like passing from a place of torture to a perfect world:

> I am ruminating a new symphony, which I'd love to go and finish near you, at Sorrento or Amalfi—(Go to Amalfi!)—but it's impossible. I'm in the breach and must hold it. I have never led such an agitated life. . . . My followers send me a mass of prose and verse, and my detractors anonymous threats. One of them . . . advised me to shoot myself—isn't it delightful? . . . This is a sort of life I like about as much as you do, but by dint of tumbling among the breakers we should manage to tame them and keep them from rolling over our heads.
>
> And so you're in Rome. M. Ingres will surely welcome you, especially if you will play him our Adagio in C-sharp minor of Beethoven and the A-flat sonata of Weber. I greatly admire the fanaticism of this great painter's musical passions, and you will heartily forgive him for loathing me when you remember that he adores Gluck and Beethoven.
>
> How I enjoy chatting with you tonight! I love you so, Liszt. When shall you come back to us? . . . I've had a severe bronchitis, which for a while made me think of Gluck's ode "Charon calls you" . . . Why am I so gay? Our friends are for the most part sad. Legouvé has a painful gastritis. Schoelcher has just lost his mother. Heine *is not happy*. Chopin is ill in the Balearic islands. Dumas drags his chain, which feels heavier day by day. Mme. Sand has a sick child. Hugo alone stands calm and strong. . . .
>
> Please remember me to Mme. d'Agoult. I sincerely thank her for her interest in the success of my doings. She does it from affection for you, but I am not the less grateful. Farewell. Farewell. I embrace you with my whole soul and wish you a north wind—since you are in Rome. Your friend.

The life of "tumbling in the breakers" was more tedious than the image suggested. The regular turning out of copy for the newspapers, the business calls, the correcting of proofs (the *Benvenuto* overture was coming out in full score), and the pelting succession of operas, virtuosi, and ballets—they had to be seen to be reviewed—all broke up the inner stream of thought indispensable for creation, not to say necessary to a humane existence. Berlioz' constant subacute irritation from these causes did not contribute to peace at home. Though the certain signs of a domestic rift cannot be pointed to for another eighteen months, it is likely that already at this time Hector and Harriet were in disharmony. She, wounded in her professional pride by repeated failures, knowing that her debts were a drag on her husband's career, and feeling that this lessened her right to demand more of his time, became restless, jealous, and in the end more demanding than she herself wished to be. True, there were visitors, friends, plenty of activity and no lack of intellectual excitement in the home. And there was Louis to love and the household to take care of, but Harriet's difficulty with French interfered with all these pleasures, just at the time when her physical charms were waning and her late-awakened love for Hector was reaching a peak of possessiveness.

He, on his side, harassed, nervous, impatient, always rushing into his workroom to dash off a *feuilleton* or seize a musical idea in its flight, must have been equally unsatisfactory as a married partner. He was extremely fond of his little boy and played with him in whirlwind snatches of gaiety, but even this may have seemed to Harriet a further exclusion. Hector was lavishing his affection, his energy, his zest on everyone but her; she had no means left to center them again on herself—or so it seemed.

Despite later insinuations and the odd reasoning that because Berlioz met singers and ballerinas, and his wife was jealous, he must have given her cause for jealousy, no rumor at the time even hinted of infidelity on his part. Considering the degree to which the lives of all Berlioz' contemporaries, and his own, were reflected in the daily press, it is unlikely that his enemies would have left us ignorant on this score. Again, it is not likely that Berlioz, if in love with another woman, would have yielded to such *épanchements de coeur* as we saw him addressing to Liszt. And given the "mechanism" of Berlioz' genius, the musical love scene he was beginning to compose argues rather the absence of love than its possession. When we add that the love music being written made use of still another boyhood melody associated with Estelle, we may infer that Berlioz was only longing or ready to love, and we shall not be surprised at the later breakup of his marriage. At the moment he was too busy, too exhilarated by Paganini's gift of freedom, too full of musical strength—exuberant in his previous score, latent in the *grandissime symphonie* now in progress —to engage either in flirtations or in a passionate affair. In the last resort, Harriet could, for a time, rely on Berlioz' strong family feeling and thoroughly bourgeois sense of dignity.

In April 1839, his beloved Adèle was married to Marc Suat. It would have been a great satisfaction to go to the wedding, but how could he, with or without Harriet? If she went, she might be snubbed; if he went alone, it would be a victory for provincial prejudices. He pleaded the perfectly real pressure of duties, but he would have been less than human had he not felt regret; and inevitably associated with this feeling were Harriet's inadequacies. With her loving tact, Adèle proposed that she should come to Paris after her marriage and take back with her little Louis, who would thus have a vacation in the country and be his parents' advocate in the hearts of his Dauphiné relatives. Hector was touched, though he could not help noticing that no one but her had written to him since the wedding. Harriet first consented to send the boy away, then wept, then agreed again. The father felt he must warn his sister: "He is the most charming and badly brought-up child you ever saw. He threatens everybody with his sword and utters all sorts of insults when crossed. He swears like—like his father . . . withal he is charming, and enchanted at the idea of picking peaches and strawberries with his grandfather, but I don't know how he will take his parents' absence: he can't be away from them for one evening without tears. Well, you'll see when you come to Paris."

Despite more illness, due to nerves and bad weather (it was a freezing cold spring) the writing of the new symphony was proceeding. At the same time, a certain thawing out of officialdom was noticeable—as if after all *Benvenuto Cellini* had been a success. On May 10, the Comte de Gasparin awarded Berlioz the Legion of Honor, and the next month, on the death of Paer, the press urged the Institute to elect Berlioz. Paganini's words, "the successor of Beethoven," had become a catch phrase embodying another consecration. Berlioz, not yet thirty-six, seemed the master of instrumental music in France. Nor does it look different in retrospect: between 1830 and 1860, no one in Europe was writing music of comparable power.

Berlioz was not to enter the Institute so soon. He learned that the aged and embittered master whom he so deeply admired, Gasparo Spontini, was a candidate for the vacant seat and he withdrew. He also spurred on his friend, the poet Emile Deschamps, to write a pamphlet on behalf of Spontini's election. To this, the tactless Spontini returned "an incredibly ridiculous letter" which he made public, but he was elected just the same. Berlioz was wise enough to overlook the older man's blunder, knowing that musical genius does not preclude wordly ineptitude.[1] He continued to admire and to soothe in his last unhappy years the master whose career in some ways resembled his own.

When the new symphony was near completion, Berlioz undertook a new project looking to his vindication at the Opera. Since nearly everyone but himself had blamed the libretto for his failure, he would secure one from the best manufacturer, Meyerbeer's own appointed tradesman, Eugène Scribe. On August 31, 1839, after approaches and interviews, Berlioz wrote to him: "I shall not take the liberty of telling you the kind of dramatic ideas that would suit me best: you know perfectly well what they are. However, in seeking a subject which would afford occasions for broad musical developments, and passionate and unexpected effects, it may be useful for me to tell you that certain individuals and groups are deeply uncongenial to me—Luther, for example, the Christians of the Lower Empire, and those brutish Druids."

Berlioz goes on to say that he wants a *simple* love plot, however passionate, combined with scenes of terror "in which mass action would have a place." The Middle Ages, he says, or the last century (that is, the eighteenth) would suit him equally well. "I should greatly love an antique subject, but I apprehend the costumes and the prosy positivism of our audiences. Naturally, this does not mean that one must keep always in the heroic or dithyrambic style. On the contrary, I am fond of contrasts." "The antique" stood here for Berlioz' cherished Virgil, just as the rejected eras and persons stood for the cruelty which he abhorred. A Virgilian libretto by Scribe would no doubt have engaged Berlioz' fullest attachment and robbed us of the epic *Trojans,* fashioned altogether by Berlioz twenty years later; but the popular playwright knew better than to make such an attempt.

By an odd coincidence, as Berlioz was writing of scenes of terror, a woman living in his apartment house went mad and threw the other tenants into a panic. Berlioz had to remove his wife and child for a few days, just as he was about to write to Kastner concerning the new symphony: "I have finished, quite finished, what might be called altogether finished: not another note to write, Amen, amen, amenissimen."

The full title of the work was *Romeo and Juliet, dramatic symphony for chorus, solo voices and orchestra,* and Berlioz at once set about getting a hearing for it. For three whole months he had been practically a free man, a composer working on unmortgaged time. Now the business of copying parts, rehearsing, and reviewing others' works claimed him again. In addition, he found himself appointed Special Master by an equity court, and charged with arbitrating a suit pending between the violinist Charles de Bériot and three different publishers, French, English, and German. Berlioz had to work up the facts and render justice without letting his equal involvements with colleague and publisher affect his judgment.

Meanwhile, his friend Dietsch was rehearsing the choruses in *Romeo.* Berlioz was himself gathering his orchestra, sending out requests and notices by hand, procuring special instruments, or scouring the town for two good harpists. Because of the shortness of time, Berlioz devised the method of rehearsing his instrumentalists by groups—strings, woodwinds, and brass and timpani in separate places. Thus the two days for each section plus two for all together became the equivalent of six or eight rehearsals. As soloists he had Dupont (who had ably succeeded Duprez in *Benvenuto*), Mme. Stoltz (the Ascanio of the same opera), and Alizard. In his favorite Salle du Conservatoire, "resonant like a good violin," Berlioz would have two hundred performers. The date of the *première* was November 24, 1839.

A week before, advance publicity began to appear. Janin in the *Débats* summoned the faithful, promising (in Berlioz' very words to him) that "the symphony by itself and without the accessories of Shakespeare's play, will make known to you the sum of passion contained in the original." This was the essence of the dramatic symphony as a genre, the literal "music drama." The same day, a society columnist, the poetess Delphine (Gay) de Girardin, reported that the seats were sold out and that the fashionable world was busy haggling and trading for them. "Come, dears: you will hear wonderful things. Just see the libretto . . ." and the writer filled up her column with verses quoted from an advance copy of the Prologue.

CHAPTER 12

VOX POPULI

Some day a grateful France will raise a proud monument on his tomb. . . .—WAGNER on Berlioz.

The first time that the Paris audience—now more than ever enriched by the presence of foreign artists[1]—heard the *Romeo and Juliet* symphony was a critical moment in Berlioz' career. The work was new in every way, hence difficult to grasp. It might be hissed like *Benvenuto* by those who wanted to confirm their own adverse judgment or carry on the war against the Bertin family; or worse, the symphony might be chillingly received, politeness emphasizing disappointment. But Berlioz had not even finished conducting Part Two when loud, sustained, and spontaneous applause broke out. The "Ball Scene," or rather Bacchanale, broke the ice; the scherzo and Finale completed the victory. At a second concert a week later, the performance was technically far superior and the public acclaim spread more widely over the work. At the end the performers rose and kept up their bravos so enthusiastically that the composer-conductor almost lost his poise.

For his father's pleasure, Berlioz went into details about both occasions. At the *première* the Queen had failed to come, but the two young Princes were there. Balzac, looking over the assembly, had described it as "the brain of Paris." As regards receipts, it appeared that nearly 1500 francs' worth of tickets had been bid for in vain. The hall was full, and in spite of numerous press seats, the gross was 4559 francs. These details Dr. Berlioz conveyed in his turn, with a tub of butter, to his daughter, adding that the news gave him a fresh lease on life. In proving himself, Hector had proved his alarming boyish predictions of sixteen years before.

The third concert on December 15 was still more satisfactory for the artist: both performance and appreciation were more exact; comments and criticisms by trusted friends gave Berlioz the pleasant feeling of good work done, which might be further polished and improved for years to come. The press was almost uniformly favorable and the younger men were wholeheartedly for the young master. Stephen Heller, the pianist and symphonic composer, wrote to his older friend Robert Schumann how gratifying it was to see the progress that public opinion was making about a genius who refused to commercialize his art.[2] Gautier attested the triumphant result of Berlioz' "unshakable will" which he declared indispensable to an artist in polemical times like theirs, for "originality acts on the French public like a red rag on a bull."

It was the first time in the history of French music that anyone had dared to give the same symphony three times in close succession. Knowing that he must be played often to be understood once, Berlioz undoubtedly helped to establish the practice which many concertgoers now follow, of deliberately subjecting themselves two or three times to a work that is new and strange. For this privilege, the Parisians paid a total of 13,200 francs. Deducting expenses, Berlioz earned for a year's composition and two months' conducting, exactly 1100 francs. "Once and for all, serious music does not keep its man. . . . Paganini is in Nice . . . enchanted with *his* score: it certainly is his score, for it owes its existence solely to him."

On hearing Berlioz' symphony, Wagner, aged twenty-six and a struggling unknown in Paris, experienced what he himself called "the revelation of a new world of music." This was due partly to the power and precision of the orchestra, partly to the music itself. As the composer of two very slight operatic scores and a few overtures and songs, Wagner could reasonably "feel like a child" in comparison with his elder by ten years. But even then, if we are to credit the recollections of forty years later, Wagner was critical of the Dramatic Symphony. He could not accept it for what it was but attempted in vain either to reduce it to the traditional pattern of the symphony or to programmatize it into the semblance of an opera.

When Wagner had heard three more Berlioz symphonies, had returned to Germany, and had begun to grope towards his own dramatic synthesis, he disparaged *Romeo and Juliet* with little regard for his own debt to it.[3] He had learned from Berlioz what the musico-dramatic problem of the century was, and from the substance of *Romeo* he had absorbed enough to serve him in a number of his own later works. Mr. Gerald Abraham was not the first to notice the exact coincidence between Romeo's reverie and Tristan's motif for a similar situation, but he was the first to trace in detail the intimate connection between the two dramas. He concludes: *"Romeo and Juliet* was written when Berlioz was at the zenith of his power; *Tristan* when Wagner was at his, but *20 years later."* (Italics in the text.)

It was therefore a just but incomplete critique which described Berlioz and Wagner as "the two enemy brothers descended from Beethoven." Wagner later proved to his own satisfaction that music cannot yield drama without being linked with words, nor be associated with an action unless the action is staged. Berlioz, we know, was not averse to writing dramatic music for the theater, but he made every effort to preserve music formally and dramatically independent from its associates. He preferred to compose discontinuous "scenes" and indicate in printed words their locale, rather than to link musical ideas to unmusical discourse or behavior. To make up for this self-imposed limitation, he strove to extend the inherent expressiveness of melody, harmony, rhythm, and tone color. Berlioz' way is the way of imagination; "rich music's tongue," as Shakespeare instructs him, is to tell "the imagined happiness." This avoids literalism and keeps open the possibility of multiple interpretations; it is suggestive and symbolic instead of "realistic," though the reality it suggests is no less solid for being unconfined.

But this reference to music drama must not make us think that with his *Romeo and Juliet* of 1839 Berlioz had said his last word, nor suppose that Wagner had uttered his first. One had created a masterpiece; the other had been awakened by it. Both were still young, and so was the century. The slight difference of age between the acknowledged and the incubating genius might reasonably suggest that they were to run on parallel courses. Yet Berlioz at thirty-six had accomplished half his work, and by the year 1840 just beginning, his specifically "French" period was virtually over.

January 1840 saw Berlioz undergoing the inevitable depression. Exhausted and irritable, he was also worried about Harriet's health. She had tonsillitis and respiratory trouble which made him fear a recurrence of pleurisy. Young Louis, who had attended one of the concerts with his mother, was now down with measles. Being closeted, sick, with a sick family, after the excitement of victory, brought on the old spleen. "Everything bores me, disgusts, offends, and revolts me." This mood made him oversensitive to the malicious inanities of a critic like Alphonse Karr, and overhardened to the touching gesture of an English admirer of Beethoven's who bought from Berlioz' publisher the baton with which *Romeo* had been conducted. The collector had insisted on the article's genuineness being guaranteed. "I guarantee it," wrote Berlioz, "and may God grant that the merit of the work will justify, at least in part, the admiration expressed in this novel way."

It was clear that Berlioz at thirty-six should have been exclusively concerned with music—its composition, conducting, and criticism—not with publicity, management, Bertin politics, and the turning out of *feuilletons* about nothing: the fresh call to renewed musical activity for a first concert in 1840 (on February 6) pulled him out of the dumps as nothing else could. Carrying out an original idea sponsored by the *Gazette Musicale* and very probably due to Berlioz himself, this concert was free to the subscribers of the magazine. The Schlesinger publishing house supported both enterprises; that is to say, substituted a musical premium for the usual kitchenware or set of classical authors with which subscribers have been immemorially enticed. At this first symphonic dividend, Berlioz' *Cellini* overture and *Harold* symphony were played with admirable finish. The rest consisted of arias and virtuoso pieces by other hands.

The effort and pleasure once over, Berlioz relapsed into gloom. It was not all weariness or temperamental failing. Berlioz had reached the high point of his possible career in Paris and saw what it was worth. He could subsist only by exceptional means—such as the gift from Paganini, which had prepared and publicized *Romeo* as a gala occasion. Only then would the fashionable world reinforce his 1200 followers. The net gain even under the best conditions was meager, and galas could recur only at wide intervals. As for the subscription concerts of the *Gazette Musicale,* they afforded merely a modest conductor's fee and a chance to repeat certain works. Berlioz, for all his estrangement from state politics, noticed and reported the discouragement of the thoughtful as they observed the greed and folly of the "railroad decade:" [4] "These are unlucky times, when artists ought not to be alive . . . when people, beholding them, only think: 'We are bored and it is you who are boring us.' "

The Romanticist generation, just in proportion as it had shed its undergraduate pose and gained mature solidity, ceased to interest a public that wanted chiefly to gape and to scorn what it gaped at. The bourgeois monarchy having given up all risk and all appeal to the imagination, whether through the drama of domestic politics or through a clear-cut foreign policy, was relying on the most selfish of self-interest to keep the nation occupied and untroublesome. The prime minister who ruled after 1840, Guizot, despite his stern and noble view of constitutional liberties, was soon reduced to corrupt means of ruling and answered all demands for a wider franchise with the phrase *"Enrichissez-vous." Things* were in the saddle, as Emerson said, riding mankind. Boredom was the unexpected result: wild speculation expressed the desire for excitement at any price—an excitement which the variety of civilized intellectual products no longer gave. Beethoven, observed Berlioz, had lost his snob appeal: "The dilettantes in the boxes no longer feel they have to keep up the pose which they had been assuming for ten years past. They are frankly bored."

But so far Berlioz and his fellows of 1830 were disgusted and bored only by the outward shape of things. Their inner life was just as fresh and exciting as it had ever been, even though they no longer put on a show to enrage the bourgeois. Their task was now to accomplish what they could in the teeth of passive resistance. By mid-March 1840, a new ministry being in power, Berlioz approached M. de Rémusat with regard to a possible commission. The plan of a Funeral Symphony had been in the composer's mind since his return from Italy, and it would seem fitting to carry it out for the tenth commemoration of the July Days. On the spot where the Bastille had stood until 1789 a column was being erected which would be dedicated on the anniversary day. The ashes of those who had died fighting for liberty in 1830 would be transferred to a cenotaph at the foot of the column. Hence the procession would require a funeral march of military character—a "funeral triumph."

But by what magic could the difficult and strongly intellectual art of Berlioz remold itself to the proper shape? The revolutionary ideal of art for the masses, which Berlioz inherited in purified form precisely because he was not contemporary with its beginnings, has often been invoked and talked about; it is another thing to put it into practice. For in spite of the broad human feeling required, the artist must tread a very narrow path if he is not to fall into alternative dangers—on the one side, condescension to his untutored audience; on the other, platitude. Nor must he simply *depict* common emotions for the pleasure of the sophisticates; he must find original ways of being at once elevated and simple. There are always people who need only to be told that a composition is scored for two hundred wind instruments in order to act like the critics of *Tom Jones* who (as Fielding tells us) "called it low and fell agroaning." But what Berlioz planned and Wagner was to admire was something else than brass and blaring. It was, in Wagner's words, "a composition altogether popular in the most ideal sense. . . . I should indeed call it national rather than popular," in short a piece of democratic high art.

And this raises a second question: how did the artist whose contempt for politics we know manage to feel and think like a true democrat? His birth, prospects, and elevation of mind obviously made him an aristocrat.[5] At times he seemed like many others deluded by the mirage of the Napoleonic legend. Does this imply a hankering after absolutism? The *Funeral and Triumphal* symphony itself had its genesis in recollections of Bonaparte's Italian campaign, and later the *Emperor* cantata expressed something of Berlioz' faith in the nephew of the great man. There is here a fundamental conflict which affects all great art, and which Hazlitt was the first to discuss. In speaking of Shakespeare's *Coriolanus* he points out that we side instinctively with the hero and against the crowd because of his greater nobility, courage, and breadth of mind. The observation suggests its counterpart, which is that in order to represent a crowd as hero, the artist must choose its highest, most selfless emotions. If these are fine but simple, their mere multiplication will raise their esthetic merit. One rogue weeping—to use Hazlitt's language—does not move us, but a mourning nation, regardless of the cause, is a mighty spectacle.

Berlioz discusses music in similar terms, insisting that it is "like great poetry, aristocratic." The truth is that the ordinary contrast of democrat and aristocrat breaks down in describing the artist. What Berlioz despised in politics was the partisanship which divided persons and ideas that he wanted to keep joined, while it took no cognizance of the ideas that mattered to him as a craftsman and creator. For art means discrimination, judgment, selectness, superiority—which count as aristocratic virtues; and art means also the urge to cut through the crust of convention and reach down to the simplest realities of common feeling. It is in this sense that Berlioz' *Funeral and Triumphal* symphony is—like the last movement of Beethoven's Ninth—popular. Berlioz' conception of a national art transcended the contemporary views of nation, class, and culture, and he created works more broadly human than France could until recently assimilate. Even in this country and century of populism, most persons are so unused to the intent of social art when it is divorced from current propaganda, that hearers of this symphony still find the last movement vulgar, regretting the varied "elegance" of the first two.

In the year of its composition, "popular" meant still another kind of art—that which flourished in the various opera houses and provided their patrons with well-seasoned commonplace. This automatically excluded Berlioz. By accepting the government commission for the symphony, he was taking the one opportunity to be played without financial sacrifice to himself. The Opera continued to maintain toward him the attitude of a hibernating bear; Scribe was in no hurry to provide the libretto he had promised; nor was Duponchel, as may be imagined, eager for a second *Benvenuto* which in all probability would be still newer in form and contents.

Yet Duponchel was in trouble. Meyerbeer had refused permission to have his new opera (*L'Africaine*) put on. He could afford to wait, for, as his mother-in-law boasted, he did not have to earn a living, and he wanted the public to work up an appetitie for his fare by being disappointed at other hands. This left Duponchel with only Donizetti's *Martyrs,* which would probably not carry the overhead. The director might have to resign. In these straits, managers or their entourage are likely to have a fit of memory and bethink themselves of masterpieces: there was talk of reviving *Freischütz.* But the idea was soon dismissed after debating how the work could be "arranged." An unsigned note in the *Gazette Musicale,* very likely written by Berlioz, concluded: "The plan is given up, fortunately for poor Weber. The danger is past."

On May 27, while Berlioz was hopefully at work on his Funeral Symphony, Paganini died. In the *Débats* a week later, Berlioz expressed his sorrow and admiration. Although he had never heard his benefactor play in public, he was familiar with the virtuoso's innovations in technique and style of composition, both for violin and for orchestra. Berlioz was also impressed by the accounts of the improvised duets which Paganini playing the guitar had engaged in with his friend the violinist Sina, and which no one had ever been admitted to hear. The article on Paganini turned into one of those excellent biographical sketches which Berlioz has left us about Beethoven, Spontini, Chopin, Lesueur, and others. More than any of his contemporaries, Liszt excepted, Berlioz understood and sympathized with Paganini's strangeness. He could feel the reserve and *contemptus mundi* behind the affectation of eccentricity, and he easily responded to the Shakespearean juxtaposing of deep feeling and boisterous humor such as Paganini had indulged in at their meeting after the gift. Berlioz himself would later develop something of the same forbidding exterior, quickly melting at the touch of genuine emotion or artistic intelligence. Meantime he had shown his gratitude and reverence for the old man dying in Nice by serving as his go-between in a pending lawsuit.[6]

During the completion of the July Symphony (as Berlioz usually called it then) his artistic nourishment from without was meager. The Conservatoire did give Beethoven's Pastoral again, together with fragments of Bach and Handel, but Berlioz was pleased neither by the performance nor by the music of the two older masters. He was downright academic about Bach's harmony, not knowing enough of the work to grasp its idiom. A later concert brought a psalm of Handel's which Berlioz found magnificent, but these two composers, with whom Berlioz had certain esthetic affinities despite divergent traditions, remained alien to him until almost the end of his life.[7] The narrowness of the concert repertory in any epoch, as well as the rigidity of style with which works outside the common choice are played, is responsible for anomalies of the kind, which exist to a far lesser degree in arts other than music.

Berlioz consoled himself for the "desperate sameness" of operas and concerts by rereading Virgil, Molière, Shakespeare, La Fontaine, Cervantes, Bernardin de St. Pierre, and a few moderns: Balzac, Vigny, George Sand, Victor Hugo. The last-named had in fact just published a new volume of verse, *Les Rayons et les Ombres,* which chimed in with Berlioz' somber thoughts and his musical activity as well: the last poem in the collection was on "The Return of the Emperor" and the Preface was postdated so as to make its appearance fall on the anniversary of Napoleon's death.

Like the *Requiem,* Berlioz' new symphony had to be finished one month before the date of its performance, which was July 28. This had the same effect of cramping the working out of the last movement in each composition, and it took the same toll on the body and nerves of the composer. The work being scored for military band, Berlioz had to keep in mind the desire of all the participating groups to have a share in the performance. Large forces were available, though not distributed ideally among the instruments. Moreover, the piece had been commissioned for the procession through the boulevards to the Place de la Bastille, and outdoor music is unsatisfactory except under specially arranged acoustical conditions. To increase the number of players does not help—they must play together, they must be led by a visible leader, and the proportions of various kinds of timbre must be kept sounding coherent. This is difficult if the performers have to march and reverberators are lacking. Berlioz gathered 207 musicians, some of them professionals who would help lead the less competent sections of National Guardsmen. Among the trained instrumentalists were the visiting band of Bavarian cornets who had recently given concerts in Paris.

Berlioz again followed his system of rehearsing by groups which saved both money and energy. And these preparations exposed him again to the usual malicious rumors that make the Paris *boulevardiers* feel they control the destinies of art. Berlioz' symphony, it was said, was unfinished; complete rehearsals could not begin; the partial ones were going badly. The fact is that by July 19 the rehearsals were going quite well and Berlioz was arranging for a public dress rehearsal, indoors. To this performance, which would at least be audible, he invited friends, critics, and notables. Chopin's ticket, signed by Berlioz, is still extant. Put into English it reads:

Sunday July 26 at 11.30 A.M.
Concert Hall rue Vivienne
Dress Rehearsal of the Military Symphony
Composed by M. Berlioz
For the Funeral Ceremony of July 28
H. Berlioz
This card will admit two.
Funeral March, Hymn of Farewell, Apotheosis.

For a government as frail and composite as that of the July Monarchy, the "Twenty-eighth" was necessarily a political occasion—it was not yet a patriotic day for the whole nation. The fête had accordingly been planned in order to give the bellicose Parisians the impression of still being the heroes they were during the first revolution and Napoleon's Empire, and by means of this external pomp to reconcile them to a very cautious and unmilitary foreign policy. The people's demand for glory had something in it of the artist's attack against Philistinism: populace and artist both aspired to make life serve nobler ends than trade. But just as an artist must live—even a Berlioz sacrificing fame and comfort to his ideal—so the people grumbled at social and political conditions which they felt restricted life without the compensation of glory. Hence the cry of Reform. On the morning of the twenty-eighth the comic weekly *Charivari* came out printed in white on a black cover, with a cartoon showing mortuary remains and bearing the caption: "Funeral Procession of Liberties Dead for the Citizen, in step with the Procession of Citizens Dead for Liberty." Further on, with a pun on his name, there was a dig at Berlioz, "who will perform his defunct funeral march. A few unlubricated carriage wheels will add to the effect of his composition."

Thus Berlioz appeared to the agitators as a minion of princes, a favorite of the government, even though his feeling about that government were precisely those of the opposition. The people and the artist could apparently not enter into the natural relation of expressing and responding to a fundamental feeling which they sincerely shared. The *Charivari,* which employed another genius neglected by public and government alike—Honoré Daumier—was blind to this social and cultural contradiction. And being ignorant of music it needlessly feared the "noise" of Berlioz' Fourth Symphony. In spite of its two hundred performers, Berlioz tells us, the work "resounded very little or very imperfectly." Once for all, serious outdoor music was unpractical. Wearing his own unifom of National Guard and conducting with his sword, Berlioz could lead only the few front ranks of his marching orchestra. Down the open boulevards, amid the shouting people, the political altercations within the crowd, and the panic caused at one point by the near upset of the fifty coffins piled on a flag-studded dray (twenty-four horses could scarcely set it in motion) Berlioz' majestic sonorities hardly carried. Only when the parade stopped at a point where the sound was reflected by houses and trees did the music have a chance. By then, the performers, having repeated the March several times, were blown and miserably broiling under the noonday sun.

Finally, an hour or more after noon, the procession reached the Place de la Bastille. The burial service was elaborately performed and silence at last secured for the symphony. Berlioz' band occupied bleachers from which all could see his decisive beat, and he was on the point of raising his sword to signal that arresting rhythm on muffled drums which begins the Funeral March, when the legion of the National Guard which had been on duty at this spot since 8 A.M. (it was now 3 P.M.) could no longer contain itself: it wanted to parade and go home. Their own drums beat and 60,000 men tramped across the Place for two hours, to an accompaniment of yells from the crowd. Of Berlioz' symphony, as he himself reports, "not a note survived."

This was but a temporary extinction. Owing to the simple presence of his name on the program, more people heard of Berlioz in one day than if he had given concerts or written operas for twenty years. The very fact that his composition had not been heard kept it fresh, and a concert featuring the work would be sure to draw. He quickly mustered his men again, adding string parts to relieve the monotony of the brass bass, and sought to carry out his frustrated intentions for the last movement by setting as a choral climax a few lines by Emile's brother, Antony Deschamps.

On August 7, an audience of standing-room size jammed the hall rue Vivienne, and the unfilled demand was such that three more performances were planned amid general enthusiasm. Only one took place, on August 14, 1840, because a piece of unsettling news diverted public attention from art to politics: while Berlioz was re-creating in sound the Revolutionary-Napoleonic legend, its heir-apparent (in both senses of apparent) had attempted his second coup: Louis-Napoleon had landed at Boulogne. He too had been arrested, like the symphony, but not extinguished. For in these days everyone outside the government was a Bonapartist, even the Republicans, who could stress the liberal side of Napoleon's career. Indeed, the government itself was Bonapartist to the extent that it wanted to be national and that it did not want to be more liberal. In May the Chambers had voted to bring back the ashes of the Emperor to Paris, to rest "among the people that he loved so well." It was a cheap substitute for war or administrative efficiency.

Still the nephew's attempted *coup d'état* put a different complexion on the uncle's return, and a new sense of caution at once affected Berlioz' availability as a musician for official occasions. His "Fifth of May," an ode on the death of Napoleon, composed five years before to Béranger's verses, was about to be published and he had asked permission to dedicate it to Louis Philippe. Berlioz' old friend and protector in Roman days, Horace Vernet, who steadily painted Napoleonic scenes for the government at the rate of one hundred thousand francs each, had offered to obtain for Berlioz an audience with the King. But after Louis Bonaparte's raid on Boulogne the opportunity was gone, the King never replied, and it became compromising to associate one's work or person with Napoleonic sentiments.

Yet that association remained in the mind of one observer, who may himself have been under the spell of the Emperor. Writing years later about Berlioz, Wagner declared that he always visualized him "at the head of his troops, leading the orchestra like a Napoleon." Very likely Wagner had been in the crowd on July 28 as he had been at the *Romeo and Juliet* and subsequent concerts. He knew Berlioz by sight, for he had submitted articles to Schlesinger, the owner of the *Gazette Musicale,* who had published them on Berlioz' advice. This was Wagner's first emergence from obscurity since he had come to the capital. Desperately poor and doing hack work, he was passing judgment on native and foreign music and also acting as correspondent for the Dresden *Abendzeitung.* To that paper he was soon to contribute a sizable essay on Berlioz, in which after describing his character at second hand he paid respect to the man's determined will to create without heed to money or vulgar opinion. Finally, Wagner gave his views on the *Funeral and Triumphal* symphony: "I am inclined to rank this composition above all Berlioz' other ones: it is noble and great from the first note to the last. Free from sickly excitement, it sustains a noble patriotic emotion which rises from lament to the topmost heights of apotheosis. When I further take into account the service rendered by Berlioz in his alogether noble treatment of the military wind band—the only instruments at his disposal here, . . . I must say with delight that I am convinced this Symphony will last and exalt the hearts of men as long as there lives a nation called France."

CHAPTER 13

MUSIC FOR EUROPE

Whoever lived and cheered (as I did) at the time of Berlioz' concerts in Germany can bear witness that never was any dazzling musical phenomenon ever greeted with such excitement and enthusiasm. . . . His music came as a fiery meteor above our heads.—HANSLICK forty years later

A *Funeral* symphony that Berlioz also called "Military" was by no means out of place in the summer of 1840. Threats of war were in the air. France's exclusion from the European conference over Egypt had aroused patriotic anger in Paris, and Thiers gave orders to increase the army and navy. The flare-up of Bonapartism led to cries of "Avenge Waterloo!" and "Reconquer the Rhine!": Europe's most incorrigible aggressor nation since the fall of Spain seemed once again on the warpath. But the time was the nineteenth century and the Germany that France threatened was but a cultural entity. Desire for counteraggressiveness existed as yet only in the minds of a few, such as the patriotic poet Becker, who bandied rimes with Musset in a pair of silly poems about the intrinsic nationality of the river Rhine.[1]

Nonetheless Louis Philippe pushed forward the completion of the Paris fortifications. But the populace felt even more revolutionary than nationalistic: they were sure these ramparts were meant to be used against them rather than a foreign enemy; so they grumbled loudly, though less effectively than their comrades in London, who presented to the Queen the first People's Charter bearing 1,280,000 names and rose up at

Newport in "Jack Frost's Revolt." The class struggle was being given doctrinal form in Louis Blanc's *History of Ten Years,* in which the bourgeoisie was named and charged as the enemy of the people. A change of ministry purged these warlike feelings of the French. Guizot came to power and a decade of grim devotion to pocket-filling began.

Almost the last event capable of arousing the historical or poetic imagination was the entombment, at the close of the year, of Napoleon's remains in the chapel of the Invalides, where Berlioz' *Requiem* had resounded two and a half years before. The entire Orleans family was present to do homage to Napoleon's memory, and 150,000 soldiers were on parade, but all the guest of honor's living relatives were either in prison or exile. The government—curious to relate—had asked Berlioz for a new triumphal march to grace the occasion, but he had wisely refused, saying that a suitable work could not be improvised in two weeks. He did not want to dim the effect of his *Funeral and Triumphal* symphony by a hasty variation on the same theme, and he took a malicious pleasure—so he told Adèle—in seeing what Auber, Halévy, and Adam would do when faced with the task. At the dress rehearsal of their pieces, some of the musicians came and congratulated Berlioz instead.

In reporting the ceremony to his sister, Berlioz made a remark about Mozart's *Requiem* which was used for the service: "*Despite the fact that it is a masterpiece,* it made a poor showing . . . under the dome of the Invalides; it is not fashioned in scale with such a celebration." [2] Berlioz' feeling for appropriate *mise en scène*—a feeling he expressed just as readily to his detriment when he admitted the total blotting out of his own symphony—also made him criticize other parts of the Napoleonic ceremony: "I had only a few moments of partial satisfaction with what the gunners did; they fired just as though it were the baptism of the Count of Paris or some other embryo Prince. I should have liked, instead of those five little cannon afflicted with a head cold, some five hundred mortars bursting with flames as the cortege entered. Nothing of the kind. Everything missed, muffed, even the artillery."

This is a good instance of the grounds upon which the sophisticated Parisian public considered Berlioz a madman and a corrupter of the national tradition: he was never content with the half-baked conception and slipshod execution of an idea; he wanted the complete and concrete fulfillment of it, especially when the occasion concerned an eminent fellow-performer such as Napoleon. Whatever one's loathing of tyranny and violence, one could not forget that the Emperor had overrun Europe from Spain to Russia carrying death to the old regime. There was a difference of scale between this and the paper war through which the hotheads of 1840 were venting their bellicose emotions, and the difference exactly matched that between Adolphe Adam's genteel chorus and the military *Te Deum* that Berlioz was already planning in his mind.

Meantime, although the comic papers of the day had pictured him carried to heaven in a broken bass drum, Berlioz sought once more to show the would-be musical, would-be national, would-be Napoleonic operagoers what a grand celebration should be. To underline his purpose he coined the term Music Festival, which has remained attached to the genre. The preparation of this concert, scheduled for November 1, 1840, required the usual diplomacy in order to circumvent the jealous opposition of colleagues. The Opera's new director, Léon Pillet, was favorable, but the conductor was still Habeneck, then sixty years old, whose opinion of Berlioz shifted according to circumstance. The question now was, would Habeneck give up the podium to the younger man? The press took a hand and sarcasm did not sheathe its fangs: " 'Wouldn't you like to hear something new and strange?' asks M. Berlioz. 'Well, I bring you marine trumpets, wet drums, broken timpani and cracked saucepans . . . I want an orchestra, two orchestras, ten orchestras. I have composed humanitarian symphonies, lethal masses, and an opera which will never be popular.' " [3]

This was one way to announce the double bill planned by Berlioz and consisting of four numbers from the *Requiem,* fragments of the *Romeo and Juliet* and *Funeral and Triumphal* symphonies, the first act of Gluck's *Iphigeneia in Tauris,* some Handel and a madrigal of Palestrina's. Worse than the Parisian jokes was the rumor that, with Habeneck's encouragement or consent, the players were going to sabotage the performance. If Habeneck did not lead them, said one paper, they would rather go and build the fortifications. Yet the rehearsals were in progress. Berlioz again used his new method of rehearsing the players in separate groups meeting in separate places—three choral sections and three instrumental. This was efficient, but in going from one to another and beating time for entire days, Berlioz lost his voice from fatigue and grew more and more nervous as November first approached.

Habeneck had decided to yield his place and Berlioz was conducting. To insure perfect ensemble, he had placed three subconductors among the mass of four hundred and fifty performers. They took their beat from him and prevented the voices from dragging as so often happens in large choral groups. The act from Gluck went well and so did the numbers from the *Requiem*. Between the two works, Berlioz went to inspect the trumpet crooks to make sure that no joker or foe had tampered with them. His good friends among the players reassured him, and even reproached him for doubting their loyalty. At the end of the *Lacrymosa,* the practically full house broke out in thunderous applause.

In the ensuing intermission a distressing incident occurred. A journalist named Bergeron sought out Emile de Girardin, the editor of *La Presse,* and slapped his face.[4] Mme. de Girardin, in the box with her husband, had hysterics. The slap in the face obviously had political intent and a garbled report of the incident spread panic in the house. The Bonapartist coup was still in everyone's mind, as well as the attempt that summer to assassinate Victoria and the Prince Consort. People both feared and looked for significant violence. The cautious part of the audience went home, which left only a few to hear the second half of the program. After the Handel and Palestrina and before the *Funeral* symphony, political feeling boiled up even in that small knot of people. Someone called for the "Marseillaise." The police commissioner, who was present, thought fit to defend his King and Master and shouted, "No Marseillaise!" The evening ended with a handful of somewhat frightened and very inattentive listeners; which enabled the comic papers to print the taunt that Berlioz had organized his festival in order to receive an ovation from his close friends and relatives.

Ridicule was the one comfort left to the lesser men of a deeply disappointed generation. The final split had come between the creators and the naggers living on in envious dejection. This meant that by and large the burden of the artist's life changed from a struggle against academicism to a struggle against the journalistic spokesmen of Philistinism. From this moment on the careers of Hugo, Vigny, Delacroix, and Berlioz became a ceaseless guerrilla. Within three years of this Berliozian fiasco, the failure of Hugo's drama *Les Burgraves* would be interpreted as marking the end of Romanticist art in France, but what is marked rather is the end of its being tolerated—the Revocation of the Edict of Nantes for serious art. Thereafter, not simply the still productive Romanticists, but every school was treated as heretical and subjected in life and death to abuse and ridicule.

Typical of the new state of mind, in the same year as the *Burgraves,* was the anonymous publication of a satirical novel which directly involved Romanticism and Berlioz. *Jérôme Paturot in Search of a Social Position* begins by showing its hero, who makes cotton nightcaps, aspiring to be a poet; then winning wealth by a fluke, and before entering politics seeking to be a patron of the arts. Accordingly he, or rather his wife, hires a long-haired composer-conductor to give a festival for a charitable purpose. The account of the fete unmistakably alludes to Berlioz and his works. "The walls of the concert-room," we are told, "were solid and withstood the noise. Lives were safe, but not one's ears." Louis Reybaud, the author (who, by the way, was an economist) devotes half a dozen pages to a musical description, of which only one or two phrases are telling: "Princess," says the composer to a patron, "I shall find again for you the Hymn of Creation, lost since the Deluge." The novelist spoils this fair thrust by adding: "More than once I had heard it said that the inventor of festivals had devised a process by which he put public and private life into music." And soon the satire turns to slander: "The hero of the evening, worn out by the emotions of childbirth . . . escaped and hastened away to compose the review article with that same hand which had written the score and wielded the baton. Modern geniuses are like that: they multiply their claims to fame and are equal to every task."

This last quip was in keeping with the author's debunking of Napoleon and was well-fitted to earn the approval of Thackeray, who, seemingly doomed to failure, preferred Reybaud to Balzac and was inclined to meanly admire mean things: " 'Give me a mutton chop and a thousand a year.' In the fortunes of honest Paturot this moral is indicated with much philosophical acumen . . . there is perhaps a great deal of sound thinking and reflection hidden under [his] cotton nightcap."

The intellectual eclipse that Renan ascribed to the second Empire beginning in 1852 had in reality begun a decade before. Berlioz noted it in his reviews of symphonic concerts: "One sees there pale women raising their eyes heavenward in a studied manner, and red-faced men trying hard not to fall asleep. . . . Clearly the audience cannot understand anything but martial sounds, crude contrasts, or flirtatious melodies. . . . If [Beethoven] had been alive, they would say he had failed, for the first movement of the *Eroica* was applauded by almost eight people, the Funeral March by ten or twelve, the Scherzo by fourteen or fifteen, and the Finale by four or five. It has cost me a handkerchief, which I somewhat damaged with my teeth."

There comes moreover a time in the life of every artist when the attitude of the public towards him is set. He is a hero or a wit or a saint or a devil once for all. He seems all of a piece and he must die, or at least become a senile Grand Old Man, before his reputation changes. Berlioz having become known early, his treatment by the Parisians hardly changed, though he himself was still developing in both character and technique. He was the "fiery romantic," the man whose opera had failed, the excessively mental composer who was not tuneful. He stayed, in short, at the stage of "notoriety" rather than fame, and this largely because he continued to be his own producer instead of winning the one sign of musical fame understood by his century, success at the Opera.

It was not for want of trying. As far as he could Berlioz campaigned on all fronts. While forwarding his festival plans, he was composing small works to balance the monumental with the *intime:* "I want you," he wrote to Legouvé, "to hear what I composed last week on your charming verses about the Death of Ophelia . . . If you like the music, I shall instrument the piano accompaniment for a pretty little orchestra and will have it played at one of my concerts." For his other good friend Théophile Gautier, and upon his verses, Berlioz had likewise composed the six great songs, *Nuits d'Eté,* which he published in June 1841. And within the same months he was still scheming to obtain the vaguely promised libretto from Scribe. For this purpose he even endured the agony of going fishing with him, at the cost of missing an afternoon with Delacroix.[5] But Scribe's name was such an open sesame at the Opera that its bearer would not readily commit himself; he pleaded that he was extremely busy. Berlioz then tried to induce him to collaborate with Frederic Soulié in the making of a half-ghostwritten libretto. Failing this there was the possibility of reviving Weber's *Freischütz* and being put in charge of the enterprise.

This did succeed, but not without incredible complications which show that it was neither Berlioz' personality nor his musical technique that created confusion around his undertakings, but an absolutely vicious tradition of musical management. In March 1841, the Opera announced that Berlioz would direct the rehearsals of *Freischütz.* This meant that he would also compose the necessary recitatives and perhaps a ballet, since the operagoers could tolerate neither spoken dialogue nor a masterpiece unrelieved by dancing. The proposed title—*Robin des Bois*—was that of the absurd but successful arrangement of Castil-Blaze, whom Berlioz had denounced sixteen years before. One result of trying to capitalize this past publicity was that, in spite of repeated protests from Germany, the rights in the opera remained the property of Castil-Blaze and Sons. Since they had despoiled Weber, the Blaze family now felt—on the principle of "set a thief"—that Berlioz was robbing them.[6] So the press campaigns against Berlioz began anew. An anonymous article in the *Revue des Deux Mondes,* doubtless written by Henri Blaze, sought to discredit Berlioz as a conductor of works other than his own. He, who had never replied to a single criticism, felt obliged to refute the accusation of adding parts to the old masters. The reference was to his recent festival concert:

"*Iphigeneia* was performed exactly as written; therefore no one can have heard any ophicleides in it. As for Palestrina 'a few sopranos' cannot have been 'sufficient for him' since his madrigal . . . is in four parts. The critic must moreover have been oddly absent-minded if he found the work 'crushed under instrumental pomp,' since I performed it, as written, without accompaniment. These are the misstatements I wish to have corrected, for they libel me in my capacity as interpreter of the great masters."

The periodical did not print Berlioz' letter but alluded to it jokingly. Jokes took care of everything, including unspent aggressiveness. "Our musical world," wrote Berlioz early in 1841, "has been rent of late by a thousand rival ambitions, which go beyond the bounds of patience and reason and attain the pitch of envy and hatred."

By April, Berlioz was at work supplying *Freischütz* with recitatives written in the style of Weber himself, as well as arranging the *Invitation to the Dance* and other fragments for the ballet. Just then Liszt came back from Italy indignant at the pitiable sum that had been raised throughout Europe for the projected monument to Beethoven. To raise more money he and Berlioz gave an all-Beethoven concert on April 25. It consisted of the E-flat piano concerto and the Pastoral: the public expressed its satisfaction by clamoring for Liszt's "Fantasia on Themes from Meyerbeer's *Robert le Diable.*"

The next month the Opera was rehearsing Weber, and quite appropriately the *Gazette Musicale* asked the young German musician Richard Wagner to write one or more articles for it on the subject of the opera. Berlioz had especially liked one of Wagner's previous essays—an imaginary visit to Beethoven—and had drawn attention to it in his own column in the *Débats.* Wagner now wrote two which, had Berlioz been like his French colleagues or like Wagner himself, he would certainly have "edited" or suppressed. For without having heard or seen a note of Berlioz' recitatives, Wagner condemned them —politely enough, but in a way to prejudice the public against the entire revival. Besides setting himself the precedent of passing judgment on Berlioz without knowledge, Wagner assumed that Berlioz' recitatives would be fiery, dramatic, "personal," and would therefore kill the airs and choruses that they introduced.

Berlioz let the articles appear, with only a heading to the effect that Wagner was judging the work from the point of view of German tradition.[7] This, of course, Wagner had every right to do, condemning in so many words any change from Weber's originally spoken text. But he also and illogically concluded that if *Freischütz* must be made into a grand opera, no one could do it better than Berlioz, "a man of genius whose poetic verve is of irresistible energy." [8]

As so often in their relations, it is Wagner who is hasty, impetuous, and incoherent, and Berlioz who knows what he is about. Berlioz' aim was to rescue and restore Weber's masterpiece. This he did with a solicitous care to which his manuscript testifies. He copied out the translated words under the parts himself so as to make sure that neither rhythm nor melody should be destroyed for prosody. The recitatives might seem overlong—that was unfortunately determined by the number of words—but they were written as tightly as possible and not at all to show off Berlioz' "energy." The ballet music came from Weber himself, directly from *Oberon* and *Preciosa,* indirectly through Berlioz' orchestration of the *Invitation to the Dance.* In that task, Berlioz could truly say, "not a note has been changed." Berlioz knew his Weber and respected his work.

At first the cabal led by Blaze dimmed the success of the opera, but it overcame their efforts and even made money—almost as much as the Meyerbeer repertoire and a great deal more than *Don Giovanni.* Wagner fulfilled his prediction of not liking it. He uttered his distaste in a serial for his Dresden paper, largely devoted to congratulating himself on being a German and hating everything French.[9] Of Berlioz' obvious feeling for Weber or the faithful musicianship of the revival, there is hardly any mention.

Although Berlioz had not come to the end of his tribulations with the *Freischütz,* it was dropped from the repertory within six months. Nevertheless it served him while it lasted by helping the sales of his *Nuits d'Eté.* This success at this time only shows again the advertising power of the Opera. Two months later that establishment performed large parts of Spontini's *Cortez,* which Berlioz was able to enjoy as an uninvolved spectator. Like the *Freischütz,* the work of Spontini enabled him to relive the enthusiasms of his youth. "I feel a hundred and ten years old." He felt bound to express his admiration direct to the old master, sketching in the course of his letter the idea of a musical center for Europe. There the great masterpieces would be given with the utmost care, at wide intervals, before a prepared public. These performances would correspond to the great religious ceremonies of ancient Greece. Music would be sought out in a receptive spirit "instead of finding the art relegated to public charity . . . like a waif that the world is trying to turn into a prostitute."

By this metaphor, Berlioz passed judgment on the Opera—he thought it "music's house of ill fame"—as well as on the social pressures that dictated its taste and forced composers like him to submit or starve. One form of the pressure could be shown by the fact that his minor share in the *Freischütz* brought him automatically more than two hundred francs at every performance, tax free, whereas the gigantic efforts of his symphonic concerts rarely netted over one thousand francs once and for all. At his last "Festival" he had had to forego the five hundred francs agreed upon as his conductor's fee and even to pay three hundred and sixty francs out of his own pocket; for upon every "amusement" the Ministry of Public

Charity levied for the poor one eighth of the receipts. The music of Berlioz and Beethoven thus helped square with God the accounts of a grasping bourgeoisie.

In September 1841 Scribe at last delivered the first act of the new libretto. The subject, under the ghoulish title of *La Nonne Sanglante,* was drawn from a recent translation of Lewis's *Monk.* Scribe thought the midnight mood of the *Huguenots* and *Robert* still strong with the public, but Berlioz set to work with only superficial alacrity.

Even if this operatic theme had been more congenial, Berlioz had grave preoccupations which might in any case have lamed his inspiration: a break in his domestic relations seemed inevitable. For many months now life with Harriet—and life for the child—had become increasingly difficult. Ever more jealous, she greeted her husband's daily return with scenes so violent as to terrify young Louis. She suspected Hector of love affairs with every woman he mentioned in conversation or in reviews; she scrutinized his mail. From an unhappy woman she had become a scold, and finally she took to drink.

On his side, no doubt, he had little strength left for conciliation. He came home with frayed nerves from a weary struggle kept up by constant self-repression, only to face the grind of writing articles which too often required the same kind of diplomacy.[10] He would have needed still more to deal with Harriet in whom he found, instead of affection, reproaches. Even had his temperament been more easygoing, less electric, it would have been difficult for him to maintain his love illusions about her. She was getting stout; reclusion and drink made her slovenly. Although she had in the past courageously shared Berlioz' views of artistic integrity, she had no direct interest in music and she now strenuously opposed his ancient purpose to give concerts in Germany. In all their discussions, moreover, his flashing mind and superior command of language must have given him an advantage that only aggravated her misery. Their marriage was doomed.

Given this state of things, there was after a time cause for Harriet's jealousy. On his first trip out of France since the Italian journey, Berlioz was accompanied by a young singer, Marie Recio, who thirteen years later became his second wife. The first marriage was not wholly destroyed. It died hard, the agony lasting from 1841 to the final separation in the autumn of 1844. In a more enlightened time and place, an uncontested divorce might have regularized this painful situation. As it was, Berlioz' position, and even more that of his son, was left ambiguous yet unchangeable—a perpetual moral burden. He naturally continued to support wife and child, though some of his contemporaries found this quixotic, and it is amply evident that after the separation Berlioz continued to bestow much thought and affection on Harriet. He had said, "I will never leave her." He came to feel that he must leave her, but not completely, never finally. He was so constituted that his "tenacity" would not let him yield anything on which he had once set his heart, even if it were a dream like the love-image that he had fastened on the unfortunate Harriet Smithson.

His feeling for Marie Recio was very different. She was a half-French, half-Spanish singer of mediocre talent, but of pleasing exterior and lively disposition, who succeeded in catching Berlioz' attention when perhaps others in the Parisian theaters had failed.[11] She doubtless saw in him an aid to her career, but must also have found him attractive and lovable since she clung to him even after the end of his willingness to help her succeed. For him, the love affair seems to have been a weaker repetition of the Camille attachment. Marie, too, was a musician, had a watchful mother (though a far better woman than Mme. Moke), and knew how to cast a spell. For a long time, now, Hector had been starved of womanly sympathy. Harriet's late-awakened passion was too aggressive to be endearing, and we may read in Hector's virtual love letters to Liszt and to Adèle, as well as in the tenderness of the great music written in this period (the songs especially) how balked his outgoing affections were. Just then, too, he was at the critical turn from mature to middle age. Ever conscious, he dropped a word of his feelings to the faithful Ferrand: "I feel that I am going downhill very fast . . . The idea that life has an end, I notice, occurs to me frequently. So I find myself snatching rather than culling the flowers on the stony way . . ."

It meant a shift in bearing and manner, half organic, half conditioned by the changing times. He writes to the same trusted friend: "Believe it or not, there has come over me, in place of my former artistic fury, a kind of cold-blooded poise, a resignation, or contempt, if you like, in the face of whatever offends me in current musical practices. I am far from being alarmed at this change in myself. On the contrary, the older I get the more I see that this outward indifference saves my strength for a struggle where passion would cripple me. It's like love again: if you seem to flee, you will be run after."

With Marie Recio he went to give two concerts in Belgium on September 18, 1842, but on his return a month later went back to his own home. His carefully planned tour of Germany was to begin in mid-December and he intended to go alone, but Marie persuaded him to let her accompany him. When she insisted on taking part in his programs, making scenes at the very thought of any other prima donna, he tried again to shake her off. Marie caught up with him at his next stopping place and he resigned himself. He sanctioned their relations by designating her, during an awkward social moment, as his second wife, and she soon gave up her pretentions to a singing career and loyally devoted herself to helping him. She kept his accounts, and, when he was in Paris, provided him with a quiet and well-kept home. He bore the expenses and included her mother in the arrangement; the two women were good managers and their *intérieur* must have been a relief after the disorder of Harriet's house and the spectacle of a badly reared child in violent and intemperate hands.

The first phase in the dissolution of Hector's marriage to Harriet occupies the period from the fall of 1841 to the September following, when Berlioz and Marie Recio left for Brussels. This twelvemonth had not been without important musical activity on Berlioz' part, nor without further signs of the gradual decay of the Orleanist regime.

In November 1841, possibly under the stimulus of the work he had done on Weber's piano waltz, Berlioz began to publish in the *Gazette Musicale* a series of articles on instrumentation —the first draft of the later epoch-making *Treatise.* He had given two more concerts, at one of which Artot had played a new composition of Berlioz' for violin and orchestra, *Rêverie et Caprice.* The work is unimportant save as an indication that Berlioz could with a little practice have turned his hand to "slick" money-making stuff. Written as a favor to his violinist friend, the short composition has no program or significance beyond the contrast indicated in the title. It suggests Wieniawski without being as successful as he in his genre, and here and there it also suggests the real Berlioz without sustaining that impression.

During the summer, Berlioz received permission to dedicate his *Funeral and Triumphal* symphony to the Duke of Orléans, who now and then bestowed his genuine regard upon artists and intellectuals. In October the work was played again at the Opera; the last movement, *Apothéose,* was becoming Berlioz' indestructible war horse. Meantime the Prince had been killed in a carriage accident and many hopes for the future of the regime died with him. The grief of the seventy-year-old King at his son's death was both personal and dynastic. A regency was spoken of, but popular unrest made the prospects of any orderly succession very doubtful. The July ninth elections had gone against the government, even though the franchise was limited to two-hundred thousand wealthy men, each casting his ballot on behalf of approximately fifty unrepresented adult males in the nation. If this voting aristocracy was turning more liberal, the monarchy was in danger. News from England confirmed the feeling that further reform was making headway. Feargus O'Connor agitated and produced a second People's Petition, so large that it had to be cut into portions and carried into Parliament by sixteen men. On its being refused, he called a general strike. "The sacred month" succeeded in the midlands, though it only led to his arrest in London. Two more attempts were made to assassinate Victoria. Both in England and in France, moreover, the industrial revolution was achieving social and cultural, as well as political expression. When Guizot undertook, as a sincere doctrinaire liberal, to "fight tenaciously against anarchy," he saw the middle class as "the rational mean between two absurdities, divine right and popular sovereignty," which he also called "the threat from below." He feared the proletarian agitation stirred up by Louis Blanc's widely circulated *Organisation du Travail,* Proudhon's "Property is Theft," and the less economically conscious views of hosts of republicans.

In this atmosphere, the decline of Romanticism, which is to say the settling down of artistic effervescence, was no individual phenomenon within each creative mind. Rather, it resulted from a redirection of public energy—toward railroad building, speculation, and agitation for reform, no less than toward the repression of democracy. The demand of the well-to-do for entertainment at any cost was the counterpart of volcano-sitting and stock-market nerves. The steam engine was in fact transforming mankind's sensibility by changing its responsiveness and its pace. Berlioz, who took his first train trip in these years, reports how backbreaking the new convenience proved. But it was astonishing to cover sixty-five leagues in a few hours, which enabled one to leave Leipzig, rehearse in Dresden, and return to Leipzig in time to hear Mendelssohn the same day. Whereas the Prince's runaway horses had killed one man by a relatively clean death, the dreadful Versailles railroad accident had mangled, charred, and suffocated sixty persons as undramatically as our rudimentary airplanes do today.[12]

Berlioz's compatriot and fellow-romantic Stendhal was therefore well advised to die, of natural causes, that same year—within a week of Cherubini, Berlioz' earliest official enemy. Only three people attended Beyle-Stendhal on the way to his grave, and forty years were to pass before anyone in France dreamed of taking his books seriously. In 1842, he was merely a salon wit who had died of apoplexy like the *bon vivant* that he was. Berlioz' slight contact with him in Italy had probably slipped his memory, or if present, had only reminded him of a Rossini fanatic who was too much of a littérateur to be a judge of music.

Cherubini's death was another thing. It left a vacant seat at the Institute, to which Berlioz had reasonable claim. His competitors were Adam, Auber, Onslow, and a younger man, Ambroise Thomas, who had been Lesueur's last pupil. Berlioz' name was carefully omitted from the first list presented by the musicians of the Institute to the full body, thus confirming Swift's dictum that "when a true genius appears in the world, you may know him by this sign, that the dunces are all in confederacy against him." Berlioz withdrew his name and Onslow was elected.

Berlioz had meantime written an obituary review of Cherubini's career, in which he did his former oppressor full justice. He knew what qualities to look for in the limited art of the Franco-Italian master, and he pointed them out to the public. This act of impartiality was by no means due to the hope of flattering Cherubini's colleagues at the Institute; Berlioz knew better than to think justice to the dead would flatter the survivors. He acted simply on critical principle, as he did whenever he wrote about Rossini's *Barber, William Tell* or *Comte Ory:* he hated Italian music and disliked in Rossini the cynical affectation of commercialism, but he could not refrain from praising genius. Anecdotes and bon mots were something else again, reserved for lesser occasions.

This disinterestedness carried Berlioz still farther. Cherubini had been Director of the Conservatoire and it was likely that the leader of its orchestra, Habeneck, would succeed him. This would leave the conductorship of the Opera orchestra vacant and Berlioz sought to obtain it, even though its acceptance would disbar him from having any work performed at the official theater. As early as October 1841, he had written to Ferrand, "I was and still am in line for Habeneck's post at the Opera. It would be a musical dictatorship of which I should hope to make the most in the interest of art." In other words, he would use his influence to raise the level of musical performance through respect for the written note, since as mere conductor he could neither choose what to perform nor submit works of his own composition. The advantages to him would be the salary and the good will of the players. We can again infer from this voluntary choice of Berlioz' that the Scribe opera did not tempt his musical daemon to manifest itself. The fragments that he composed make us glad that the libretto did not blossom. How could it? It was neither Virgil nor Goethe nor Shakespeare, and Berlioz had not included it among those flashing intentions of his thirtieth year.

The orchestra post was not reassigned. Auber was chosen head of the Conservatoire and Habeneck stayed where he was. Berlioz therefore pursued his plan to visit Germany and give concerts. It was an ideal time for him to leave Paris where journalism, domestic life, and public apathy were alike inimical to art. On this first trip, between mid-September 1842 and the end of May 1843, Berlioz visited Brussels twice, then Frankfort-on-Main, Hechingen, Carlsruhe, Stuttgart, Weimar, Leipzig, Dresden, Brunswick, Hamburg, Berlin, Hanover, and Darmstadt. In eight months he gave nineteen concerts. He was not able to arrange performances at all the places he visited, but everywhere he established friendly relations and studied the local resources of musical talent. Long before, Weber had thought of writing a guidebook for orchestra conductors who had to travel in Germany, but the work was never finished and Berlioz had to develop from scratch the technique of the musical conquistador. With stretches of residence in Paris and London, this was to be his life for twenty-five years: his mission did not end until within two years of his death. If in the twelve years since the *Symphonie Fantastique* he had, as d'Ortigue wrote, accomplished a musical revolution in France, he was now, like a second Napoleon, carrying it to the four corners of Europe.

CHAPTER 14

THE CONDUCTOR-COMPOSER

As far as I know, all writers repeat his observations on orchestral technique. They do not always acknowledge the author . . . But Berlioz' subtlety of construction is beyond the cerebral powers of authors of pedagogical treatises.—VAN DIEREN in 1935

Berlioz' first trip to Germany was also an opportunity for renewing many old friendships. Companions of youthful days were now established men nearing middle life. Ferdinand Hiller—Camille Moke's former admirer—was musical director in Frankfort. Schloesser, Berlioz' classmate at the Conservatoire, held a post at Darmstadt. At Leipzig, besides Robert Schumann whom he had never met but who had publicly invited him six years before, there was Mendelssohn occupying a well-entrenched position. Berlioz' discreet letter of inquiry from Weimar drew from his friend of Roman days a cordial invitation. Berlioz replied on January 26, 1843:

You are wonderfully good and kind, as I was sure you would be. Luck is on my side these days: the concert went well and this morning I received your letter. . . . Yes, indeed, I should very much like to give concerts in Leipzig. If it does not depend on someone's special permission, granted as a favor, I should like to give two, since I see that expenses are moderate. . . . Though it irks me, I shall have to begin with my old stuff, my latest scores being still in Frankfort, whence they are being forwarded. So please thank the directors [of the *Gewandhaus*] and tell them I shall be happy to present on the 22nd the Finale for three choruses from my *Romeo and Juliet* symphony. But they must be warned that the part of Friar Laurence requires a first-rate bass.

This letter illustrates Berlioz' problems and procedure. From one center he prepared the concert for the next by arranging for a personal invitation and, if possible, securing the co-operation of a friend. From Stuttgart he had written to Meyerbeer at Berlin, and to an old Conservatoire man, Chelard, who directed the Weimar "chapel"; and from Weimar to Karl Lipinski, concertmaster at Dresden, where Wagner, just turned thirty, had become court conductor. At Stuttgart, where he had no acquaintance and where no one spoke French, he (who knew no German) managed pretty well by speaking with Dr. Schilling in Latin.[1] Everywhere he was known through his *feuilletons* which for three years had been reproduced in German, chiefly in Schumann's *Neue Zeitschrift für Musik.*

The financial arrangements varied. Berlioz bore the cost of transporting himself and his music, as well as of any extras on the spot—he usually had to import at his expense one or two instrumentists such as the harp and English horn. He supervised the rehearsals and, if the local rules allowed it, conducted. In return he received half, or sometimes less, of the net profits. This was no lavish compensation, for the halls were generally small, the price of admission low,[2] and his own outlay considerable. He had with him "500 pounds of music," which the railroads in their infant weakness were unwilling to carry with any guarantee of delivery. So the parts and full scores had to go by mail coach at exorbitant rates. Traveling and living in hotels was also costly, especially for a man of reputation who could not scrimp too obviously. As keeper of the purse, Marie was of great help, for she had habits of economy which she could exercise on Berlioz' behalf with complete propriety. He was thus able to send a good part of his earnings to his wife and child, which supplemented the royalties from the *Freischütz* that he had made over to them.

From the start of his tour, Berlioz' art and person made him many new friends. At Brussels, the guitar virtuoso and music critic Zani de Ferranti became an enthusiastic advocate; at Hechingen the Prince took part in a performance specially arranged by Berlioz for a very small ensemble; the King of Württemberg also proved very gracious; at Dresden, Baron von Lüttichau, superintendent of theaters for the Saxon King, seconded Berlioz' efforts with great courtesy; at Brunswick, he made a lifelong friend of the composer and critic Robert Griepenkerl; in Berlin, Alexander von Humboldt introduced him to the King of Prussia. In turn, Berlioz introduced the harpist Parish-Alvars to Chelard, and many other instrumentists and singers to officials who needed their services or might help them. It was a musical round, and Berlioz had to charge his memory with the names, capacities, and concerns of dozens of artists in order to act efficiently in his new role of impresario for himself and musical missionary at large.

In setting out, Berlioz had been under no illusion about the difficulties ahead. Although a few years before Liszt had written him an open letter, saying, "Germany is the country of Symphonies; it is therefore yours," Berlioz knew better than to take music for a universal language. His very devotion to certain masters implied that there was not one Music but many musics. And he knew from Liszt and others that in Germany too, the Italian sort prevailed. His own was neither Italian nor German and he was also burdened with a mission implying a set purpose. This purpose was, as a composer, to develop dramatic music on "Shakespearean" lines, and as theorist to defend the German or symphonic conception of the genre against the Italian; in other words, Gluck, Mozart, Beethoven, and Weber as against Pacini, Vaccai, Donizetti, Bellini, and the lesser works of Rossini.

This was no mere partisanship. Berlioz' conviction rested on three postulates: 1. That modern music was a new and independent art. 2. That music possessed intrinsic significance, which he called "expressiveness." 3. That music could not be judged by pre-established scholastic rules, but only a posteriori, through experience, by ear—in a word, pragmatically. Against the upholders of routine and convention he preached expressiveness and psychological or dramatic truth; and against the theorists who wanted to subordinate music to stage effects or poetry he preached the formal unity of musical structures and the sensuous pleasure they can give apart from expressiveness. The belief that the *genre instrumental expressif* was the youngest birth of the human spirit, just come to maturity, Berlioz derived from direct observation and creative fiat. His touring of Europe was meant to teach his ideas through his works by training musicians to play them and hear them.

The most rewarding moments of this first trip were the concert and visit at Weimar; the meetings with Mendelssohn and Schumann at Leipzig; the lively discussions with Lipinski and

Wagner at Dresden; the enthusiastic ovation at Brunswick. Elsewhere the response to Berlioz' music varied from respect to hatred, just as the performances varied from poor to perfect. Marie's desire to sing did not make for success, but her pretensions were soon reduced to one song, "Absence," which Berlioz orchestrated for her. It was at Weimar that he shook her off for a time, before this compromise arrangement had been reached; and it was there that he enjoyed the pleasure of a successful concert combined with the free run of a town whose artistic associations were, to him, particularly vivid.

The memories of Goethe and Schiller and Mme. de Staël, the smiling aspect of the countryside, the neat walks in town and outside, and at night the mild moonlit sky, enchanted him. The fever and sore throat that had plagued him at Frankfort disappeared. Invariably the atmosphere of intellect and art proved a cure for ailments of nervous origin. The one flaw in his enjoyment of the ducal city was his discovery of Schiller's narrow dwelling: "Can it be that these two small windows light the garret where . . . the great singer of every noble feeling wrote *Don Carlos, Mary Stuart, The Robbers,* and *Wallenstein?* Is it here that he lived like a poor scholar! Ah! Goethe ought never to have allowed it. He, a rich man and minister of state, might surely have softened the lot of his poet friend—or was this illustrious friendship not genuine? I fear it was genuine chiefly on Schiller's side . . . Ah, Schiller, you deserved a less human friend." [3]

At Leipzig, Mendelssohn and Berlioz greeted each other like old companions, long separated, who both shy away at first expecting a rebuff. But nothing of the sort ensued; on the contrary their earlier friendship was cemented for life. Mendelssohn still sincerely disliked Berlioz' music and Berlioz knew it. Yet Mendelssohn helped to rehearse and produce it, and Berlioz no less sincerely admired and praised his friend's works till his death and after. Curiously, it was Berlioz' orchestration that Mendelssohn could not stomach: "It is so entirely slovenly—scrubbed up anyhow—that one has to wash one's hands after reading one of his scores." [4] The melodies he rather liked, and most of all he liked Berlioz as a man, knowing after renewed contact what qualities of mind and heart lay behind the distant or ironic exterior: "It grieves me [that Berlioz should compose as he does] because Berlioz is intelligent, cool, and sensible in his judgment, and always thoughtful." Mendelssohn helped him, says Berlioz, "like a brother

. . . His patience was indefatigable." They exchanged batons, and Berlioz, remembering his boyhood admiration of James Fenimore Cooper, wrote a gift card comparing the batons to tomahawks and themselves to Indian chiefs.

Close to Mendelssohn was Schumann—who had praised and played Berlioz' earliest works—and with him Clara, his pianist-wife, whom Berlioz had met at the Bertins' house in Paris. Schumann was already plagued by the depression which marked his latter years and hence exceedingly taciturn, but he let drop a word which deeply touched his visitor: "The Offertory [of the *Requiem*] surpasses everything." At the concert, the *Symphonie Fantastique* was applauded, together with *Rêverie et Caprice,* played by the virtuoso concertmaster Ferdinand David; but the public as a whole was rather of Mendelssohn's opinion. Despite Schumann's discreet but single-minded propaganda, *die Tante* (as musical Leipzig was familiarly called) found Berlioz a dangerous revolutionary.[5]

Why, asked the critics, did he not write harmonies like everybody else? Why did he use instruments not generally found in the classical masters—harp, ophicleide, English horn? The summing up, though adverse, was perceptive: "Berlioz refuses to please us; he wants to be 'characteristic' . . . he seeks to liberate music, tolerating neither shackles nor boundaries. His fancy alone he regards as law. . . . After the Witches' Sabbath of the *Symphonie Fantastique,* Weber's 'Den of Wolves' is a lullaby." Mendelssohn's friend Moscheles was similarly stung: "His barbarous and wicked counterpoint seems to want to show that ours is pedantic."

At Dresden, hallowed for him by the memories of Weber's conductorship, Berlioz heard Wagner direct *The Flying Dutchman.* Although the score did not move him deeply, and he is said to have found the instrumentation excessive, Berlioz saw as soon as anyone else that Wagner was an artist worthy of special attention. He admired the "uncommon energy and precision" with which Wagner conducted. But the two men seem to have had few opportunities to converse. Baron von Lüttichau—"a tall thin man with a hard, dry face" (Wagner's description)—monopolized whatever time was not taken up with rehearsing. In the brief intervals of relaxation Berlioz chatted with Karl Lipinski who, like Lobe at Leipzig, was already a stout disciple. Lipinski suspected Wagner of obstructing Berlioz' efforts, but the two concerts were none the less successful, well attended, and financially profitable. The performers were so enthusiastic that on the day of departure they serenaded the composer under his windows.

After a second turn in Leipzig, a racking ten-hour trip in an open coupé brought Berlioz by March 1st to Brunswick, where he was greeted by his old friends, the four brothers of the Müller quartet, and where the orchestra proved to be *"excellentissime."* At the first trial of the Queen Mab scherzo, however, the players broke down in confusion. This gives us a good idea of the average technical ability in an unusually good orchestra, or rather, it confirms Wagner's estimate of four years before when he first heard Berlioz conduct in Paris: the new music was composed for, and had to be played by, virtuosos. The conception of the orchestra was being transformed, and the thing itself reshaped into a new instrument.

After fatiguing rehearsals, the conductor-composer had his reward. The audience stood up and cheered and the players invited their leader to a banquet of one hundred and fifty covers. There were speeches, toasts, reiterated invitations, and what is more, the critic Griepenkerl wrote a pamphlet expounding Berlioz.[6] "I confess," wrote the composer to Heine, "that these demonstrations made me very happy." Hamburg gave him equal satisfaction. As Berlioz wrote to his father after the first of these triumphs, "I have been wanting to write to you for quite a long time. I do not know what instinct made me wait until I had a really great success—greater than the rest—before telling you anything. I do not think I shall ever have another like this recent one. The performance, first of all, was marvelous. . . . Then they put crowns of laurel on my score, on the stage. . . ."

In Berlin, the composer had his first experience of the disagreement-in-reverse which may occur between public opinion and the critics' judgment: the audience cheered and the papers damned. Meyerbeer—Spontini's successor in the post of royal music director—was officiously present, helping Berlioz and keeping up the instructive relations he had initiated in 1829. Frederick William IV, King of Prussia, came to the concert, heard *Romeo and Juliet,* and was charmed. He came a second time, all the way from Potsdam, and finally gave a small party in Berlioz' honor—only a dozen guests or so; but after a space the curtains at one end of the apartment flew open and three hundred musicians under Wieprecht, the bandmaster, played the *Francs-Juges* overture.

It was now late May, 1843. Home again after two more concerts, Berlioz' first care was to see Harriet and his son. The meeting must have been painful, and to live with them again disheartening, for he wrote to Adèle: "Your children are, I hope, in good health. Harriet often speaks to me of your quiet and happy household. She envies you. Louis has grown up . . . and will write you a letter. Harriet is beginning to grieve again because I have had another offer from the London Philharmonic to conduct a concert . . . But the trip is not yet decided upon; they have not replied to the musical and financial stipulations I made. We both send your husband greetings, and kisses for your little daughters, and we kiss you *into the bargain* . . ."

While London was pending, Berlioz wrote to Ricordi, the music publisher at Milan, where he remembered hearing the fine orchestra of La Scala. The possibility of a concert there was tempting, but nothing came of the suggestion. Meantime there was enough to do in Paris. The score of the *Funeral and Triumphal* symphony was being published and Thalberg wanted to make a free piano transcription of the Apotheosis, which required complicated adjustments between two publishers. As for operatic plans, the libretto of the *Nonne Sanglante* still hung fire. Berlioz had made but little progress with the first act. If his voyaging in new lands had stirred him up spiritually, as was probable, the result was not immediately apparent, nor was it likely that the impressions gathered from new aspects of nature and fresh musical emotions would suit Scribe's banalities. Rather, the German countryside had awakened recollections of his early fondness for Goethe's *Faust*.

Of more immediate importance was the forthcoming publication of Berlioz' *Treatise upon Modern Instrumentation and Orchestration,* which was a revision and expansion of the series of articles published since 1842 in the *Gazette Musicale*. For the version in book form, Berlioz had illustrated his chapters with musical quotations from the masters and himself. As the best and most objective proof of his "science," the volume must now be launched throughout Europe. Already the previous year, an unauthorized German translator had brought out a version of the essays, and with his slim collection had prepared an audience for the complete *Treatise*.

It proved to be an immediate and lasting success. Translated into several languages and re-edited in small details down to the present, it has remained standard. There is hardly a composer since 1844 who has not at some time or other looked into the book. Many have taught themselves from it, and we know from spontaneous testimony that it has served as the inspiring guide of many a distinguished beginner—Mahler, Delius, Elgar, Moussorgsky, Busoni, Vincent d'Indy, and Debussy are among those who have told us so. In its day, besides giving instruction in a new medium it "came as an awakening and a message which no one in the world of music could afford to disregard."

But at that time it brought the author little or no material returns. Berlioz had to resume his journalistic duties—his "semi-critiques," as he called them; for residing as he did in Paris he could scarcely say all he felt about his colleagues. Yet in the course of supplying the market these colleagues necessarily submitted their scores to Berlioz' judgment, just as if the works had not been commercial products—semi-works of art. Berlioz' first *feuilletons* on returning from abroad consisted of letters from Germany—reports and anecdotes on his recent trip, which enabled him to thank his recent hosts, and which formed the core of a volume of musical travels to be published the following spring. Destined for the *Débats,* these letters detailed the conditions under which the art of music was carried on in the middle of the nineteenth century, and their substance was preserved for inclusion in the later *Memoirs.*

For the *Gazette,* Berlioz combined not fact but fiction with musical ideas long pondered and produced a notable document: the serialized novelette called *Euphonia,* in which he set forth the ideal conditions for producing the great works since Gluck and Beethoven. The imagined Euphonia was a city organized for music the way Paris or London were not even organized for making boots. Besides anticipations of Dalcroze eurhythmics and modern conservatory teaching, Berlioz' plan is the blue-print of Bayreuth.

Pressing practical affairs also occupied him. Through his influence, Marie Recio had been engaged at the Opéra-Comique. She again failed to attract notice, which marked the end of her musical career. Berlioz henceforth supported her and her mother, relying on the care and affection she gave him as well as the quiet which he could no longer expect at home. Nevertheless he was frequently to be found at that home, with his old unhappy love and their son.

During his absence in Germany, moreover, a project he had discussed with his friend Baron Taylor had taken shape. Under the title of Association of Musical Artists, a group of Paris musicians had agreed to band together for mutual aid and the furtherance of modern music.[7] Berlioz was a charter member. Shortly the Association decided to sponsor symphonic concerts, with a view to relieving the individual composer of just those risks that Berlioz had so long shouldered alone. By September 1843 a festival was planned which Berlioz was to direct in December. In between, a concert of his own at the Conservatoire earned him a rousing ovation and a few hundred francs. The program included—among more familiar pieces—a trio from *Benvenuto Cellini,* the *Rêverie et Caprice* for violin (played by Alard), and the great song "Absence." The Apotheosis from the fourth symphony brought the audience to its feet. The press for once was short of jokes. Berlioz' single-handed efforts were termed "a prodigy of human will power," and it was noted that the audience listened ". . . with religious silence" between its salvos of applause.

Habeneck of the Opera was annoyed by Berlioz' success as a conductor. He managed to prevent the concert of the Association from taking place. Despite all his hard-won success, Berlioz' position was as precarious as ever. As a free lance he was a menace to others and hence to himself; for if one of his enterprises failed, he must redouble his efforts in the face of lost prestige; and if it succeeded, it only closed the ranks of the placemen against him. Aptly reflecting on "our culture and our form of government, which victimize the artist in proportion as he remains an artist," [8] Berlioz drew out his score of *Benvenuto* and, reliving its vigorous inspiration, was inspired to compose on two of its themes a new overture, the now well-known *Roman Carnival.*

Worked up symphonically, this felicitous by-product occupies in the complete *Benvenuto* the place that Beethoven's *Leonore* overture does in *Fidelio.* Each sufficiently anticipates elements of the music drama so that it seems a pity to play it ahead of the second act. Yet the music so clearly belongs to the larger work that its separate performance is a tantalizing hors d'oeuvre. Berlioz played his *Roman Carnival* (separately of course) at his first concert of February, 1844, and the new work was encored. The overture soon became a general favorite and finally a concert "war horse." Being simple in its contrast of love song and dance, it was found "melodic," it was compared to Schubert, and it even caused a few of Berlioz' fanatical enemies some embarrassment. "What is the fascinating overture you have been playing?" the conductor Seghers was once asked. "That was the *Roman Carnival* by Berlioz." "Well! I must say—" "You're right," broke in one of Berlioz' friends, "I agree he ought to be ashamed to go against an honest man's prejudices in that way."

On the same program Berlioz, still fresh from Goethe's Weimar, had announced the hitherto unperformed Gretchen song from his *Eight Scenes* of 1828. It again remained unperformed because the singer was ill, but his revived interest in the score was to last and to bear fruit. At the moment, the chief novelties on the program were two songs from the *Irish Melodies* of his youth. He had revised them, and one, the *Chant Sacré,* dating back still further, to his second prize cantata, was to go through yet another transformation which happens to mark a date in the history of instrumentation.

Three years before, Adolphe Sax, a young musician with a scientific turn of mind, had come to Paris from Brussels with thirty francs in his pocket. His plan was to develop systematically the wind choir of the orchestra, and he needed the support of eminent performers and composers to obtain the necessary financial backing. One interview sufficed to convince Berlioz, who gave him a public endorsement in the *Débats.* Meyerbeer, Rossini, and Kastner followed suit with testimonials such that all other instrument makers leagued themselves against Sax. When he developed an entirely new instrument, later named saxophone, his rivals took steps to oppose the patent on the ground that it was not new. He defied them to produce its like and once again enlisted Berlioz' support. The composer could write stingingly and from experience about such conspiracies. Would he also score a work for the new reed instrument and the other wind improved by Sax? Berlioz fell in with the idea of a "propaganda concert." His old "Prayer" from *Herminie* which had become a six-part chorus, he now arranged for two clarinets (soprano and bass), two bugles (large and small), a small trumpet, and a saxophone.[9] The new version was only a qualified success, largely because Sax's new instrument was still imperfect—the saxophone "leaked"—and the inventor-performer forgot the fingering. Berlioz' little work was not repeated, though Sax and his friends gratefully serenaded the composer at home with the same instruments, much improved, later in the year.

During the spring and summer of 1844 five more concerts either featured Berlioz' music or consisted entirely of his works. The *Roman Carnival* and the Weber-Berlioz *Invitation to the Dance* had, together with the Sax venture, renewed the public's interest in the composer. A helpful catchword began to pass current: Berlioz was the foremost *instrumental* composer of the day (*i.e.,* don't, my dear, expect coloratura effects or wonders at the keyboard). Still, the tyranny of the piano was now unshakable and at one of these concerts the *Roman Carnival,* whose structure and atmosphere are wholly orchestral, was rendered to thunderous applause by eight hands on two pianos —the forty fingers being those of Pixis (the arranger), Heller, Hallé, and Liszt.

Stephen Heller, who also composed, could well wonder "why do we not hear Berlioz played by the Conservatoire [that is, by the Concert Society]. He is the greatest French composer. Must he first make up his mind to sleep the long sleep? Once dead, he will live for a long time. The cry of 'Berlioz is dead' will make thousands shout: 'Long live Berlioz!' "

In May the *Voyage Musical*—part autobiography, part music criticism—went to press with a dedication to his royal highness the Duc de Montpensier. The two handsome volumes, priced at fifteen francs, appeared in August and sold very well. In four years they were out of print, and whether he knew it or not, Berlioz had given status to a new literary genre—that which his great forerunner Weber had not lived to establish firmly and which his great follower Wagner would amplify still further. Opposite the title page of the *Voyage Musical* was a lithograph of the author as conductor—his first portrait, excluding caricatures, since Signol had painted him at the Villa Medici. A little later at Vienna, Prinzhofer drew a finer portrait in a similar pose. It shows Berlioz as he was in the full strength of maturity, at the height of his second period of fighting success. This is the way he looked and remained to the thousands of European musicians who played or spoke with him during the first campaign of 1843-1855, and who did not see him in the later one, as an old man.

Holding his public position as orchestral virtuoso by main strength of composing, conducting, and organizing, Berlioz cast about, in the spring of 1844, for his next occasion. That summer the first great exhibition of industrial products was to be held in Paris. Always interested in science and technology, Berlioz saw no reason why the show should not close to the accompaniment of music. He and the violinist Strauss (the master of the dance in Paris as his unrelated namesake was in

Vienna) petitioned the Ministry for the right to present a double program—a serious celebration in the afternoon, a program of dance music in the evening.

The idea being new and perhaps profitable, it raised enormous opposition. Everyone expressed a different fear. The police commissioner thought that the mob might storm the Tuileries. Why the mob, if so minded, could not do it without music was not explained. Again, though Berlioz did not intend to fill the afternoon concert with his own works, he could not play every living composer's hymn or march. Hence the omitted musicians formed a cabal, under the natural leadership of Habeneck.

Berlioz was busy unknotting every intrigue when Strauss fell ill and the whole burden of organization dropped on his partner's shoulders—from overseeing the printing of handbills and filling out requests for constables and firemen, to gathering from all over France and rehearsing in Paris the twelve hundred singers and players who would participate. In spite of the careful drilling of this small army, the dress rehearsal on July 31 was a near-fiasco: in the vast hall of machines, the carpentering of stands and the dismantling of steam engines made music virtually inaudible. At last, leading seven subconductors, each with his battalion, Berlioz created order and music out of noise and disarray. That night the stands had to be altered under his direction because the chorus blocked the orchestra. A preliminary survey of ticket sales was wholly disheartening.

But the next day the people rushed in a whole hour before the concert, and from beginning to end applauded the music. Berlioz himself had composed a short *Hymne à la France* which, as he said on another occasion, "not having been done with the aid of time would not be preserved by it." Still, his magic has touched the work at more than one point, in the rhythm especially, and in the breath-taking economy of the orchestration.

The hall being lined with curtains, flags, and other decorations, the volume of sound pouring down on the audience was by no means a Niagara, on the contrary. The preceptor to the King's sons, Cuvillier-Fleury, who was also a colleague of Berlioz at the *Débats,* gave a firsthand account to the Duc d'Aumale immediately after the event: "No spot could have been more badly adapted to the purpose, for the hall is entirely lacking in the resonance necessary to favor Berlioz' attempt, which was patterned after that of the German musical societies. But where else could he put his 1200 performers? He would not give up a single contrabass—so everyone rushed to his aid when he called. The crowd was a brilliant one. Your young brother, the Duc de Montpensier, was in a box to which I had the honor of being invited, and he was seen—to everyone's satisfaction—applauding with all his might the refrain of the chorus from [Halévy's] *Charles VI,* 'Never will the English rule!' The execution was truly formidable because the entire audience joined in." This enthusiasm caused a governmental tremor. Louis Philippe was at the moment on good terms with England, which was of course sufficient reason for the public's singing defiance. Berlioz was haled before the Prefect of Police, who charged him with having provoked the demonstration. This was easily refuted, since the program had been posted and approved in advance. In spite of the police rebuke, the Duc de Montpensier sent Berlioz a congratulatory letter and a handsome piece of china.

As might have been expected, Berlioz was nearly dead. During the intermission he was wet to the skin, his teeth were chattering, and his face was unrecognizable. For a moment his alarmed friends among the orchestra did not think it safe to let him go on. They sent for fresh clothing and set up an improvised screen of harps with their slip covers, behind which Berlioz mopped himself, changed, and caught his breath. Marie, who was singing in the chorus, saw him safely home. The reaction came less than three weeks later, in the form of a fever diagnosed as possibly typhoidal. His old teacher, friend, and physician Amussat bled him and ordered him out of Paris for a complete rest. Berlioz went to Nice.

It was at Nice that nearly fifteen years before he had spent the twenty happiest days of his life, after Camille's treachery and the mad attempt to commit suicide. He found again the "sublime sea" and serene skies of his "return to life." He found the old tower up in the rocks, and soon, under the spell of nature and memory, he began to compose the overture which he had sketched at the same time as the *King Lear* and *Rob Roy*. But though the mood was propitious and the will and musical daemon in working order, the tired body put obstacles in the way. The overture was finished and christened, for association's sake, *Tour de Nice,* but at a first hearing in Paris the next year, Berlioz put it aside for recasting—the later

Corsair overture. A new melody also came to him, *La belle Isabeau,* and found more favor in his eyes, since he published it at the first opportunity.

He came back to Paris restored and found that an entertainment king by the name of Franconi wanted him to direct a festival at his establishment, the *Cirque Olympique.* This time, at least, Berlioz would not have to do his own managerial chores. Just then the mind of musical Paris was being stirred by the revelation of a new musician, Félicien David,[10] who for ten years had been composing unplayed and unknown. Now at a concert in the Conservatoire, for which David had had to borrow twelve hundred francs like Berlioz in 1825, he displayed a talent for atmospheric pieces of oriental coloring which infatuated the public. As a disciple of Saint-Simon, the doctrinaire socialist who advocated a Christian technocracy, David wore clothes of a utopian light blue, and with hair falling to the shoulders paraded on the boulevard with a gay band of fellow-believers who sang his party hymns. They came to the concert, and celebrated on the streets afterwards to such effect that the citizens who had stayed at home were sure it was a new revolution.

It was not even a revolution in music. David's most famous piece was a "Caravan Procession" from an oriental suite, *Le Désert,* which suggests rather too much the Pilgrims' March from *Harold in Italy.* The form of David's *Symphonic Ode* was likewise derived from Berlioz' early essays at a dramatic symphony. But this did not keep Berlioz from seeking out David, asking him for works to put on his programs, and giving him a cordial and detailed boost in the *Débats.*

Meanwhile rehearsals for the Franconi festival were begun, but not satisfactorily from a musical point of view because the oval bowl made sound reverberate unpleasantly. The four scheduled concerts took place once a month from January to April 1845. At the first, despite bad acoustics and a ragged performance, the *Tuba mirum* of the *Requiem* and the *Hymne à la France* came through. This was music, said one critic, "fitted to electrify the masses." It was then that Berlioz heard his *Tour de Nice* overture and decided to lay it aside.

The second concert was given over to David and the pianist Leopold von Mayer, who performed a new "Moroccan March" of his own composition. At the third concert, in March, Berlioz introduced Glinka to the Paris public by playing excerpts from *A Life for the Czar* and *Russlan and Ludmilla.*

The two composers had met when both were still students in Italy and had found their views of music highly congenial. Both were more or less consciously founding new schools of dramatic music upon a solid background of national traditions, and it was no accident that their paths should cross again in 1844, nor that later their musical tendencies should merge in a common influence upon the Russian Five. In a long article in the *Débats,* Berlioz followed up his presentation of the music with criticism and biography, and Glinka, whose main object in coming to Paris had been to study Berlioz at close range, declared himself more than rewarded. He heard the music, read Berlioz' new works in manuscript, and felt that his own talents had been at once consecrated and fertilized during the encounter.

The fourth and last concert in April was chiefly devoted to Berlioz' own works—those that he felt were least known and undeservedly overlooked because of their mild and subtle coloring—his Impressionist movements, so to speak, such as the Offertory of the *Requiem* and the Queen Mab scherzo. His performers were now playing at the top of their form, and he was musically well satisfied, but public support was dwindling as other novelties drew the crowd away from Franconi's *Cirque.* The impresario lost money and the decline unfortunately coincided with the finest rendering of Berlioz' finest work.

With hardly time to catch his breath, but only to be bled again, Berlioz left for Marseille where his friend the cellist Lecourt was eager to have him conduct. The local talent, especially the singers, were worse than inadequate, yet Berlioz managed to inspire them with some rudiments of musicianship by June 19. Like many a Berlioz *première* before an unprepared audience, the concert left everyone cold. A second performance on the twenty-fifth went better, musically and financially.

On the way back to Paris, Berlioz stopped at Lyon where George Hainl—soon to be a devoted friend—directed the Grand Theatre. To the regular orchestra, Berlioz added amateur singers and other instrumentists bringing the total to two hundred. Among these, he had included his old teacher Dorant, met by chance on the streets of Lyon. He was the versatile player of several instruments who had taught Hector the guitar at La Côte and helped him with his first harmonizations. In presenting him to the orchestra as a first violin,

Berlioz took occasion to express his affectionate old memories in a characteristic little speech: "Gentlemen, I have the honor of presenting to you a very able teacher from Vienne, M. Dorant. He has in our midst a grateful pupil—myself. You may shortly be thinking that his pupil is no great credit to him, but I beg you to welcome him as if you thought otherwise, for this is in any case what he himself deserves."

The public of Lyon was as slow as that of Marseille to like anything but the sure-fire pieces. It responded not at all to the Pilgrims' March, but rose to the March of the *Fantastique*. The *Apothéose of the Funeral Symphony*—to us the least interesting of movements when detached—was found sublime. A second concert, after the orchestra had learned a little more and had serenaded their trainer, caused greater pleasure and even stirred the local gentry to entertain their fellow countryman.

By July 25, Berlioz had just one week to turn around in: back to Paris to write a few columns overdue by reason of his absence, to thank by letter all his friends, hosts, and helpers in the provinces; then off again for the great musical event he had been dreaming of: the inauguration of Beethoven's statue at Bonn.

CHAPTER 15

FAUST AND PHILOSOPHY

This word "damnation" terrifies not him.—MARLOWE'S Dr. Faustus, about himself

In the course of his dozen visits to the still disunified "Germanies," a land still full of artistic internationalists, Berlioz made many friends but even more important, he soon drew from the cultural contact the inspiration that produced one of his most resplendent scores, the *Damnation of Faust* of 1846.

The fourteen months that saw its completion began most appropriately with Berlioz' departure for Bonn, on August 1, 1845. Beethoven's statue was to be dedicated in this, his native town, after the usual incredible obstacles had been overcome by Liszt,[1] and the unveiling on the fourteenth was to be preceded by numerous musical events including Liszt's commemorative cantata.

Berlioz' account of the proceedings in the *Evenings With the Orchestra* gives us an excellent insight into the musical manners of the period. Berlioz had had nothing to do with the arrangements of the fete, beyond contributing twenty francs toward the statue and conducting without fee Liszt's money-raising concerts. Liszt and Liszt alone was "the soul of the festivities" and the "delegate from the wide world." But even Liszt's money and zeal had not been enough to galvanize Europe or the Bonn Committee. Though Frederick William of Prussia attended, with Queen Victoria and her Consort as his guests, and though musical celebrities from England, France, Russia, and Central Europe came to demonstrate their faith,

Beethoven's eminence was far from an established fact. Italy sent no representatives, neither did the Paris Conservatoire. In fact, all the French musicians present were there unofficially. The Conservatoire had refused to give a concert for the benefit of the collection when Liszt petitioned for it. And there were other notable absentees: Wagner, Glinka, Mendelssohn, Schumann, Marschner, to say nothing of the crowd of French and Italian opera makers.

The local Committee, it is only fair to say, had issued its invitations somewhat casually and had made no provision whatever for the reception of any but titled guests. To get to hear the Mass in C in the cathedral and avoid being crushed to death by the Bonn citizenry, Berlioz had to slip in through the artists' entrance; and later, for the unveiling of the statue, to vault a fence. "Taking one thing with another, the invitation I received from the Committee in charge of the festivities did not actually prevent me from witnessing them." Still worse, the Committee had neglected to call on the best available performers, and the orchestra purposing to honor Beethoven with his own music was needlessly inadequate. "To do the right thing would have been not only possible but very easy," adds Berlioz, "But it would have meant overcoming narrow nationalistic ideas, which in circumstances of this kind can only have disastrous results, and which are besides infinitely ridiculous to all sensible people." [2]

Nor did prejudice affect only nations. "It will be asked how and why there could be any ill-will against Liszt . . . to whom the credit must go for initiating and carrying out whatever has been successful at Bonn . . . It is chiefly this deserved credit . . . which gave offense. Some had a grudge against him because of his extraordinary talent and success; others because he is witty, and yet others because he is generous, because he has written too fine a cantata, because the others' compositions . . . were unsuccessful, . . . because he speaks French too well and knows German too thoroughly, because he has too many friends, and doubtless because he has not enough enemies. . . ."

As is usual in celebrations, some unfamiliar works of Beethoven were played, and some well-known works played for the first time as written. *Ad hoc* songs and hymns by venturesome living composers filled the subsequent programs. From lack of foresight, one of these outdoor cantatas remained inaudible. The final program, reorganized by royal order, joined to an overture and songs by Beethoven the Weber piano concerto. This was played by Madame Pleyel, Berlioz' onetime fiancée, whom he praised in his review. Then came virtuoso pieces—mostly variations on operatic airs—finally a small musicale was given at Bruhl by the King of Prussia, to which Berlioz was invited. There he heard Jenny Lind for the first time. "Her voice, of an incisive metallic timbre, great power, and incredible flexibility lends itself equally to mezzo-voce effects, to impassioned expressiveness, and to the most delicate embellishments." At the same concert, Berlioz' favorite artist and good friend, Pauline Garcia Viardot, sang three pieces "exquisitely," and Liszt and Meyerbeer played. Midnight struck and Berlioz returned to Bonn by railway "dead drunk with harmony, wearied with admiring, feeling an irresistible need of silence and calm." He found lodgings in a cottage at nearby Königswinter, where he collected his thoughts and wrote his article. In the course of its skillful combination of reportage, anecdote, philosophizing, and music criticism, he found a place for drawing the artist's moral, obvious and self-interested, but eternally right and needful:

"It is very fine to glorify in this fashion the demigods who are no more. . . . But it comes too late. This Beethoven in bronze is unaware of all this homage, and it is sad to think that the living Beethoven, whose memory is thus honored, might not have obtained from his native town in the days of suffering and destitution which were so numerous during his troubled life the ten-thousandth part of the sum lavished upon him after his death."

Back in Paris after this spiritual bath, Berlioz found nothing to keep him on that exalted plane but his own thoughts. The Opera "is in a state of madness, beastliness, and feeble-mindedness to the very tip of its long ears." Scribe's verses and plot reminded him of their destination. Berlioz dropped them where he had left them and took up instead a double project—to revise and enlarge his "Eight Scenes" into a complete dramatic work based on Goethe's *Faust* and to pursue his musical mission by "invading" Austria. Early October 1845 found his plans laid for leaving later that month. Before setting out he had tedious business to attend to: suing a delinquent vicomte who owed him five hundred francs on a bill of exchange, and turning out some pieces for harmonium which had been commissioned by his friend, the organ manufacturer Alexandre.

The three pieces add nothing to Berlioz' stature, though one of them again exemplifies a characteristic mood and technique in the solemn religious fugato of the "Hymn for the Elevation of the Host."

On the way to Vienna, Berlioz had to stop at Nancy, being ill. He soon recovered, though he and Marie missed the steamer at Regensburg and had to go by post chaise. They arrived in Beethoven's second home town on November 2, 1845. Cordially received on the strength of his earlier German reputation, Berlioz was immediately in the musical swim. A concert with which he had nothing to do, but to which he was urged to go, showed him what a thousand Viennese amateurs (four hundred instrumentists) could do. To his surprise they played with extraordinary "verve and precision" the *Magic Flute* overture—"that wonderful work, of which the motion is so fleet and the texture so tightly and delicately woven."

His own rehearsals were a delight, only topped by the knowledge that he was in the Theater an der Wien whose boards Beethoven once trod. Moreover, musical Vienna was agog at the recent discovery of Gluck's place of burial. Discovery implied forgetfulness and Berlioz could not refrain from exclaiming, "Viennese! you are almost worthy of inhabiting Paris!" But they had not forgotten how to be lively at concerts. At Berlioz' first they encored the *Roman Carnival* overture, and divided on the rest of the program. The press and the green rooms were buzzing with discussions of the "new esthetic." Two more concerts in November brought the composer's local fame to a high pitch and secured him a new batch of affectionate devotees. The audiences, as he wrote to a friend in America, "are most gracious to me; they applaud fit to shatter their knuckles and make me encore as many as four numbers in one concert." One of these was a charming bolero, *Zaïde,* which Berlioz had just taken from his unpublished melodies and orchestrated.

On the eve of Berlioz' birthday, that is on December 10, a hundred and fifty musicians gave a banquet in his honor and presented him with a baton of silver gilt, bearing the titles of his works, as well as the names of the first forty subscribers to the presentation. Baron de Lannoy, the Austro-Belgian composer, former director of the Vienna Conservatorium, in speaking for the musical home of Gluck, Mozart, Haydn, and Beethoven, expressed the hope that the stick would remind Berlioz of the music lovers who now joined in the cry of "Long live

Berlioz!" In his reply, the composer immediately associated the other French musicians then in Vienna (naming Félicien David) as sharers in this token of fraternal feeling.

Berlioz had to extend his stay. In the course of it, he visited the famous hall where Johann Strauss and his choice band produced the waltzes which had added a new glory to Vienna's musical renown. Greatly impressed by the quality of both the music and the dancing, Berlioz did not hesitate to call Strauss a genuine artist and to commend his orchestra as superior to many more pretentious bands. He also noted with pleasure the rhythmical variety of Strauss's compositions which "made use of every beat in the bar" for syncopation or secondary rhythmical lines, in a manner that Berlioz himself had advocated earlier against the proponents of squareness and the strong beat.

For the additional concert Berlioz had proposed to give the Dramatic Symphony, *Romeo and Juliet,* and the suggestion had been eagerly taken up. "And all this," as Berlioz wrote to Desmarest in Paris, "is due to our dear old *Symphonie Fantastique.* The Scenes in the Country and the March to Execution have turned their hearts inside out. As for the *Roman Carnival* and the 'Pilgrims' March,' they are now popular pieces. (Things have gone so far that pies are named after me.) The musicians are first-rate, and the orchestra is young —half Czech, half Viennese—and trained by me, since it was only made up two months ago. It is now as strong as a lion. This morning, I rehearsed in addition the Kärntnertor orchestra (the leading orchestra in the Germanies) for . . . my concert tomorrow. . . . On the 30th I shall have the chorus and orchestra of the theatre, doubled in numbers, for *Romeo and Juliet* complete. For Friar Laurence I have Staudigl, who is a fine strong bass. And what a musician! . . ." Other details follow of a more intimate nature: "Marie is radiant with pleasure at all this success. . . . What is the exact amount of the tailor's bill outstanding . . . ? Will Latte [the publisher] pay his usual price of 200 francs for *Zaïde?* I am going to bed a little weary from rehearsing."

Romeo and Juliet, given on January 2, 1846, proved too difficult a dose for the audience, but the performers having grown familiar with it felt, like a later New York critic, that the work "had come to stay." As the double chorus ended, they raised a great shout for the composer, as well as a banner bearing commendatory verses. Berlioz had not conducted and thus had heard his score for the first time with relative detachment, jotting down numerous alterations for a future edition.

Despite the hurly-burly he was in a composing vein. His new sketches for *Faust* were taking shape; notably the Enchantment scene, which had grown into three variations upon the original theme of 1828. It was encouraging—and so different from the Parisian battle—to have one's musical output understood, even if sometimes rejected; for partisanship here seemed to be about his work, not about his affiliation with the Bertin family or his relations with the minister of the day. Though no one was calm enough—as the critic of the *Theaterzeitung* wrote—"to assess his extraordinary talent, . . . wherever he goes with his music love springs up and hate also. Berlioz acts like spiritual yeast and causes a general ferment of the mind." A fifth concert, spontaneously organized to honor him as he left, and an audience with Metternich completed Berlioz' round of pleasures.[3]

Now for Prague, whence there were signs of Berliozian "ferment" even before the trip was thought of. Young Dr. Ambros, the critic and musicologist, urged the visit and took upon himself all the preparations for it. Schumann's review of the *Fantastique* was familiar to the younger crowd of composers and a new conductor-composer-professor, Johann Friedrich Kittl, had just begun to impose Beethoven on the conservative townsmen's taste. This undoubtedly fortified them for the advent of Berlioz. Three concerts in mid-January 1846 insured him a reception as enthusiastic as Vienna's. The musicians especially took fire. Classes from the Conservatoire came to learn his ways of rehearsing. Tomaschek, the dean of Czech composers, then over seventy, declared himself "one-third won over." The intellect and aristocracy of Prague were similarly split but with the larger fraction favorable.

A more regrettable division was that of the gate receipts, much diminished by complimentary seats, and by the theater manager's levy of twelve per cent. "The only thing to do is to render unto Caesar, as usual, what does not belong to Caesar." Berlioz promised to return soon if *Romeo and Juliet* could be rehearsed in his absence. It is clear that he was deliberately working, not for public applause, but for the approval of the next generation of composers, determined to give them his richest and most advanced thought as exemplified in the Dramatic Symphony. The audiences at large were obviously better able to appreciate his first works first.

Meanwhile Vienna wanted still another concert, scheduled for February 2, which Berlioz returned to direct; and by that time Buda-Pesth was feeling the "musical earthquake" (so said the *Wiener Theaterzeitung*) and was clamoring for his presence. A friend advised Berlioz to bring the Hungarians an orchestral version of one of their national airs. Berlioz chose the so-called Rákóczy theme, and spent the night preceding his departure fashioning the now famous March. He was still in the flood tide of his creative urge and what he made of the military tune was a short symphonic poem of irresistible effect.

The story of its first performance is told in full in the *Memoirs,* its most interesting points being the various signs of the Hungarians' nationalistic fever, which was to burst forth two years later. M. de Horvath, to whom Berlioz showed his new score tried to warn him: "Your exposition of the [Rákóczy] theme is marked *piano* and we are in the habit of hearing it start *fortissimo*. . . ." Berlioz would be affronting national honor, but he kept calm. "Yes," he said, "your Zigeuner play it *ff,* but never fear, you will have a *forte* such as you have never heard. . . . In all things one must look to the end."

The effect was what he foresaw. The gentle woodwinds and strings which state the theme after the rhythm-setting fanfare, lead it gradually into the battlelike climax with dull pulses of the deep drum on the off beat. Dismayed at first, the hall was electrified at the end. In the green room, Berlioz was embraced and wept over. An unprepossessing, haggard veteran, seizing his hand, told him in halting French, " 'Monsieur, monsieur . . . me poor devil Hungarian . . . Forgive excitement . . . the French they revolutionary . . . know how to make music for revolutions.' It was almost frightening," adds Berlioz, "it was sublime."

The Hungarians, as well as Berlioz' Viennese and Czechish friends, were going to be plunged in revolution sooner than they thought, and the composer might have told them that the art thereof can generally be made only after the fact, when the feelings can be recalled in tranquillity and given form.

Berlioz' muse continued active. His plan for *Faust* was clear in his mind, and its music came into being of its own accord. Having lost his way one night in Budapest, he wrote the refrain of the Peasants' Dance on a street corner, under the lamppost. At Breslau, his next stop, more numbers came, including the students' song. Everywhere he is "furiously at work." But suddenly he misses his old Paris comrades and "the whirlwind of ideas in which one moves." So he told his affectionate brother-in-arms Joseph d'Ortigue, in all sincerity, for Vienna had just offered Berlioz the post of Imperial Kapellmeister. He declined without hesitation, which with him argues previous thought: Paris tugged at his heart, of course, but he also must have considered that his critical post at the *Débats* was a necessary and induplicable weapon of defense, while at the same time its obligations left him free to carry on his European mission. The Imperial Chapel would fetter him. In the foreign-speaking city, once his musical honeymoon with the Viennese was over, he would be merely another working musician in a provincial colony of outsiders. No. The mission was paramount—and besides, there were Harriet and Louis for whom he felt responsible in more than a material way.

Once again in Prague at the end of March 1846, Berlioz made new converts with his *Romeo and Juliet* and two other concerts. The supper following the dress rehearsal was graced by toasts; Liszt drank to Berlioz' "erupting crater of genius" —drank so effectively that he was with difficulty prevented from fighting a pistol duel "at two paces" with a Bohemian nationalist.

Pleased with his latest corrections in the score of the Dramatic Symphony, Berlioz was still, as Lesueur had said long ago, "streaming music from all his pores." One night he was awakened by the thought of a melody which made him "tremble lest he forget it." He used it for the angels' greeting to Margaret which closes the *Damnation of Faust.*

Before returning to Paris Berlioz had taken on a collection of errands and messages to and from musicians: he was to buy two violins in Paris for the Prague Conservatoire; another Czech musician, the young Hanslick, who in those days was still favorable to modern music, wanted a recommendation to Liszt; the Vienna clarinetist Tropianski wished to transfer to Paris—and more of the same kind. To Mendelssohn, Berlioz sent greetings and congratulations on his *Midsummer Night's Dream,* which he had heard for the first time at Breslau: "I have never heard anything more deeply Shakespearean than your music. . . . I would have given three years of my life to embrace you. Farewell, farewell. Please believe that I love you as much as I admire you, which is to say, a great deal." [4] Finally on April 19 a "very brilliant and very profitable" concert at Brunswick—where he had so many close friends—marked the close of the second campaign.

The "whirlwind of ideas" in Paris turned out, when near at hand, to be mostly wind. This did not include Berlioz' circle of intimates, all of whom were as weary as he, though with rather less to show for it. Gathering his impressions of musical life, he could see that when compared with Central Europe Paris was stagnant. It was no longer the hub which it had been three decades before when the Conservatoire, with its faculty of over one hundred, seconded the numerous theaters and private societies in attracting quantities of foreign musicians, many of whom came to stay. Although no other center replaced Paris, that subtle but perceivable fluid which accompanies the motions of the spirit was flowing in the contrary direction. Prague now had a great Conservatory, Vienna the best orchestra, and the separate German states an enormous urge to produce and perform. Though this activity owed much to decentralization, to the diversity that comes of pluralism, it seemed also to go with the desire for national unification. The goal of statehood and constitutional liberty aroused strong feelings bent on something greater than self; whereas in France the *status quo,* moderately good but monolithic, aroused only hatred and self-contempt. In politics, disgust was held in check by despair, and in the arts a kind of torpor overcame even the best minds. "Here," wrote Berlioz to a German friend, "we have nothing but shabby scores, sprinkled with shabby melodies, accompanied by shabby orchestras, sung by shabby singers, and listened to by a shabby public, which fortunately never listens to them twice and forgets them at once." [5]

The Opera, to which this refers, had in fact died in its tracks and the public had begun to notice it; the press was up in arms against Pillet's directorship. As for Berlioz, strengthened in his own faith by his trip abroad, he had dropped all operatic schemes. Though for brevity he spoke of the *Damnation of Faust* as a "concert opera," it is no such thing. The form had grown out of the Eight Scenes and was a further extension of the dramatic symphony. Its completion and instrumentation were going satisfactorily throughout the summer, with but one interruption. Jules Janin, amiable and everready, had written a cantata for the opening of the Northern Railway at Lille on June 14. He naturally applied to "friend

Berlioz" for the music, which was put together in a few nights.

This *pièce de circonstance,* like half a dozen others in Berlioz' output, does not greatly signify. As the composer put it, "If I had had three *full* days, it would have been fit to live 40 centuries more." Yet in addition to further proof of the composer's speed, one finds one or two passages of real beauty in this song celebrating Peace, the Nation, and the Workers. Berlioz went to Lille—"the most musical town of the French provinces"—in order to conduct the work. Three military bands would also play, beforehand, the *Apothéose* of the *Funeral* symphony. At the end of this the local National Guard wanted to discharge its artillery. "The cannon are on the program," they told Berlioz, "the public expect them, and we cannot back out." Berlioz consented, conferred about the signal for the explosion, and proceeded to conduct. But on the final chord, no cannon: the fuses had burnt out to no purpose. The rest was silence and Berlioz dashed to his other chorus and orchestra, indoors, to conduct the cantata.

The social aspect of music continued to occupy him. In order to celebrate—and to feed—the musicians of Paris, their Association planned a festival like the one projected three years before. The *Apothéose* of the *Funeral and Triumphal* symphony was to be played, and this time the concert took place with the aid of forty regimental bands. Berlioz being in sympathy with the object but having had no share in the arrangements, could judge them with some detachment. He concluded once more that open-air music was a delusion and that the organizing powers of his compatriots were not equal to their tradition and opportunities: "The French, who fought the campaigns of the Revolution and Empire, and who made good the July uprising, cannot manage to build a concert hall." Behind this lay moral defects. "What we lack is seriousness, gravity, calmness . . . , the qualities that make the adolescent superior to the child and the mature man superior to the youth. . . . We lack the ability to rise above petty passions, petty ideas, petty objects. We lack the ability to examine instead of half seeing, to listen instead of overhearing, to think before speaking. We lack the ability to scorn maliciousness and the wretched popularity that we gain by it; we lack the ability to believe—and to believe steadfastly—that the spirit that creates is superior to the spirit that destroys."

Suiting his action to his ideal, Berlioz set on foot a celebration for the anniversary of Gluck's death. Baron Taylor and the Musical Association were for it; the indestructible opposition was against it. Part of the objections may have been due to the fact that the work chosen by Berlioz and the Association was the *Requiem;* but the other, greater barriers were raised from sheer hatred of seeing something succeed. Berlioz circumvented the willful obstructionists, collected his musicians, trained them by sections, and gave at the Church of St. Eustache on July 29 a performance of his *Requiem* which the participants long remembered.

Berlioz was by now a seasoned commander-in-chief. He could make up programs, cope with officialdom, draft publicity notices, watch the accounting, see that notables were sent tickets, and kindle the zeal of janitors; he could rehearse, conduct, train the amateurs, cajole the professionals, disarm the grumblers, and impart passion to the mass. He knew how to word reminders and sugarcoat admonitions; he could induce the press to write, the printers to print, and the public to come. His mind was an electric distributor which gave the well-timed spark to each cylinder of his vast machine. He did this without the aid of secretaries, telephones, dictographs, typewriters, automobiles, or benzedrine. It was a princely expenditure of nerves, and Berlioz disliked the impression of coercive pushing which it could not help generating like ozone in the air around a dynamo: "Thanks to the ill-will provoked by my criticism in the *Débats,* and to the raging anger of envious natures, I can make my way in Paris only like a red-hot cannon ball that hisses, burns, and shatters. I have noticed that this hostility increased during my absence in Germany."

Meanwhile the invisible inner mechanism, the demon inside the cannon ball, was still functioning in the frictionless world of thought. On a trip to Enghien, Berlioz found the rhythmic finale for Part II of the *Damnation;* at Rouen, where he went to see his son at school, and to rest from practical affairs, he wrote the love duet of Part III and began the polishing and fusing of all the scenes and parts. "I am working strenuously," he wrote to his father, "on a large work which is nearly done and which I want to put on in Paris by the end of November." And a new faculty, long latent, was developing: "I have had to be poet and musician both, because my score, begun and pursued across country, in Bavaria, Austria, Hungary, Bohemia, and Silesia, was going faster than my versifiers in Paris and I was thus compelled to do without them. It quite surprised me to be able to."

For another six weeks he worked with "all the care and patience of which I am capable," and on October 19 he dated the last page of the completed score.

CHAPTER 16

SONG IN TIME OF REVOLUTION

That singular Republic of 1848, which managed to shoot down, imprison, or deport all the real-republicans, leaving at the head of affairs only royalists.—SAINT-BEUVE in 1869

The *Damnation of Faust* was ready to be heard by the end of November 1846. To a journalist, possibly one of the Escudier brothers, who published music as well as the weekly *France Musicale*, and who had turned suddenly favorable to Berlioz, the composer dashed off a typical preconcert note:

Dear Friend,
Here are three notices just as they come. I am groggy with making arrangements. We rehearse all day today, but I shall try to go and see you about four o'clock. Yours . . .

To d'Ortigue Berlioz also wrote, asking that if he were to quote anything from the text it should be the verses: *Nature immense, impénétrable et fière*. The article moreover should not stress the daring of the conception and enterprise, but should on the contrary say that this concert form ought to have been tried long since. The "daring" lay in the gigantic risk Berlioz was taking in the production at his own expense of a work which though not an opera was of comparable dimensions, and which was to provide the sole entertainment of the afternoon.

He had hired the Opéra-comique—the only available place —for two Sundays a fortnight apart. The rehearsals were very satisfactory. The tenor Roger sang Faust in excellent style and the other soloists were adequate. Berlioz had a bad turn when it was announced that on the same day as his *première* the students of the Conservatoire were giving a concert for the benefit of flood victims. But the Comte de Montalivet, who was Minister of the Interior and who respected Berlioz, postponed the students' concert. For over a month the "Berlioz press" prepared the public. The Duc de Montpensier and his new duchess notified the composer that they would attend, and the composer mustered his faithful: Gautier, Janin and the rest.

But the public was not to be wooed. If anything was to take its mind off political agitation and resentment against every established thing, it must be novelties like the English troupe of men and women who, in flesh-colored tights, posed in protracted tableaux that the eager viewers agreed to call artistic. In the summer just past, two more attempts had been made on the life of Louis Philippe, bringing the total to seven; while the guerrilla in North Africa which was to be an outlet for restless nationalism remained inconclusive. Revolt was in fact brewing in various parts of Europe, much of it engineered by refugees in Paris. Prussian and Austrian Poland rose; Portugal was rent by civil war; and the Franco-British entente was broken, precisely by the success of the Duc de Montpensier in winning the Spanish princess.

In Paris, business was in depression. "Money was hiding," as the animistic phrase has it. The flood victims were only a few of those suffering from want. High prices and layoffs had provoked a riot in that weathervane district, the Faubourg St. Antoine. No masterpiece, were it ten times as irresistible as the *Damnation,* could overcome the fever of uncertainty, the self-centered fear now gripping the Paris bourgeois. Even if the citizen with money in his pocket had wanted to break the current of his gloomy thoughts, he would have turned away from Goethe, Berlioz, and Romanticism, and toward the cozier side of art—toward Scribe or Ponsard for drama, Auber or Clapisson for music.[1] In all the arts, an instinctive regrouping had come about, vaguely known as the School of Common Sense. That the days of Shakespeare and *Faust* were far in the past, Berlioz could feel when he climbed the podium and bowed to a half empty hall.

The performance naturally suffered, though two of the numbers were encored. Berlioz did not despair—yet, for he had a second chance on December 20. But the reviews were more sharply divided than before. Gautier after the dress rehearsal had set the seal on Berlioz' position as the one musician in the vanguard of French art: "With Hugo and Delacroix, he completes the trinity of Romanticism." But the irritable Scudo at the *Revue des Deux Mondes* frothed at the mouth. In the lobby, Adam gloated over Berlioz' apparent defeat. Janin ended a truthful report of divided opinion with a superb: "I pity Berlioz and I envy him."

In the face of the disaster, the convinced admirers among professional musicians felt that they must mediate between Berlioz and the public. D'Ortigue, always precise, went into details: "Being wholly absorbed in his innovations, . . . M. Berlioz loses sight of his audience and goes beyond the bounds where their perceptions stop. M. Berlioz is of the stature of the great masters, and has gone farther than Mozart, Beethoven, and Weber, not because he is superior to them, but because in his hands art has taken a step forward . . . He will continue to fight the good fight, but there will always be a gulf between the way in which the mass of the public conceives of art—owing to the theories commonly taught—and the way M. Berlioz conceives it."

Before the next performance it started to snow, so that on December 20 the hall was only a quarter full. Those present formed such a select group that they were enchanted with the music, even though Roger declined to sing the Invocation to Nature.[2] To solace the composer, his admirers organized a banquet presided over by Baron Taylor, and had a gold medal struck in honor of the work. Offenbach made a speech in the name of German music, Osborne in the name of English. The romantic contrast between glory and wretchedness, greatness and misery, could not have been better contrived by fiction. Homage and failure greeted this work which was to be resurrected thirty years later as the productive mainstay of the Colonne repertory, and to be accepted without effort as "the masterpiece which is the *summa* of nineteenth-century French music."

Meantime Berlioz was financially ruined. In a letter to his sister Nanci he could but thinly cover up his profound depression; he was later to say that this indifference of the Parisian public had wounded him more deeply than any previous blow. To insult and misrepresentation he had grown hardened; neglect was more galling. Nor could the investment of time and energy be recouped by later concerts as he had done for earlier compositions: "There is no concert hall in Paris." This was now true, for the Opera was dead set against Berlioz and controlled the Italian theater, while the Conservatoire, as we know, had made a rule that no "outsider" could use its hall during the season. "Moreover the government is becoming economical in a fashion that was unthinkable five years ago. The Minister in whose jurisdiction the arts are placed cares about them rather less than he does about the grocery business. There is nothing to be done in this ruthless country and I can only hope to leave it as fast as possible . . . I am like a beast of prey, forced to seek my food afar: only barnyard fowl thrive on the manure heap. I have made up my mind. Despite the cold weather, I am going by land next month to St. Petersburg."

A feeling of resentment verging on sour grapes was not Berlioz' sole motive. St. Petersburg had been in his mind for two years past, and even before that time he had been attracted by what was reported of the success of his *Requiem* there.[3] Vernet had visited Russia in 1840 and been well received, and more recently, Balzac had returned from his courting of his future wife, Mme. Hanska, and was extravagant in praise of the country's welcome to artists. "You will not be able," he told Berlioz, "to come back with *less* than 150,000 francs." And as a sort of pledge for his prediction he offered Berlioz the loan of his fur coat.

Before Berlioz could leave he must settle his new debts. Friends helped out: Bertin of the *Débats* advanced five thousand francs; Hetzel, the kind and intelligent publisher of Victor Hugo, a thousand; Adolphe Sax, twelve hundred. On the point of leaving, Berlioz had another gleam of hope that he might after all entrench himself in Paris. Pillet's management of the Opera was doomed, and a public scene by the power behind the throne, the singer Rosine Stoltz, hastened its end.[4] The winning team for the new directorship was Duponchel, former director in the days of *Benvenuto Cellini,* and a mediocre writer named Nestor Roqueplan. This partnership, not as yet appointed, had backing from the Rothschilds as well as from the *Débats*. It could be inferred that Berlioz would be made conductor. This was in fact promised by the eager candidates but soon written off as a pre-election promise. Berlioz must leave France. In February 1847 he wrote to Balzac, taking him up on his offer of the coat, which was duly delivered. It must have been made of *peau de chagrin* if it fitted the thin musician after housing the rotund novelist. At any rate on St. Valentine's day Berlioz set off alone by way of Belgium and Germany. The comic papers signalized the departure of M. Berliozkoff in a bass drum drawn by four horses.

The composer had no expectations on the scale that Balzac forecast and he meant to take every precaution against further losses. Accordingly, he stopped off at Berlin and obtained from the King a letter of introduction to his sister, the Tsarina.[5] The trip thence was extremely uncomfortable and more than usually cold, especially from the Russian frontier onward, four days and nights by sleigh.

A first concert was planned, prepared, and carried off with lightning speed within two weeks of Berlioz' arrival, that is to say on March 15. The Tsarina was present as well as the nobility and the representatives of the arts—a gala occasion which was also a memorable success: "Encores enough to make one dizzy. The program included the *Roman Carnival* Overture, Parts I and II of the *Damnation,* and the *Funeral and Triumphal* Symphony." After shaking the hands of many new friends and drinking a bottle of beer, Berlioz inquired about the receipts: eighteen thousand francs—a clear profit of twelve thousand. "I unconsciously turned my face southwest . . . and murmured, 'Ah, my dear Parisians!' My life was saved." A second concert met with equal success. The Tsarina and her sons (of whom the elder became Alexander II) showed the visitor marked attentions, gave him valuable gifts, and went wherever he performed. "If the Parisians chose to punish me for having composed my latest work, the Russians have amply made it up to me."

Four more days in a sleigh ("which shakes one up like shot in a bottle") brought Berlioz to Moscow, where the orchestra and choruses were by no means so good as the picked German group in St. Petersburg. But the applause on April 10 and the profits that went with it were equally gratifying. "The Russian aristocracy has grown delirious over *Faust.* . . . While I am giving these concerts in Moscow . . . the Grand Theatre [in St. Petersburg] is rehearsing *Romeo.*"

The return to the capital was slowed up by the spring thaw, but this delay only heightened the pleasure of finding on his return the large well-trained ensembles playing and singing *Romeo.* He rehearsed them in sections as usual, and gave himself wholly to "the divine Shakespearean poem." The excitement of the performance and the warmth of the public response were too much for him. After many curtain calls, he retired to the green room where Ernst the violinist (who had played in the *Harold* symphony) found him dissolved in tears. " 'Nerves,' " said Ernst, " 'I know all about it.' And he let me weep like an hysterical girl for another 15 minutes."

Another strain on the thirtieth for a repeat performance was followed by a depressive reaction. He experienced one of his fits of loneliness in the midst of friends. He thought of Liszt, newly in love with the Princess Carolyne Sayn-Wittgenstein, who was temporarily in Russia, and wrote him a long letter for her to deliver by hand. "I think a great deal about you, and the opportunities of speaking of you here are many, for people love and admire you as much as I do. Don't you think you and I go around a good deal? Just now, I am sad, sad enough to die of it. I am having one of my bouts of *isolation;* and it is the playing of *Romeo* that brought it on. In the middle of the adagio I felt my heart contract, and here I am, caught by the evil for Lord knows how long. My wretched temperament!

"But enough of this. I have played a deal of music here. . . . Now the King of Prussia has had me notified by Count Roeden that the Berlin Opera is at my disposal to put on *Faust* entire. So I'm going to Prussia, but my heart is not in it. Will I recover it? There I go lamenting again. What misery to be an electrical machine that can be electrified. The Princess tells me that you compose a great deal. When is your *Sardanapalus* due in Vienna? . . .[6]

"Farewell. I embrace you. I should like to see you. The sun shines as in Italy—34 degrees of heat [93.2° F.]—a torture. Come hither ice, fog, insensibility! Farewell again, don't laugh at me: if you do I shall know it wherever you are."

Berlioz' sense of isolation, brought on by overwork or the aftermath of battle, was his old trouble, rooted farther back than adolescence; it was the passion for Estelle, for solitude in the fields, mingled with yearning for a love he never knew and never was to know. The absent Marie was not the one to make him feel that his real experiences were being shared. Worldly in a small-minded way—as her P.S.'s to some of Berlioz' letters attest—she had ceased being either spirited or naïve. Alone and brooding, Berlioz easily deluded himself into thinking that he loved one of his choristers, a modest young woman who lived by her needle and was betrothed by her family's will to a man on his way to Sweden. She took pity on the great artist in his distress. It was an innocent affair: they walked arm in arm along the Neva and talked—for she knew French fairly well—or Berlioz would sing to her. He knew she did not love him, but she spoke like Faust's Gretchen as she wondered what he could see in so ordinary a creature as herself, and the poetic and musical associations redoubled his grief masked as love.

However much the mind might stand off and judge it, this was no trumped-up feeling on Berlioz' part: it was the imagination of love, out of which, for gifted and erotic but unsensual natures, all art springs.[7] "There are so many sorts of love," Berlioz confided months later to a friend. "The kind I feel is the true, grand, poetic love. I have known it since the first time and nothing is more beautiful. With the love of art, there is no other divinisation of the human heart. With it the world grows bright, horizons enlarge, all nature takes on color and vibrates in endless harmonies, and—one loves, that's all, one loves!"

From this first visit in 1847, Russia felt that Berlioz' music was pregnant and prophetic and wanted to keep his scores at the Imperial Library. But Berlioz had no copies and could not leave them. He did leave warm supporters, notably Vladimir Stassov, Alexis Lvov, and Count Michael Wielhorsky, whose appreciation of his work had considerable effects on the national art. He on his side had received an unforgettable impression from the liturgical music of Bortniansky.

On his way to answer the Prussian King's invitation, Berlioz stopped at Riga, where he gave a concert by arranging some of his scores for fifty musicians, playing even the Chorus of Sylphs for orchestra alone. The audience was sparse, for the population was at the docks along the river, watching and trading as hundreds of ships unloaded grain. But in return for his pains he had "the great good fortune" of seeing *Hamlet* well performed. "I was again, as always, all stirred up over this marvel by the greatest genius who ever lived. The English are right to say that next to God it is Shakespeare who has created most. One ought not to allow his masterpieces to be shown before a haphazard gathering of dolts, half dolts, semi-literates, grammarians, schoolteachers, baby nurses, ladies of fashion, *demi-mondaines,* old crones, dandies, wheat brokers, horse traders and traveling salesmen . . . [even if] God has put them on earth in order to keep artists humble and clip the wings of their ambition."

Four days later Berlioz was in Berlin assembling his forces for the *Damnation*. In two weeks all was ready, but it was

June 19, the season was far advanced. The horse races had just begun, and the King used his privilege to request that the concert start at six. Half the audience therefore came an hour late. Still, despite this handicap and that of two inferior singers, several encores were called for. Frederick William asked him to Sans Souci; they talked where Voltaire had lived and Bach had played; walked in the gardens and parted pleased with each other. The King awarded Berlioz the Red Eagle, but the Berlin returns were slight. A truer compensation in artistic form roused Berlioz from his growing fatigue—"*La Vestale* entire, that is, as scored, without cuts. In spite of the [singers'] inadequacy it made—especially at the rehearsal—a profound impression. The last aria, which is never sung in Paris, is sublime."

In Paris, as Berlioz could see from the newspapers, the Opera after five months was still being tussled for. "In three days we overturn a dynasty, but it takes all this time to pass from Pillet to Coignard or some other. . . . In truth, it is everywhere the same. The King of Prussia has a superintendent who in all matters goes against the public, the artists, the court, and the King himself. Yet the King keeps him, though Meyerbeer is giving up from discouragement."

When Berlioz reached the French capital on July 7, the new directors had been in office one week. Within a month, the pair with the Flaubertian names, Duponchel and Roqueplan, had forgotten all their pre-nuptial courting of the powers, including Berlioz and the *Débats*. But with the composer once more in residence the comic papers had really fresh material for their wit tinged with envy: "M. Berliozineff has been made a prince. . . . He has had his armorial bearings engraved on his guitar." Berlioz quickly gauged the Opera situation and by mid-August sent a note to the new heads giving them back their latest word.[8] He had released to Scribe full rights to the libretto on Lewis's *Monk*. He had also accepted a complex but apparently attractive offer to go to London. The musical businessmen, Marie and Léon Escudier, had acted as intermediaries between Antoine Jullien, a French impresario married to an English wife, and Berlioz. Jullien was to open a new opera company at Drury Lane, of which Berlioz was to be conductor. Out of his salary of forty thousand francs a year, Berlioz would pay four thousand to Escudier, plus ten per cent on any contracts for special concerts that Berlioz might give under Jullien's management. The high rates were due in part to the computation in pounds sterling (London was expensive) and in part to Jullien's views of big business in art, which he had hitherto made profitable. Berlioz wrote up his Russian and German trips for the *Débats* and looked forward to England.

On the strength of his new engagement and in order to be in physical shape for it, Berlioz took a vacation; and since tangible success always put him in mind of his father, he went home to La Côte, taking with him his pale, blond little boy of thirteen. Berlioz did not manage to see Humbert Ferrand, who despite his real affection could never bestir himself in time to meet his old friend. But Berlioz kept him informed of his doings and read with appreciation the ex-poet's gentle brochures on politics.

La Côte had hardly changed in fifteen years, except that Dr. Berlioz was of a spectral thinness and near his end. His gastritis reduced him to an insufficient diet and to a steady course of opium. Partly deaf and very much alone, he was a pitiable old man of seventy-one. The sight of him shocked Hector, who nonetheless succeeded in enlivening him with anecdotes of his journeys, and even made him laugh. For young Louis, life in the open air with his father was a gleam of unimagined happiness. They romped together as if they had been brothers, and Hector himself was rejuvenated. But in the evening, he and the Doctor could only talk of the approaching end, or of the death, earlier, of those whom neither had seen at the last: Hector, his mother; Dr. Berlioz, his son Prosper. The old man was also likely to dwell on questions of inheritance and could not be turned from the subject. Berlioz left at the end of his fortnight knowing he would never see his beloved father again.

The month of October was devoted to preparations for the London trip. Berlioz now had a faithful copyist and guardian of his mounting pile of music, Roquemont, from whom he could reliably order parts to be made, counted over, or dispatched. This aid lessened the necessity of carrying everything with him and it would be indispensable in Berlioz' new post abroad, where he would need the music of others. Before leaving, Berlioz had singers and instrumentists to engage, endless errands to run, and quantities of proof to read. He found time to notice and encourage a young contralto, Mlle. Charton, whom he did not know but in whose future he believed as soon as he heard her. She repaid him sixteen years later by creating the role of Dido in his *Troyens*. But for the moment art in France seemed to him "dead, putrefying . . . The more I see of foreign nations, the less I love my native land. Forgive the blasphemy."

Sensing as he did the decay of an epoch and feeling inwardly chilled at the thought of his father, he preferred to make the journey to London in solitude. It required "a series of *coups d'état*" to obtain from Marie the right to go alone. Not that he had any intention of abandoning her or of taking up other attachments. He continued to support four people in two separate households, giving time to Harriet (whose apoplectic condition had become alarming) and to Marie and her mother. But he did not want to mar his first meetings with his English colleagues by letting Marie's heavy-handed ways overshadow his tact and *savoir-faire*. On his way to England, he accompanied Louis to his boarding school at Rouen, where two good friends, Méreaux and Baron de Montville, made his unhappy youth a little less solitary.

On November 5, 1847, after an easy crossing, Berlioz arrived in London. He lodged with Jullien at 76 Harley Street and was aghast to discover the size of megalopolis. It took three quarters of an hour to go from the house to Drury Lane, where his orchestra (for the first time *his*) greeted him most cordially. He knew a good many of the French and German players, and he found that his English was adequate to his needs. He spoke with a relatively slight accent, but took a little time to catch all that was said to him.

Rehearsals began for the first scheduled opera, Donizetti's inevitable *Lucia*. This was to break in the public gently. What Berlioz looked forward to was the staging of Gluck's *Iphigeneia in Tauris,* Mozart, and possibly Spontini. Jullien also had the notion that Berlioz should flatter the British by composing on "God Save the Queen" something like his Hungarian March. This absurd suggestion forecasts Jullien's approaching insanity.[9] Naturally, nothing came of this proposal, though Jullien's natural extravagance grew alarmingly. He wanted a two-act ballet from Gautier at a thousand francs an act, and Berlioz had to arrange for it as well as for the choreographer and the music by local talent. He had to entice Mmes. Dorus-Gras and Barth-Hasselt who had been vaguely engaged. Despite the artist's businesslike catching up of the irresponsible businessman's errors, things went quickly downhill. It came out that Jullien had lost fortune and credit *before* taking Drury Lane, so that he now cut all salaries by one third, which was a trifle since he did not pay them. *Lucia,* though excellently done, was only a moderate box-office success, and Balfe's new piece which followed was no hit.[10]

Linda di Chamounix was the next choice and by January 1848 Berlioz was "working like a dray horse," rehearsing all afternoon, conducting all night—a twelve-hour day. London, like Paris, was suffering an epidemic of midwinter grippe, which Berlioz caught. He "took as medicine the chores and the drafts of Drury Lane," since the situation could be saved only by energy. Meantime, Jullien's advisers gathered and took counsel of Berlioz. He proposed to enlist public support by means of a striking *artistic* novelty, such as Gluck's *Iphigenia in Tauris,* and he explained its requirements. Jullien's response was: "There are helmets, we are saved!" Berlioz finally gave up by the end of January 1848, taking to his bed with a serious bronchitis. "They are playing *Linda*. . . . I have the good luck to be ill." He recovered in time to put on the *Marriage of Figaro* in a manner to impress Wilhelm Ganz, but it did not draw. Berlioz had received altogether one month's salary; Jullien was bankrupt and planning to start again in New York.[11]

Berlioz' spirit was a prey to many dark thoughts. Mendelssohn had died the day before Berlioz landed, and his posthumous oratorio, *Elijah,* was being performed in his memory. "How wonderfully great and beautiful it is," wrote Berlioz. "We have all been deeply moved by the loss of this superior artist, whose death is a stout blow inflicted on our art." But the *Antigone* of Sophocles, given with Mendelssohn's incidental music, had failed. The perpetual need to overcome resistance, to persuade by will and convince by material gain, was depressing. In his fever and lassitude the musician thought of the superb concerts "imperially run" under order of the Tsar, and he longed to be at last somewhere put in charge of what he could do best—produce music. From France the news was disquieting. The republican banquets of December 1847 presaged trouble—or less likely, reform—which the concluding of peace in North Africa only postponed for a time.

Other thoughts of Russia assailed Berlioz. He had written to his friend the cellist Tajan-Rogé at St. Petersburg enclosing a note for the little singer Berlioz had loved, feeling himself to be "a young fool of over forty," and he had received a reply—a last reply full of good sense, honesty, and affection. "I am grateful to her," he wrote in thanking Rogé, "for reviving in me the pain I was trying to forget." But brooding in bed was useless and was in fact a forbidden luxury, for Drury Lane being on the rocks, Berlioz had scheduled a concert of his own works for February 7. His new friend J. W. Davison, music critic of *The Times* and founder of *The Musical World*, was helping him to get on his feet and make his music known. The mission was in its third phase.

To help the concert, Berlioz asked Vigny for a letter of introduction to Count d'Orsay, with whom Vigny was on terms of close affection, and who could give Berlioz entree to the artistic circle of Lady Blessington. Berlioz was already in touch with Macready, who gave a dinner in his honor, and with theatrical writers and critics, thanks to whom Berlioz saw a good many plays.[12] Sir Henry Taylor's *Philip van Artevelde* was the novelty of the season but Berlioz preferred *Othello* and the to him suggestively entitled *New Way to Pay Old Debts*. In answer to Berlioz' request Vigny wrote a very warm letter to d'Orsay who soon replied that Berlioz had quickly become one of theirs: "He is a friend of . . . all the shepherds of our time, society being composed only of those and of the numberless sheep." This *esprit de corps* had the useful result of making the critic of the *Athenaeum*, Chorley, change his mind about Berlioz' music and write of it pleasantly for the first time.

London concertgoers had for five years past heard a few of Berlioz' overtures but this February concert was to be a full-dress presentation. The volatile Jullien, however, had tried a last stroke to recoup his fortunes. Taking with him Berlioz' best players he was touring the United Kingdom in a series of promenade concerts. The orchestral rump that was left had to be rehearsed five times and the chorus eighteen. In the end things went well enough, the public cheered, and the press was almost entirely favorable. One of the converts was Edward Holmes, the friend of Keats and biographer of Mozart, who had come strongly prejudiced. *The Times* and the *Illustrated London News* led the chorus of enthusiastic and discerning praise. "Jullien," said the latter journal "may be forgiven much for giving the London public a chance to hear Berlioz. . . . Had he been named Musical Director at Drury Lane and not merely chef d'orchestre, it would have been better for himself and better for the interests of Lyric Drama."

Once again honor was safe and intrinsic success achieved in the face of material loss: Berlioz began to plan a second concert; but Jullien had just wits enough left to appropriate the money of the first without paying anyone anything. The orchestra that Berlioz had trained was therefore disbanding. The music publisher Beale, it is true, was willing to issue a good many fragments and piano arrangements of Berlioz' work, but royalties would be distant and probably not large. The ancient Society of British Musicians gave Berlioz a testimonial dinner at which—against the custom of the society—a toast was drunk to the guest of honor. Berlioz replied in a manner which he says was contrary to his custom too, for "I was cool and self-possessed and was thus able to properly thank the public, the musicians, and the critics."

When Berlioz wrote this to Brandus, the French publisher who had taken over the *Gazette Musicale,* still another "Reform Banquet" had been planned and prohibited in Paris. The prohibition had been a declaration of war between the people and the government. The February Days (twenty-second to twenty-fourth) had begun to the cry of "Long Live Reform," Guizot was down, barricades were up, and the insurgents marched, with the troops, to the Tuileries. While the Chamber discussed a Regency of Louis-Philippe's grandsons under the Duchess of Orleans, a mob which included the Swiss painter Arnold Böcklin interrupted the proceedings. A provisional government headed by the poet Lamartine, the scientist Arago, and the political theorist Louis Blanc, was appointed by acclamation. The Republic of 1848 was born.

For each section of society, reform means the reform of the abuses it feels most, and Berlioz naturally hoped for the end of monarchical interference in the arts: no more tax levies on concerts, no more censorship of songs, no more arbitrary disposal of the means of production. "I hope, in short, that we shall at last be free to be free—unless we are in for a new mystification." The silence of his French friends was alarming. "What's happened to M. Bertin?" Being an Orleanist, the Director of the *Débats* was rumored to be in hiding. But what could make Desmarest the cellist and Brandus the publisher keep mum? Berlioz begged Morel to tell him what had happened "to all our precious villains, as Shakespeare calls them."

By the middle of March 1848 the answer was self-evident. Cultural activity had utterly ceased in France; it was "dead, rotted away, and buried." Berlioz must face the task of building himself a new position in England. Revolution was now aflame in Prussia, Austria, and the Rhineland; in Rome, Naples, Ireland and Bohemia. Short of Russia, there was no dwelling place for music on the Continent. Jullien had converted Drury Lane into an equestrian circus, and having no liquid assets feared no lawsuits. He had blithely defaulted on all his contracts. But Berlioz could not default on his four dependents in France and must use his pen to earn his living. He proposed critical and travel articles to Davison, but as one can tell at a glance, *The Times* is not a French newspaper, which can accept casual copy from outsiders. Berlioz inquired of the new Minister of the Interior whether his one hundred and eighteen francs a month as curator of the Conservatoire Library would still be paid. He had no reply.

Yet he found time to hear and comment enthusiastically on Mendelssohn's *Italian* symphony, which he much preferred to the *Scotch*—"fresh, lively, noble, and masterly . . . a superb piece." This was given at a concert of the Philharmonic Society, which Berlioz' well-wishers would have liked to see extend a welcome to the French composer. But the directors were conservative and cautious. The directors of Covent Garden, on the other hand, were interested in a Musical Shakespeare Night in which Berlioz' *Tempest, Death of Ophelia, King Lear,* and parts of *Romeo* would figure. But opposition developed: Berlioz was caught again between the equivalents of the Conservatoire and the Opera.[13] He worked at piano arrangements of his works for Beale and at a vocal version of the *Apothéose* of the *Funeral* symphony, which had aroused cheers at his concert.

Beyond this, his only capital was himself and his achievements. Pondering them, he took out the two volumes of his *Voyage Musical* and set to work making of them an autobiography, filling in the gaps, beginning at the beginning—his birth forty-four years before, in another era of European massacre. His career might be over, but the artist's memoirs of his experiences might survive the flood and be of use.

As he sketched in his Preface the circumstances under which these memoirs were being written, during the last week of March 1848, the tide of revolt touched London. The Chartists assembled to cries of "Down with the Ministry. . . . The Charter and No Surrender!" They planned another mass meeting, a petition, and a march to Parliament. To fend off revolution, 170,000 special constables were sworn in, one of whom was Louis-Napoleon Bonaparte, nephew of the late Emperor. Troops were quartered in the houses and the Tower guns mounted. The Duke of Wellington was put in charge of all the government forces and a proclamation was issued against "assembly for disorderly purposes." "Time presses," wrote Berlioz. "Republicanism sweeps with its steamroller over all Europe. The art of music which for so long was everywhere dragging out its life is good and dead today. . . . England, where I now live, has shown me a noble and cordial hospitality, but at these first quakings of the continental thrones, swarms of bewildered artists seek asylum here. . . . Will the British capital provide subsistence for so many exiles? Will it lend an ear to their songs of sorrow amid the proud clamors of neighboring peoples which are crowning themselves kings? Will it resist such an example? *Jam proximus ardet Ucalegon.*[14] Who knows what will have become of me in a few months—I have no assured means for myself and my family. Let us therefore make use of the flying minutes. . . ."

The moment was doubly bitter, for the financial needs of Harriet and Marie had brought the two women into a cruel tangle, after which Marie had decided to rejoin Berlioz in London. He could obtain money due him neither from Jullien (who was at last in debtor's prison) nor from the vicomte who owed him five hundred francs. Worst of all, the Escudiers had been made bankrupt by the revolution and although "they cannot be compelled to pay me what they owe, I shall be compelled by the original contract to pay what I do not owe them." He had to borrow at revolutionary rates to provide for Harriet and Louis, while he and Marie moved to modest lodgings in Regent's Park. "I am convinced that I am *de trop* in this world."

By sheer will he busied himself about another concert. French musicians were arriving in droves and they lent him their services. On June 29, at the Hanover Square Rooms, after eight months of virtually continuous overwork, he gave a brilliant concert which was worthily received and brought little. It was evident that musical London, like Paris, was intellectually ready to appreciate what was new, vigorous, and unconventional, but was not in any way organized to support it. The paying institutions in London were the two Italian theaters, which ran a handful of favorites by Bellini, Rossini, and Donizetti—and not their best works at that—and the orchestra and oratorio societies, monopolized by Handel, Mendelssohn, and their living imitators.

As for Paris, it was swimming in blood. Three days before Berlioz' concert, from the twenty-third to the twenty-sixth of

June, the unemployed in the national workshops—the original WPA—had risen in protest against the threatened cessation of their dole. Entrenched in the eastern part of the city, they faced the government like a foreign army and were treated as such. General Cavaignac brought reserves and battered down the barricades with field guns. It was civil war. The Archbishop of Paris was killed trying to stop it. The rebels finally surrendered, and with a savagery to which both sides had been led by equal fear, the government deported wholesale and without trial all the prisoners taken. Public feeling turned sharply in favor of strong rule and against all popular social aspirations. All parties, all citizens, were now legitimately afraid. Had Cavaignac not loyally believed in republican government, he could have made himself dictator; the situation was in the pre-Napoleonic stage of 1795, the pre-Cromwellian of 1651. Paris was a stricken field.

This was the City of Light that Berlioz had loved, had made his name in, and was now compelled to return to. He entertained no illusions. In May, even before the second outbreak had attested France's social and political alienation from art, he had written to the architect Louis Duc, his old companion of the Villa Medici, a letter which summed up the facts and reflected the many lights thrown upon them by Berlioz' mind:

London 26 May 1848

My dear Duc:

Our piece (the *Apothéose*) has at last come out. It was thought necessary to tamper with my sub-title. I had written: "Composed for the inauguration of the Bastille Column," and farther down: "Dedicated to M. Duc, architect of the *Bastille* Column." This made it clear why the column came into it at all and wherefore the dedication was appropriate. But since the last Chartist agitation, the London bourgeois has a deep dread of whatever is related from far or near to revolutions, and in consequence my publisher refused to consider any mention on the title page either of your monument or of those to whom it was put up.

I have sought in vain an opportunity to send you the score, together with the Scotch airs you asked for. Instead, I send you the *Apothéose* by itself, for a package of the kind you request would cost a great deal. The Hungarian March for four hands has also been published by Beale, and the Chorus of Sylphs will appear shortly. Our piece would I think be quite impressive if sung by a large chorus and instrumented. I may have it performed in Paris if it becomes possible to give music there. Meanwhile you'll have to be content with the piano score.

Speaking of Paris, the reproaches that my friends utter about my absence are scarcely founded if they think that my staying away is doing me harm. A man must have a tricolor flag over his eyes to fail to see that music in France is now dead, and that it is the last of the arts to which our rulers will pay attention. They tell me I am sulking at my country. I certainly do not sulk at it: that is putting it too mildly; I flee from it as one flees a barbaric shore when one is looking for civilization, and this I have done not merely since the Revolution. For a good while I have stifled in myself the love of France and uprooted from my heart the foolish habit of centering all my thoughts upon her. During the last seven years I have lived solely from what my works and concerts have earned me in foreign lands. Without Germany, Bohemia, Hungary, and especially Russia, I should have starved in France over and over again. Friends write to me of "positions" to take, of "posts to apply for." What position, what posts? There aren't any. Isn't Auber at the Conservatoire, Carafa at the Gymnase, Girard at the Opera? What else is there? Nothing. And the love of mediocrity—has that been swept out of French minds by the Revolution? Possibly, but in that case it will have been replaced by the love of worse men and things (if there is indeed anything worse than mediocrity).

No, I have nothing to do in France, except cultivate the friendships that are dear to me. For my career I have attempted enough, suffered enough, waited enough. I shall not fulfill it there. In France I have undergone nothing but vexations more or less disguised; I have found only a stupid opposition because the national mind is stupid about the higher reaches of art and literature. I have an invincible and ever-growing contempt for those "French ideas" of which other peoples have not an inkling. Under the previous government I found nothing but scorn and indifference; I shall now find nothing but grave preoccupations added to scorn and indifference. I wrote three times to Louis Philippe when he was King requesting an audience. I did not even receive *a reply.* I wrote to Ledru-Rollin recently and he was of the same politeness as the King. There is only one lyric theatre in Paris—the Opera, which is managed by a nitwit and closed to me. Don't you suppose that if Duponchel is dismissed, they will not find twenty others like him? Some day, perhaps, I shall be approached, when I shall be very old, very tired, and no longer good for anything. But at that time I may not have lost my memory, and this belated confidence in me—*if it comes,* will only be the more painful.

I have therefore nothing better to do than what I am doing

now. If I am a savage, I hold on to my freedom, I keep going as long as the earth will have me, as long as the woods have wild life and deer; and if I often feel weary, and sleepless, suffer from cold, hunger and the insults of the pale-faces, at least I can dream alone above the waterfall and in the silent forest, worshipping nature and thanking God that he has left me the sense of her beauty.

I saw *Hamlet* recently. . . . What a world is that masterpiece! And what ravages *that fellow* makes in one's heart and soul! Shakespeare meant to depict the nothingness of life, the vanity of human designs, the despotism of chance, and the indifference of Fate or God toward what we call virtue, crime, beauty, ugliness, love, hate, genius and folly. And he has cruelly succeeded. In the performance, this time, they had deigned to give us *Hamlet* as written, and almost uncut—an unusual thing in this country where one finds so many people who are superior to Shakespeare. . . . For that matter, they do the same to music, Costa has instrumented and corrected for Covent Garden Rossini's *Barber of Seville* and *Mozart's Figaro* and *Don Giovanni*.

Here ends the message of explanation, expostulation, and resignation. But the writer must have been conscious of excessive and self-centered seriousness in addressing a friend to whom he says *tu* and whom he wished first of all to please by a dedication and a gift. So Berlioz adds a paragraph or two in another vein:

Let me tell you, by way of stopping this verbiage, that I am preparing a concert . . . for June 29. That is all my news. . . . I may say, I miss our delightful, easy, unpretentious conversations at Mme. Vanderkelle's, and the fine wit and cultivated opinions with which M. de Montville flavors them, and your own enthusiastic shouts and leaps at whatever is beautiful, and your admiring words shot through puffs of tobacco (I mean smoke), and the reclining position of the ladies while we discuss.

Only one thing has always shocked me in those gatherings—a dull and indecent thing which Mme. Vanderkelle does her best to conceal and yet fails to, a thing unworthy of a house like hers, and one that offends all good company. I mean her upright piano. No, madam, in a house appointed like yours, it is not permissible to sport such a cupboard; it is not permissible, in a choice circle such as your salon, to let an instrument like that be heard. It is indeed a crime of *lèse-art*. On this pun,[15] I shake you all by the hand, and beg you—what was I going to beg you? Ah, yes, beg you not to let Duc sing the *Apothéose*. A thousand heartfelt greetings.—H. Berlioz

Even before the second outbreak in June, the spirit of 1848 had already shown its deeply disruptive character. The initial success of the revolution had in fact been made possible by the general decline of authority and intellectual power which had been going on for about half a dozen years. So that Berlioz was neither mistaken nor purely self-centered when he saw in the revolution not merely the end of a regime but the end of an epoch. Like many others—ranging from Renan and Gobineau to Leconte de Lisle and Baudelaire, he was ready to support a republic that could both proclaim and defend new freedoms, and as we shall see he gave it a try. But his skepticism as to the outcome was soon verified by events. The explanation is not simply that Berlioz had reached mid-career and made a reputation with the aid of kings and princes, but that 1848 in France represents a new mode in revolutions, and one inevitably inimical to culture as Berlioz understood it. If 1830 was a sixth and last attempt to entrench the liberal claims of 1789, the republicanism of 1848 was the first bid for the establishment of the populist, collectivist society which our century is still struggling about. We may therefore generalize and say that 1848 split the century in half, and by creating new conditions of life for artists wrecked the careers of all those who remained true to what Lionel Trilling aptly calls "the high and exigent culture" of the prepopulist era.

Besides Berlioz' enforced exile in London, where Chopin, Roger, Hallé, and other French musicians soon joined him, Sainte-Beuve and others had to find literary work in Belgium or Switzerland, or else be destitute. The poetess Desbordes-Valmore subsisted on charity; Musset's librarianship was abolished; Gautier's and Vernet's livelihood was curtailed and Adolphe Adam went bankrupt. The rest of Europe was soon affected. Verdi, who had just bought a house, saw his new opera fail at Trieste; the cessation of music in Germany killed off a fifty-year-old journal such as the *Leipziger Allgemeine Zeitung,* and from all parts exiles began to stream into England —all this to an accompaniment of shootings, lynchings, arson, vandalism, and panic. It is easy for the distant observers to see in great popular uprisings the inspiration of whole artistic periods. What art can spring from or represent such chaos? And at the same time, how is it that Romanticism is the true culture of the French Revolution? Obviously the true culture of a revolution comes after the event, the culture makers being either opponents of, or, if indifferent, opposed by the revolutionary forces. In any case, the conditions of a going revolution are especially inimical to art: there is no wish, there is no preparation, and there is no money for art because, strictly speaking, there is no need for it. When art is consciously used by revolutionists as a means to prestige or propaganda, the result in the artist is even worse than when, as in 1848, it is treated with contempt. In a word, there can be no song in time of revolution.[16]

CHAPTER 17

VISION OF A VIRTUOSO

I am a composer and was born to be a kapellmeister . . . [the rest] is with me a side line.—MOZART in 1778

The city to which Berlioz returned on the doubly revolutionary date of July 14, 1848 was an intellectual desert and a visible shambles. The narrow crooked streets, which had made the raising of barricades easy, showed scars of the fighting, looting and arson. Violence had not quite ceased. "The people kill the poor young constables whenever they catch them alone." The angel of liberty on Duc's column, Place de la Bastille, had a bullet through its gilt body, and the Tuileries were a mass of litter.[1]

Of Berlioz' friends, many were abroad, others stayed with relatives in the country, still others were out of circulation as they made shift with menial jobs. Berlioz saw a pianist playing on the streets for pennies; painters served as crossing sweepers. "I am again living as when I was a medical student in the Latin Quarter, on 80 or 100 francs a month," wrote Berlioz to his brother-in-law. His only source of income was the *Débats,* for "nothing is left of what used to exist in the way of art . . . No one even thinks of it or talks about it."[2] "We attended the opening of the Opera," said Berlioz in his first *feuilleton,* "and some malicious wit suggested that the word should be taken in the sense of 'autopsy.' "

The Chamber did vote "aid" for the dispossessed and unemployed artists, but it was far short of adequate. "Besides, in order to economize, they take back with one hand what they give with the other. Thus, the committee on the Conservatoire proposed yesterday to abolish my post in the library and to divide my salary among the other employees." It is true that Berlioz' office was a sinecure, but he himself was just proposing to the authorities that his status be changed. "It was not my doing if the Conservatoire failed to use my services more actively: the musical views of the previous Director [Cherubini] always kept me at arm's length . . . Yet I could, for instance, hold a chair of Instrumentation. This modern branch of the composer's studies is not taught anywhere, and general opinion has it that I possess the requisite knowledge and that I have even made contributions to it."

The "Citizen Minister" of the Interior did not establish such a chair, but through the influence of Louis Blanc's brother Charles—an engraver and art critic who was the new Director of Fine Arts—Berlioz' post and salary were maintained. It was fortunate, for the newspapers had cut their rate of pay to half, and his expenses were increasing by reason of Harriet's worsened health. She was nearly paralyzed and must have constant attendance. Adèle's husband, the faithful and intelligent Marc Suat, lent Berlioz some money. At the same time, Adèle told her brother of her apprehension at their father's condition: he died a few days later, on the twenty-eighth. "The agony of the last days," she wrote again, "was dreadful. He looked like a galvanized corpse, shaking continually . . . and asking us for impossible things . . . Our caresses would calm him down . . . I held him in my arms with frenzy when he was at his worst. Nanci would run away in terror . . . He was shown your portrait and called you by name, and immediately asked for pen and paper . . . One day, seeing his eyes in search of something, I asked if he wanted anything. 'Nothing, daughter,' he said in the tenderest voice, 'I am looking for your eyes.' This fatherly word reduced us all to tears."

Berlioz could not go to La Côte until the following month. He did not see the long train of sincere mourners—patients and poor people—who followed the country doctor to his grave. Berlioz, still at work on the Death March for *Hamlet* which he had begun in London, could not help associating it with the death of his father, and consequently would never trust himself to play it. In these months an angry kind of worry over the ways and means to keep alive was his normal state. It would have been infuriating to go under (as did his friend and early benefactor De Pons who took poison) when so many idle and useless functionaries were managing to survive. "These people are our enemies—a thousand times more so than the wretches who kill on a barricade. . . . The only problem is for us to avoid dying and to take our time about it." [3] This abstract fury masked affectionate apprehension about his friends in Vienna and the Germanies, and especially about Liszt. As soon as Berlioz heard from Belloni, his friend's secretary, who was in Paris, he could write: "Everyone asked me about you in London, but I had absolutely no idea on what European barricade you stood. . . . So many bankers have failed that I very much fear you have suffered losses. Farewell. I hope to see Belloni tomorrow and to make him talk about you. . . . Your forever devoted: H. Berlioz."

Berlioz left for his birthplace on August 18 and stayed in Dauphiné until September 10. The empty house and familiar horizons, the reunion with his dearly loved Adèle and her kind husband opened up his heart. Nanci came too and he melted to her also despite their mutually uncongenial ways. The subject of inheritance likewise had to be discussed. Each of their shares was worth about 130,000 francs, but since the whole consisted of real property it would be unwise to try to liquidate it at once when the market was stagnant. The three nevertheless had to go to Les Jacques, near Grenoble, to sort out personal effects, and it was there that looking across the river valley Berlioz thought again of his Estelle and decided to go on a pilgrimage to the site of his ideal childhood love. The account of this visit, given in one of the best pages of the *Memoirs,* was doubtless written soon after the event. From his relatives Berlioz found out what was known of Estelle, now Mme. Fornier, a widow of fifty with four children, one of whom was finishing law school in the same class with a young cousin of Berlioz'. Hector took what he termed "the strange liberty" of writing to her, excusing her in advance if she chose to "laugh at the grown man's recollections as she had done at the child's worshiping." He received no reply.

In Paris, grimmer feelings were to be his lot. About the middle of October, Harriet suffered a fifth stroke—while Berlioz and her son were with her, fortunately—but when her doctor was out on call. "For two hours, Louis and I scoured the neighboring streets of Montmartre without finding any physician in. The poor woman was all this time unconscious and more like the dead than the living. Finally her own doctor arrived and bleeding brought her round. . . . One result, however, is that her speech is more impaired than before and it is almost impossible to understand her."

Berlioz accompanied his son back to Rouen and kept him informed of his mother's condition: "She is still in bed and under orders not to talk. The least emotion, too, would be fatal to her. So please do not write her a letter like your last one to me. It is distressful to see you giving yourself up to moping and idleness; you will be eighteen [in four years] without having any career to go into . . . You keep telling me that you want to be a sailor; you must want pretty badly to leave me behind, because once you are at sea God knows when I shall see you. If I were free and independent I should leave with you and we would seek our fortunes in India or elsewhere, but even to travel takes means. . . . And my career as a composer keeps me in France. I would have to give it up if I left the Old World for the New. I write to you as to a grown boy. You will think all this over and you will understand. For no matter what happens, I shall always be your best friend, *the only one* entirely devoted to you and full of unchangeable affection for you. I know you love me and that will make up to me for everything. . . . Tell me again about your teeth: have they been thoroughly cleaned? Farewell, dear child, I kiss you with all my soul."

The heartfelt attachment expressed in this letter—the first that remains of Berlioz' correspondence with his son—does not conceal a certain remorse which Berlioz doubtless felt at having left Louis for six or seven years alone with his mother, or still more alone in boarding school. The causes of the boy's melancholy indolence were perfectly evident to the father, who also sensed the child's desire to retaliate and "leave him behind." Not that Berlioz had abandoned his son; but in those years of travel to Moscow and back, and when Berlioz had come within sight of solid material success, he had been too preoccupied to be anything but deficient as a father. And those same years had transformed the winsome, "badly brought up" baby into a shy despairing adolescent. His "qualities of heart," said his aunt Nanci, were "of a rare sort and most endearing." And she lectured her brother, trying to prove that a good heart was much better than a brilliant mind.

Toward the end of October 1848 Berlioz, aided by Baron Taylor, prepared and led a concert for the benefit of the Musicians' Association. Organized under extreme difficulties, it was intended in part as an inducement to the new Republican leaders to think better of the arts. Four hundred and fifty performers were gathered in the theater of Louis XIV at Versailles, which the public had been admitted to only twice since its construction. The prices were moderate and the program was to suit all tastes without any condescension: Rossini, Meyerbeer, Gluck, Mozart, Beethoven, and three small works by Berlioz. Both orchestra and audience shunned elegance of dress and made up for this populist pride by showing their pleasure a little rowdily. The event turned out badly for Berlioz, by reason—as always—of political interpretations.

His willingness to make music "for the people" was felt to be ill-timed because everyone now predicted the coming of "an Emperor." Louis Napoleon had been elected to the Assembly by four districts, had had his election returns disputed, then validated, had shrewdly declined to take a seat that "might embarrass the government," but declared himself ready to follow the people's will. Whereupon he had been reelected by five districts. The glorious associations of his name and the disgust felt at the Republic's squabbling incompetence made Bonaparte a likely winner of the presidency. At this date the Empire was not inevitable, yet it was widely spoken of as the next step, its presumed style and dignity contrasting with the bad manners that had, among other things, given offense at the Berlioz concert. On that occasion, it seems, "little old Marrast" the president of the Constituent Assembly, had slouched in the armchair of Louis XIV and had appeared, in his lemon-colored gloves, to be enjoying himself altogether too much.

The Republic, though slow, was not ungrateful. It kept Berlioz in his Librarianship, paid the arrears of his salary, and added five hundred francs "to encourage him as a composer." Cavaignac, the republican soldier, was doing all he could to restore the popularity of the regime which the sabotage of the National Workshops and the bloodshed in June had nearly destroyed. The campaign for the presidency in December had been the last chance for staunch republicans and socialists to prove that the country deserved self-government. When that chance failed by producing instead a demagogue, all but a few felt that their hopes had been illusions, and that a true republic could only be the work of a later generation. In the interim between his Republican concert and Bonaparte's success, Berlioz summed up the situation for one of his Russian friends: "What changes since then [1847] in our unhappy Europe! What cries and crimes, what follies and blunders, and what cruel mystifications . . . Paris is still in a fever and has attacks of delirium tremens. To think of the peaceful works of the mind or to seek the beautiful in art and letters under such conditions is like trying to play billiards on a storm-tossed ship. . . ."

Berlioz worked nonetheless. In his reconquered Library at the Conservatoire, he went on with his *Memoirs,* parts of which might make salable articles. He had finished the Death March for *Hamlet* in late September and joined it to the "Death of Ophelia" and the "Religious Meditation" to form a volume which he entitled *Tristia* (after Ovid's "Sad Pieces"). It appropriately signalized for Berlioz a year of exile, defeat, and mourning. He had also revised *La Captive,* the melody that had charmed Rome seventeen years before, making it now into a miniature symphonic poem for voice and orchestra. These small but beautifully finished works once behind him, he could begin the new year with a fresh enterprise: a companion piece to his monumental *Requiem* in the form of an equally large-scale *Te Deum.*

The germinal idea dated back to his Italian notebooks of 1832, only part of that inspiration having gone into the *Funeral* symphony. Berlioz' plan, it will be recalled, was to celebrate the nation's great dead with a vast symphony in seven movements. The idea did not recur to him now because of any similarity between the heroic first Napoleon and his nephew the President, elected in December 1848. Citizen Bonaparte had stumped the country like a vulgar politician, promising peace and plenty, and pretending attachment to republican institutions. The Berlioz *Te Deum* on the contrary was to be a religious and military fresco more closely related to the revolutionary era of which 1848 had revived certain aspects—war, grief, and the terror of divine justice. As for the political fact, Berlioz did desire an Emperor such as Napoleon to put an end to the "grotesque and disgusting farce" and "pretentious stupidities" of the Republic, yet he abstained from voting "so that I shall be sure not to have contributed to any catastrophe."

Composing had to go on to an accompaniment of brain squeezing for the "relentless" newspapers. The *Débats,* reduced in size, was paying little—only eight francs a column, but the *Gazette* kept appearing weekly and paid by the line. Berlioz' printed remarks on the new operas were thus not so concisely witty as the comments in his letters: he could not afford it. "Meyerbeer," he informed Count Wielhorsky, "has begun rehearsing his *Prophète;* he is a very courageous man to risk launching a work of those dimensions at a time when riots or a change of government . . . can cut him short, however great his eloquence. Halévy has just won a tremendous success with his *Val d'Andorre* at the Opéra-Comique. It is really good. There are in his score some charming melodies and things of a high and just style. *I said what I thought* when I wrote of it. It is quite the other way with [Clapisson's] *Jeanne la Folle:* no ideas, no style; it's simply gross, dull, and flat. You will wonder how grossness can combine with flatness. I do not know how the composer did it; it is one of his trade secrets."

A few months later, to Berlioz' delight, the second act of *La Vestale* was put on by the Conservatoire, whose public was properly overwhelmed. By that time (February 1849) Liszt was again in touch with Berlioz, exchanging confidences and even offering financial help which Berlioz did not have to accept. The pianist was himself going through a bad time as regards both money and personal relations.[4]

"I was much upset," Berlioz writes back, "as you can well imagine. But I know how energetic and decided you can be in crucial moments . . . Still, your project [to go to the United States] seems to me *violent*—to cross the Atlantic to make music for Yankees who just now think only of California gold! You are the best judge of the advisability of such a trip. As for what can be done here, I really don't know: it changes with the riot-meter.

"The Italian Theatre flaps only one wing; the Opera never had any, but they say *Le Prophète* will supply the want of them. . . . When the crowds who are coming to the Industrial Exhibition have gone, when the new Chamber is elected and seated, when the emotion caused by the premières of *Le Prophète* has calmed down, maybe you can try something here. We are all impatient to see you."

The reference to the several "first nights" of the new opera alludes to the special effort Meyerbeer made just then to win over Berlioz by inviting him to a private rehearsal. At the same time, possibly at Meyerbeer's instigation, the Conservatoire asked that Berlioz allow something of his to be played at their concerts. The German composer whose mastery of the operatic world was unchallenged seemed eager to have the approval of a less variable judge than the public, and perhaps to share with Berlioz the artistic ground which Meyerbeer in his own mind knew that Berlioz occupied. At any rate, he addressed him as

"Dear and Illustrious Master," and expressing his "love" and "fear" of him, invited him in successive messages to several of the rehearsals, signing the last note: "Your devoted and trembling Meyerbeer." [5]

The day before the occasion of this curious testimonial, two excerpts from the *Damnation of Faust* were given by the Conservatoire. This sudden reopening of a symphony society which had been closed to him since the early days of the *Rob Roy* overture (sixteen years) made Berlioz feel nervous about the outcome. The gracious invitation might prove another blow, especially since his erstwhile admirer Narcisse Girard, who had been eclipsed by Berlioz as conductor, would lead the orchestra. The players anyhow were very friendly and as it turned out the audience also. The composer could feel that his success was like "the overturning of a barrier . . . If the other Great Walls of China that still hem me in . . . should likewise collapse, perhaps the music I have composed might receive the same welcome here as in the rest of Europe and I might be forgiven for being alive and French. Perhaps I might also produce new works, more important than those I have been engaged on . . ."

Right or wrong, Berlioz felt that recognition on home ground was necessary to his career. "You cannot imagine," he wrote to Janin, "with what heartbreak I sit down to my task when I am convinced that my work will be well received only abroad." Though he kept counseling himself to be patient, he doubtless seemed to his friends impatient and certainly unresigned. Yet he had gauged the French temper accurately for a century to come, and he knew better than his friends the difference between working for a well-disposed steady audience and working in the void. It was not long after this artistic interregnum in Paris that for poignant practical reasons Berlioz denied himself the right to compose a symphony of which the ideas came to him in sleep on two successive nights. His phalanx of twelve hundred in the best days of the 1830's had not disappeared but they were discouraged too, and even more distraught. The continuity of mind and will which he could maintain through all vicissitudes could not be expected of them—it could not even be found among his enemies. Thus Fétis, who was present at the concert of April 15, 1849, begged permission to produce Berlioz' symphonies in Brussels. "The man," wrote Berlioz to his sister, "who has written so much to prove that they are anything but music—what puppets!"

The *Te Deum* was growing slowly amid the usual interruptions. Liszt had given up the trip to America and was planning to come to Paris instead, and join with Berlioz in a concert which could be linked with the much-touted Industrial Exhibition. Meanwhile Meyerbeer's advances constituted a diplomatic problem. Berlioz could not help seeing in him an ambiguous sort of well-wisher who exploited others' musical and dramatic inventions without saying so, yet was not wholly ungrateful: in Berlin Meyerbeer had assisted him and later had been a prime mover in the presentation dinner after the *Damnation of Faust*. He was moreover a genuine musician whose artistic conscience was real as far as giving the operatic public full value for its support. But Meyerbeer was also an intriguer who had "captured" the Opera and posted his henchmen—such as Girard and Alexandre—in key positions. According to an expressive exaggeration circulated by Heine, the musical boss had "bought his way for the next hundred years." [6]

Berlioz' review of *Le Prophète* was therefore hard to write. On the surface a eulogy, with its few objections tactfully cushioned, it really expressed a very qualified approval of the opera. One has only to compare this cool judicial report with Berlioz' no less critical but thoroughly life-breathing studies of Gluck to assess the difference and to conclude—as against certain critics—that the art of Meyerbeer did not enthrall him. A letter to his sister shows the extent to which Berlioz felt constrained: "I am also free of my article on *Le Prophète*. . . . Meyerbeer has the good sense not to take amiss the four or five reservations I put into my ten columns of praise.[7] I should have liked to spare him the pain . . . but there are certain things that must absolutely be said out loud. I cannot let anyone think that I approve or even condone the compromises which such a master makes in favor of the bad taste of a part of the public. . . . The score contains some very fine things side by side with feeble and detestable ones. But the splendor of the show will make everything pass muster."

Sincere even in his diplomacy, Meyerbeer chose to head the delegation which in July presented the medal struck in honor of the *Damnation:* it had been impossible during the two years since the banquet to find the gold with which to make it —a fortunate delay, for it brought the token to the composer after the success of the two excerpts at the Conservatoire instead of after the failure at the Opéra-Comique.

But family concerns for the moment outweighed all else.

Harriet had caught the cholera during the spring epidemic—Berlioz suffered only a bout of grippe—and he had nursed her during nights of continuous vomiting. Now Nanci developed an undiagnosed ailment which despite Hector's less than complete affection for her caused him deep uneasiness. It turned out to be cancer of the breast, which carried her off a year later and made of Berlioz a convinced advocate of euthanasia.

Harriet at last recovered and seemed even in better health than before, though still paralyzed and incoherent of speech. As for Louis's plans, Berlioz furthered them with the help of the Bertins who put him in touch with a Captain Page, recently reduced to half pay by the Republic, but still enthusiastic about the sea. So much so that Berlioz' own wanderlust revived: to hear the sea! to travel! He yearned to leave Paris and smell again the poplar woods along the Arno, which a friend in the diplomatic service alluded to in a letter; he wanted to forget the *feuilletons* ("they will kill me in the end") and settle down in solitude at Les Jacques, which was to be his share of the family estate. He planned a reunion in Grenoble so that he might see Nanci in her illness, take stock of the property, and renew acquaintance with old friends of his mother's—"if any are left": in short he was alive with outgoing emotion that was virtually objectless.

In Paris, the "hair-raising comedy" was going on: near-riots, provincial delegations dressed in the garb of 1793, and endless debate and gossip as to the fidelity or the deep designs of the new Prince-President. The no less new American President, General Taylor, was giving the deriders of republics cause to jeer when the report of his inaugural quoted him as saying: "We are at peace with all the world and the rest of mankind." Elsewhere reaction was seeping back into power. By treachery and savage force Austria, Italy, Hungary, Bohemia, Prussia and Denmark were won anew to kings. Constitutions were torn up and rebels indiscriminately shot. Two of Berlioz' best friends in Austria faced firing squads. Richard Wagner, who had rioted and made speeches in Dresden, fled before the enemy and took refuge in Paris. He arrived just in time to see another insurrection fomented by the news that French troops under Oudinot were helping to overthrow Mazzini's republic in Rome. President Bonaparte quelled the Paris republicans while his general chose July 14 to announce the reconquered sovereignty of Pius IX.

Wagner's loss of place and livelihood was somewhat compensated for by a fine gesture of Liszt's, supported by Berlioz: Liszt was putting on *Tannhäuser* in Weimar and sent a long eulogy of the opera to Berlioz, who reproduced it in full in the *Débats* with a cordial introduction.[8]

Berlioz' trip to Dauphiné had to be given up: Harriet was too ill. And Nanci had gone to take the waters at La Mothe.

When doctors send a patient to a watering place, it is generally because they are at their wits' end. . . . I cannot tell you, dear sister [this was to Adèle] what sad and deep thoughts bind us three to whatever is a reminder of our wonderful and excellent father. The memory of him will never leave me. The approaching anniversary of his death gave it fresh and painful force. I have his book, as you know, annotated by him, and I have just read it. His pencillings showed him pondering and correcting with great care, and I was struck afresh by the fine integrity with which he practiced medicine, as well as by his sagacious mind, which should have shone in a wider circle. But his ineffable goodness and the attentions he lavished on us children are far deeper motives for our regret. . . . I should like to see you both; give me at once some wholly truthful news of Nanci. I shall write to her soon.

I have got back to my work (music, I mean). I am finishing, polishing, completing my new score. A sort of feverish impatience grips me because with regard to music I am still revolving a *number of projects.* And I want to set them down as soon as possible. This ardent occupation is the only one that can help me to repress a growing love of travel. I dream only of ships, seas, distant isles, adventurous explorations. My musical voyagings through Europe have only developed this half-buried instinct of old. I can see its futility, its childishness, but can do nothing about it. Were it not for my obligations here, I would again take a chance on productive tours in [Scandinavia] and in Russia, where I was so well received. Perhaps I may be able to go to Holland this winter: it's three steps away, thanks to the railroads. Travel on land is so easy and so cheap these days. . . .

No single document, perhaps, conveys so naturally the interlinked emotions, sensations, and intellectual interests to which Berlioz responded and out of which he achieved in his art a balance of contrary tensions. Nor is it farfetched to see in the longing for ocean voyages and Pacific isles a first sign of the European artist's repudiation of industrial urban life, later acted out by Rimbaud, Gauguin and others.

During the first week of October 1849, the *Te Deum* for three choruses, organ, and orchestra was finished, and Berlioz had to begin devising an occasion for the usual test by audition. He obtained an audience from the President of the Republic, but was preceded by a deputation of sixty long-winded provincials. He waited an hour and a half and got only excuses for his pains. Not seeking a second chance, he detemined to try emancipating himself and the art of music in France from dependence upon the state. The means was to be a Philharmonic Society, which he at once set about organizing.

Dietsch, of the Opera, would conduct the chorus, many devoted friends would play for modest shares of the early profits, and the choice of pieces would be made by a representative committee. But the idea of a private person starting any such enterprise was too new in France: it lasted only eighteen months. Its cash reserves were inadequate, and Berlioz' connection with it was enough to consolidate a resourceful opposition. Still, it gave a dozen concerts, it publicized the idea that was too new, and it established the foundations upon which the later organizations of Pasdeloup, Colonne and Lamoureux were reared. By a just return, it was these orchestras that made known to the French the more accessible parts of Berlioz' concert works. Meantime an independent, unofficial society, neither limited in repertory like Seghers's "Saint Cecilia," nor politically doctrinaire like David's "Union," would satisfy the composer's undeviating musical ambition. What he called his "life sentence at hard labor," namely journalism, he knew to be the merest sideline. "Give me orchestras to lead," he promised, "give me rehearsals to go through, let me stay eight or even ten hours on my feet, practicing with the chorus, singing their parts when they miss, while I beat time for the rest until my arm gets cramped and I spit blood; let me carry music desks, double basses, and harps; compel me to correct proofs during the night time, and I will do it. . . . I have done it and can do it again."

The Philharmonic Society received from the outset more spiritual than practical encouragement. There was a distinguished list of sponsors from the worlds of music and fashion. The press favored the plan without grasping its difficulties: "The society comes into being just at the right moment, in a musical twilight when among artists and audiences alike the desire to act was succumbing to paralysis." But the "action" came from Berlioz' will power and stayed there. For a year and a half he assumed the gigantic task of corralling and rehearsing the players, handling the publicity, watching the finances, soliciting aid, and arranging or composing music for the programs. In the flush of initial success he was a whirlwind of versatility and good humor; at its decline a year later he was sick to death. In between, the problem was threefold: finances, authority, and musical fare.

The first concert on February 19, 1850 brought in four thousand francs and was hailed as a triumph. The net profit amounted to twenty-seven hundred francs, which had to be divided in equal shares among ninety instrumentists and one hundred and ten singers, plus three shares for the chorus master, Pierre Dietsch, and four shares for Berlioz as conductor and General Director. This meant that for three rehearsals and one concert, each performer received thirteen francs and the two leaders about fifty francs apiece.

For such poor sums, the Society could not command prompt and faithful attendance at rehearsals, nor did its outlay secure anything but a very poor hall. What was even worse, the group was divided in allegiance: the singers—Opera people—"belonged" to Dietsch; the orchestra was devoted to Berlioz. This might have gradually been forgotten had not Dietsch fancied himself as a composer, and had an accident not brought the division to the surface.[9] At Angers, in mid-April 1850, a corps of troops marched in step across a bridge and the rhythm broke it. Hundreds of officers and men were drowned and the whole country was in mourning. The Philharmonic Society proposed to give a benefit for the victims' families at the Church of St. Eustache, and the question came up whether a mass by Dietsch (he had four on hand) or Berlioz' *Requiem* should be played. After some wrangling within the Committee, after Berlioz' offer to reisgn so as to let the benefit proceed, and after a protracted dispute between the singing and the playing members, the *Requiem* was given, under Berlioz' sole direction. It was an impressive performance which netted a large sum.

Henceforth, Berlioz made every effort to find other modern music than his own to put on the program. Remembering his difficult beginnings he had provided in the statutes that each year the Society would play the work of a young Rome Prize composer after his return from Italy. None had yet been submitted. Berlioz' friend Morel, a founding member of the Society who had left to take up duties at Marseille, had an overture which was played. Then a rich amateur named Cohn proposed a work which he would pay to have performed. The Committee reserved the right to consider it, and ultimately had it played to a house full of M. Cohn's friends. Works by Weber, Halévy, Spohr, Léon Kreutzer, Mendelssohn, Gluck and Beethoven were passed on and put in rehearsal. An Italian prima donna named Frezzolini and loaded with jewels was exhibited as well as allowed to sing.[10] But it was only too plain that apart from the great classics, the only music that drew the public and elicited important notice was Berlioz' own. During its short life, the Society accordingly played (besides the *Requiem*) two of the symphonies, parts of the *Damnation* and several of the small choral works, to which Berlioz had now added two: *La Menace des Francs* (March and Chorus) and the "Shepherds' Farewell," the first completed movement of the later *Infant Christ*.

Yet it was impossible for external and internal reasons to have the Philharmonic Society feature Berlioz alone. The fact was that in France certainly, and in Europe almost to the same extent, there was in 1850 no one else on whom to draw. It was indeed a twilight, and far from rejoicing at being *facile princeps,* Berlioz felt it with acute wretchedness. "I am utterly sad —Spontini is dead." Lesueur, Chopin, Mendelssohn, and now Spontini. Schumann was entering his last decade in ill-health and mental darkness; Liszt was given over to conducting and virtuoso work and was so far only planning his symphonic poems; while Wagner as far as anyone knew was still far from his true path. In the *Débats,* Berlioz wrote Spontini's obituary, and to his friend Morel he dropped a word about him that reveals the sense of void in which he felt himself working: "I had come to love him by dint of admiration." [11]

One result of this situation was to help create the legend of Berlioz' egotistical scorn of his contemporaries and satisfaction with his own merits. He gave offense by his admiration of the great dead, for he seemed to claim kinship with them and so to reproach the living mediocrities who—to the onlooker—seemed just as good. No public can understand why an artist who is conscious of great powers would enjoy feeling humble in the company of the mighty, nor has criticism yet taught the world to differentiate between an artist's impersonal egotism and the common brand of self-love. The world thinks that a Beethoven or a Berlioz, a Wagner or a Delacroix, should be ashamed to feel the reality of his genius, or should have at least the decency to say nothing about it.[12]

And yet we know that the Lord looked upon his handiwork and found it good. We fail to draw the inference: the power to create implies the power to judge, and occasional failures of judgment in mortal creators prove nothing against the rule. Berlioz could see how the modern world was corrupting, or at least confusing the artist's proper self-regard: "The vanity of actors and authors," he wrote on New Year's Day 1851, "is no longer caused by love of fame, but by the crass love of money, by avarice and the passion for luxury, by insatiable material greed. They want hyperbolic praise because this alone stirs the crowd and leads it to this one or that. And they want the crowd because it alone brings money.

"Hence today one no longer finds artists able to limit themselves to the making of a few polished, unlucrative works, preferring a moderate and painstaking output to the constant exploitation of their overworked minds."

Spontini's death had left a vacancy at the Institute, and to fill it Berlioz was the logical candidate. He paid the necessary calls. At the first ballot a younger man of the theater, Ambroise Thomas, was elected by a majority of thirty. The remaining eight votes were split among Niedermeyer and Batton. Not a single vote was cast for Berlioz.

While certain persons were trying to "dephilharmonize our society," that is, bring disunity into its ranks; and while "the rascally Italian press" (Scudo and Azevedo) were trying to chill the enthusiasm of the instrumentis.s, Berlioz learned the truth about Nanci's desperate condition. He tried, in the teeth of hopelessness, to give her courage by chatty letters of Parisian doings: Hugo's salon was full of ugly old ladies, but at least there was no bad music served. Dumas had a daughter of nineteen, "too much like her father to be pretty, but whose somewhat gracile quadroon appearance . . . heightened by a sequin headdress, made her look like an odalisque from Madagascar. Farewell, poor dear sister. God grant that you may have read this letter to the end, and that it may have helped you forget your pain for two minutes. I shake your good Camille by the hand. Farewell again; I kiss you."

Then a month later, to Adèle: "Give me at least some news of yourself. Your silence is disturbing. I am afraid of your grief, though you must have suffered a thousand times more than I while watching the torture and agony of our poor dear just delivered. . . . Are you ill? In that case, let Suat write to me. Farewell, I kiss you. Poor sister! We are now only two."

In June 1850, news came that Balzac was back from his second Russian journey and married to his long-courted love, Mme. Hanska. Berlioz wrote to him immediately: "Since the eve of my trip to Russia, I have not seen you once, which makes three enormous years. Have you ever thought of the anguish that would be felt by certain passionate beings at seeing the features of their idol only in mirrors thrice removed? That is the way I feel not having seen you. . . . In less roundabout fashion, let me ask you when I can go and shake your hand and beg you to introduce to Mme. Balzac one of her most devoted servants." The simile of the mirrors betokened, among other things, Berlioz' physical weariness. He had constant stomach cramps, headaches, and the need of sleep. The pace he had set himself was, *mutatis mutandis,* the pace that Balzac had followed too, and that carried him off two months after Berlioz had greeted him—another void among the ranks of his peers.

That winter of 1850, filled with the business of the Philharmonic, Berlioz' son set out on his apprentice voyage to the West Indies. The father was on tenterhooks until he received his first letter, from Haiti. It had taken fifty-three days, and thus began for Berlioz' apprehensive mind a fresh source of torment. The letter reported good health, good spirits, and also the death of a friend in the new world, to whom Berlioz had recommended his son. This led Berlioz to review the losses by death which he had suffered for three years past, besides his father and sister: Balzac and Chopin, Mendelssohn and Spontini, Frédéric Soulié and numerous foreign musicians or patrons of music for whom Berlioz felt regard and gratitude—Alfred Becher and Count Batthiany, both shot, in Austria and in Hungary respectively; Prince Lichnowski, mobbed by peasants; and the oldest friend and patron of all, Augustin de Pons (he had lent the money for Berlioz' Mass of 1825) who being destitute had taken poison.[13]

Louis's return to France in the spring of 1851 dissipated some of Berlioz' gloom. The boy looked grown up and well, and both were pleased, for Louis had made the flattering discovery at Haiti and other ports of call that he was the son of a famous man on whose account he himself was readily invited. On his side the father found in his boy signs of maturing intelligence and responsibility. The second apprentice cruise would still have to be paid for, but after that the young sailor could support himself.

Together they went to see Harriet who still lived in the

house at Montmartre where Louis had been born. She could sit in the garden, see her boy during his shore leave and her husband when he had a free hour between rehearsals. The climb up the hill to her house was easier now that steps had been built and Berlioz came often, for she needed attentions that only he could interpret to her nurses: she spoke even less French than before, virtually none at all, and enunciated very imperfectly.

During this period also Berlioz succeeded his good friend Bottée de Toulmon as Chief Librarian of the Conservatoire. This brought a slight increase in salary and an opportunity to add to the teaching resources of the library by creating a collection of instruments. A few weeks later, the Minister of Commerce appointed Berlioz to the jury which was to judge musical instruments at the forthcoming London Exhibition of 1851. Though this was everywhere hailed as a great honor, Berlioz foresaw the delicacy of the task ahead: "I am very much afraid . . . that there will be . . . a stormy contest between the instrument makers of Paris and those of Berlin. All are friends of mine and I shall be caught between hammer and anvil. But I am resolved to be a Minos worthy of such assizes and not to render Injustice. The Lord knows (or rather, I wager that He does not yet know) where I shall find lodgings. . . . The Minister . . . cannot say whether the English management has kept a kennel for us in the Crystal Palace or elsewhere . . . But then the Minister is very young—only four days old."

A trip to England at this juncture of the Philharmonic's affairs was most opportune. Berlioz could leave the Society with honor instead of sinking with it, dragged down in part by the desire of some to make it pay at all costs. Berlioz' English friends expressed delight at the news of his mission and at the prospect of seeing him again, for as the *Illustrated London News* had said, he was "an excellent classical scholar, a choice wit, and full of fine enthusiasm." There were, in addition more than casual hints that a great musical project might be set on foot if he were in London to lead it: the score of the *Te Deum* was ready for performance if some great occasion, musical and national, should call for an original work.

CHAPTER 18

VICTORIAN LONDON

Music is good to the melancholy, bad to those who mourn, and neither good nor bad to the deaf.—SPINOZA

Berlioz paid his second visit to England in the spring of 1851, officially for the purpose of judging musical instruments at the Great Exhibition. But he hoped at the same time to be able to recoup the debacle in which he had been involved three years before by Jullien's mismanagement. By good fortune he soon found among his English acquaintances the almost ideal backer. T. Frederick Beale, the barrister-musician who was a partner in the publishing house of Cramer and Company, had faith in Berlioz as man and artist and the confidence was returned: "I am dealing with a business man of a rare kind—honest, intelligent, charming, and rich." The plan was to establish a new concert society.[1]

Beale put Berlioz on salary from the moment of his arrival (£600 a year) which not only relieved the composer of a good deal of journalism, but also helped him out as official delegate, for France was acting in the most niggardly fashion towards its representatives. It paid their expenses while in London, but not the cost of going there and returning, and it set a limit to their stay regardless of the duties undertaken. Berlioz, who liked to see things through, stayed last of all the French committee "in order to see justice done. . . . France comes out ahead beyond any possible comparison: Erard, Sax, and Vuillaume. The rest is more or less in the class of penny whistles and pots and pans."

Together with Sterndale Bennett, Thalberg, George Smart and six others, Berlioz had to examine and listen to all the instruments from piccolos to organs, submitted by the makers of five nations. Even the composer's worst enemy might consider that he suffered on this occasion more than was his due. "It splits your head to hear these hundreds of wretched machines, each more out of tune than the next, three or four excepted." But for once trade and art happened to combine their claims upon his trained ear. As a practiced flute player, he was especially interested in Böhm's latest designs and could assert that in comparison with the product of twenty years' experimentation, the old eight-hole wooden flute still in use when Berlioz began was "only fit to be played at a fair." These, of course, were his casual pronouncements. The final report he wrote for his "Section" was as precise and dignified as any chancery could wish.

The contrast in the quality of the wind instruments aptly symbolizes the kind of progress which the entire Exhibition—the largest and richest yet assembled—was to illustrate. The Prince Consort had had difficulty in obtaining consent to his "extravagant" plans, but their practical success won over the envious and the timid. Coming so soon after the troubles of 1848-1849, the gathering was feared by Continental rulers, who saw themselves being conveniently massacred under one roof. In England, some had forecast hooliganism on a large scale as a result of letting "the people" out of their hovels. To the contrary, the most impressive feature of the show was the respect, good nature, and self-discipline of the huge crowds. It was estimated that at one time one hundred thousand persons milled about in the nineteen acres of Hyde Park covered by the Crystal Palace. This structure, by the way, although we tend to associate it with garishness, was in fact the fulfillment of fifteen years of new thought in architecture and the first piece of genuine industrial building in glass and metal.[2] It was the first of the many exhibition buildings out of which came the Eiffel Tower and the Galerie des Machines, themselves forerunners of twentieth-century architecture in steel, glass, and concrete. We may thus date the beginning of the combined mass age and machine age from 1851. So new was it to the human imagination that Berlioz had to explain to Adèle how unlikely it was that he could find his uncle Félix Marmion by chance in the crowded enclosure. The two men's letters had miscarried and though both were in London for some time, they failed to meet.

But despite Tennyson's call—

Uplift a thousand voices full and sweet
In this wide hall with earth's invention stored

no music in keeping with the age graced the Exhibition itself. Modern painting, too, was represented elsewhere, in Litchfield House, St. James's Square, to which Delacroix sent his "Moorish Cavalry Charge." Berlioz had to content himself with drawing up a plan for a possible concert which would represent European composers and performers while furnishing the visitors with four opportunities to hear a program of monumental music ranging from Handel and Bortniansky to Rossini and Berlioz' own *Te Deum*.[3]

The only monumental music available in London was the concert of charity children at St. Paul's which he describes in the *Evenings with the Orchestra*. This "musical impression" moved Berlioz and some of his colleagues to tears, while it furnished a practical demonstration of his views on this type of mass art. "There," as he wrote to d'Ortigue, "is the realization of a part of my dream, and the proof that the power of musical masses is absolutely unknown, on the Continent at least."

At the very same moment, Berlioz was also entranced by the diametrically opposite style: a Frenchman named Rousselot had organized in London a Beethoven Quartet Society, of which Berlioz' friend Heinrich Ernst was first violin. Berlioz lodged in the same house with Rousselot and was invited to sit in on the rehearsals. At times when Berlioz had to write his article for the *Débats,* he would keep the doors open between rooms, even though this stopped all writing. "Enter, ye sublime melodies! . . . Where, where can Beethoven have found these thousands of phrases, all so poetically characteristic and all different? What unexpected turns! But what's this, what's this?—a prima donna is beginning an aria! John, shut the door."

Besides the less-known Beethoven, the London offering just then gave Berlioz a chance to hear *The Marriage of Figaro* and, still rarer, *The Magic Flute*—". . . those wonderful pages, in which Mozart has used the style which might be called antique-religious . . . Beauty reigns throughout—expression, melody, harmony, rhythm, instrumentation and modulation. Never before Mozart had anyone approached such perfection in the genre, and I fear no one will approach it again after him. It would be folly to attempt it. . . . Nothing equals this grandeur, serenity, strength, and sweetness combined. . . . The earth and its sad passions are forgotten. . . . We are on the threshold of the infinite."

These impressions Berlioz could gather in spite of the indignities practiced upon the score by Michael Costa, director of Covent Garden and himself a "composer." Ill-rehearsed in ten days and sung mostly in the rowdy Italian manner, Mozart's work was further defaced by "trombonization"—"a three-part continuo with bass-drum and attached-cymbal obbligato . . . The bovine instrument couches on Mozart's delicate orchestration as aptly as would a trowelful of mortar on a painting by Raphael. . . ." Critical honesty made Berlioz utter this just complaint, although self-interest would have indicated a discreet silence, for Costa was a great power in London music. Like a second Habeneck he was in charge both of the opera and of the chief orchestra, the Philharmonic. It was enough to be defying him in action, Berlioz' backers having planned to set up a New Philharmonic and to impose on Covent Garden *Benvenuto Cellini* or any new work for the stage that Berlioz might write. In keeping with this prospect, though Berlioz went back to Paris in August and reported on the Exhibition, he had leased an apartment in London for 1852.

Benvenuto was in the air because Liszt wanted to produce it at Weimar. Berlioz was touched by the thought, and a look at the score acted like a tonic. "It will be a great pleasure for me to see this poor brainchild revive, or rather, be born under your direction. I have sent the score to my copyist who is repairing it and making a few necessary changes." These changes ultimately amounted to the thorough revising of the dramatic plan—three acts instead of two with only two changes of scene; a swifter denouement;[4] and the removal at once of verbal irrelevancies and of some consessions demanded by singers and managers in 1838. "What ravages those opera people forced me to make then. . . ! It's devilish lively, and I shall never again find such a shower of young ideas. But this only makes it the harder to perform: theatre people, singers especially, are so devoid of *humor*. But I count on you to Pygmalionize all those statues."

By February 1852, Liszt had been working at the opera for four months and the *première* was set for the sixteenth. He invited Berlioz to come and stay with him and the Princess Wittgenstein at the spacious Villa Altenburg.[5] Berlioz tactfully declined: "You can guess that Marie, who has never heard *Benvenuto,* wants to join me . . . so don't press us, but be good enough to reserve a small suite for us at the Hotel de Russie or elsewhere . . . My arrangements with Beale," added Berlioz, "are now concluded and I have to be back in Paris by the 24th at latest."

Berlioz never left Paris. Before the scheduled opening, *Benvenuto* had to be postponed. Liszt explained that Beck, the tenor, and a small group of his "followers" were sabotaging the work and spreading the rumor that it would ruin the voices of the participants. "It surprised me greatly," replied the hardened Berlioz, "that some such thing had not yet occurred . . . The worst thing about this tenor is that his ill-will goes with a lack of capacity, and that his crowd . . . may form a cabal on the first night. But I shall say nothing to discourage you further. I am behind you in exact proportion to your own noble persistence. Act as if I were not involved . . . If the tenor spoils his role, perhaps the audience will notice it; besides, if the rest comes through I'll be more than content. . . .

"Farewell. No need to recommend Joachim to me: I know him of old and esteem him highly.[6] I leave [for London] in a few hours. The Paris papers must have told you the facts about the New Philharmonic Society. It has devilishly stirred up London and I shall have on my neck, as soon as I arrive, all of old England in a fury. Anderson, Costa and the rest are the angriest. But if Beale lets me have the *needful amount of rehearsing* I snap my fingers at their opposition. Farewell, dear Liszt . . . write to me in London—*the truth* as always: I have faith only in you. . . ."

The six months that Berlioz spent in Paris between the Exhibition and his return to London had seen a change in the government. In December 1851 Louis-Napoleon had by his first *coup d'état* made himself Prince-President for life and virtual dictator. The Second Republic was certainly overthrown by force, for quantities of resisters were arrested, shot, or exiled, but the change could not be called a revolution and many liberals took it with resignation or indifference.[7]

On his side, Berlioz noticed that the rise and fall of regimes brought no alteration in the state of music. Meyerbeer held the stage at the Opera: when *Le Prophète* was off, *Les Huguenots* was on. The Opéra-Comique, always happy-go-lucky, assimilated anything whatever. " 'For the belly, everything counts' as Sancho Panza used to say. That doughty squire would have been such an intrepid follower of comic operas! . . . Of Gluck and Mozart this breed will never know anything. It thinks *Don Giovanni* was written by Musard because the latter unquestionably wrote quadrilles on themes from the opera."

Within that half year a few concerts had taken place at which Berlioz was performed, not under his baton. With him gone, his Paris Philharmonic disintegrated completely. It had played the work of a gifted young man, Ernest Reyer, who had put up fifteen hundred francs for the performance, but it could not be mustered when Berlioz received a later offer of two concerts.

Berlioz, being neither in politics nor close to it, remained as unmoved as Delacroix by acts that would once have aroused his indignation—for instance the treatment of Hugo and other intellectuals. The power to react had been blunted by overuse. Both Delacroix and Berlioz hoped that a stable government would favor their respective arts, more dependent than literature on official favor. If the Prince-President held views similar to his uncle's, and if the regime were proud and decorative, it might provide occasions for grand ceilings and *Te Deums.* What Péguy said of Victor Hugo's Bonapartism certainly applies to the other two members of the artistic trinity: *"Le vrai Napoléon, c'est le Napoléon où l'on rythme."* [8]

Even so, it may be deemed fortunate that it was not Berlioz' *Te Deum* that was chosen in January 1852 to celebrate the brummagem pomp of the nascent Second Empire. Berlioz was in fact suspect to the new regime. He belonged to the house of Bertin, whose Orleanist opposition continued *in petto;* he had played for the Republic and been protected from its rigors by the Director of Fine Arts, Louis Blanc's brother Charles. He was, above all, an independent mind, whom official theaterdom and the "sound" people could not overawe. In a word, he was *persona non grata*—again just like Delacroix—to the dubious new authorities. For this was not a Napoleonic regime but rather the first modern dictatorship—demagogic in tone, bourgeois in manners, anti-intellectual in both capacities.

Before leaving for his London engagement, Berlioz conducted two concerts for Heinrich Ernst, and since no music of his own was played, he could publish an account of them. They were great successes which somewhat redeemed the dead level of ordinary music, even if it was the violin of Ernst and the piano of Leopold von Meyer that drew the crowd. Elsewhere, said Berlioz, the public does not even like what is bad. . . . We artists live in a state of death. . . ." This could not be the view of a government which like its predecessors found the Opera a good instrument of rule: patronage, women, a means to celebrate glory and to show off stability. With reckless honesty, Berlioz wrote a *feuilleton* on behalf of his fellow musicians who, he said, had such just grievances that on an official occasion they made audible murmurings and the Prince-President found it expedient to withdraw. By an oversight, the article passed the censor and came out in the *Débats* as the sole outburst of criticism in a muzzled press. Berlioz was swamped with visits and letters of congratulation. The working half of the Opera now loved him, the other half cursed, while Louis Napoleon's shady entourage put him down among those to keep a watchful eye on.

Urged by his advisers, Berlioz wrote the Prince's private secretary a letter to show that his published remarks signified neither defiance nor blackmail. His attitude toward the Prince for "pulling France out of the morass . . . could be summed up as one of grateful admiration." The letter was sincere; it was necessary and yet impossible to make convincing, therefore useless and—what is worse—unbecoming for a man in the position that Berlioz should have occupied. He derived no benefit from it, for one has to be of the chameleon blood to profit from acts of submission, and it was plain that future acts of independence would occur. This was all the more likely that after the suppression of political news, Bertin counted on Berlioz for extended treatment of whatever subjects were in the air. The canny editor and opposition leader was even loath to let Berlioz go to London.

By the spring of 1852, Beale and his partners had launched the New Philharmonic and subscriptions were coming in. The rate was two guineas for six concerts; artists were entitled to half price. Exeter Hall was chosen, despite Berlioz' strong feeling that it was too large for musical and practical results. The investment of over £2000 had persuaded his backers that they needed box-office returns in proportion. "I have an excellent orchestra," wrote Berlioz to Adèle, "and a choice chorus, so that everything goes as it should. Only the soloists defy all efforts to animate them; they sing like marble monuments. . . ." Berlioz and Marie had a small but comfortable place on Old Cavendish Street and the composer, who read Dickens and took in matinees, became more of a Londoner than ever. He liked the green squares and parks, and took walks into the country, finding delight in the "luxuriant vegetation not to be matched anywhere on the Continent."

As on earlier visits, he received many invitations "of which the British are very lavish" to clubs and private houses, and like all persons whose character combines reserve with lively feelings, he found quite congenial the formal—even stiff—manners of Victorian intellectuals and men of business. For Adèle's peace of mind he had to refute French superstitions about English brutality. "Your opinions about cockfighting and other such things you'll allow me not to answer seriously . . . They are ideas which date back to the Empire." Berlioz felt especially welcome at the house of Harriet Grote, wife of the historian, whose salon brought together statesmen and artists of all nationalities. His contacts with the musical and theatrical worlds were of the most cordial and he had the respect of all the critics without exception.

Before the first concert, due March 24, Berlioz heard good news of *Benvenuto* at Weimar. "My dear, good and wonderful friend," he wrote in reply to Liszt, "I am overjoyed . . . to have this new proof of your friendship for me. I embrace you with all my heart and say 'Thank you' without making phrases. . . . Don't forget to transmit my gratitude to the artists of the Weimar theatre for the talent and the work they have put into seconding your efforts, and you can add some words of excuse for the difficulties which my score entails. Tell them that in performing as they have done such whimsical and impetuous music, they have given the greatest proof of musicianship that anyone could ask of artists today."

Berlioz also wrote a well-turned letter in answer to Princess Carolyne's congratulations and, at her suggestion, another to the Grand Duchess of Weimar. To the Paris newspapers he merely communicated a part of Liszt's victory bulletin: "Hail the Master-Goldsmith! . . . *Benvenuto Cellini,* which was performed here yesterday, revealed its full stature as a work of art. . . . I thank Berlioz most heartily for the noble pleasure that the attentive study of his score has given me. It is one of the most powerful works I know, at once gorgeous filigree work and living sculpture of true originality."

This vindication of his musical drama must have strengthened in Berlioz the retrospective mood which had accompanied the revision of the score, for we find him revolving the idea of a complete edition of his works, including the *Treatise on Or-*

chestration. He had begun going over his printed scores, tabulating errors, replacing older instruments, and making other corrections based on recent rehearing. On the flyleaf of one of the scores we find a significant note: "Twenty-five works at an average of 10 francs each would make the set 250 francs. I should like the complete works to be sent to the Chapels or Philharmonic Societies of Brunswick, Hanover, Carlsruhe, Berlin, Vienna, Weimar, Munich, Bremen, Hamburg, Dresden, Leipzig, Amsterdam, London, and St. Petersburg."

This task occupied only leisure moments during several years, for republication under one imprint was beset with difficulties. For the time being, Berlioz could only draw up a list of all the available items, with a description of each and the name of its publisher. Bearing the date 1852, this catalogue argues the author's awareness of the meaning of his career.

The first six concerts of the New Philharmonic were a series of triumphs—a demonstration that Berlioz' mission was anything but mistimed or misplaced in England. While Liszt was conducting the second night of *Benvenuto,* Berlioz was presenting the "Jupiter" symphony, Beethoven's triple concerto, Weber's *Oberon* overture, Rossini's *William Tell* overture and the first four parts of the *Romeo and Juliet* symphony—all of which the audience and the press received with enthusiasm. It was, according to the *Musical World* "the commencement of a new epoch" in English orchestral music.

At the second concert, the *pièce de résistance,* garnished with solos and trifles, was Beethoven's Fifth. For the third, besides repeating on request the excerpts from *Romeo,* Berlioz had determined to force down large fragments of Spontini's *La Vestale* against a British prejudice of twenty-five years' standing. He meant to commemorate the composer's recent death and would brook no opposition. All by himself he incarnated the Spontini tradition, the last phase of the reformed opera style based upon the works of Gluck and Mozart. On the afternoon of the concert, Berlioz received an oblong package with a letter from Spontini's widow: ". . . Allow me to offer you the conductor's baton with which my dear husband used to direct the works of Gluck and Mozart as well as his own. How could it be better used than by your able hand. . . . Tonight, as you conduct *La Vestale,* it will remind you . . . of him who loved you so much and so greatly admired your works. . . ."

At this same concert, by a coincidence easily explained, Mme. Pleyel—the former Camille Moke—played the *Concertstück* of Weber: she now had connections with the *other* firm of French piano manufacturers, Erard, and Erard was Spontini's brother-in-law. He had escorted to London his sister and the "queen of pianists," who at the final concert was also to play one of Liszt's great pieces. There was in fact a duel of virtuosos between Camille Pleyel and Liszt's pupil Wilhelmine Clauss, whom Berlioz thought highly of. In her anxiety over this championship bout, Camille complained to the trustees that Berlioz had accompanied her badly in the Weber. No one else had noticed it, and she lacked the wit to see that although Berlioz might at one time have shot or strangled her, at no time would he commit a crime against Weber.

For the fourth concert, Berlioz produced Beethoven's Ninth, which had been mangled once by Costa and had remained for most listeners "a sort of disagreeable acrostic." Under Berlioz' baton, and with the plentiful rehearsals which he called for, Beethoven was vindicated, even though George Grove, hearing it for the first time "could make very little of it." The work was greeted with storms of applause, the conductor being recalled six times at the end. Clara Novello, Martha Williams, Sims Reeves and Berlioz' favorite bass, Staudigl, sang the solo parts. Berlioz felt that the symphony had sounded even more impressive than at the Conservatoire. In the chorus, the sopranos and altos were remarkable. "One has no conception in Paris of these Englishwomen's voices, still less of the musicianship of choristers who in three sessions learn *by heart* the most complicated scores." The orchestra was a picked international group and as before it had "sung like a quartet."

Berlioz' passion for Beethoven was just then enhanced—if that were possible—by the appearance of a large work on the master from the pen of Berlioz' Russian friend Wilhelm von Lenz.[9] It was the fruit of twenty years' research and the first attempt at a scholarly presentment of Beethoven (both biographical and critical) in opposition to the grudging or hostile opinion still prevailing in many quarters. Berlioz reviewed the two-volume work in great detail and found time as well to compose out of his own published essays, short stories and fictional critiques the entertaining volume entitled *Evenings with the Orchestra*.[10]

The scheme of the book is well known: the imaginary narrator spends his evenings with the members of an orchestra while they play in the opera pit of "a civilized town." When a bad work is being performed, good talk or the reading of a good book indemnifies the instrumentists. We come to know some ten or twelve by name, point of view, and physical traits, chief among them being Corsino, first violin as well as composer, who often serves as Berlioz' mouthpiece. All converse on an equal footing until one of the group improvises or reads aloud the piece that Berlioz wishes to reprint from among his articles. When an operatic masterpiece is being played they attend to their parts and there is no soiree.

The wit and artistic fervor of the book are equalled only by the author's virtuosity in modulating from subject to subject. As for the felicity of the satire, it may be sampled by quoting its underlying "myth": since "even in an ordinary opera" the absence of the leading orchestral parts would be noticed, the performers take turns, and "it follows that when the conversations and literary studies languish in one corner, they revive on the other, and the fine talkers on the left take up their talk when those on the right take up their instruments." On one occasion, therefore, after a particularly dull opera, the conductor was moved to admonish his orchestral intelligentsia: "Silence, gentlemen, the performance is over!"

In this volume also we have the biographies of Spontini, Méhul, and Paganini; the major essays on the state of music in France and England, on the monumental style, and on Euphonia; the account of the Beethoven celebration at Bonn and of Lenz's biography of the master; together with half a dozen humorous extravaganzas and innumerable observations on the life of art, some of which have supplied the most pregnant quotations in these chapters. As Ernest Newman remarked, considering Berlioz' irritation at having to write continually about nonentities or abuses, "all the greater must our admiration be for the artistic detachment that enabled him . . . to stand at a distance from the cause of his sufferings and see them objectively as subjects for the art of letters, to universalize them, and to sprinkle them with the salt of an irony that has kept them fresh. . . . He has really left little more to be said on such sempiternal topics as tenors, professors, coteries, claques, Philistines, opera houses, and the curious belief of the English that there is something vastly more creditable in playing an orchestral work or putting on an opera badly after two rehearsals than there would be in doing it well after ten."

By the end of May, his book finished, Berlioz had two more

London concerts to conduct. England's favorites, Handel and Mendelssohn, occupied the fifth program, together with Berlioz' *Francs-Juges* overture. At the sixth and last, the Ninth Symphony was repeated by request, and two parts of the *Damnation of Faust* were performed for the first time. Enthusiasm again rose to a high pitch. Berlioz took bow after bow amid the shouting crowd, a wreath was tossed on the stage, and the press was all but unanimous in praise. The "but" was Chorley of the *Athenaeum,* a born operagoer who deplored all the "new" music since Mozart as delirious and unintelligible.

Berlioz had found his London "twelve hundred" and perhaps more. Unfortunately, the cost of doing things right had exceeded the returns, and the backers of the New Philharmonic had a deficit to face. This fact seems to have served the ends of Henry Wylde, one of the founding members, whose ambition was to conduct and play his own works.[11] In any case, the Committee did not engage Berlioz again for 1853. Berlioz' adequate rehearsals were certainly expensive, and Wylde was probably most economical in this regard.[12]

After the glory and deep satisfaction of the London season, it was dismal to return to Paris and its predictable routines and drudgeries. To these was added the grimness of Berlioz' private situation. Harriet was "quite well, that is to say, just the same," attended day and night by two reliable nurses. While Berlioz was in London, young Louis, who was back from his cruise, had suddenly decided to give up the sea. Fearing opposition, perhaps, he expressed his wish with impudence and also intimated that he was losing his mind. This brought down a remonstrance from Berlioz together with a one-hundred-franc note, necessitated by the boy's spend-thrift ways. Louis was in Paris when his father returned, and the boy's indolent, pointless existence was a double burden, spiritual and financial. He was finally persuaded to continue in the merchant marine. He reembarked in August. To augment his resources Berlioz was ready to sell Les Jacques, but there were no acceptable offers.

Unlike the unattached epicurean Stendhal, tracing in the dust with his cane the words "I'm going to be fifty," Berlioz at the same age was not in the mood to deplore missed opportunities of romance. Those he had taken were costing him his very blood in worry and effort. His hair was almost all gray and his nervous energy so depleted that he left rehearsals in the condition of "a wet rat" and spent intervening days in bed. "I cannot work during the night too," he wrote to Hiller, "for I find I have to have sleep . . . Even if I had to be guillotined at nine in the morning, I should all the same want to sleep till eleven." But wit was only temporary relief and the therapy of grumbling has its limits. His season over, he must once again drag the reviewer's chain and ball for a living. At ten francs a column, he had to write from four to six columns a week about "pot-pourris of waltzes and galops . . . platitudes, turpitudes, things that are no-things . . ." An offer, it is true, had come from the United States to conduct a series of concerts, but he awaited better terms. "If ever I accept . . . it will be solely in the hope of being able on my return to give up this job of music critic which is my shame and my despair. If you knew what I have had to hear since I came back from London, and what they want me to praise that I will not praise. . . ."

The paradox of his role, "not of critic but of article clerk [*articlier*]" was that Berlioz' satiric dramatization of it was bringing him reputation, even popularity. Though the publisher of the *Voyage Musical* declined the *Evenings with the Orchestra,* another snapped it up and sold an edition very rapidly. Berlioz might well have feared the effect of becoming known in a double capacity, for his literature was obviously closer than his music to the standard of consumers' goods. Yet given a fit occasion, his music was not forgotten. In the fall of 1852, Baron Taylor was asked to carry out those provisions of the will of another connoisseur, Baron de Trémont, which concerned the five "artists' unions." [13] He suggested that Berlioz' *Requiem* be given in honor of the little old man who had been so generous a patron of the arts. This accordingly was done at St. Eustache on October 22.[14] The best singers and players of Paris took part as simple choristers or second desks under Berlioz' lead, and the audience was equally choice. The reviews were highly laudatory and the question arose whether the composer's *Te Deum,* as yet unheard, would be chosen for a coming official fête.

Louis-Napoleon was touring France and selling the idea—as our elegant modernism has it—of Empire. More accurately, he had bought all the politicians with munificent salaries, and he was now seducing the peasants by proffering the gold brick of peace with empire. The rest of Europe could afford to see these moves with greater serenity than they had felt at the struggles of the Republic. Central Europe was quiet, its chief excitement being the sale at auction of Germany's fleet, first formed in

1848. No one as yet could foresee the consequence of Bismarck's being sent as Prussian envoy to the Federal Diet and securing Austria's adherence to the Zollverein.

It was to this becalmed Germany, purged of politics and once more steeped in culture, that Liszt bade Berlioz and Marie from Weimar for a "Berlioz Week" beginning November 17, 1852. On the first night, *Benvenuto Cellini* won a still warmer reception than it had eight months before. The next two days were given to rehearsals for his own concert, at which young composers and virtuosos—friends of Berlioz or pupils of Liszt, such as Hans von Bülow, Klindworth, and Pruckner—were happy to play the lesser percussion instruments. On the twentieth an ovation greeted *Romeo and Juliet* and the first two parts of the *Damnation of Faust;* after which the Grand Duke conferred the Order of the Falcon on the composer-conductor. A second performance of *Cellini* followed a ducal dinner, and was itself topped by a banquet and ball in Berlioz' honor. He was accompanied to his train at a late hour by a shouting band of ecstatic admirers.

More important than official and friendly tribute was the winning over of the young. Bülow was a devotee from the first, calling himself fortunate to see Berlioz at work and proclaiming that the latter's mission was giving European music fresh vigor and a new start in the right direction. *Benvenuto,* he felt, restored the style of singers and orchestra to a "correct dramatic expression" which had been lost in Germany since the time of Gluck and Weber owing to the popularity of "French and Italian trash." For public enlightenment, Bülow wrote a series of articles on *Benvenuto Cellini* calling its author "the hero of our modern music" and the "immediate and most energetic successor of Beethoven." The "grandiose work," *Cellini,* deserved study for its "numberless beauties."

Liszt, who knew how much he owed artistically to Berlioz' genius and spiritually to his friendship, was repaying his debt in a princely manner, which Berlioz appreciated to the full. "Our ill-wishers," he wrote to the Princess, "seek for the *motive* [of Liszt's actions], and that they will never understand." What Berlioz could not know was that Liszt's different and unobligated fondness for Wagner was causing him some embarrassment. For Wagner, without knowing the music of either *Cellini* or the *Damnation,* was casting doubt on Liszt's judgment of them by offering his own: "The poem of

Benvenuto Cellini is bad, and the composer has been put into the unnatural position of having to fill with purely musical inventions the lacunae which only the poet can fill. Berlioz will never be able to rescue his unfortunate *Cellini,* but tell me which is worth more—Benvenuto or Berlioz? Let the first go and save the second. It's horrible for me to watch these efforts at resurrection. Let Berlioz write a new opera . . . for only one thing can save him, and that is drama. . . . Believe me, I love Berlioz despite the capricious distrust that keeps him distant from me. He does not know me but I know him. If I expect something from any composer, it is from Berlioz, but not if he follows the line that has led him to the platitudes of his *Faust* symphony."

This letter, written by one who asserted that "he knew Berlioz" although he had neither heard the two works he attacked, nor could have studied them since both were still unpublished (moreover mistaking the *Damnation* for a symphony),[15] shows merely that Wagner sensed the purport of Berlioz' dramatic method and rebelled against it a priori. The remark about "gaps that only the poet can fill," and the belief that "Berlioz can only be saved by drama," reveal Wagner's conception of opera and his essentially literary bent, diametrically opposed to Berlioz' "purely musical inventions." Possibly Liszt had described to Wagner how Berlioz treated the Carnival scene in *Benvenuto* and this went against the grain of the other's genius—so much so that he thought of becoming Berlioz' librettist. Himself still uncertain whether his genius drove him to playwriting or to music, he admired Berlioz enough to want to propose to him a drama on *Wieland the Smith.*[16]

As for the objection that Wagner put forth when Liszt revived *Benvenuto* we do not hear of it when a similar effort went into *Lohengrin* or *Tannhäuser,* nor is there any hint of "capricious distrust" when Berlioz reprinted, with a warm introduction, Liszt's eulogy on this last-named opera. The triangular situation—half friendship, half enmity—must have been very trying to Liszt, for he knew that Wagner had launched a major attack on Berlioz in a massive work entitled *Opera and Drama,* which had not yet been translated or excerpted, but which sooner or later would be brought to his older friend's notice. Meanwhile the author of these ambivalent gestures resented the fact that Berlioz, their victim, was keeping his distance.

In France a second plebiscite had been held and doctored in order to make an indubitable emperor out of a Prince-President. The success of Berlioz' *Evenings* coinciding with this development, there was a bare chance that the Imperial chapel would be entrusted to him. He even sketched a project for adjoining to the Chapel an up-to-date school of music, but the post went to Auber who was already Director of the Conservatoire as well as on the list of prospective Senators at thirty thousand a year. Auber was seventy and had never achieved anything like the success of his *Masaniello* a quarter century before, but he was a tireless courtier and Lothario, endearing qualities to a ruler of the same cloth. The official beginning of this Second-Empire style of life was promulgated on the anniversary of Austerlitz, the Bonapartes' lucky day, December 2.

The new year 1853 opened for Berlioz with continued praise of his *Evenings.* His enemies themselves granted that he had the "wittiest, most imaginative, most ingenious and poetic mind." His manner, it was said, recalled that of Diderot. In the same month, too, his English friends succeeded in having *Cellini* accepted at Covent Garden over Costa's opposition. The libretto had to be translated into Italian, and Berlioz made further musical revisions, the fruit of two hearings at Weimar and of suggestions from Liszt. He also corrected proofs of an Italian edition of the *Requiem.* Little else occupied his real mind. After long bargaining he yielded to Richault the rights to the *Damnation:* what proved to be twenty years later a fortune for this publisher was exchanged under pressure of necessity for a few hundreds. Berlioz' financial position was exactly what it had always been: respectable but strained. Louis had returned, and while taking a scientific course at Le Havre, had to be supported there. This was the period to which Berlioz refers in one of the most moving episodes of the *Memoirs*—that of the symphony that he voluntarily suppressed.

Berlioz had by now three completed scores in his portfolio, for besides the *Te Deum,* he had finished the *Corsair* overture (out of the former "Tower of Nice") [17] and had expanded his "Shepherds' Farewell to the Holy Family" into what is now the second part of *The Infant Christ,* namely "The Flight into Egypt." In one way, Berlioz' career was enormously successful. His music, his training of performers, his ideas, were impregnating Europe and germinating in hundreds of minds. But the facilities which his achievement should have brought him were still withheld, and the feat of endurance by which he pursued the even tenor of his mission was beginning to tell on his physique.

After a bout of his old ailment—sore throat and fever now invariably accompanied by nervous gastritis—his energy and morale recovered. His articles once more sang the praises of work. "Keep going, ignore small hurdles and small men, small emotions and all smallnesses in the world. What is done is done; that is the great challenge: *to do something.*" [18] This valor, coinciding with the return of spring, went into tasks of musical upkeep: correcting the parts for the London *Benvenuto;* preparing a manuscript of the *King Lear* overture for Liszt, who wanted to make a piano reduction and play it; and dealing with Edouard Bénazet, the manager of the casino at Baden-Baden, who wanted good music and proposed to put on some or all of the *Damnation.* At last on May ninth, the *Benvenuto* rehearsals having begun, Berlioz left for his fourth London journey.

Covent Garden was then almost exclusively an Italian theater. It appealed to a public of dilettanti who came for the singers and who considered vocal feats the *raison d'être* of all opera. The singers in turn freely embroidered their parts, each acting to the gallery while the orchestra played a very modest second fiddle. Berlioz was in the enemy's house. Costa knew it, but he behaved in the most friendly and courteous manner. The score of *Benvenuto,* requiring an exact balance between *bel canto* and orchestral precision, and so highly organized for ensemble effects, could easily succumb to individualist tactics in the normal opera style. Though all but Tamberlick (Cellini) found their parts unusual, they took their cue from Costa and gave Berlioz their best co-operation. The rehearsals were arduous but satisfactory. Costa had also agreed to Berlioz' giving a concert at the *Old* Philharmonic. Berlioz was therefore rehearsing (for May thirtieth) a program consisting of the *Harold* symphony, the *Roman Carnival* overture and the *"Repos de la Sainte Famille"* from his *Flight into Egypt.* His good friend Sainton played the viola in *Harold* and did it so superbly as to win great applause despite the competition of a prolonged thunderstorm.

Three and a half weeks later, *Benvenuto Cellini* met with disaster. It was hissed practically from the beginning, despite the presence of the Queen and Prince Consort. The innocuous *Roman Carnival* overture was hissed even while playing, though as in Paris earlier, the *Benvenuto* overture proper was asked for twice. Berlioz did not repeat it, deeming it too long. The whole occasion partook of madness. Two or three of the songs were encored; at other times the hissing began before the singers opened their mouths. At his entrance and at the end, Berlioz was enthusiastically called for and applauded. He of course declined to appear at the final curtain.[19] Victoria and her Prince held their ground to the very last. The cabal of the dilettanti was provable by the fact of preparatory meetings and their behavior during the performance,[20] but a good many independent critics opposed the score by reason—as usual—of evil features which it did not contain. By an oversight, Costa had not asked the reviewers to the dress rehearsal and they heard only the tumultuous *première*. Berlioz withdrew the opera the next day.

The most curious result of the occasion was Chorley's candid revelation of the real trouble: "It will surprise those who only recollect *Benvenuto Cellini* by its performance, on going through the published music, to find how considerable is the amount of real idea existing in it. In no other of its writer's works is the melody so abundant or so natural." After telling how he had had his ears opened at the Weimar performance, "the excitement of which was remarkable—almost amounting to a contagion not to be resisted—" Chorley reverts to "the beauties" of a work that made him "almost forget the partisanship which belonged to it."

Two days after the London fall, two hundred and twenty singers and players gathered and sent delegates to Berlioz to express their indignation at the treatment his work had received. They spontaneously offered their services for a testimonial concert of his own works at his own time. Independently of this, a subscription was taken up among musicians and publishers, and the sum of £200 was presented by Beale to the composer as a token of good will. Berlioz declined the gift, and shortly thereafter the proposed concert as well: "My dear Mr. Smythson," he wrote to the chorus master, "The concert for which the artists of Covent Garden so generously promised their aid cannot take place. I am none the less deeply touched by the kindness shown me by these artists on this occasion. Please thank them on my behalf and tell them I feel more happy and proud at this proof of their friendship than if I had given the most splendid concert in the ordinary way. Let me say, too, how grateful I am for the pains you took in rehearsing *Benevenuto Cellini.*"

On the same day Berlioz also wrote his thanks to Costa and less formally to Sainton, who being permanently settled in London as teacher and performer, was Berlioz' spokesman to the profession: "I am leaving on Saturday and have so much to do tomorrow that I cannot possibly accept your kind invitation. Do excuse me . . . I am also writing to Beale to thank the members of the committee—of whom you are one—for their delightful idea of publishing an English edition of my *Faust.* Nothing could be more delicately kind-hearted and artistically thoughtful."

In these notes, as in those that Berlioz dispatched to intimates in France, there is no hint of bitterness or self-pity. If Berlioz felt either, he was too great a gentleman to let it contaminate his expressions of gratitude to friends, or of civility to enemies who, like Costa, had behaved honorably and helpfully. Just as he had kept quite cool while conducting his work through the racket—hissers had even been posted in the wings—so now he was unshaken and indeed prophetic as to the inherent virtues of the work: "*Between ourselves,* I am sure that a real future is in store for this score (in Germany first and later in France). . . . Whatever may be its present fate . . . it is to my mind a new sort of music, of unconquerable vitality." [21]

CHAPTER 19

RELIGIOUS HISTORY

Perhaps he thought of God only when he wrote L'Enfance du Christ, *that tender masterpiece. And, who knows? perhaps also God in his goodness took it for a prayer.*—BARBEY D'AUREVILLY

The two years measured by Berlioz' fourth and fifth visits to London (July 1853 to June 1855) represent the harvest time of his career. He had sown in Paris for a quarter century, in Central Europe for almost fifteen years, in England for seven. Everywhere recognition, honors, and spontaneous devotion were his to reap. He would still be alone and overworked, still attacked, but the active musical minority now sided with him and some of the old irreconcilables—Fétis, Moscheles, Adolphe Adam—were beginning to act reconciled. As composer, organizer, man of letters, and man of the world Berlioz was in demand. The financial reward was slight but with the small income from his inheritance and the trickle of royalties, he enjoyed a fair livelihood. He could occasionally buy his freedom from journalism for a seaside vacation, and he repeatedly received more musical offers than he could accept.

These coming rewards Berlioz had no means of foreseeing. Returning from the London failure of *Benvenuto,* he had the prospect of going the next month to conduct at Baden-Baden and the immediate task of proofreading three unpublished scores—the *Damnation,* the *Te Deum,* and the *Flight into Egypt.* Fatigue put him in two minds: "After [these publications] the Lord knows what I shall decide to do. I am torn between the love of art and disgust, between lassitude about the known and eagerness for the unknown, between obstinate tenacity and Reason which cries 'impossible!' " Seeing too well around his own position and observing that Liszt's recent effort on behalf of the new music exposed his friend to the same intrigues and insults, Berlioz voiced an ironic doubt: "Could it be that we are simply imbeciles, possibly even impudent rogues, with our private pretensions?"

He then modulates to a touchy subject that Liszt had brought up: "I am as convinced as you are that it will not be hard for me to mesh gears with Wagner, if he will only put a little oil in the wheels. As for the words to which you refer, I have never read them and hold no grudge on their account. I myself have too often fired into the marching throng to be anything like surprised at getting broadsides in return." The allusion was to Wagner's ambivalent attack in *Opera and Drama* two years before. As for the meshing of gears, it did not take place for another two years, Wagner being still an exile in Switzerland, and Berlioz in the interim shuttling back and forth between Paris and Germany.

The reason for Berlioz' engagement at Baden was the presence there of Edouard Bénazet as holder of the gambling concession. He was an adroit entrepreneur who had studied a little at the Conservatoire, mingled with artistic and diplomatic society, and who now undertook to make the Baden waters an unusually chic resort by providing a season of artistic notables matching the high society. The great lounge known as "the Conversation" was made into a concert hall, and there on August 11, 1853 some three hundred listeners indoors (and twice as many outdoors) heard Parts I and II of the *Damnation of Faust*.[1] Though this was not Berlioz' dream of Euphonia, his task was made agreeable by Bénazet's closing of the gaming tables for the day. The "King"—as the impresario was called—had also provided at his expense additional instrumentists from Carlsruhe. To rehearse them, Berlioz covered the twenty-five miles by train. He and his men were hospitably cared for by the croupier-Maecenas, who thenceforth offered Berlioz a yearly opportunity to direct.

From Baden Berlioz went to Frankfort-on-the-Main, gave two concerts, and with the local music societies projected a Shakespeare evening at which he might hear the appropriate numbers of his *Tristia*. Back in Paris, two *feuilletons* "leaped at his throat," but he shook them off to prepare for Hanover where the young blind King especially delighted in Berlioz' music. Brunswick and Leipzig also put in bids for the composer's presence. At Detmold, without his help, the reigning family of Lippe was preparing an audition of *Romeo and Juliet* entire. The Prince would sing Friar Laurence and the young Princesses joined the chorus. About this time, too, an offer came from England which sounded so attractive that Berlioz became suspicious and asked for a deposited guarantee lest he fall into the hands of another Jullien. "They agree to everything, which frightens me." In Paris, the opening of Meyerbeer's new opera was being coddled by a new device—the press conference—and Berlioz had to attend the solemn gathering at the Café de Paris. As he was leaving for Germany, it mattered little to him that the Institute, just then stimulated by death to take fresh thought, omitted Berlioz from its list and elected Reber.

Ample compensation was in store at Brunswick where Berlioz' two concerts created a lasting commotion. He was played by the Park band, serenaded, given a silver-gilt baton, smothered in laurel, and hugged on the streets by perfect strangers. The musicians' fund was named after him, and the orchestra, which had the reputation of being "tough," followed his lead to his extreme satisfaction. In two rehearsals he had "broken the muscle-bound rhythms" which he feared for his works. Not losing sight of the future, moreover, he had asked Joachim to play the viola in *Harold,* "one of my main motives for giving *Faust,"* being, as he wrote to the virtuoso, "that you should hear that score complete." For Joachim was "a superb talent," young, and ambitious of fame as a composer.

Griepenkerl, the critic and theorist, followed Berlioz to Hanover and began to arrange for a Leipzig concert. The Hanoverian rulers had heard *Cellini* hissed in London, and their subjects had been rather cool on Berlioz' first appearance ten years before, but this time warmth was universal. Diamond-studded gifts were added to the wreaths and plaudits. The King was beside himself with joy. "I cannot see you conduct, but I can sense how you do it." Most touching of all, the orchestra voted not to take its usual fees and to turn them over to the composer-conductor. Berlioz accepted, on condition that it should never happen again. Goethe's (and Beethoven's) Bettina von Arnim, aged seventy-two, came out on purpose, not to *see* Berlioz, as she said, but to *look* at him.

The next step was north to Bremen for a single concert, then diagonally across Germany to Leipzig, the citadel to be stormed again and again. Liszt came, accompanied by the faithful: Peter Cornelius, Richard Pohl, Klindworth, Remenyi, Pruckner, Raff, Joachim, and others. Before the concert, the *Kapellmeister,* Ferdinand David, gave a soiree at which Liszt played piano arrangements of Berlioz, including a comic fantasia by Bülow on two motives from *Benvenuto.* The concert the next day was an unqualified success, and a second ten days later brought excitement and banqueting to effervescence.

The press was divided as before, but the reminiscent critics could report Berlioz' visible advance in public esteem. "He has convinced us," said one interpreter, "that he possesses not only a musician's spirit and an artist's mind, but a heart also. He likes to express . . . the most tender and ethereal feelings. . . . Each voice in his orchestra is an animate thing. . . . His music is truly polyphonic, and those who deny its organic unity are in error. . . . For a long while Shakespeare's *Hamlet* was held to be obscure, inorganic, full of enigmas and contradictions. One day Goethe found its meaning and the marvelous work became clear and intelligible: just so with Berlioz. . . ."

Otto Jahn, the great Mozart scholar, continued to jeer at all modern music ("there is no other God but Berlioz and Liszt is his prophet"), condemned its lack of melody and roughness of texture and, arraigning its supposed program, went on to criticize Berlioz' Roman Carnival because it did not match *his* conception of the occasion. The term "modern music" had been used by Berlioz himself in an interview given to J. C. Lobe and published in the *Fliegende Blätter für Musik.* Feeling as he did about systems and pedantry and knowing history, Berlioz naturally refused to limit the scope of either music or modern music. He pointed out that a commentary on the present state of the art would fill a volume (he had just published one and had written enough for three more) and that the issuing of manifestos went against his principles: "I have not the slightest ambition to *represent* anybody, nor to be deputy, senator, or consul. . . . Besides, if I had such a wish, it seems to me I need not do anything more in order to earn the approval of my fellow-practitioners . . . than to imitate Coriolanus . . . and bare my breast to show the wounds received in defending our territory.

"As for my own confession of faith, is it not . . . in my works . . . in what I have done and what I have not done?

What music is today, you know as well as I do; what it will be, neither you nor I can tell. . . . Music is the most poetic, the most powerful, the most alive of all the arts; it should be the freest, though it is not yet so. Hence our artistic travails, obscure devotion, weariness, and despair. . . ."

Berlioz then recurs to the symbol of Perseus whom he had already used in his opera on the theme of art, and develops a parable whose luxuriant imagery merely veils its precision: "Modern music, music proper (and not the courtesan one meets everywhere under that name) is like the antique Andromeda, divinely naked and beautiful, whose burning glances break into many-colored rays by shining through her tears. Chained to a rock on the edge of a boundless sea . . . she awaits the conquering Perseus who will break her chains and destroy the Chimaera named Routine. . . . I believe that by now the monster is getting old: his motions are not so energetic as of yore . . . his heavy paws slip on the edge of Andromeda's rock. And when the devoted lover of the sublime captive . . . has restored her to Greece, at the risk of seeing his passion repaid with cold indifference, it will be vain for neighboring satyrs to laugh at his ardor and cry: 'Leave her in chains! How do you know that once freed she will be yours? In bondage she is easier to possess . . .' The loving lover wants not to wrest but to receive. He will save Andromeda chastely, and would . . . even give her wings to augment her liberty.[2]

"This," concludes Berlioz, "is the only confession of faith I can make, and I make it solely to prove to you that I have a faith. Many have none, and unfortunately I have one, which I have too long proclaimed from the housetops, in pious obedience to the gospel."

In other words, Berlioz declined to bind himself or anyone else by a program, and to assume the role of leader of a school. His faith was clear from his deeds and parables, and strong without the buttressing of a cosmic philosophy. He knew the danger of so much self-reliance: "It is not true that 'faith is the only salvation.' On the contrary, faith is the only perdition, and by faith I shall be damned." This was prophetic. Berlioz had not read "the lines" by Wagner which Liszt referred to, and which later served the doctrinaires as a systematic weapon against Berlioz' "lack of a scientific esthetics." But Berlioz chose the right part for him, and now that Wagner's theorizing appears in all its inconsistency, Berlioz' decision to stand on his accomplishment rather than on a platform appears also as sound judgment. How could he, arguing for freedom, be a party to boxing up his art within a creed? Nor, believing as he did in the integrity of the individual artist, could he claim the liberation and renovation of music for himself alone. He knew what he had done but as he said in explaining to Adèle his successes in Germany, "it is *Time* which has moved ahead . . . and the great number of young artists newly established in Hanover. . . ."

Berlioz' meditations on artistic faith were not remote from those other feelings which from his twelfth year had linked in his mind music and religion. Lately, the gentle and intimate aspects of that association of ideas had borne fruit in the little score of *The Flight into Egypt,* which he heard for the first time entire on November 30, 1853. Everywhere the final section entitled *"Le Repos de la Sainte Famille"* had been so well liked that he was thinking of enlarging the work by means of a sequel—*The Holy Family in Egypt;* and since his two nieces, the daughters of Adèle, were especially devout and especially desirous of seeing their names on a score, he promised them the dedication.

The original number, as is well-known, first bore another name than that of its composer. And the genesis of that germ tells us again that "character" in Berlioz' art came first: shortly after finishing the *Te Deum,* during a social evening made dull for him by everyone else's playing cards, he began to sketch a four-part andantino for organ. His old friend and fellow guest, Louis Duc, prodded him to write instead a parlor piece for his album, but "a certain character of primitive, pastoral mysticism" in the melody led Berlioz to invent an occasion for it: he imagined the shepherds bidding farewell to Jesus on the eve of the Holy Family's flight into Egypt. He wrote appropriate words and then thought of a further embellishment:

"Now," he told Duc, "I am going to put your name to this. I want to compromise you."

"That's absurd! Everybody knows that I know nothing about writing music."

"That is indeed a brand-new reason for not composing, but wait! Since vanity prevents your adopting my piece, I am going to make up a name out of yours. I shall call the author Pierre Ducré, whom I hereby appoint music master of the Sainte-

Chapelle in Paris during the seventeenth century. My manuscript thus acquires enormous antiquarian value."

The remaining parts of the *Flight into Egypt* were soon added and when in 1850 the little work was performed, it was under the name of Ducré. All but one of the critics fell into the trap, although the original "Farewell" contains a characteristic Berliozian modulation which gives away the hoax. Berlioz shortly published the work under his own name, though keeping the caption "Attributed to Pierre Ducré, imaginary chapel master."

The decision, three years later, to enlarge the work occurred just when Berlioz met Brahms, whose favorite within the Berlioz repertoire turned out to be this very score.[3] Then aged twenty, Brahms and his first works made a strong impression on Berlioz: "I am grateful to you," he tells Joachim, "for making known to me this shy young composer who is bent on writing modern music. He will have much to endure . . ."[4] Meanwhile in Weimar, another young musician, Peter Cornelius, who called himself

> *A pale and candid Lisztian*
> *To his last breath and tone;*
> *A Berlioz-Wagner-Weimar-Christian,*
> *And yet Cornelius-like in mind and bone . . .*[5]

was hard at work supplying or revising the German for several Berlioz scores, and spurred on by his study of his chosen masters was beginning to compose his own delightful comic opera, *The Barber of Bagdad.* Admittedly reminiscent of *Benvenuto Cellini,* but revealing a distinct personality as well, this gay opera, in which a modern critic finds "beautifully polished workmanship and something more—a dash of real genius," was later to provide a test of Weimar's toleration for the new music: Liszt produced the work; it fell and he resigned.

But this was still five years away. As yet Cornelius came before the public only as a disciple, though a vigorous one. It was Cornelius who in an article published in Berlin in mid-January 1854, launched the slogan of the "three B's"—the *original* three B's: "On the heights where Bach and Beethoven already dwell, there will the third great B first find recognition. For if I mistake not, the specific polyphonic musician in Berlioz controls the poet in such a way as to create within the symphony a dramatic form fit for his variegated expression. . . . Allow me then in concluding to sound a small fanfare for my favorite modern master, for the proud and daring hero, Hector, for the many-voiced composer and many-sided writer Berlioz, who is also one of the great humorists of our nineteenth century . . . three cheers, now: 'Bach! Beethoven! Berlioz!' "[6]

When this apotheosis took place, the subject of it had been back in Paris for only a fortnight. The change of occupation should have brought rest from the rehearsals, the correcting and shipping of parts, and what Matthew Arnold used to call the battle for life with headwaiters. But it had brought no relief because there were as many letters and errands to do as on tour, more proofs to correct, and rehearsals to boot. Seghers of the *Sainte Cécile* society wished to perform *The Flight into Egypt,* and being a feeble conductor, he had to be helped. At the same time the battle for life took the form of an unexpected lawsuit. A Polish count was suing the Opera on grounds which must have delighted Berlioz: the count had bought a ticket which promised Weber's *Freischütz* and had been given only a cut and patched version. The lawyer for the defense, however, tried to exculpate the Opera by throwing the blame upon Berlioz, who twelve years before had supervised the mounting of the work and had composed recitatives. The press, with its professional short memory and love of dogfights, represented Berlioz as guilty and receiving his deserts at last.

This confusion of the facts due to the Opera's legal smoke screen caused Berlioz a great deal of worry, fury, and real harm. Though he at once wrote letters to the Paris newspapers and to his German friends, the mischief had been done.[7] Angry letters came from music students, and newspapers throughout Europe copied from one another the garbled facts. "This stupid business," wrote Berlioz to David at Leipzig, "vexes and outrages me as you can readily understand: I have spent fifteen years of my life as critic combating correctors, arrangers, and mutilators. When *Freischütz* was put on at the Opera, I prevented its being shorn of a single note; I managed to have it performed in full, and now I am accused of having cut it up myself, though the cuts were made during my absence from the country, without my being notified, and by a Director with whom I am not on speaking terms. . . . It is revolting by its absurdity and injustice."

On top of this annoyance, whose repercussions were not soon over, the owner and director of the *Débats,* Armand Bertin, suddenly died. Berlioz mourned him as a friend who had stanchly supported him throughout their association. His death might mean Berlioz' removal from his entrenched position, for Louise Bertin had given up music and her brother Edouard—a childhood friend of Delacroix's—was a landscape painter. Without a Bertin to head it, the newspaper would be sold, possibly to the government. Fortunately Edouard gave up painting and Berlioz kept his post. Among his duties immediately after this scare, was to give an account of that "world-shaking event"—so said the *Gazette Musicale*—the opening of *L'Etoile du Nord* at the Opéra-Comique. With this score (known also as *La Stella del Nord*) Meyerbeer's monopoly of Paris theaters was complete. Louis Napoleon and Eugénie his new Empress led the applause, and Berlioz had to praise the show. But he took much of it back in a daring last paragraph which conveyed what he thought of the patent formula for producing this kind of work.

Meanwhile at the concert of *Sainte Cécile,* Berlioz' *Flight into Egypt* had been warmly received and he was composing the remainder. "The Arrival at Sais," much longer than the first part, was finished by January 1854. This in turn called for an opening section to balance it. Musical ideas came in abundance, and the present first part, "Herod's Dream," was ultimately the longest. But the organizing of the whole had to wait, for the proofs of the massive *Damnation of Faust* were still being run off and the time of the engagements in Germany was approaching. Suddenly, Harriet took a turn for the worse. Summoned, Berlioz flew to Montmartre, but she lingered on. On Friday March third, just after he had again left, she died.

Louis had been spending four days with us and had gone back to Calais the previous Wednesday. Fortunately she saw him again. . . . I had to take care of everything myself—registry office, cemetery—I am in misery today. Her condition was dreadful. Paralysis was complicated by erisypelas and she had difficulty in breathing. She had become a formless mass of flesh—and beside her that radiant portrait which I had given her last year, where she looks as she was, with her great inspired eyes. Nothing left. My friends have stood by me. A large number, with Baron Taylor leading, followed her to the cemetery. . . .

And the dazzling sun, the panorama of the plain of Saint-Denis—I couldn't follow. I stayed in the garden. I had gone through too much the previous day while going to find the Pastor. By a barbarous chance, as so often happens, my cab had to go past the Odéon where I saw her for the first time 27 years ago, when she had at her feet the intellectual elite of Paris[8]. . . . The Odéon, where I suffered so much—we could neither live together nor leave each other, and we have endured this torture for ten years past. We each suffered so much at the other's hands. I have just come from her grave. She rests on the side of the hill, facing north, towards England, to which she never wanted to return.

I wrote to poor Louis yesterday. I shall write to him again. How horrible life is. Everything comes back to me . . . her great qualities, her cruel demands, her injustice, and then her genius and her woes. . . . She made me understand Shakespeare and true dramatic art. She suffered penury with me; she never hesitated when we had to risk our savings for a musical undertaking. Yet contrariwise, she always opposed my leaving Paris. . . . If I had not taken decisive steps I should still be virtually unknown in Europe. And her jealousy, *without cause,* which ended by altering my whole life. . . .

I have no taste for anything. I care about music and the rest about as much as——. I have kept her hair. I am here alone in the large living room next to her empty bedroom. The garden has buds. Oh! to forget, to forget! . . . We all live so long—and now here is Louis so tall, he is no longer like that dear child I used to see running down these garden paths. I see here his daguerreotype portrait at the age of 12. It seems to me I have lost *that* child, and the big one whom I kissed six days ago does not console me for the loss of the other.

Don't be surprised if I sound strange. What a deadly faculty to remember the past. Is it the reason why I have so cruelly succeeded in arousing similar impressions in some of my works? Yet everybody says we must be glad she is no longer suffering. It was a dreadful life; but I have nothing but praise for the three women who tended her. Farewell, dear sister. . . . Take care how you write to me; your letter can help me bear up or break my resistance further. Farewell. Fortunately there is Time which keeps moving and crushing, which kills everything, sorrows and all.

Harriet's passing was signalized in the press by articles written to honor her relation to Berlioz and recall her earlier glory. Alexandre Dumas had a kind word, Gautier praised her, and Jules Janin wrote a fine evocation, quoting at the close the litany from Juliet's Funeral March in Berlioz' symphony, "Strew on her flowers . . ." Liszt wrote a consoling letter assuring Berlioz: "She inspired you, you loved her and sang your love of her, her mission was fulfilled."

Adèle, to whom Berlioz kept pouring out his overfull heart,

was her usual loving self. "Dear, admirable sister: You are right to say that I should feel thankful at having been near. I cannot face the thought of her dying all solitary. . . . I go to the cemetery every morning; it hurts me less than if I kept away." Then since the province-bred little sister, surmising perhaps that her brother would legalize his relation to Marie, asked a practical question, he replies: "Yes, of course there was a marriage contract. I have just reread it. How can it be of use to Louis? Against whom? Not against me, I suppose. We were married under the law of community property, with the following conditions: I was not held accountable for her debts prior to our marriage, though I acknowledged them and they have been paid long since. . . . The survivor is entitled to property worth a thousand francs from the estate. I shall take nothing; I give everything to Louis absolutely. . . . I tell you all this without precisely grasping the point you raise in your letter. . . . Unfortunately, Louis is still such a child that I am forced to give him but little at a time and myself to buy some of the things he needs."

Louis had in fact been for six months a midshipman on the cutter *Le Corse.* He had passed his examinations well, was earning forty francs a month and had sworn off prodigality. Having interested Admiral Cécille in the boy's career, Berlioz had reports that those in charge of the young officer-in-training spoke well of him. Berlioz was beginning to believe that the man was emerging from the child when a new source of worry assailed him. The year 1854 began with preparations for war against Russia and Louis Berlioz was in line to see active duty.

Meanwhile the legal settlement took longer and was more complicated than Berlioz at first imagined, the boy being a minor and the estate subject to registration. Adèle's lawyer-husband finally straightened everything out. As for Louis, we can imagine him working out in his customary solitude his difficult emotional problems. In the only extant letter from him, we see how close was the temperamental kinship between father and son, the exact counterpart of the resemblance between Berlioz and *his* father: "Since my poor mother's death," he writes to his Aunt Adèle, "I have several times meant to write to you, but the shattering memories that I would then have aroused held me back. My poor mother! What a sad life she has had! No, one cannot regret life on her behalf; now that she sleeps in her grave she does not suffer. I have always lived far from her. While still a child, I left for Rouen and then saw her only at long intervals, so in the short times I had with her I had to hide my desolate heart under a laughing face. Sometimes my courage failed me and I would leave abruptly, so that some people thought me a bad son. . . . She had to die far from me. I couldn't follow her to her grave, any more than I was to walk her on my arm or see her on the stage. It is all over. I have only my father left, my poor kind father. I can't love him more than before, for I love him as he does me and only God sees the depth of the friendship between us. I have caused him grief sometimes but I am very young, dear aunt, and young people go through terrible times. Since the loss of my mother I feel new strength and I want to use it to spare every kind of grief to him who is dearest to me in all the world. God willing, he will be proud of his son. I can't speak of the day when he will have to quit this earth, because, as I have felt since I reached the age of reason, that day will be my last. The thread of my life is but the continuation of his. When it is cut, both lives are at an end. . . ."

Louis then goes on to news of his ship and touching remarks about his young cousins. He was eager to spend some time with Adèle who had invited him. Berlioz supplied the money but war orders prevented.

The return engagement at Hanover came for Berlioz as a release from brooding, and in the two concerts (one at Brunswick) he even surpassed his earlier performance.[9] One of his objectives this time was Dresden, where Karl Lipinski as of yore, and the newly arrived Bülow, desired to have Berlioz appointed Music Director. Not liking what he had first seen of the Saxon court, Berlioz had been reluctant to go, but he yielded now and strove to make a perfect showing. On April 22, the *Damnation of Faust* was received with acclamations. At the dinner following the concert, a Royal minister attended. The press was favorable except for the ubiquitous old guard who repudiated Beethoven's later works and accepted only some of those in the "second manner." Mozart was the god with whose unconscious aid Berlioz was damned, and when the words "pure" and "classic" failed, the charge was that Berlioz lacked inspiration and "ciphered with notes."

Other criticisms were more alarming because still farther off the point. Berlioz was French, and this in many quarters was becoming a serious handicap. Since the failure of the Frankfort Parliament and the quasi-national "humiliation of Olmütz," patriotism had grown touchy and some persons let Berlioz feel it directly. He spoke no German (though he could at need write out his programs in that language) and therefore used French, English, or Italian while rehearsing. Once, too, a piece of irony had miscarried: when advance news of the Dresden directorship had leaked out in Paris, Berlioz had denied it in a squib saying he would leave his beloved Paris only to direct for the Queen of the Hovas in Madagascar. Whereas this was a dig at the Parisians, a German journalist took it as an insult to the German musical princes. Such stupidity was unanswerable.

Nor was this all. Berlioz was playing his *Faust,* composed on what had become since Goethe's death a national poem.[10] Critics objected to the disfigurement of the lines and the plot. Berlioz had to explain in a Foreword to the score just then in press that the German text was "a translation of a translation," while the whole was a reworking of the legend. Berlioz always resented having to explain himself and "prove to people that you do not mean to dry up the Caspian Sea." [11] But expostulation did not help. He was accused of having "libelled Mephisto" by making him deceive Faust. "For you must know," Berlioz wrote to Griepenkerl "that Mephisto is a virtuous and honest devil whose word is as good as his bond." Further, Berlioz was made out to be another of those immoral Frenchmen for having written in the students' Latin chorus that they went by moonlight *quaerentes puellas per urbem*—"seeking girls through the town." German students, Berlioz was informed, had never done such a thing. "I had to read this with my own eyes to believe it."

Though Berlioz had to give four concerts instead of two, the Dresden offer did not materialize, whether because of national feeling, or because it would have meant victory for the conspiring modernists—Liszt, Bülow, Cornelius, and Lipinski (with Wagner in the offing) or again because of Marie Recio's indiscreet remarks about Wagner's latest attack on Berlioz. Fragments of *Opera and Drama* were being reprinted and discussed, and the old guard enjoyed seeing one of the innovators manhandle the other in print. Though Berlioz was willing to follow Liszt's advice and "grease the wheels," it was clear that Wagner was pouring sand. Marie, lacking equally in tact and self-respect, could not refrain from drawing indignant comparisons between Berlioz' reprinting in the *Débats* Liszt's praise of *Tannhäuser* and Wagner's deliberate assault in his book. Bülow then took a hand, with just as little judgment as the annoying woman. He urged Liszt to caution Berlioz that Dresden was still faithful to Wagner, not seeing that a word of caution to Wagner was also necessary if the moderns were to show a united front.

Berlioz, who after all had not thrust himself in but had been invited, tried to keep aloof and remained grateful throughout for the hearty welcome he had received. "There are rascals in Germany as elsewhere," he concluded, "but one must confess that there is in that country much more cordiality and a deeper feeling for art than in the rest of Europe. I have been treated with understanding, respect, and affection, which touches me to the bottom of my heart. Moreover . . . it is only owing to this dear country that I keep alive."

During the next three months (May through July 1854) Berlioz finished his triptych on a sacred theme, *The Infant Christ.* He dated the manuscript of this quiet "page out of a missal" on the twenty-fourth anniversary of the day when he won the Rome Prize, the opening day of the July Revolution raging outside. Louis Philippe seemed far away. Already the Louis Napoleon who had protested that "the Empire means peace" had turned into a swashbuckler at war with Russia; and a third Louis—Berlioz' cherished son—grown into a naval officer, was caught in the foolish enterprise. It was already known that a French army was dying of disease in the Danube delta and that to prepare a landing in the Crimea a diversion must be made in the Baltic. Louis Berlioz, on board the *Phlegeton,* was part of this diversion. The father bade him farewell and concealed his apprehension under encouraging words, but letters to Adèle and others show his real thoughts: "I look for a letter from him every day. He wrote to me that the *Phlegeton* is assigned to carrying despatches only. . . . Even so, at night I get terrible spasms of the heart. . . . The vessel, they tell me, will not be in the battle but I don't believe it."

He was right. In August the ship took part in the bombardment of Bomarsund. "I have been in torment these last few days. . . . He tells me nothing of his impressions but I can imagine what the poor child who has never even seen a skirmish must have felt in the midst of that hell which is called a naval battle. I had gone to spend a week . . . at the seashore

. . . when a local paper mentioned the ship. I came back to Paris as soon as I could for news. . . .

"What intoxicating air I breathed a week ago, stretched out on the cliffs of St. Valéry, with the calm sea softly swishing three hundred feet below my green bank. What marvellous sunsets, what peace on those heights and what purity in that layer of the atmosphere! Only such passionate interviews with nature as these can make me forget for an instant the griefs of outraged love of art. But these very same sights quickly kindle them again more burning than before: all is interlinked."

Before leaving for the country, Berlioz had once more been a candidate for the Institute, making the necessary calls on people who he knew would not elect him. They chose Clapisson.[12] "Having begun, I am bound to persevere. The place is worth 1500 francs [a year], which means a good deal. I don't speak of the honor, which is a fiction when you consider who belongs and has always belonged to the Academy. I have tried only twice. Hugo knocked on their door five times, Vigny four; Delacroix after six tries has not been admitted yet; Balzac never did get in. . . ."

By the sea, recovering from Paris and the Institute and suppressing dark thoughts, Berlioz wrote two more chapters of the *Memoirs*. The text itself records the strain the writer was under. At the mention of Louis, Berlioz breaks out with his buried imaginings about a fight at sea: "These enormous guns which he has to *serve;* these red-hot cannon balls, these congreve flares, this hail of shrapnel, fire, the hold filling up, exploding steam! I shall lose my mind. I cannot write." Louis was reported safe. The diversion was over. He would return to France and set out again for the Crimea. During the interim, Berlioz took the opportunity of going to La Côte for a family reunion. The familiar sights stirred memory again, and Berlioz resumed the abandoned chapter, which he dated on his return to Paris, October 18, 1854. On November 1, Louis landed at Cherbourg. "The fullest joy of the soul is mine. Louis is here. . . . I wrote to him at Cherbourg the news that you may already know—that I have remarried. He replied to me with affection and good sense."

The day after he had brought up his *Memoirs* to cover the time of Harriet Smithson's death, Berlioz ratified his liaison of fourteen years' standing, and Mlle. Recio became Mme. Berlioz. It was done, as he said, without ostentation or concealment. "My situation," he wrote to Louis, "is more fitting thus, being more regular. I make no doubt that if you harbor in your mind any painful memories or unfriendly feelings for Mlle. Recio, you will conceal them utterly out of affection for me." Louis proved not only affectionate but self-possessed and quite a man of the world. He was beginning to seem so even to others. Not long since, he had called on Liszt's daughters Cosima and Blandine, who were vising Paris, and they reported that he impressed them as an entertaining young blood.

Simultaneously with these events, the score of the *Damnation* appeared and attracted notice. It was almost a curiosity in a world occupied with war and fed on Meyerbeer's cumulative successes. The spirit of innovation had become as outmoded as the liberties that Napoleon III had extinguished. "In the thirties and forties," said *La France Musicale,* "fresh blood revivified art; men were in the grip of a fever, but also of a faith . . . It was then Hector Berlioz appeared, an eagle-eyed pioneer. Today the arts languish; we have lost that inward energy which keeps the soul aloft in the realms of poetry."

It could not be denied that Berlioz had maintained his course through those realms in spite of all discouragements and against all likelihood. He was even then preparing for the thankless capital two great musical events—first the performance of *The Infant Christ* ("I expect to lose some eight or nine hundred francs by it") and second, the use, in connection with the Great Exhibition of 1855, of his *Te Deum.* The man seemed indestructible and his music took after him: even before these new musical projects, and independently of any move on Berlioz' part, the manager of Covent Garden had put *Benvenuto Cellini* on the list of operas for the coming season. This act of reparation did not take place, but why announce a work so recently and throughly hissed, unless there were qualms stirring in the commercial conscience? The truth is that the exhibition years were like moral holidays taken from business life, and not only for Berlioz but for Delacroix and Courbet, 1855 marked a sudden glorification after the long struggle against hostile neglect.[13]

The first of Berlioz' concerts was set for the day preceding his fifty-first birthday, December 10, 1854. He invited some of his old intimates of the 1830's now in seclusion, such as the invalid Heine and the retired Alfred de Vigny, to whom Berlioz wistfully addressed "farewell, dear invisible poet." Contrary to his forecast, the concert proved a financial as well as an artistic success. Repeated on Christmas eve, the work netted its author eleven hundred francs and was immediately asked for by the charitable foundation known as The Infant Jesus for a benefit in January. The *première* was, according to Cosima Liszt, the most important event of the season. "The whole hall was stirred to the depths. . . . In a word, Berlioz' work achieved a gigantic success." [14] This was perfectly true and the press (saving only Scudo) was unanimous in praise. Heine apologized to Berlioz for having questioned his melodic gift seventeen years earlier in speaking of the *Requiem*. The Empire's official newspaper said: "Berlioz has garnered in one day the fruit of many years of struggle and patient labor."

All this the composer took with a grain of salt. "The good people of Paris say that I have changed my manner, that I have reformed. I needn't tell you that I have only changed my subject. . . ." The reception of his new brainchild, he told Liszt's Princess, "is insulting to its elder brothers"; and to Liszt himself: "So be it—I have become a good little boy, human, clear, melodic. I am at last writing music like everybody else. We are all agreed on that score." The favor he now met with in his compatriots' eyes came to him on three counts, which they took care to specify for his information—as composer, as conductor, and as poet. For the words of the trilogy were entirely his, and though he was still diffident about his versifying, the approval it received as literature encouraged him in the planning of his next two works.

At the third hearing, Berlioz substituted for the Haydn symphony and Mendelssohn trio which framed his oratorio, a piece of occasional music that he had written earlier on the foolish words of a Captain Lafont. Entitled *Le Dix Décembre,* it celebrated the Empire, and Berlioz later renamed it *L'Impériale* or *Emperor* cantata. As music, it shows what technique can do to supply breadth of style when this does not arise from genuine feeling: it yields an artificial pearl. Berlioz seems to have valued the work chiefly for one orchestral "find," [15] and for the help it might give in getting the court to authorize the *Te Deum*.

The year 1854 closed with undertones of worry beneath the artistic satisfactions. Berlioz had grippe, Marie was suffering from hives, Louis was halfway to the Black Sea, at Malta, and then not heard from. Nevertheless the German concerts had to be prepared. On top of this, a dispiriting contretemps spoiled a London victory which might have matched that in Paris:

two weeks after Berlioz had accepted a moderately good engagement to conduct two concerts of the New Philharmonic, he heard from Sainton that Costa had resigned from the Old and that his post was for Berlioz to take. It amounted to a recognition of Berlioz' pre-eminence over all living conductors, and carried with it honor, money, and opportunity for acclimating the moderns in England. The fame of Beethoven and Mendelssohn earlier had been entrenched by this very society. Berlioz tried to obtain an honorable release from Dr. Wylde who, thinking himself Berlioz' rival, took care not to grant it. The Old Philharmonic, also disappointed, turned to Spohr and failing him, to Richard Wagner.

At Hanover early in February 1855, *The Infant Christ* brought Berlioz further acclaim and the Order of the Guelfs. At Weimar a second "Berlioz Week" presented the same work. But after the "pious" new score, Berlioz had Liszt put on the "impious" melologue, *The Return to Life,* now renamed *Lélio, a monodrama.* It was cut down as to wordage and excellently performed as to music. To speak more accurately, the Episode in an Artist's Life was given in full—first the *Symphonie Fantastique,* then its vocal and pantomimic sequel—in which Liszt played the piano part as well as that of the Chinese gong. The public was somewhat taken aback by the speechifying but was charmed by the music; it liked even better the pieces with which it was now quite familiar: *Romeo,* the "Chorus of Master Goldsmiths" from *Cellini,* the "Concert of Sylphs" from the *Damnation,* and the orchestral song *La Captive.* Liszt played his E-flat concerto, "dazzling with verve and power," said Berlioz, "as always."

So full of verve, indeed, that he and his acolytes gave Berlioz the greatest triumph of his career. It was the high point of his harvesting season: Liszt was still his alter ego; Lauchert painted him; Cornelius was ready to exchange "any opera" for *La Captive;* and at the banquet of Weimar's notables, the poet Hoffmann von Fallersleben improvised a Latin toast which Raff at once set to music and the guests sang: Berlioz was called *Hospes Germanorum,* was told he had fulfilled their desire, and was bidden to remain *"amicus Neo-Wimarorum."*

At the same time, a more lasting effusion of feeling was taking effect at the Altenburg. Liszt and Princess Sayn-Wittgenstein in their long intimate talks with Berlioz filled him with the zest to undertake a large new work on the subject he had dreamed of since youth—the *Aeneid. L'Enfance* had strengthened his belief that he could deal with the antique otherwise than in the narcotic manner of the Opera, and it had shown him that his best librettist was himself. At the height of his worries about Louis, while brooding by the sea, he discovered that his "Passion for music, or rather for all art, takes on inordinate proportions. I feel within myself powers that are stronger than ever, and that are impeded only by material obstacles." Only his practical sense of these barriers made his lust for creation seem to him inordinate. It was therefore a blessing that Liszt and the Princess, moving in the freedom of luxury, should impart to Berlioz a little of their sense of power. The result was that composing words and music for his Virgilian subject occupied him for the next three years, filled though these were with English, German, and Parisian concerts, besides the usual load of private cares.

CHAPTER 20

VIRGILIAN MUSIC DRAMA

. . . thou that singest
Ilion's lofty temples robed in fire,
Ilion falling, Rome arising,
Wars and filial faith and Dido's pyre
Landscape-lover, lord of language
Thou majestic in thy sadness . . .
I salute thee,
I that loved thee since my day began.
TENNYSON on the nineteenth
centenary of Virgil's death

Berlioz' new task, at once literary and musical, was to be his passion and raison d'être for thirty-nine months, despite interruptions by concerts, journeys, and ill-health. But it may be noted in passing that the mood of *The Infant Christ* had not vanished all at once. Naïve religiousness produced another flower, the *Children's Morning Prayer,* on a text by Lamartine, which Berlioz scored for two-part female chorus and which has been likened for touching simplicity to some of Herrick's verses.[1] This afterglow of inspiration shows that Berlioz could probably have continued, at any point in his career, the production of music in any given style that had found favor. The determination with which after each major score he turns his back upon success and seeks out a new field to till is a feature of his creativeness that explains why he remained, for his own time and for a good while after, a musicians' musician.

Home from Weimar, Berlioz suffered the usual letdown, with aggravating circumstances. The "intestinal inflammation," which was diagnosed only later, now occurred as a regular symptom added to his old ones of sore throat, fever, and headache. It seems likely that Berlioz never had a disease properly so-called his whole life long. His nervous system when strained produced functional disorders, which in time became localized lesions and finally killed him. Until then a congenial musical task would "cure" his most violent pains, so that he may be said to have died a professional death rather than a casual or self-indulgent one.

A week in bed partly restored him for his concerts in Brussels, where he met again Adolphe Samuel, a young composer of thirty who greatly admired the French master and soon became one of his confidants.[2] Meanwhile Belgian rehearsals proved trying. "Whatever does not come down on the first beat makes them lose their heads. . . . They made me suffer like Hurons." Only the final concert satisfied the conductor, but at all of them the music was new—or rather, the public was, and its response correspondingly uncertain. Fétis, as we know, had revised his views a second time and thus regained his original position of somewhat alarmed admiration for Berlioz. At dinner he found Berlioz "a man of wit and great intelligence, both general and musical . . . unfortunately the richness of his imagination does not come up to his acquired technical skill." [3]

More wholehearted was Edgar Quinet, Michelet's friend and fellow historian, whom Napoleon III had exiled: "I had the other day the great joy of receiving a visit from Berlioz, whom I did not know and whom I have always admired in the teeth of public opinion. I love and admire this artist who follows the Muse without flattering the public. Berlioz himself attracts me as much as his music: his will power, his energy, his pride are as fine as any of his symphonies. What a fine work is the life of a true artist! He had my admiration, he leaves with my friendship. Moreover, we didn't only converse. I twice heard his oratorio *The Infant Christ,* which contains songs that Raphael might have created." [4]

On his return to Paris Berlioz was greeted by the first performance of the *Corsair* overture which he had recast in London and dedicated to his friend J. W. Davison. The next musical move was the preparation of the *Te Deum* and other concerts in connection with the Great Exhibition. Berlioz as usual did all the organizing, from finding the advance capital and the instrumentists to supervising the publicity and the building of stands. "The expenses alone come to 7000 francs.

It's enough to give you the shivers." Doubtless recalling the setback of the *Damnation* and hating the thought of debt, Berlioz formed a virtual partnership to divide the risk. The profits were allocated in advance: the Church would receive fifty per cent, the district commissioner of the poor twenty per cent, and himself thirty per cent. Despite the share allotted to the Church for its trouble and to the poor for theirs, the Archbishop at the last minute threatened to stop the enterprise. By an adroit use of the press, Berlioz coped with this impediment; but in between errands and rehearsals he had to lie down, feverish and writhing in pain.

On April 28, 1855 the public dress rehearsal of the *Te Deum* took place at St. Eustache. The critics were lifted out of their usual apathy, and their enthusiasm insured the financial success of the public hearing two days later. The church was full to overflowing and everything went without a hitch. The former director of the Opera, Roqueplan, who had treated Berlioz so shabbily, came forward with many others and warmly congratulated him. "The end of the world is near," was Berlioz' dry comment to Princess Carolyne. And to Liszt, in saying farewell, "I am taking to my bed."

His stay in bed must have been short because in early May he was calling at the Ministries for authorization to give subsequent Exhibition concerts. Of the seven that were planned, he was put in charge of three, including the first. Yet pain and fatigue still plagued him and we find him giving Liszt explicit instructions for publishing the *Memoirs* if he should die suddenly. "Forgive me for writing to you in this testamentary tone." Before the beginning of the London season to which he was committed, he had proofs to correct, piano reductions to oversee (young Saint-Saëns was doing *Lélio*), and the usual *feuilletons*.

In London with his wife by June 9, Berlioz had the weaker of the two orchestral societies to conduct in two concerts. His first included Mozart's *Magic Flute* overture and G Minor Symphony, fragments of *Romeo,* and the *Templar* overture by a young composer named Henry Leslie. Richard Wagner, of whose presence in London Berlioz heard from Liszt, was in the audience. He had been badly handled by the press for his conducting of the other orchestra, but was reported calm in spirit and sure of "dominating the musical world in 50 years." This first concert of Berlioz aroused the subscribers so mightily that their cheers, according to a witness, made the walls of Exeter Hall vibrate. And the loyalty of the oldtimers was such that protests were received at the omission of the choral parts of *Romeo*—an omission due solely to the lack of the right voices.

The second concert on July fourth featured *Harold in Italy* (viola solo by Ernst), the *première* of Henselt's piano concerto in F minor, and a scene from Meyerbeer's *Prophète*. The composer was in England to aid in the mounting of *Stella del Nord,* for which Queen Victoria lingered late in the capital. Berlioz moreover conducted a benefit at which, after Rossini's *Stabat Mater,* no less than eight prima donnas of both sexes sang fashionable airs. Ernst played little pieces on the violin and the success was complete. On the next day Berlioz would leave England for the last time.

Before his departure, however, he and Wagner had had their first and only long, uninterrupted conversation. It was at the house of Berlioz' friend Sainton that the two spent an evening together informally, and came as near knowing each other as it was granted them to do. Their previous meetings had been brief interludes in the midst of action, and the well-meant efforts of Liszt, Bülow, and others had only resulted in developing as much difference as kinship between them. It is usually difficult to make one's friends become mutual as well as common friends, and with men who have ideas the attempt may be fatal. Besides, just as Davison (who disliked Wagner's music and conducting) was not slow to represent to Berlioz how violently Wagner attacked him in print, so there were those in Germany who stirred up Wagner to a comparable though unmotivated resentment. Since, finally, Berlioz' assurance to Liszt of a willingness to forget Wagner's attacks was not encouraged by Marie (she took her husband's magnanimity for laxness in self-defense) it might have been expected that the evening at Sainton's would be, at best, stiff.

It turned out precisely the opposite. Immediately after, Wagner was writing to Liszt:

> One real gain I bring back from England—the cordial and genuine friendship which I feel for Berlioz and which we have mutually declared. I heard a concert of the New Philharmonic under his direction and was, it is true, little edified by his performance of Mozart's G Minor symphony, while the very imperfect execution of his *Romeo and Juliet* symphony made me pity him.
>
> A few days later, we two were the only guests at Sainton's

table. He was lively, and the progress I have made in French while in London permitted me to discuss with him for five hours all the problems of art, philosophy, and life in a most fascinating conversation. In that manner I gained a deep sympathy for my new friend; he appeared to me quite different from what he had before.[5] We discovered that we were in reality fellow sufferers, and I thought that upon the whole I was happier than Berlioz.

After my last concert he and the other friends I have in London called on me; his wife also came. We remained together until 3 o'clock in the morning and took leave with the warmest embraces.

On his side Berlioz had written to Liszt:

We spoke a great deal about you with Wagner recently, and you may imagine with how much affection, since, on my word of honor, I believe he loves you as I do. He will no doubt tell you of his stay in London and of all he has had to endure from prejudiced hostility. He is superb in his ardor and stoutness of heart, and I confess that even his violence pleases me. It seems fate itself is at work to keep me from hearing his latest compositions. . . . If it is true that we both have asperities [of character] those asperities dovetail into each other thus:

What Berlioz, with a tactfulness Wagner did not emulate, refrained from telling Liszt was that he had not enjoyed his new friend's conducting "in a free style, the way Klindworth plays the piano . . . *sempre tempo rubato,*" nor that just before leaving, he had at last been shown the words of Wagner's attack.[6]

Liszt rejoiced. "I am delighted," he told Wagner, "at the news of your friendship with Berlioz. Of all contemporary composers he is the one with whom you can talk in the simplest, openest, and most interesting manner. Take him for all in all, he is a splendid, honest, tremendous fellow."

A witness to the second meeting in London, Wagner's friend Praegor, makes an interesting comparison enabling us to picture Berlioz at this time: "Berlioz was of an excitable temperament, too, but could repress it. Not so Wagner. He presented a striking contrast to the polished, refined Frenchman, whose speech was almost classic through his careful selection of words." And to complete the portrait we may quote Guizot writing to his daughter about a soiree at Legouvé's. Gounod, Gustave Doré, Gautier, and Theodore Ritter (of whom we shall hear more) were present: "A moment later I saw next to me a gentleman of spare frame, with a tousled head of hair, a piercing eye, and a spirited and quite noble countenance. Legouvé approached him and said, 'My dear Berlioz'—we were introduced. He turned out to be a true enthusiast, not at all talkative, until the moment when his enthusiasm grips him, and then he becomes full and eloquent: a striking contrast with the skeptical and sensual writer Théophile Gautier." Later Guizot said to his host: "I have met many illustrious artists at your house, but none has impressed me like M. Berlioz. *There* is an original being!" Legouvé, who had known Berlioz for twenty years, concurs: "He was an extraordinary mixture of enthusiasm and sarcasm; his mind always gave forth the unexpected. His conversation kept you in suspense by the very unevenness of its flow."

Judging Berlioz' and Wagner's conducting in one season, the public at large received a corresponding impression: polish and precision as against impetuosity and self will. Moreover, "Wagner, embittered by his long struggle against poverty, depreciation, and failure, . . . [was] in a very unfit condition to make friends, even if he had been the most genial of men. He appears to have set everyone by the ears. . . . Berlioz, on the other hand, resembled Mendelssohn in the charm of his manner and the desire to be affable. It was by a mere chance that . . . he did not settle in England, or at least make it to a large extent his home." Certainly his English friends, admirers, and backers formed an ever enlarging group and seemed a more compact and active following than any he had met. The British tradition of Handelian oratorio favored an understanding of Berlioz' dramatic forms. During his stay he had arranged for an English publication of *The Infant Christ,* and had signed a contract with Novello for a revised edition of the *Treatise on Orchestration,* to which the author agreed to add his essay on "The Art of Conducting." The trip as a whole had been materially and spiritually profitable.

Awaiting him at home was a mass of arrears. The *Te Deum, L'Enfance,* and *Lélio* were coming out together. "I do nothing but read proof from morning till night." Since the *Te Deum* was being published by subscription, Berlioz must also write letters to possible buyers. *Benvenuto Cellini,* widely called for in Germany, was being engraved at Brunswick. On top of this, Berlioz was again on the jury for musical instruments at the Paris Exhibition. It was "enough to kill off a resuscitated man." The heat was unusually great; Louis, who had been quite ill in a naval hospital at St. Mandrier, was recovering slowly; and there were already premonitions of the next war.

Nevertheless, the *Treatise* was revised and issued and four musical works, one of them in two distinct editions, were published and distributed. In September, declining Wagner's invitation to visit him in Zurich, Berlioz wrote: "So you are melting the glaciers as you work upon your *Nibelungen.* It must be splendid to compose in the presence of Nature. That is another delight I am deprived of: beautiful scenery, high peaks, and the grand aspects of the sea absorb me entirely instead of prompting thought. At such times I can only feel and not express. I can only draw the moon by looking at its reflection in a well.

"I should like to be able to send you the scores you so kindly ask for. Unfortunately my publishers no longer give me any [of the earlier ones]. But there are two, in fact three —the *Te Deum, The Infant Christ* and *Lélio* (a lyric monodrama) which will come out in a few weeks and these at least I can send you. I have your *Lohengrin;* if you could let me have your *Tannhäuser,* it would give me much pleasure."

The next month the Exhibition would close and rehearsals must begin for Berlioz' three concerts. This was "a furnace in which to broil alive," for although the conductor expected to be worn out in the usual way, he now found himself faced with an Imperial Committee that interfered at each step and "co-operated" destructively. Like the Quaker housewife, Berlioz had only strength enough to do things by himself. "Yesterday," he writes to Liszt's Princess on November 6, 1855, "I began my rehearsals, my struggle with the architects, the copyists, and so on. I have nine days to go, baton in hand from nine to four. . . . The whole of Paris wants to sing, blow, and scrape, and one has to tune all these voices, instruments, and pretensions."

For good measure he sandwiched in a few errands for his correspondent and her lover, seeing to the shipping of saxophones and claiming of unpaid royalties. Liszt had composed two symphonic poems which Berlioz wanted to know more about in order to publicize their existence, and Liszt had finished a long essay on the *Harold* symphony, with sidelights on *Benvenuto* and Berlioz' method in general. He now wished Berlioz to have the essay published in Paris.

The first concert began at noon on November 15—prize-giving day—in the presence of Napoleon, Eugénie, Prince Jerome and the Duke of Cambridge. After the parade, Berlioz began his *Emperor* cantata, now or never appropriate, and moreover quite short. But the Emperor himself interrupted it by getting up and fingering his speech. The remainder of the concert—works by other composers—was similarly hashed up, but the performers cheered the conductor in spite of protocol. The next day, with no officials but an immense audience, the whole program, from Beethoven and Berlioz to Handel, Gluck, Meyerbeer and Rossini, was acclaimed. He had massed his cohorts on and around the Imperial platform, which was the correct acoustic spot, and the effect lived up to his design. In the *Te Deum* March for the Review of the Colors and the *Apothéose* there were two hundred drums.

But this was nothing to the armies corralled on succeeding days by other conductors: Gounod led sixteen hundred singers one day and forty-five hundred later on. Berlioz gave his program with his smaller, better balanced and better trained forces a second time and received most of the notices. They were hardly musical judgments, but Berlioz was used to that. His irritation, as the year ended, was spent on Liszt's behalf; for after a concert in Berlin where his friend had played his own setting of the thirteenth Psalm, the critics had served up their old arguments against expressive music on religious subjects. "So the Berlin Ph.D.'s are riding their Rosinante to tilt at the religious paradox again! Materialist music—dramatic—passionate—worldly! They want the Christian to pray as a statue would if it could . . .

"And these same heavyweights who find modern music wrong in being thus expressive . . . make no objection whatever to the nonsense contained in the innumerable [operas] with which Europe is flooded. . . . In short, Raphael and Michelangelo committed a crime against religion in painting when they used color; they should have used only black and white, and even so their Madonnas have faces that are too expressive and meaningful. . . . The Gotha concert will definitely take place on February 6. I have another at Liège on January 29, and one here in Paris on the 23rd. I'll send you a list of the ladies who are killed or injured."

At the Gotha concert Berlioz received two hundred thalers, a cross from the Grand Duke, and a visit from Liszt, who was unwell. Together they went to Weimar, where the pianist, now a Perfect Wagnerite, hoped to make Berlioz a convert by playing him large portions of the operas at the keyboard. The occasion of Berlioz' stay was really a third "Berlioz Week," beginning with *Benvenuto Cellini,* which proved as successful as before; but Berlioz was made to feel that Liszt had adopted a new idol which he, Berlioz, could not add to his own Olympus. The friendship between the old companions of 1830 was as real and affectionate and serviceable as ever, but a new doctrine—as Liszt explicitly admitted later—was depriving it of artistic significance. Liszt had every right to like and to champion any music he chose, and Berlioz was too great a mind to question that right for an instant. But he could not concede the Wagnerian theory of musical evolution, namely that Wagner's new art superseded that of Weber and Beethoven.[7]

There was something a little crude in Liszt's attempt to make Berlioz agree to this proposition, something a little blind in accepting it himself—what room did it leave for the very works of Berlioz which Liszt continued to conduct and eulogize in print? Moreover, there was as yet not a single work answering to Wagner's description. *Lohengrin* and the original version of *Tannhäuser* were not "works of art of the future." Berlioz and Liszt thus bogged down in painful and futile debates which by common consent they did not renew.

What made the situation critical for each of them was that the three men involved were producing: Liszt had taken fire orchestrally, Wagner was also approaching the fulfillment of his long preparation, and Berlioz was taking the step by which the dramatic symphony and dramatic legend were adapted to the stage in a music drama of epic style and proportions. For despite the setbacks of illness and concertizing the Virgilian project was taking shape. Letters from his "encouragers" as he called Adolphe Samuel in Brussels, the Baron von Donop at Detmold, Auguste Morel in Marseille, and Liszt's Princess as well, kept him from yielding to the "inert and glacial" atmosphere of Paris. There Prince Jerome was an island of comfort, being desirous of "establishing" this French composer with a European reputation whom Paris maintained only as a critic. But the Emperor, the source of all power and possibility, was unapproachable, perhaps because "he execrates music like ten Turks."

Instead of the signs of quickened life, the spring of 1856 brought home to Berlioz rather the watchful presence of death. Not only did he himself experience unpleasant spells of faintness, but many in his circle were mortally stricken. First, young Fumagalli died, a pupil and friend of Liszt's, aged twenty-eight; then Mlle. Pleyel, Camille's daughter—also a pianist and very like her mother in looks—from galloping consumption at twenty; then Montfort, who had won the Rome Prize the same year as Berlioz. Also Heinrich Heine, who had matched wits with Berlioz for a quarter century, and whom Berlioz had continued to cheer by visits during the last years of the poet's invalidism. Likewise Berlioz' doctor, Amussat, who had once been Hector's teacher at Medical School, and another physician, Vidal, always a stout Berliozian, though attached in a professional capacity to the Opera. "I am always at the cemetery," writes the survivor, "the good Lord is mowing us down. . . ."

Louis was another source of worry. After his illness, the young man wanted to leave the Navy and enter the merchant marine. Berlioz tried to secure dispensations in order to avert loss of rank. In the end, the boy's position had to remain as it was. But the general rise in prices compelled Berlioz to move to a smaller apartment, at 4 rue de Calais, in the Clichy district. And Caesar's economics, as usual, was affecting things belonging to God: the occasions for serious musical criticism were becoming fewer. The small Salle Herz, built the preceding year, held in its couple of hundred seats all those who cared for genuine music. At the Opera the great attraction was *Le Corsaire,* a ballet by Adolphe Adam, the popularity of which was largely due to the real ship which could be seen in the last act. "Music! That's the last thing anyone thinks of."

At the instigation of a Swiss publisher, Berlioz had just revised his *Nuits d'Eté* and completed their orchestration. Fresh music too was stirring within him. "I am gathering my strength," he writes in mid-April, "I have blocked out the main lines of the great dramatic business that the Princess takes so much interest in. It's beginning to take shape, but it is huge and therefore dangerous." This was to Liszt; a month later, he informs the Princess: "Day before yesterday I finished versifying the first act. It will be the longest and it took me ten days to write it—the first ten I have had clear since my return from Weimar. . . . I have been a dozen times on the point of throwing everything into the fire and giving myself over to the contemplative life. But now I am sure not to lack the courage to reach the end. The work has got hold of me. Besides, I reread your letter from time to time to spur myself on. Usually, I feel discouragement at night but come back into the breach in the morning—in the day's youth. Now I can hardly sleep: I think of nothing else and if I had my time wholly free, in two months the mosaic would be finished."

No statement ever described more briefly or more exactly the overcoming of inertia at the beginning of a great work, that psychological dead weight which has nothing to do with the nature of the task, the author's preparation for it, nor even his desire to be at work, but is an emotional resistance due to the disparity between the world of created things and the world of the uncreated. The conception on its way to birth,

Like the red outline of beginning Adam

is unreal and, as it seems, superfluous—reality being complete without it. In Berlioz, we know, this sense of the folly implied in creation was heightened by his knowledge of practical affairs. Paris under the Second Empire virtually forbade the kind of enterprise he had in hand.

The artistic problem was to form a dramatic sequence of musical scenes from the narrative contained in Books II and IV of the *Aeneid,* that is, the story of the sack of Troy, followed by the landing of the Trojans at Carthage and the tragic love of Dido for Aeneas—a subject which has traditionally attracted dramatic musicians from Monteverdi and the masque composers to Purcell and Piccinni. In keeping with his habit, Berlioz did not want long explanatory passages, nor the usual operatic dialogue (accompanied by gesticulation) which hitches the plot forward. Hence the planning of his "book," not to speak of the lines, was bound to be a delicate task.

He interrupted it to stand for the Institute: Adolphe Adam had died suddenly. This time the academic musicians put Berlioz at the head of their list and he was elected; but only on the fourth ballot lest popularity should go to his head. In effect, Parisian circles took the event as a revolution—a second was in store for them when Delacroix succeeded to the same honor six months later. The admittance among the officially immortal of these two young men (aged fifty-three and fifty-nine respectively) marked a date in France's recognition of modern art. It was also a triumph for the loyal Horace Vernet. Berlioz was chiefly glad of the fifteen hundred francs a year which helped reduce the number of necessary *feuilletons,* but he also knew how his new title would impress the public and his outlying relatives. Parodying Talleyrand's retort to Napoleon he wrote to his soldier uncle: "I was sitting on a bayonet, now I am in an armchair."

By this time (mid-June 1856) Berlioz had finished the third act of his drama. During the cab rides to the houses of the members who were to vote for him, "I thought not of what I was going to say . . . but of what I ought to make my characters say." Ten days later the last scene of Act V was in progress. "I grow more impassioned about the subject than I should, and I resist the blandishments that music exerts to have me attend to her. I want to finish everything before I begin the score. Yet last week I could not help composing the Shakespearean duet:

In such a night as this
When the sweet wind did gently kiss the trees, etc.[8]

So the music of this litany of love is done. But I shall need another fortnight to file down, carve, polish, correct, twist and untwist the verses such as they are. . . . I have still twenty-two confreres to call on and thank. I saw fifteen this morning, and I was obliged to stand the embraces of a number of those who voted against me. . . . Forgive the triviality and coldness of this letter: could it be that already I——? No! My Institute uniform has not even been ordered. . . ."

By July, the tentative title *Les Troyens* was adopted. "But that is of no moment," wrote Berlioz in sending the Princess his manuscript, "the question is one of music and you will see what an enormous score this text presupposes." Unlike Wagner, supported by friends and trusting tradesmen in his Swiss retreat, Berlioz could not count on long stretches of free time. No sooner had he been elected to the Institute than he had to sit on the Rome Prize committee, after which he was detailed to study and conduct a Mass by Niedermeyer. This done, he had his regular stint to do for Bénazet at Baden.

From there on August 12 he wrote to the Princess thanking her for comments on his text: "What an excellent analysis!

That is what I call entering into the author's intentions! You wanted to cheer me along and I shall not be deluded by your words. You go so far as to credit me with the beauty of Virgil's poetry and praise me for my thefts from Shakespeare! Have no fear: I have the grit to carry on to the end; it was not necessary to lure me forward with eulogies that I do not deserve—it is beautiful because it is Virgil; it is striking because it is Shakespeare. I know it. I am only an interloper; I have ransacked the gardens of two geniuses, and cut there a swath of flowers to make a couch for music, where God grant she may not perish overcome by the fragrance. . . . As for Dido's scene with her sister . . . it is a simple mirage of love which I have conjured up in order to avoid the invariable *dream* of the classics."[9]

Berlioz then turns to the musical side, saying that when he is once again in Paris he will free himself as much as possible for the strenuous task ahead. "May all Virgil's gods come to my aid, else I am lost." It is at this juncture that he states for the first time in relation to one of his own works his conception of the proper role of music in music drama. This of course leads him to mention Wagner's contrary view, too reminiscent of eighteenth-century literary theories to suit the man who all his life had worked to make music free and independent:

The great difficulty [throughout] is to find the musical *form*—that form without which music does not exist, or exists only as the humbled slave of speech. There lies Wagner's crime: he wants to dethrone music and reduce it to expressive *accents.* This is to outdo the system of Gluck (who most fortunately *did not succeed* in following his own impious theory). I am for the kind of music that you yourself call "free". . . . Music is so powerful that in given instances it can conquer alone, and it has a thousand times earned the right to say with Medea:

"Myself, which is enough."

To want to bring music back to the old recitation of the antique chorus is assuredly the most incredible and, luckily, the most useless folly in the history of art.[10]

To find the way of being expressive and truthful, without ceasing to be a musician; to endow music, rather, with new means of action—that is the problem. . . . Another hurdle in my path is that the feelings to be rendered move me too much. That is bad. One must try to do coolly things that are fiery. This is what held me up for so long in the *Romeo and Juliet* adagio and the finale of Reconciliation. I thought I should never see my way. . . . Time! Time! He is the great master. Unfortunately he behaves like Ugolino, he eats his children. . . .

At Baden, Berlioz had conducted Beethoven, Gluck, and Mozart, together with an excerpt from *The Infant Christ,* but the audience was small, for the August weather was mild enough to make the outdoors pleasant even at midday. Feeling unwell after the confusing interruption of this session, Berlioz returned to Plombières, the French water resort, where he had spent two weeks before going to Baden. He had while there met the Emperor and been invited by him to a soiree at which Vivier the horn player, mimic, and raconteur had entertained a small group.[11] It was clearer than ever that Napoleon III took not the slightest interest in serious music, even when composed by a newborn academician. During his second stay at Plombières Berlioz rested, which means worked at *Les Troyens* while strolling in the woods. He quickly recovered his health, was full of gaiety and could dash off amusing *feuilletons* without qualms since he had composed three scenes of his music drama.

By virtue of a neurosis which he seems to have dimly observed, his return to Paris was always gloomy. He necessarily found the old worries and obstacles, and found them as if he were still in the desperate straits of his twenties, when Dr. Berlioz had said "Do or die" and had loaded the option by cutting off funds. In Paris, Berlioz felt, "I seem to hear nothing but the resonance of empty or extinguished souls." His illness returned and was diagnosed on November 14 by Alphonse Robert, the cousin (now famous) with whom he had first come to Paris to study medicine in 1821. But diagnosis seemed no avenue to cure. The prescription was six drops of laudanum in a spoonful of water. "It leaves an inner tremor which is rather disagreeable." [12] Abdominal pain gripped him so hard and so relentlessly that he had to spend whole days in bed, and he came to think that he might not live to finish his work. Nor did he lack mental afflictions. Louis was still making himself a burden by his free spending and his disinclination to go on with any career.

Nevertheless, by January 1857 the first act of *Les Troyens* was virtually completed. In consequence, after fifteen years of straightforward enmity, Berlioz must once again be concerned with an institution he despised: he would soon have a score designed for the stage, and the Opera was the only large stage available. But while he was rejuvenated by creation[13] the Imperial theater was supersenile: it could not or would not even give *William Tell* entire. Access to the ministerial controls was even more remote than in the days of good King Louis-Philippe. Only, Napoleon's manners were better, and he took care to send Berlioz a medal for his part in making the Exhibition of 1855 a success.

Despite the prospect of never hearing his *Troyens* live in sound, Berlioz worked on. Music was pouring out of him for several scenes at one time, out of sequence, the while he steadily furbished up the lines, withdrawing foolish concessions to current taste and nourishing himself on Virgil and Shakespeare. "I am quite transported by some words of old Nestor in Shakespeare's *Troilus and Cressida.* I have just reread this amazing parody of the Iliad, where none the less Shakespeare makes Hector even greater than Homer did. Nestor says that Hector raising his sword aloft to spare the trembling Greeks as he sped through battle in his chariot made him think:

Lo, Jupiter is yonder, dealing life! [14]

What a painting that would make! . . . God in heaven but it's beautiful. . . . I feel my heart will burst when I come across lines like that. . . ."

Each scene would be composed in the rough within a space of two or three days and then instrumented and polished during as many weeks. Being ill gave Berlioz an excuse not to be sociable, though his duties as critic brought on the periodic "calamity" of having to go to the Opera. The Italian Theater meanwhile teased him with hints that they might put on *Benvenuto Cellini.* Was it to purchase his good-will? In the houses of friends where he felt at home, there was always the danger of being involved in artistic discussions, which just then Berlioz was not in the mood for. Thus at Mme. Viardot's (Pauline Garcia) he ran into Delacroix, old, nervous, and ailing like himself, and the two masters of Romanticism, differing on pinpoints, would end by annoying each other. Yet when the next Institute vacancy occurred among the painters, Berlioz urged Delacroix's election. It took place on January 10, 1857, at the ninth attempt. So few were left who had understood the message of the century in the thirties and persevered in giving it form! The neoclassical reaction was in full swing, aided by the vague political drift which likened Caesar and Napoleon the First with the present incumbent. The narcotic playwright

Ponsard was winning a reputation for depth and originality by lectures proving that Shakespeare lacked artistry. "Noodle!" exclaims Berlioz in his correspondence, "overripe cucumber!"

Music was still streaming "in floods." He timed the first act and found it ran one hour and ten minutes. This meant that "all the rest must be as compact as possible to keep the whole within reasonable proportions." He would invite certain of his instrumentist friends and have them play some of the "solos" (*i.e.,* outstanding melodic parts) while he accompanied them sketchily on the piano. "The Opera clarinetist (Leroy) is a first-rate virtuoso, but cold . . . My piano was a little low, so our two instruments were not in tune, the virtuoso phrased 'only approximately,' finding it *very pretty*—which made me devilishly mad. . . . What a torture *approximation* is in musical performance! Yet I think the young man will end by understanding his solo if I make him study it bar by bar. . . ." This was the sublime scene without speech in Act I, where Andromache leading her orphaned son walks past the Trojan women to pray at the altar and receive Priam's blessing.

Was it a good omen for such conceptions that the Parisians had taken a sudden liking for Weber, whose *Oberon* was filling the Théâtre Lyrique? On first being told of the projected production, Berlioz had echoed Rossini's famous, "What? All of it?" and wound up thinking "Poor Weber!" But he had lent a hand at the rehearsals, and it now seemed that "the burghers are actually amazed to find they like this music which, although far from perfectly executed, is nevertheless better done than it would be at the Opéra-Comique and much better than at the Opera." The old question whether the public likes what it gets or gets what it likes could be debated apropos of this musical surprise, and Berlioz would have to make up his mind about it before venturing his *Troyens.* He inclined to the view that the public was more often corrupted than corrupting.

The love music which fills the fourth act was now complete and instrumented. The pillars of the edifice being in sight, the masses and proportions could be inferred. At a dinner given by Prince Jerome for Academicians, Berlioz had the pleasure of seeing his dear friend Vigny again—for the last time—and of meeting Disraeli.[15] A few weeks later at the Tuileries, he was presented to the Empress who charmed him by her classical knowledge (Mérimée had been her tutor) and by her great beauty. Berlioz spoke to her of his work and was graciously told he might read his poem to her.[16] Nothing came of this purely imperial promise, but the idea remained with Berlioz of creating interest in his work by reading the poem. Moreover the experience of *The Infant Christ* had taught him the importance of minds prepared by a knowledge of "the story." He gave two readings of *Les Troyens*—at the Bertins' and at his own house —which considerably impressed the listeners.

This was in March 1857. The next month he conducted a concert for his favorite protégé, the composer and pianist Theodore Ritter—the son of Berlioz's friend Bennet. Berlioz admired the young man's musicianship, he was forming his taste, and he enjoyed in his company something like a father-and-son relation of the kind that poor Louis could not help denying him. Ritter showed his gratitude by making the piano reduction of *Romeo and Juliet*—the best so far (according to Berlioz) of all the arrangements he so disliked.

Paris was now as full of musicians as of writers and painters. One could find as many as eight recitalists all striking their first chord simultaneously before as many audiences. In one of his reviews Berlioz gathers the names of one hundred and sixty-three performers who had just given or were on the point of giving recitals. One hundred and fifty he could arrange in riming couplets: the other thirteen had neither rime nor reason. It would soon be necessary to pass ordinances: "No concerts given here," or "Commit no music on these premises." Paris was as far as ever from Euphonia.

"Nothing," he wrote to Morel on the subject now much in his thoughts, "will keep the public from going to the Opera—whence a complacent carelessness on the part of the management which is beyond belief. . . . You should hear the music that is occasionally played at Court. And now here is the poor King of Prussia who has lost his mind; I do not know whether his brother shares his feeling for art. The small German courts where music is really prized are not very wealthy, and Russia (like England) is monopolized by the Italians. There remains Queen Pomaré, but Tahiti is rather far away." [17] Berlioz had thought of giving the *Damnation of Faust*, "which is unknown in Paris," but he could find neither hall nor singers. Moreover Pasdeloup's expanding orchestra raffled whatever instrumental talents might be momentarily unused.[18] Berlioz could have gone to Sweden, from which an offer came, but he preferred to keep working at his score. One event that gave him pleasure at the end of this season at the Institute was the award of the Rome Prize to a promising youth named Georges Bizet.

It was now midsummer and the Baden concerts loomed. Berlioz and his wife went first to Plombières, and since the Emperor was not among the visitors, the town was quiet, propitious for country rambles and steady composing. After a month, the Festival brought him again into the freehanded, regal atmosphere of Bénazet's realm, where his old friends the musicians of Carlsruhe, and his German admirers—Princess Stephanie of Prussia, the Duchess of Baden, Countess Kalergi, and others—made him feel he had a place in their affections. This time they heard and applauded no less than five of his works, including the *Judex crederis* from the *Te Deum.*

Between early September, when Berlioz returned to Paris and the end of November, the third act was composed, but in a growing musical isolation for its author. The Second Empire's honeymoon with art was over. Like other new regimes it had shown a few years' excited awareness, followed by a relapse which seems to say: "Whew! We've done our duty." [19] Berlioz' old friend d'Ortigue was now almost exclusively interested in his studies of plainsong, and shortly Liszt would also appear in Paris as the herald of an orthodox religious withdrawal from the world. Carvalho's Théâtre Lyrique had followed up *Oberon* with *Euryanthe,* which had fallen utterly flat, for reasons Berlioz could understand: "I don't believe that any one ever put on the stage comparable nonsense. It must be difficult to be so stupid. We all agree in praising the music . . ." Yet the failure made Berlioz "sad all over."

This feeling must have been aggravated by the rise of the pro-Wagner crusade—an obvious answer to the prevailing platitude of Parisian offerings, but based on the principle of *omne ignotum pro magnifico.* Those who preached the new gospel knew at most the one opera produced in Weimar—*Tannhäuser* —and unrevised at that. But the converts, who naturally included the best and liveliest minds, were full of doctrine and spoke with confidence of a new score "which would be still more stunning." Even the rumors uttered by Wagner's enemies helped, for they roused men like Gautier, Reyer, and a little later Baudelaire, to defend with indignation the beauty and power of the fragments they knew. Gautier was asking for a "solemn test" of *Tannhäuser* at the Opera. This might prove either good or bad for *Les Troyens,* but the proposal hardly respected the claim to public attention that Berlioz had the right to exercise before anyone else.

This unwitting injustice was at bottom due to cultural politics rather than to musical feeling. To these half-informed devotees, Wagner was the dark horse who stood a better chance than the war-worn Berlioz to vindicate art against Philistinism.[20] Wagner's campaign literature was abundant, mysterious, and solemn. He was beginning to acquire the status of a national artist, interpreting the deep Germanic soul to the world —a close parallel to the Italians' conquest of French opera in the eighteenth century. Berlioz had already witnessed a recurrence of Italianism in the 1820's and had next endured Meyerbeer's monopoly. Having suffered a great deal from blind attack, he was by no means unwilling to see justice done to Wagner's works. He himself was eager to hear them. But Wagner's admirers were bent on creating still another monopoly, exclusive and doctrinaire, and on making Berlioz admit that in music as in industry the latest was the best. To the Princess, he replied very philosophically about being pushed against his will (he might have added, against chronological fact)[21] into the conservative position: ". . . it is so easy to abstrain from certain discussions and there are so many other points on which I have the good fortune to agree with you that I hope in future not to be drawn into such sanguinary debates."

The great work went on. "I go at it with a concentrated passion which seems to increase as I satisfy it." But it took a heavy physical toll requiring systematic rest. This did not keep Berlioz from assisting in the establishment of a Beethoven Music School —a private venture begun by the singer Louis Paulin, who wanted Berlioz to teach Instrumentation. In the end, Berlioz could not spare the time for the course, but he helped defend the new enterprise against the attacks of the monopolistic Conservatoire.

The question of teaching carried Berlioz back many years, just at a time when his Brussels friend Samuel was complaining of the difficulties inherent in earning a living while doing "one's own work." Berlioz tried to cheer him by matching woes. "You *give* lessons; we *receive* them here, from every Tom, Dick, and Harry. . . . I should have answered you at once, but I was feverishly gripped by an impassioned scene in my fifth act, which I really could not tear myself from. I finished it this morning and I breathe a little easier.

"I wonder what I am about to undergo in the way of burning regrets and vexations when I have completed this huge musical and dramatic construction. The time is near. In two months it will be all done. Where shall I then find the theatrical manager, conductor, and singers that I need?[22] The new opera will lie there like Robinson Crusoe's canoe until the sea comes up to set it afloat—if there is such a thing as the sea for works of this nature. I am beginning to think that the sea is only a dream of shipbuilders."

In January 1858, Berlioz' disease held him bedridden. Liszt, he heard, had again been ill. Meanwhile Wagner had come to Paris and had called. The object of his visit was to find an opening for any one of his operas at some official theater. He and Berlioz agreed to meet again at Emile Ollivier's, the present Minister of Justice, who had just married Liszt's daughter Blandine (Cosima's elder sister) and was thus Wagner's patron in Paris.[23] Berlioz returned Wagner's call, but their London entente was not easily resumed.

Shortly after, Berlioz again read his poem before a cultivated gathering at the house of his fellow-academician, the architect Hittorf.[24] Though the result was not intended, such a reading could only set Berlioz and Wagner as runners in a race to reach the first vacant stage. Prince Jerome, always friendly to Berlioz, declared the Opera hopeless, impregnable. Meanwhile Liszt and his other son-in-law, Hans von Bülow, were doing all they could to take Berlioz into camp by writing him long letters, putting excerpts from his works on their programs in Germany and thus trying to assign him his role as elder statesman in the Wagnerian movement. "The young man," wrote Berlioz to his son about Bülow, "is one of the most fervent disciples of the extravagant school known in Germany as the music of the future. They will not give up their determination that I should be at their head as standard bearer. I say nothing, write nothing, and let them have their way. Sensible people will know what to make of it all."

There is little doubt that if Berlioz had accepted this part of John the Baptist which the younger men thrust upon him, he would not have been cast into the semi-obscurity of his last and immediately posthumous years. But he would also have been purchasing a position at the price of lost integrity. Besides, he was not an elder statesman or titular chief but an originator still, with energy for several bouts to come. Perhaps the young Wagnerians took it as a counteroffensive when Berlioz helped another German musician, Henry Litolff, to give concerts in Paris. The truth is that Berlioz sincerely admitted Litolff's music, which was somewhat influenced by his own; and that Litolff, though opposing Wagner, was an old friend of Liszt's. He was also a music publisher in Brunswick who on Berlioz' journeys there had been affable and helpful and had just brought out an edition of *Benvenuto Cellini*. Berlioz was paying a debt of gratitude—and most effectively, since the concerts were very successful.

Toward the end of the same month (February 1858) all but the final scene of the gigantic *Troyens* was finished. Berlioz gave another reading at his house, always noting the effect and the comments of his picked hearers. The day before he wrote to Samuel: "I have worked at the poem with extreme patience and will not have to make major changes. Why should we not have patience?—I was reading yesterday in a Life of Virgil that he took eleven years to write the *Aeneid,* yet so unfinished did it seem to him that as he lay dying he ordered his heirs to burn it. . . .

"I think you will be satisfied with my score. You can easily guess what the scenes of passion, of tenderness, or of nature, whether serene or stormy, must be like; but there are other scenes of which you cannot as yet have any idea . . . It no longer matters to me what happens to the work—if it is produced or not produced. My musical and Virgilian passion has been sated. . . ." Berlioz pushes this philosophic calm to the point where it passes into its opposite: "Farewell, dear friend, Patience and Perseverance! I may even add, Indifference: what matters anything?" But this skeptical question is itself open to doubt: "You know my Pyrrhonism," he tells the Princess, "I believe in nothing; that is to say I believe that I believe in nothing. Wherefore I believe in something. Just see what words are good for and where logic takes you! Nothing is real but feelings and passions. Another absurdity I am saying! What of pain, and death, and fools . . . and a thousand other too real realities? I wish you would ask Liszt to be good enough to compliment Mme. Milde for me on the way she played *Alceste. . . ."*

Pyrrhonism and Perseverance in Berlioz only seemed to cancel each other; as he practiced them they really created fruitful tension while protecting the will with a Stoic's buckler. The Princess's sympathy was valuable but also enervating. Berlioz appears much more lively and free in his letters to Liszt, Bennet, Louis or Adèle. These and his *feuilletons* prove that when gastric pain did not pin him to his bed, his energy was unabated. He had been thinking, among other things, of "an exhibition of my whole output in ten concerts"—a project to be undertaken only after the present score was done.

Meanwhile he had innumerable offers—to conduct for five months in New York, Philadelphia, and Boston for twenty thousand dollars; to inaugurate a new concert hall in London; to celebrate a royal wedding in Sweden. He must also busy himself about numerous concerts of his works given without him in Vienna and elsewhere, but which required scores, biographical notices, and injunctions to managers. Early in April 1858 he has so much to attend to that every morning he makes a list of tasks and errands and despite steady going never reaches the end by nightfall. He was recruiting his people for the Baden Festival at which the first four parts of *Romeo* were to be given. He was also planning a direct appeal to the Emperor to bespeak his interest in *Les Troyens*. The letter asking for an audience and stating the motive was respectful without flattery. The tone was not that of a courtier, but of a proud warrior who has served the state and is conscious of his title of nobility; hence when Berlioz showed the draft to the Comte de Morny, the illegitimate half brother of the Emperor, the count thought it "rather unsuitable."

Wagner meanwhile had found that Ollivier's influence was not powerful enough to swing open the doors of the Opera. *Tannhäuser* was not sufficiently "economical," and Ollivier and his mother-in-law, Comtesse d'Agoult, were considered less than loyal to the Emperor. It looked as if to conquer Paris Wagner must begin the slow way, by concerts such as Berlioz had been giving these thirty years past. And even when the combination of foreign intrigue and public concerts made the Opera yield to *Tannhäuser,* it was to be another defeat, a prelude to Wagner's blackest days from which, as Bülow said, only the miracle of King Ludwig's intervention saved the composer "at the eleventh hour." The composer's lot in nineteenth-century Paris was indeed constant. "You wish to know," Berlioz replied about this time to a would-be biographer, "the causes of the opposition I have encountered in Paris for 25 years. There are many . . . :

"The principal one lies in the antagonism between my musical thought and that of the great majority of the Paris public. A host of people are bound to consider me crazy since I hold them to be children or simpletons. Any music which deviates from the little path where the makers of comic operas trot back and forth is necessarily . . . the music of a lunatic. Beethoven's masterpiece, the Ninth symphony, and his colossal piano sonatas, are still for these people the music of a lunatic.

"In the next place I had against me the instructors at the Conservatoire, led by Cherubini and Fétis, whom my heterodoxy in matters of harmony and rhythm had wounded in their self-esteem and shocked in their convictions. . . . One must also add among my opponents the devotees of the sensualist Italian school, whose doctrines I used to attack and whose gods I have blasphemed. . . . Today I am more cautious. I still abhor, as formerly, these works which the crowd proclaims to be masterpieces of dramatic music. . . . Only, I have the strength of mind to say nothing."

Berlioz had before this summed up his career in an unpremeditated epigram when, in a scribbled answer to a German inquiry for his *vita,* he had slipped in: "On my return from Italy I began my Thirty Years' War against the routineers, the professors, and the tone-deaf." In the spring of 1858 this war seemed to have reached its Peace of Westphalia; he wrote the last bar line of *Les Troyens* on April seventh, confident that "Come what may, disappointments or tribulations, nothing can prevent the work from being in existence."

CHAPTER 21

ESTHETES AT WAR

At the present moment, only we three fellows really belong together, because only we three are equals, and that is—you—he—and I.—WAGNER TO LISZT about himself and Berlioz

In the half dozen years that Berlioz devoted to composing and polishing his musical epic, he felt that the *rapprochement* between himself and the public which had occurred apropos of *The Infant Christ* was but a momentary gain. His awareness of the originality he had just put into renovating opera from within made him feel at times like a sane man in a lunatic asylum—that is, made him occasionally wonder who was crazy. For if Biletta's new work, *Rose de Florence,* was dramatic music then *Les Troyens* was folly. If the really important innovation at the Opera was to stage something by that professional amateur, Prince Poniatowski,[1] then *Les Troyens* lacked the right kind of novelty.

Berlioz' new work was monumental in a different sense from that in which the adjective has hitherto been used in these pages. That is, the drama is not scored for a great mass of performers nor for a national ceremony focusing simple emotions. It is monumental in being the longest of Berlioz' dramatic works, the most varied and grandiose in subject matter, as well as the model of the epic style in music drama. In form, both poem and score carried forward the principle of construction first shown in *Benvenuto Cellini,* the principle which underlies the *Damnation of Faust,* the Berlioz principle, in short, of choosing musical situations and linking them by the shortest path of recitative. Between larger sections there are no links. The hearer must make the mental jump with the composer. Yet such is the dramatic force of the music that one need not memorize a libretto. That Troy fell to the Greeks and that Aeneas abandoned Dido is really all the information one requires—*provided* that operatic habit has not developed in the beholder an unmusical demand for minute particulars of plot. The characteristic involvements of ordinary opera—its absurd wrangling and legal technicalities—are absent.

After a modern production in Great Britain, a critic who is anything but partial to Berlioz admitted that *Les Troyens* is "not so difficult to follow as are the changing fortunes of the gold in the *Ring*." This is because *Les Troyens* seeks to impart neither metaphysics nor the details of a legend, but only its psychological and emotional substance: "The great human interest of *Les Troyens* makes it an opera for others besides musicians—contrary again to received opinions." The work fulfills the intention Berlioz expressed to Samuel: "At least I will have shown what I conceive can be done on an antique subject broadly treated."

These facts of conception and construction explain why Berlioz apprehended on music's behalf what he conceived to be Wagner's aim of making music once more subservient and drama system-ridden. Berlioz gave no special name to the form by which he meant to improve upon current opera while avoiding the theoretical error of the "artwork of the future." But when seventy years later Stravinsky called his own *Oedipus Rex* an *opera oratorio,* musicology came to recognize the long tradition of those who had sought to liberate dramatic music from tutelage to Continuity in word or action. Before both Stravinsky and Berlioz, Bach and Handel tended to treat oratorio dramatically like opera, or opera discursively like oratorio. Between Berlioz and Stravinsky the links are Saint-Saëns's *Samson and Delilah,* Pfitzner's *Palestrina,* and Busoni's *Faust,* influenced respectively by *Les Troyens, Cellini* and the *Damnation of Faust.*

That Berlioz' lifelong striving to fuse religious, symphonic, and operatic traditions had generated the suitably flexible form is daily becoming more evident. Sir Donald Tovey's assertion that *Les Troyens* is "one of the most gigantic and convincing masterpieces of music drama" should settle the matter even for adherents of the older opera, Italian or German. Their favorite works are in fact being subtly reshaped to a Berliozian pattern through our frequent performance of them in concert form, just as Wagner's own also were, shortly after his triumph on the stage.

But all this is hindsight. What is astonishing is that in the 1860's, after thirty years of public activity and many genuine victories, Berlioz was still alone in his way of conceiving art. He had been understood, admired, and exploited, but piecemeal; and the mysterious resistance of his music to direct imitation, coming on top of his uncommon power of creating a new style for each work, gave him the appearance of a fitful fragmentary personage who had not formed a "school." Being alive to nuances and no recluse, Berlioz could sense his own uniqueness yet would not rally to either of the well-labeled parties: neither to the music of the present, which meant Meyerbeer, nor to the music of the future, which meant Wagner. No one really knew what Wagner's future music was, but his scores had the advantage of being readable and transcribable at the piano. Liszt read the poem of Berlioz' *Troyens* with delight, but he could only trust his friend's genius for the musical richness of the whole. He and his group had only penetrated *Benvenuto, Romeo,* or the *Damnation* in rehearsal and by ear.[2] The path to success seemed to lie through literary argument seconded by piano reductions. In short, by 1859 the modern trend toward digest-and-commentary, kin of propaganda and popular culture, was well under way.

Berlioz felt the tacit condemnation of his artistic creed in the new doctrines while still pregnant with a work that contradicted them. His only confidant and possible spokesman in the German camp was the Princess, who for reasons of her own feared Wagner and tried to keep him at a distance from Liszt. But she did not wholly recognize how far Berlioz was being gracious by treating her as his equal and spiritual collaborator. She presumed upon this from time to time, which inevitably led to a crisis. Ultimately, the relations of the three peers—as Wagner called himself, Liszt, and Berlioz—were rendered hopeless, and the course of public opinion was confused by the tangle of three proud artists and their women (Marie and Cosima joining in) upon the treacherous ground of esthetics.

Again in 1859 the smell of war was in the air. The Emperor's New Year message to his Austrian "cousin" held a stern threat which must lead sooner or later to a battlefield. People speculated about time and place in the cheerful old way, for war still seemed to the citizen a thing of flags and chargers and heroes holding bridges singlehanded. Berlioz was virtually alone in his truthful imagining of modern carnage and his preference for other forms of heroism. The contrast only heightened his isolation: every casual or deliberate social force was repressing his real self. He began to have the fits of a Hamlet caught in a time out of joint: "In such moments, the slightest accident produces strange results. Day before yesterday, while talking quietly with friends by my fireside, someone brought in a newspaper in which I saw announced a new biography of Christopher Columbus. At once the whole life of that great man appears to me in a flash. I see it all in one glance, like a painting, and my heart contracts at the thought of that memorable epic. I fall into a fit of indescribable despair, to the astonishment of those present. The incident was laid to the account of my disease, and I was not going to expose myself to mockery by admitting that the name of Columbus had alone brought on the fit. My trouble is an entanglement of causes and effects in which the wisest physiologists and psychologists would lose their way. . . ."

One of the causes undoubtedly was Berlioz' sense of the decadence around him. The unseemly greed for pleasure that Offenbach expressed like a second Petronius, the pre-deluge philosophy of those in power, turned all Columbus figures to ridicule and made of creative effort a joke. It was time for a Berlioz to decline battle and cease trying to nourish spirit on tainted air. He could not of course help translating his alert forebodings into the music for the Fall of Troy, but to save his integrity—like the later Melville after the American Civil War—Berlioz the artist must withdraw.

The doctors said in fact that he had a general inflammation of the nervous system and that he must "live like an oyster, not think and not feel." Yet he had much to think about. His one chance to have *Les Troyens* decently performed was to obtain an Imperial edict ordering one of the subsidized houses to play it. At the Institute his new colleague, Prince Jerome, continued favorable, but the Emperor disliked his cousin; so letters of recommendation brought no result and Berlioz ought rather to avoid his supporter.[3] It was tantalizing, for the previous August at Baden the composer had seen what power and good will could do. "King" Bénazet was a true prince: all the special performers that Berlioz wanted he obtained; the whole group were fed, housed, and courteously treated, and moreover *thanked* for their work. Nor did Bénazet lose by it—everyone worked twice as hard. There were eleven rehearsals before the fete, and although the "musical fever" was a strain, Berlioz produced one of the finest concerts of his lifetime—Beethoven, Mozart, Weber, a Litolff piano concerto played by the composer, and four parts of *Romeo and Juliet*. "What a performance!" he wrote jubilantly to Ferrand. "Poor Paganini, who never heard the work I composed for his pleasure!" The next day, the beautiful Countess Kalergi averred she was still in tears from artistic bliss.[4] Berlioz' old colleague Georges Kastner was among the most enthusiastic and, giving up an old grudge, embraced Berlioz and took him and Marie home with him to Strasbourg.

The well-being induced by this real Utopia, this approximation of Euphonia, of course evaporated in Paris, where the Emperor had granted Berlioz an audience (with forty others) and graciously permitted the composer to present the text of *Les Troyens*. Napoleon had "his 25 below zero look,[5] and he took my manuscript with the assurance that he would read it if he had the leisure. The trick was neatly done. It's as old as the hills; I'm sure King Priam did it just this way."

At the turn of the year Berlioz had also published suitably cut portions of his *Memoirs*, beginning with the Festival of 1844 and then going back to the early chapters. He wanted to correct some of the misstatements that had appeared in Mirecourt's biographical volume three years before, and to supply once for all the details that foreign concert managers kept asking him to send. This publication brought him many encouraging letters, including a grateful one from Paganini's son, and the usual batch of strangers' poems asking to be set to music at the composer's early convenience.

The articles also brought him a round sum which he would soon need for Louis's period of study ashore. The "dear Indian" as his father addressed him, was at the Antipodes and much missed, "If your ship goes to China, shall you receive my letters?" Once again the "dear child, dear Louis, dear lieutenant" seemed in a fair way to success. He was due back in the spring of 1859 and when July came, his ship a month overdue, Berlioz went through agonies. Finally on the nineteenth Louis landed. By that time, luckily, the ridiculous war with Austria was over. Napoleon had learned with his own eyes that shrapnel and cannon balls killed the "poor people" whom he sent to war, and that the sense impressions given off by a battlefield at night differed much from those of the boudoirs to which he was accustomed. But after fifty years' lack of practice the nineteenth century no longer knew how to make a war look efficient while protracting it for full employment. Nevertheless, thanks to Eugénie, Magenta, the glorious battlefield, came to denote everybody's favorite color and dressmakers took heart.

Berlioz had by then begun to make his own vocal score of *Les Troyens.* It would be needed for any rehearsals and he found in the process an opportunity for "scraping and scrubbing into every recess of the score." In the task of rendering his many-voiced orchestration on the piano, he was aided by his friend Pauline Viardot, who was an excellent pianist as well as a great singer. Indeed, this remarkable woman, sister of Malibran and daughter of the famous Garcia, was a personage whose place in the century has not yet been adequately presented. A great actress, a superb voice, a strong intellect, a fascinating woman without petty arts and even without regular or beautiful features, she bewitched all those who came near her. She was for years Turgenev's close friend and collaborator, she deeply impressed men as diverse as Dickens, Tolstoy, and Tchaikovsky, and she inspired in Berlioz the worship which he felt for the great in art and character.

This, and the idea of a new dramatic work which he had been commissioned to write for Baden, constituted Berlioz' real present and only tolerable future. Otherwise his mind dwelt in the incredible past: Paris was changing visibly under the radical planning of Baron Haussmann, which made the old city seem to the man of 1830 "a cemetery dotted with memorial stones—here I met Balzac for the last time; there I walked with Paganini; in another spot I accompanied the Duchess d'Abrantès, a silly good woman;[6] this is the house where Madame de Girardin lived—a clever woman who thought me a fool; this is the sidewalk where I talked to Adolphe Nourrit;[7] that desolate house yonder is that of poor Rachel;[8] and so on, and so on. So many dead! Why aren't *we* dead?"

Letters from the Princess prodding and preaching a little too much, from Morel discussing the musical situation in Marseille, and from the ailing Ferrand imparting his troubles, gave the sense of a dying and shrinking world to a man who had spent most of his life in the heat of action. Being ill to boot, he went from doctor to doctor, with little faith and much Molière in his mind. Yet he lent himself to their experiments, falling at last into the hands of a certain "Dr. Noir," a Negro of great repute who had "cured" Adolphe Sax of a melanotic growth on the lip. The man, whose real name was J. H. Vries, proved to be only a more imaginative quack than the rest. A large fashionable practice daily waited from four to five hours in his anteroom and he managed to persuade the Faculty of Medicine, represented by Dr. Velpeau, to put a hospital and its free patients at his disposal. Ultimately, Velpeau's report put an end to Dr. Noir's hold on his clientele. They none the less gave him a testimonial dinner. Berlioz had by then ceased going, the few fruitless treatments having wasted too much of his time, but he had given in to the plausible manipulator's request and composed for his projected "tabernacle" a *pièce d'occasion* on a religious-humanitarian theme.

What Berlioz obviously needed was a musical life. He dreamed of music at night and recalling his dream "mentally performed . . . the adagio of Beethoven's B flat symphony [Fourth] just as we did it three years ago at Baden, so that little by little I fell into one of those unearthly ecstasies and wept my eyes out at the sound of that tonal radiance which only angels wear. Believe me, dear friend, the being who wrote such a marvel of inspiration was not a man. Only thus does the archangel Michael sing, as he dreamily contemplates the spheres . . . And not to have an orchestra at hand that would sing for me that seraphic poem. . . . Down to earth, now! Someone is coming in . . ."

As the next best thing to a seraphic orchestra, Berlioz was planning a concert for Easter Week. Louis, who was expected home before then, had not heard any of his father's music since childhood and this was an added spur. Meanwhile Paris was going to a new opera by Gounod and not liking it. The subject was *Faust* and Berlioz, though he did not say so, must have noticed that some of its best ideas came, a good deal watered down, from another *Faust* which the Parisians had scarcely listened to. The public's hesitancy about Gounod's score only showed how unpalatable was the music which came from the Berliozian quarter of the artistic world. The work being so far superior to anything that had been put on for years—classic revivals aside—Berlioz did his best to keep it afloat, but other critics had learned nothing and forgotten nothing. Gounod, they felt, lacked melody; he wrote "German" music; and—the jibe was over seventy-five years old—he "put all his effects in the orchestra." [9] Berlioz wrote a stout defense, adroitly quoting fashionable gossip about the work,[10] and pointing out to the true connoisseurs the technical and expressive qualities of the best parts.

The real success of the season was Meyerbeer's new work, *Le Pardon de Ploërmel* (in English *Dinorah*) which furnished in a Breton setting his excellent custom-made article, cut from the best material in stock. It afforded the Opera's choicest visual delights, and the press confirmed the public's entranced appreciation. By contrast, Berlioz' mingling of reasoned disapproval with his praise seemed unjust and was imputed to envy. Yet Berlioz, as before, truly valued Meyerbeer's musical gifts and only deplored their misuse and corruption in the service of an antimusical genre. The reigning form of opera he could at least deride openly: "Shall I speak of the *mise en scène,* of the artificial thunder, the broken bridge, the white goat, the sluice that opens and the cascade of *natural* water? No, No! Go and see for yourself!"

Readers enjoy prize fights between artists at any time, and they relished this satirical note, while continuing to know what they liked and to be puzzled by what Berlioz revered and desired. Hence they gave equal acclaim to the new opera and to Berlioz' new collection of squibs and essays, *Les Grotesques de la Musique,* which soon became a best seller. They liked the witty narrative and the good humor that predominated over the bitterness of the technical parables ("The right to play in F a symphony written in D"). The onslaughts on mediocrity they brushed aside on Swift's principle that a satirist aims at everybody but the reader. Besides, it gave one status to be able to "place" Berlioz, on the evidence of one's eyes, as an *esprit fin et cultivé,* an *écrivain spirituel,* a *grand feuilletoniste,* almost as *grand* as Janin, the prince of the tribe.

On April 23 (Louis still unheard from) Berlioz gave his Holy Week concert, *The Infant Christ.* The audience showed its discrimination by liking some of the more hidden beauties of the score. To Berlioz it had seemed the most perfect execution so far. "What pleased me most was that the mystical chorus, 'O my soul, what is yet left . . .' was for the first time sung with the requisite accent and nuance. In that vocal peroration the whole work is summed up, for it seems to me that the feeling of the infinite, of divine love, is in that passage."

Numberless *démarches,* visits, and readings for the sake of *Les Troyens* continued to fill the days. Surprisingly, old Véron, onetime director of the Opera, grew enthusiastic about Dido's funeral pyre and declared that if he were still in charge he would spend 150,000 francs on the show—mostly, one suspects, for faggots. "To be sure, his words cost him nothing . . . Yet they have caused a sensation in the Opera crowd. Will they come, gradually, to the Mountain?" Vain hopes, as Berlioz recognized, because of the lack of fit performers. "There is no *Priameia virgo,* no Cassandra. Dido would be sure to be inadequate and I would rather be stabbed ten times in the chest with a dirty kitchen knife than to hear anyone mangle the last monologue of the Queen of Carthage."

Berlioz was still giving the score "a good workout with the file" but he declined the Princess's suggestion that he publish the libretto. "It would be to confess a desire for literary fame, to which I do not pretend." When he had had a good day free from gastric pain, he would gather a few musical friends for chamber music as in the past, and now also for an informal sight-reading of this or that scene from his music drama. Only Berlioz could hear it as it should sound, but the others grew to like the great nostalgic melodies unlike anyone else's, and the telling harmonies in which the notes did not seem to account for the shiver that they caused. So much so that in the fall of 1859, at the Beethoven School, Mme. Charton-Demeur and Jules Lefort, with Ritter at the piano, gave two of the duets for twenty or thirty friends of the composer's. The "audience" wishing to hear some of the choral parts, they all sang, Berlioz included. Thus, long before there was any prospect of its production, *Les Troyens* was becoming a public fact; its size and purport were gossiped about in musical, literary, and official circles. Its existence partook of the ghostly, like the shade of Hector, and of the monstrous, like the Trojan horse.

In the interim Berlioz went to Bordeaux where the Saint Cecilia Society had invited him to conduct his own works at its annual concert. Two hundred and fifty musicians gave the *Roman Carnival* overture and excerpts from *Romeo* and *The Infant Christ.* The large theater was full of a cheering multitude who stood to see Berlioz crowned with laurel. Some stayed to toast him at an interminable banquet. Other calls came for scores. At Carlsruhe there was talk of *Benvenuto;* in Russia and America his shorter works were beginning to be regularly performed, and news from other Geman towns led a resentful French critic to accuse Berlioz of causing the same "subversive events" across the Rhine as at home.

Before the Baden season the international situation had become so tense that it was thought impossible to hold a festival.

Romeo and Juliet had been scheduled, by request, and Berlioz was getting ready for it, but as a result of Napoleon's clear designs upon the South German states, the Badenese wanted to "eat the French alive." They feared armed invasion, and by a metaphor which has since become a basis of national policy, they feared invasion by foreign talent. They did not think back a month or two—no nationalist does—to Hans von Bülow's "capture" of Paris to the heavy artillery of his tumultuous piano. But he had been a great success, and Berlioz had enjoyed his vivacious company and that of his young wife, the former Cosima Liszt.

Although Bénazet's plans were in suspense, he would not release Berlioz from his promise to compose a new opera for two years hence. The libretto, by the popular playwright Edouard Plouvier, was all ready. Based on an episode in the Thirty Years' War, it seemed to hold few attractions for the musician. "In it are to be found a Duke of Saxe-Weimar, a Bohemian girl, a few Francs-Juges, the Devil—and all his train. . . ." Despite Berlioz' repeated begging off, Bénazet wanted the opera "even if his project of building a theatre does not materialize. . . ." Berlioz' heartfelt gratitude, coupled with the memory of his own costly ventures, made him apprehensive: he felt obliged to produce a success. "The risk is his, but there are days when the idea plunges me into despair." At other times it seemed possible. "Perhaps the fire will catch when I once begin. Yet there would be no perhapses if it were a question of dealing with the subject you mention [*Romeo and Juliet*]. *That* fire has been lit a long while; it burns steadily, banked like a buried coal mine which we know exists only through the boiling water it shoots upward. Yes indeed, it is still possible to write a beautiful *Romeo* opera besides the symphony."

The Baden season did take place, and Berlioz was able to add to the program the love duet from *Les Troyens,* sung by Viardot and Lefort with full orchestra. But Liszt and the Princess, for whom Berlioz had mainly taken the trouble, did not come. Liszt had resigned from Weimar, his post no longer congenial. The death of the Grand-Ducal pair who had appointed him; the younger Duke's interest in plays rather than music; finally the hissing of Cornelius's *Barber of Bagdad* the previous year (for no reason except that the author was a pupil of Liszt's and Liszt was not married to the Princess) drove the pianist to pitch his tent elsewhere. Even in the pianistic world he was losing ground, eclipsed by a new star, Anton Rubinstein. The string of epithets young Cornelius had applied to himself—"Lisztianer, Wagner-Berlioz-Weimarianer"—would no longer carry meaning. The center for the new music was to move about wherever Liszt could get a foothold, and his concentration of effort upon getting the *Ring* produced would ultimately mean a second eclipse, this time as an orchestral composer, at the hands of Wagner.

The Princess was also on her travels. Berlioz heard from her at Baden that she had betrothed her daughter to Prince Constantin Hohenlohe-Schillingsfürst,[11] and that she might be visiting Paris in the autumn. In a different way from Harriet Smithson, she too had played her part in Berlioz' creative life, and this part was over and done with. They remained on the same devoted terms, just as Liszt and Berlioz did, but one by one the vivid threads were fading, the isolation, the twilight, were creeping around Berlioz, leaving clear only that narrow and stony path which leads the predestined to Colonus.

In Paris, articles had appeared about the scene from *Les Troyens* heard at Baden. All were highly complimentary. Ernest Reyer assured his readers that the score was stupendous, and that the book revealed not a librettist but a poet. D'Ortigue hinted that an earlier Napoleon had ordered the production of a comparable masterpiece, *La Vestale*. Berlioz had by now given up as beneath his dignity all attempts to interest the Imperial household. At the Opera a new *Romeo and Juliet,* which was in reality the old one by Bellini, was in production. Berlioz took this opportunity to review all earlier musical Romeos, except his own, and to conclude as he had done in his letter to the Princess, that a worthy operatic score was still to be written.

There are to date five operas whose subjects purport to be that of Shakespeare's immortal drama. The playwrights have all pretended to light their torch at the great love-sun, but all are pale tapers, three of them being hardly little pink candles. . . . Not that it is possible to make a drama into an opera without changing, upsetting, and more or less spoiling the original. But there are so many intelligent ways of committing the desecration which music requires! For example, though it is impossible to keep all of Shakespeare's characters, why has it occurred to none of the arrangers to keep at least some of those they have dropped . . . [and to drop] the entirely new ones they have introduced—these Antonio, Alberti, Cebas, Gennaro, Adriani, Nisa, Cécile and so on: what are they for?

Naturally, neither the French nor the Italians—any more than the English on their legitimate stage—have had the courage to keep Romeo's character intact and allow so much as a hint of his first love for Rosaline. How admit that young Montague could love another than the daughter of the Capulets! For shame! It would debase the idea universally held about this model lover; it would take all the poetry out of it: the public is composed of souls that are so constant and so pure!

After the failure of Bellini's *Romeo,* Carvalho at the Théâtre Lyrique announced Gluck's *Orpheus* and put Berlioz in charge of establishing the score, there having been two—an Italian and a French—both corrupt. Inversions, interpolations, "trombonization," and careless *col basso* scoring had long made the work the sport of manhandlers. Carvalho himself, with the powerful drive of the frustrated creator in an artistic profession, wanted Berlioz to use the overture to *Iphigeneia,* insert a chorus from *Armide,* and generally earn his fee. But Berlioz was an old hand at the game and he had vowed that it would be *Orpheus* or nothing, *Orpheus*—as he had said of *Freischütz*—"without *Castilblazade* of any kind." [12] Carvalho he believed to be "full of good intentions"; and he added: "his hell shall be paved with them."

It is because of Carvalho's amiability and this firmness on Berlioz' part that we owe both the preservation of the original Gluck "style" and the existence of a correct edition of the master. For as a sequel to this first task Carvalho and others invited Berlioz to oversee productions of three other Gluck operas; Berlioz coached singers and conductors, and the public responded. He wrote articles on the work of restoration, and these inspired his admirer, Mlle. Fanny Pelletan, to devote her leisure and her fortune to editing Gluck. First with the aid of Berlioz' friend Damcke, whom she chose as theory teacher, then with Berlioz' protégé Saint-Saëns, who tells the story, the work was carried through.[13] No one of Berlioz' competence had seen and studied the works of Gluck and his school so thoroughly, and he missed no opportunity to make able proselytes, young Ritter being but one of several. Mme. Viardot was now entrusted with the role of Orpheus, so Berlioz spent a few days at her house in the country giving her his views on style—equidistant from the trivial and the pompous and *varied* in successive scenes. She was a pleasure to work with; the merest hint was enough and Berlioz was in the seventh heaven.

He had a bad bout of illness while at the Viardots' and not wishing (as he wrote to Louis) "to burden and alarm this charming family," he returned to Paris. In bed he could read proof on the corrected parts of Gluck that Roquemont was bringing in. "Tonight [September 23, 1859] I finished putting the first act of *Orpheus* in order. Carvalho wants my Trojans for his theatre, but how? He has no tenor for Aeneas. Mme. Viardot suggests that she play both Cassandra and Dido . . . The public might, I believe, accept this anomaly, which is incidentally not without precedent. And so my two roles would be played in the grand style by this great artist."

Princess Carolyne was in Paris as Berlioz worked lovingly at *Orpheus* and *Les Troyens*. They dined together. Face to face she gave him such a liberal dose of the flattery and compassion which served her to express high regard that he could hardly resist living up to her image of him as a stricken lion licking his wounds. He was chronically worn out by pain, it is true, but he still had fortitude, and more than once he rebelled against her emollients. Gently reproved, she measured the strength of his creative will, and since she truly shared his passion for modern art (she was a great admirer of Delacroix) she urged Berlioz to compose an *Antony and Cleopatra*. "If my strength returns," he replied, "I will try. . . . I do not suppose that any man was ever so unfortunate as that unfortunate wretch after the defeat of Actium and his cowardly flight from his infernal mistress, his serpent of the Nile. I cannot look without shuddering on that ocean of misery. . . . But I see that the Opera is to revive Flotow's *Soul in Pain*.[14] There was an irrepressible need for all of us to hear some Flotow. . . . Farewell; a thousand greetings to Liszt, and to you all my—no, not all, but a great deal. Come, this is foolish. I must take my cup of whatever it is with ten drops of laudanum and forget things until tomorrow. *Forget*. 'Gods of oblivion'—I really wish you could have heard that chorus, but it could not be managed." [15]

Wagner arrived just as the Princess left. Possibly her sudden departure was a tactful move to forestall the need of being loyal both to Berlioz and to Liszt's new companion-in-arms whom she disliked. Not that Berlioz had as yet any reason to think a diplomatic revolution had taken place. He knew that Liszt was bestirring himself on Wagner's behalf; he did not know that for two decades to come it would be an exclusive apostolate. At the moment, the Austrian ambassador, urged by his wife, was contriving to secure the adoption of *Tannhäuser* by a Paris theater, preferably the Opera.

For Berlioz, during October and November 1859, *the* opera was *Orpheus.* Restoring the notes was a trifle compared to teaching every one how to sing, act, dress, and even dance—since the ballet had very imperfect notions of the way shades in Hades and the Elysian Fields disport themselves. There were besides a few vocal cadenzas to write, for the traditional ones were either missing or abject. Again, in one of the airs, even though Berlioz did not consider it genuine, he entrusted to Saint-Saëns the task of writing a more manageable accompaniment, saying: "How can you expect me to re-instrument the work of Gluck when I have all my life exterminated people who took such liberties?"

On the eighteenth of November the work opened and created a furore. It made Carvalho wealthy and renowned; it outlasted current offerings, and it left in the memory of numberless judges an ineffaceable impression. Michelet was transported and Dickens reduced to tears. Flaubert went repeatedly and would go to nothing else. The ordinary public had never seen anything to compare with it, and although some professional and lay critics still found Gluck detestable,[16] Berlioz was naïvely happy and made hopeful by the fact that when every detail of a production was handled with a craftsman's care and an artist's vision, even the random public responded. He may have suspected that the result of his quest for perfection had moved the beholders by contrast with their routine fare, but he does not seem to have noticed that at the age of fifty-six he had actually come before the public in a new capacity, that of opera director.

The day after the *première,* still working at his *Troyens,* he was again "intoxicated with harmony" and stirred to musical creation. The Princess's suggestion recurred to him; he reread *Antony,* and assured his correspondent that he would not have the "impertinence to disfigure Shakespeare's creation by fashioning an academic Cleopatra." He imagined a very Shavian creature, part child, part flirt, and part royal lover and sadist, fit only for a "musical fantasia." The upshot was that two weeks later Berlioz definitely made up his mind that he would not compose Bénazet's opera on the Thirty Years' War. His musical faculties were aroused and the dances in *Les Troyens* not having been all composed, the needed music came effortlessly.

Other ideas beset him, for which Cleopatra was a temporary peg. "I think I would make an attractive creature out of that torpedo. It would be different from anything I have done." Though Berlioz may not have known it, his next work was begun; naturally it would be different—different especially from nearly all that kept sing-songing around him. For while he ruminated novelties, his Institute colleague Halévy was admonishing Bizet about his *envoi de Rome:* "We urge the composer to be on his guard against certain harmonic boldnesses which may sometimes be qualified as roughness." Bizet might have been Berlioz, Berlioz Bizet. Nothing had changed since 1830.

Orpheus continued to sell out for ten days in advance. Besides bringing Berlioz appreciable royalties, this success shook the reputation of the Opera director. There was talk of replacing him with Prince Poniatowski, now more than ever beloved as "that distinguished amateur." The prince, Berlioz told his son, "loudly proclaims—*too* loudly—that he will put on *Les Troyens* if he is appointed. The prince has a work in rehearsal, which the author of *Les Troyens* will have to review: there you are—the familiar game." Meanwhile Berlioz was proofreading the piano score of *Orpheus* and doing his best to get Liszt elected as Corresponding Member of the Institute. " 'Is it as a composer or as a virtuoso that you are presenting M. Liszt?'—'As everything,' I answered, 'does that suit you?' " But Berlioz was kept off the committee, which nominated Conti and Verdi. "Wagner," he reports, "was not even brought up—such are academic bodies." The final vote put in Conti and Verdi.

Flattering for Verdi, isn't it? He had nothing to do with it and must be greatly surprised . . . For I may tell you that Verdi is a true gentleman, very proud and unyielding . . . he is as far from Rossini's railing, buffooning, and joking—sometimes stupid joking—as he is from the snakelike flexibility of Meyerbeer. Many a time he has rescued from the sin of sloth the people in the Opera and the Ministry. You must grant him your esteem at least for that. . . . As for Liszt, I am sorry that he attached to this election an importance which it has not for *him.* It was important for *us,* us alone. The Institute should attach to itself . . . the people of stature instead of taking to its bosom with a protecting air so many dwarfs who are not even worth drowning in the irrigations of Gulliver.

These activities took time, and took it from the new composition. Hardly "one hour out of forty" could be devoted to music. The rest went, among other things, for new treatments (electrical) which "do me neither good nor harm. . . . What play-actors these doctors are!" Louis was also on Berlioz' mind. He was at Dieppe preparing his examinations for a captaincy, but he seemed to his father overexcited about other matters. He expressed frenzied concern over the fate of *Les Troyens* and, as Berlioz failed to see, he worried far too much about his father's health to be able to study calmly. Of the boy's abnormal attachment to him, Berlioz knew something ("We love each other like brothers"), and on his side too, this affection was distressfully passionate: "It seems as if all the tender feelings I bore your mother were now centered on you." Long separations, anxiety and the verbal repetition of frustrated longings were unsettling to both.

Berlioz kept some of his bouts of illness from Louis, and could discuss the boy's future only with his devoted friends, Morel and Lecourt, who had cared for the youth at Marseille. But in his "troubled, anxious" state Berlioz needed something more. He found life at home unsatisfactory, "constantly grating, almost impossible," driving him either to seek calm with friends or even to consider "strong measures." We know no more, for in confiding this to his Brussels friend, Berlioz says "I can tell you no more." Whether Marie grated on him by duplicating in words what he already thought about the present impasse in his career, or whether the irritation came from her comments about Wagner's arrival, we can only surmise. We know that she was ailing too, more seriously than anyone supposed, and that her narrow-gauge spirit was ill attuned to Berlioz' lofty brooding mind in moments of stress.

The fact remained that Wagner was in Paris, had announced a series of concerts, and had gained powerful support for his opera plans. Legitimate curiosity had been aroused by his German reputation and by the novelty of an artist-philosopher.[17] The press republished chapters that Fétis had translated six years before, and "the music of the future" became a fashionable phrase. It was interpreted rightly enough as meaning that Gluck, Mozart, and Beethoven were mere approximations, preparatory sketches for Wagner's esthetic fulfillment. And by one of the magic synchronizations of history, Darwin's *Origin of Species* had just come out in England and America, and a solemn article expounded evolution in the *Revue des Deux Mondes,* as Wagner stunned Paris with his three concerts.

Some days before the first of these, Wagner called on Berlioz, and just four days before, sent him the score of his latest work. It was *Tristan* and it bore the inscription: "To the dear and great author of *Roméo et Juliette,* the grateful author of *Tristan und Isolde.*" Accompanying it was a short note: "Dear Berlioz—I am delighted to be able to present you with the first copy of my *Tristan.* Please accept it and keep it out of friendship for: Yours, Richard Wagner. January 21, 1860."

On the evening of January twenty-fifth, Berlioz left his bed to attend the first concert, comprising the *Flying Dutchman* and *Tannhäuser* overtures, the preludes to *Lohengrin* and *Tristan,* and six other fragments from the two middle works. The audience was divided between raucous enthusiasm and equally noisy condemnation. At the intermission there were near fist fights in the lobby. Berlioz was seen applauding repeatedly, but unfortunately Marie was present and giving the loose to her tongue. He, suffering from laryngitis, hardly spoke, but in the review which appeared before the third concert he mentioned "the prodigious amount of nonsense, absurdities, and even lies which are uttered on such an occasion, and which prove that in France at least, when we have to judge a type of music different from that which runs the streets, passion and prejudice hold the floor and keep good sense and judgment from speaking up."

Berlioz' review was full of praise. He had come back for the second performance and had been gripped anew by the great power, melodic insistency, and fiery orchestration of the works presented. He analyzed them with care, both technically and poetically. The *Flying Dutchman* overture "takes hold of the listener imperiously and carries him away." The *Tannhäuser* ensemble shows "such vigor and authority" that a certain harshness is "accepted unresistingly." The masterly ease in scoring and the strong characterization of themes elicited Berlioz' strong approval, which his reservations about details did not weaken. And in speaking about the *Lohengrin* prelude he was completely enthusiastic. It seemed to him "a great invention, admirable in all respects . . . a marvel of instrumentation . . . a masterpiece." In the March from Act II, Berlioz found "a period which perhaps has no equal in music for grandiose impetus."

He made, to be sure, a number of general objections, principally to Wagner's harmonic system and to his excessive repetition of certain motives, but the only work of which he declared he could not appreciate the intent was the *Tristan* prelude.

Since it was built on the same plan as that of *Lohengrin,* it puzzled him to understand why it had been put on the same program. Besides, his most attentive hearing could make out "no other theme than a sort of chromatic moan, full of dissonant chords, of which the long appogiaturas that replace the real note only increase the cruelty." [18]

In the remaining paragraphs of his review, Berlioz felt called upon to reiterate his pragmatic creed, favoring freedom, innovation, and expressiveness. If this, he said, was the meaning of the slogan "Music of the future," he was willing to be classed among its practitioners. But if it meant something else—which he outlined—he dissociated himself from it wholly, and holding up his hand said *"Non credo."*

Wagner, seizing the opportunity to prolong the public's notice of himself, affected to feel aggrieved and wrote an open letter which Berlioz readily published in the *Débats.* According to it, Wagner also repudiated the music of the future. For this term he substituted "the work of art of the future," which was to fuse all the arts, and in which music would be "supplemented and explained by poetry and pantomime." He wound up with a skillful paragraph saying how much he regretted that an intelligent critic who was also a friend, had mistaken him so badly; that he hoped that Berlioz would "let hospitable France give sanctuary to his lyric dramas"; and that he, Wagner, "awaited with impatience the production of *Les Troyens* —for reasons of affection first, of musical importance second, and lastly because of the special relation which that work must bear" to Wagner's own "ideas and principles."

The letter was a master stroke for putting Berlioz in the wrong. The implications—all misleading as to the facts—were that out of jealousy Berlioz had turned against an old friend; that *Les Troyens,* which was the cause of this treachery, really came out of Wagner's "ideas and principles"; and that Berlioz, if he were a man of honor, would out of his good grace and and great power "let" *Tannhäuser* be played. The true musical debate was adroitly shifted to "the work of art of the future," which made the "intelligent critic," Berlioz, look ignorant in addition to spiteful [19]—as if the musical analysis of three overtures and two choral ensembles were irrelevant, and as if the praise he had lavished on the bulk of them were a mere trifle.

The germ had been sown. At the moment, Paris lumped the two men together as excessively Germanic musicians, with Wagner having the better right since he could not choose but be a German. But thereafter Wagner's words brought him returns at compound interest. It persuaded the French Wagnerians of Berlioz' mean and ungrateful conduct, so that it seemed right to dismiss and discredit him. Only a few inquiring minds who had looked up Berlioz' review of the three concerts dared to say: "We have reread the article and we frankly admit that we cannot discover in it that preconceived hostility . . . which some have liked to stress so mightily and even to exaggerate."

It would be equally absurd to exaggerate Wagner's craft. Such a perfect barrage of insinuations, confusions, and imputations can scarcely be deliberately contrived; it is a gift of nature, stimulated by the struggle for life. That this was so appears most probable when we read the letter which a few weeks later Wagner wrote Berlioz in somewhat imperfect French:

> I have just read your article on *Fidelio:* a thousand thanks to you for it. It is a special kind of joy for me to hear your pure and noble accents of the expression of a soul, of an intelligence which understands so perfectly and takes unto itself the most intimate secrets of a creation by another hero of art. There are times when I am almost more transported by seeing this act of appreciation than by the appreciated work itself, because it bears witness to an uninterrupted chain of intimate relationships binding together the great minds which—thanks to this bond alone—will never fall into misunderstanding.
>
> If I express myself badly, I nevertheless like to think that you will not understand me badly.
>
> Your most devoted
> RICHARD WAGNER
>
> Paris, on my birthday.
> [May 22, 1860.]

Wagner's impulsive recognition that Berlioz understood Beethoven and that there exists a communion of genius, made it all the harder to fathom Berlioz' unwillingness to join in a movement under Wagner's aegis.[20] Pushed by Princess Metternich and a favoring tide of international affairs, Wagner was about to force the doors of the Paris Opera with his *Tannhäuser,* which he would shortly revise on this account. Drawing haughtily on his friends for his personal needs, he could give himself over to the writing and publicizing of his new large-scale works. He felt energetic and buoyant as one who sees a long series of apparently scattered efforts shaping into a public triumph. And in this generous mood he informed Liszt of the presence in the musical world of only three great equals—

Wagner, Liszt, and Berlioz. Unfortunately, Wagner always had to seek Berlioz out and he explained the Frenchman's reluctance to be Holy Ghost in this trinity by the fact of Mme. Berlioz' evil tongue. She was "ruining him" according to this somewhat distant observer who had met her twice; she was reducing the "God" to "a poor devil." Despite this puzzling disappointment, Wagner in 1860 could complacently measure the progress he had made in twenty years. In 1840 he had been in Paris, unknown, unprotected, nearly starving, and rich only in the musical revelation afforded him the preceding autumn by Berlioz' *Romeo and Juliet.* And that debt he had just canceled by his inscription in the score of *Tristan.*

Berlioz' essay on *Fidelio* had been prompted by the revival which Carvalho, urged and aided by Berlioz, had produced on May 5, 1860. The superb critical statement which aroused Wagner to admiration marked Berlioz' own spiritual revival after an almost mortal crisis: shortly after the Wagner concerts, Berlioz had been telegraphed for from Dauphiné where Adèle, suddenly stricken, was dying. Himself in acute pain, he watched by the sickbed of the one woman who had returned his love in equal measure. He could do nothing but wonder why she, ten years younger than he, happy and beloved by husband and daughters, should be the first to die. He waited until the specialist from Lyon came and declared the crisis past, assuring everyone that the patient would recover. Berlioz returned to Paris. A few days later, on March 2, Adèle was dead.

It hardly mattered then that the conductorship of the Opera went to Dietsch, that of the Conservatoire to Tilmant, that of the Imperial Chapel to a protégé of Auber's. In any circumstances these vacancies, due to the death of Berlioz' erstwhile friend Girard, would have had value only as supplying an orchestra with which to play "real music." To prestige and power the artist was now indifferent. If Carvalho at the *Lyrique* kept following Berlioz' musical direction as he had so far done, that "position" was enough. The enterprise was successful from box office to press seats, and the manager had just announced *Les Troyens.* At this juncture, however, the directorship of the Opéra-Comique fell vacant and Carvalho, eager for an official post, secured it. Under this "normal" blow Berlioz stood resigned but exhausted. Paris was obviously a squirrel cage in which headway was impossible. Ill again, he could only answer inquiry by saying that he was "dying of his life's work." Even the nighttime afforded him no relief. "I desire only sleep while awaiting something more permanent."

It was from this torpor that *Fidelio* had roused him. A bit of good news—Louis's successful passing of his first examination—combined with some excellent chamber music to restore his threatened equilibrium. For the Baden stage he was plotting a new idea, and meanwhile, at the instigation of his friend, the tenor Roger, he had orchestrated Schubert's *Erlkönig;* it would worthily supply the want of short works for the summer programs. From the finely wrought and polished score no one could suspect anything of the anxiety, illness, or conflicts in his heart and soul. It is delicate, poignant, full of insight into Schubert's masterpiece—a compendium of art concealing itself.

When he returned from Baden, where Schubert and parts of the *Damnation of Faust* had been accompanied by thunder and heat lightning, Berlioz had a new work under way.

CHAPTER 22

PROSPERO'S FAREWELL

Beatrice Benedick piques, coquetting.—THOMAS HARDY

Les Troyens being no nearer staging as the summer of 1860 ended, Berlioz drew satisfaction from the agreement he had just reached with Bénazet, to substitute a text of his own for the unarousing work of Plouvier. Berlioz' new subject was his old one of 1833—*Much Ado About Nothing*—the last shoot on the tree that the Italian skies had first brought to blossom three decades earlier. Berlioz had then made a sketch of the musical situations suggested by Shakespeare's comedy. He had now but to revise, versify, and compose it. His own work, as usual, gave him happiness, health and gaiety. "It looks as if my disease were wearing itself out," he writes to Louis, who had also complained of stomach trouble. "I feel stronger since I no longer take medicines, and I have been working so hard that the occupation itself helps to cure me. I can scarcely keep up with the music of my little opera, so rapidly do the pieces come to me. Each wants precedence and sometimes I begin a fresh one before the previous is done."

As if to reward indifference, *Les Troyens* now seemed to be on the way to production. A friend who remained anonymous guaranteed Carvalho fifty thousand francs to put on the work. The press announced the fact in late October 1860. Commenting upon it, Berlioz told Ferrand: "It's a good deal, but it isn't everything. So much is needed for a musical epic on that scale." Nor was it entirely a question of money. Carvalho was back at the Lyrique, and full of enthusiasm after having obtained official status and the means of building a new theater,[1] but the musical personnel was inadequate. If Berlioz wanted to see his Trojans properly acted and sung he must obtain a ukase to have it done at the Opera. But that inevitable and narrow gate was now blocked by *Tannhäuser,* whose endless rehearsals were to cost, together with settings, one hundred and sixty thousand francs. Wagner had entered like a prince, ahead of all other pending claimants and with all his special conditions agreed to in advance. This very expenditure of funds and good will made any repetition of it unlikely in the near future, despite the plausible reasoning that the Wagner precedent should also serve a native composer who was no longer young or unknown.

Yet Berlioz' friends urged him to argue this precedent. The influential Comte [now Duc] de Morny, half brother to the Emperor, had known about the *Trojans* for three years, but in the interim he had become a supporter and indeed a collaborator of Offenbach's: it would be useless to approach a rival poet. The new Minister of Fine Arts, Count Walewsky, might be less partial, so Berlioz gave the minister's secretary yet another copy of his work. "Everything comes to him who waits," he reflected; "if we could only live to be 200, if we could stay young, intelligent, and strong during that couple of centuries, we men of ideas—men of fixed ideas occasionally; and if meanwhile the others died at 30 or 40 no cleverer than they were at birth—then, then, the obstacles in our path would be child's play."

Unfortunately, many of the people in their forties seemed livelier than ever, and stupider. There was a redoubled lust for spiritual messages, not from contemporaries but from the departed. These came through the legs of Empire tables, or rather, Second Empire tables, and therefore not legs but limbs. Berlioz took ironic notice of this in an essay on Beethoven's "fourth manner"—the style of those compositions received through the medium of furniture, that is, the furniture of mediums:

> The spirit of Beethoven inhabits Saturn or one of its rings, for Mozart, as everyone knows, occupies Jupiter. . . . Last Monday, a medium who is very familiar with the great man . . . laid hands on his deal table to fetch Beethoven for a chat. . . . These wretched spirits, you must admit, are very obliging. In his earthly life Beethoven would not have bothered to step from Vienna's Carinthian gate to the Palace doors, even

if the Austrian Emperor had bidden him; yet now he quits Saturn . . . to join anyone who owns a deal table. What a change death brings about in one's character! . . .

Beethoven comes and says through the legs of the table, "Here I am." The medium asks the composer quite casually to dictate a new sonata. The spirit needs no urging; the table starts romping. The work is taken down . . . Beethoven goes home. The medium and a dozen startled witnesses go to the piano and play the sonata . . . , which is no half-hearted platitude but a complete, full-strength platitude, an absurdity.

After this experience, how can you believe in absolute beauty? I think we are bound to infer that beauty and ugliness not being universal, many productions of the human mind which are admired on earth would be despised in the world of spirits; and I believe (as I suspected before) that many operas which are applauded daily here below might be hissed on Saturn or Jupiter. . . . This view is not calculated to encourage great craftsmen. Several of them, overwhelmed by the discovery, are said to have fallen ill and to be on the verge of passing into the spirit state. Happily that state will last them a good while.

When he wrote this fantasy with a moral, Berlioz was feeling buoyed up by work on his new score, but the New Year 1861 brought harassment. An unexplained inflammation of the left eye and cheek was a mere nuisance, but Marie's ailing condition grew worse, and Louis's perturbations cast a pall on the helpless father's mind. The young man had passed both his examinations; he was now a captain and had at once obtained a berth which would pay him eighteen hundred francs a year. Yet he still needed money, and suddenly he felt a raging impatience to get on faster—doubtless from guilt at being dependent. Berlioz had to rehearse for him his own arduous beginnings and show the young officer that he was relatively fortunate. But sound reasoning, as Berlioz knew, hardly touches feelings like those Louis suffered from. The new-made captain, it appeared, wanted to be married—not to anyone he could name but in general. Berlioz with his two unhappy experiences of matrimony, tried to dissuade his son by sketching the despair, exasperation, and anxieties of marriage under adverse conditions. He was brief and kind on the subject, but Louis felt attacked, or else he misunderstood, and he replied in wounding words which Berlioz begged him to moderate in future. The boy also spoke of nightmares connected with boarding operations and dating back to his service in the Baltic. Clearly, Louis nursed a sense of wrong which from time to time burst through his love for his father, and demanded from him a special pity. All this Berlioz could easily read between the lines: in the paragraph following his "knife thrusts," the wretched boy wanted to know why the newspapers did not more often speak of his father. Berlioz had no resource but to be patient and try to soothe the intelligent and affectionate child who had too soon become a flayed spirit.

For a month Berlioz had not been able to touch his score. Besides illness and worry he was swamped with concerts and reviews. Death too was at work and required notice from the survivors. Scribe, Murger, and Guinot in the world of letters; Berlioz' old friend Chelard, the loyal and affectionate Weimar musician; Simon, who had also studied with Lesueur; Mme. Lesueur herself—with each extinction part of Berlioz' known world was disappearing. For a man who lives not in himself alone, who is therefore especially vulnerable to treading down by the hungry generations, it would have been good to have the protection of fame, to become at the right moment a Grand Old Man and assume the detachment of that role.

The very reverse was happening. As is clear from the *Tannhäuser* episode, Berlioz' most intimate friends—the Princess, Ferrand, the Massarts and the Damckes—were exacerbating his sense of injury. These last especially, being strongly anti-Wagnerian, aggravated Berlioz' concern over the effect of the new work and deepened his distress at Liszt's apparent desertion. The old friend and fellow warrior who had been unable to go to Baden was coming to Paris to see Wagner through the probable ordeal. Franz and Hector would have to meet: what could they say to each other? They were too intelligent and too well bred not to understand that no one's rights had been violated—Liszt had not taken an oath of eternal allegiance to Berlioz—but the emotional assumptions of a quarter century cannot be forgotten in a twelvemonth. To drown out thoughts of self, Berlioz would ask Mme. Massart to play him Beethoven sonatas. But the return to futilities in speech was upsetting. He felt dizzy: "Never did I have so many windmills to tilt at as this year. I am surrounded by lunatics." For a while Liszt deemed it best not to come after all, thinking perhaps to avoid painful meetings.

Berlioz now faced another stretch of proofreading. He had undertaken to publish the vocal score of *Les Troyens* at his own expense, being determined to hear his Cassandra and Dido and having to be ready for any opportunity. So many times before in his career will power and persistence had breached stone walls, success had so often come against all probability, that there was no point in being reasonable. For the sake of his music drama Berlioz also kept his "armed position" at the *Débats*. "So many rascals would annihilate me if they were not afraid. And yet my head is full of ideas and projected works that I cannot undertake because of that slavery." While time dribbled through one's fingers, moreover, one had to wait upon the private secretaries of the great and chat with Emperors and Ministers about the weather or the latest financial suicide. An artist was expected "to die with a gentle noise under the feet of these pachyderms."

On March thirteenth and eighteenth, 1861, the *Tannhäuser* performances, with attendant riots, took place. It was then Berlioz wrote two private letters expressing, most unjustifiably, his satisfaction at the failure of the work. His fairness and philosophy had given way together. Liszt finally came to Paris and dined with d'Ortigue at Berlioz' house. It was a doubly glum and embarrassing occasion. Berlioz spoke in a low voice, looking as if overborne by cheerlessness. "His whole being seems hovering over the grave." Possibly Berlioz was mourning the end of a long and disinterested friendship dedicated to the twin powers of love and music.

The next month, the Conservatoire orchestra played two excerpts from the *Damnation of Faust* to a delighted house. Obviously Berlioz' name could still muster out his concert public; it was even growing, though meagerly fed on scraps. To play fragments cost nothing—"hence they do it," as Berlioz remarked, thinking of what the true presentation of a complete work of art requires in brains and cash. *Les Troyens,* without changing its character, was daily becoming more impossible. At a musicale given by Edouard Bertin, several scenes from the drama were sung with piano accompaniment before a choice and presumably influential gathering. More articles appeared. But the Opera, recovering from *Tannhäuser,* shied away from a new risk. It proposed instead to revive "Berlioz' *Freischütz,*" or even better—since Berlioz had shown Carvalho how to make Gluck pay—it would engage Berlioz to help produce *Alceste*. There seems to have been a vague expectation that if Berlioz were allowed to do something at the Opera, he would be "taken care of," he would swallow the score of *Les Troyens* and no one would ever mention it again. *Freischütz* rehearsals actually started, Berlioz giving himself without stint, as usual. But after a month the idea was dropped and *Alceste* reverted to. Berlioz had to withdraw when he found that far from being asked to restore the work as he had done for *Orpheus,* he was expected to arrange it in accordance with the "desires" of the Opera subscribers. He declined. Walewski, whose word might ordain *Les Troyens,* was annoyed at Berlioz' refusal to tamper with *Alceste,* but Berlioz was adamant.

Meanwhile, Alphonse Royer, director of the Opera had "accepted" *Les Troyens,* reluctantly, under pressure from still other forces. But when it came to the point of setting a date, he seized on every excuse: the work was expensive; the five sets, mid-stage curtain, and processional costumes could not be dug out of the lumber room. Then the novelty of a double tragedy, each part requiring a pair of first-rate singers, was a dreaded obstacle. The first pair would grumble at not coming on again. Besides, the work was long; there would have to be cuts. If only the composer would consent to . . . And to clinch the matter, it was known that Gounod and Gevaert were each at work on something—something which being only rumored, not even written, obviously looked greener than any completed score presenting definite problems. Understandably, Berlioz was becoming nervous about the excess of advance publicity that his work was receiving. The history of *Benvenuto* was repeating itself. Too high expectations might prepare a letdown, and simultaneously too many near-acceptances would brand the work as unmanageable.[2] He decided for the second time to let the matter rest. "I no longer run at Fortune's heels. I stay in bed and await it there."

On August 6, Berlioz arrived in Baden ready to rehearse the *Tuba mirum* and Offertory of his *Requiem*—"to cheer up the gamblers," as he told the Princess—in reality for his own pleasure. Pieces by Verdi, Halévy, and Donizetti, together with *Harold in Italy,* completed the program. The symphony Berlioz "heard for the first time as I want it to be," and after eight rehearsals the *Requiem* numbers went well.

In Paris again by the fall, Berlioz heard a conclave of amateur singing groups perform, among other pieces, his unimportant *Temple Universel.* Earlier in the year it had been sung in London in two languages simultaneously, and Berlioz had been tempted to go and see his many English friends. He decided against it on account of expense. The possibility of a year's visit to the "Disunited States"—his own words, for the Civil War had begun—he also put off, foreseeing complications of all sorts, and surmising that the Opera would take his departure as a pretext for canceling its uncomfortable "acceptance" of *Les Troyens.*

Then, still in Paris, where he had made fruitless efforts to help Ferrand publish a book, Berlioz received from Louis the worst blow yet dealt in the boy's fitful correspondence. The father had heard nothing for two months, and what he now heard was reproaches couched in the tone of irony, coupled with the news that Louis was married and had a child—or possibly children: on this point the letter was confused. Berlioz rose to the challenge, not of the boy, but of the situation.

If I did not know what a bad influence sorrow can exert on even the best characters, I should be by way of answering you with home truths. You have wounded me to the heart, most cruelly, and in cold blood—as appears from your careful choice of words. But I excuse you and embrace you. In spite of all, you are not a bad son. If someone who knew nothing about us were to read you, he might believe that I was "without real affection" for you; that people say you are "not my son"; that I "could if I would" find you "a better position" . . . and that I "humiliated you" by comparing you to some hero or other of Béranger's to whom you allude. I must say, frankly and without recrimination, that you have gone too far and made me suffer a pain as yet unknown to me. . . . Ah, my poor dear Louis, it wasn't right.

Don't you worry about your tailor's bill. It will be paid on demand. If you want to have it off your mind sooner, give me the man's address and I will go settle it. It is true that I thought you younger than you actually are, but is this reason enough to impute it to me as a crime that I have no memory for dates? Do I know at what age my father, mother, sisters, and brother died? No. But can you infer from this that I did not love them? Really! And I see that I sound as if I were justifying myself. Once again I tell you that unhappiness has made you speak as in delirium, and that is why I can but love and pity you all the more. . . . Only tell me clearly what I can do and I will do it. . . . Farewell, dear friend, dear son, dear unhappy boy whose misery comes from you and not from me. I kiss you with all my heart and hope for news of you by the next mail.

Berlioz had yielded at last in the matter of *Alceste.* Pauline Viardot was singing the role, which therefore had to be transposed throughout, but she sang it nobly; and by consenting to be involved Berlioz was able to prevent all other alterations.

He enjoined the rest of the singers to "keep their embroidering to themselves." Still, the transposition of the soprano part gave Berlioz "shudders of indignation," for although certain airs lost little, "the effect of others was weakened, not to say destroyed; the orchestration became flaccid and dull, and the sequence of modulations was no longer Gluck's." At the same time, Berlioz' study of the score as well as of Euripides and the operas on the same subject by Lulli, Handel, and others, furnished him with the matter for no less than seven articles, published in the fall of 1861.

In effect, "his" *Alceste* was very successful and Count Walewski, mollified, offered Berlioz the royalties usually given only to authors of new works. It was a sardonic comment on the timeliness of Berlioz' musical philosophy that the only exertion that brought him easy and prolonged returns was the work he most abhorred—the "arranging" of Weber and Gluck. On each occasion his consent had been given only in order to forestall worse evils, but this preventive medicine was still bitter. He could contrast with this unhappy compromise the integrity that was his when he acted freely, not under, but above Carvalho and Bénazet.

The hours left over during these last months of 1861 went into making progress with *Beatrice and Benedict*. It had grown (as usual) from one to two acts and was nearly done. The subject and the expected audience both called for light, gay, romanesque, and restful music, which Berlioz miraculously found it in his heart to write despite the plagues of Paris, his constrained home life, and the anguish about Louis. Since the exchange of complaint and expostulation with his son, no news. January 1862 brought none. On March 2, Berlioz wrote to Morel at Marseille, who had so devotedly acted *in loco parentis:* "Could you be good enough to give me some news of Louis? Has he left for India? As I foresaw, he has not dropped me a single line. I cannot tell you anything that you haven't already guessed, but I confess this new grief is among the most poignant I have ever experienced.

"I write to you athwart one of those abominable reviews of the kind which it is impossible to do right. I am trying to hold up our unhappy Gounod who has had a fiasco worse than any yet seen. There is nothing in his score, nothing at all.[3] How can I hold up what has neither bone nor sinew? Still, I have got to find something to praise. . . . And it's his third fiasco at the Opera. Well, he's headed for a fourth. No one can write dozens of operas—not great operas. Paisiello wrote 170, but of what sort? And where are they now?"

No operas, in fact, seemed then to have longevity. Except for the occasional initiative of a Berlioz, Lizst, or Wagner, no one kept up the cult and tradition of the great dramatic masterpieces. The current output had no connection with either masterpieces or drama, and even Gounod's failure was a bad sign, for obviously the Opera director would be twice as timid as before and poorer still in pocket. The one going concern was Offenbach's *Orpheus in Hell* which still played to full houses after more than four hundred showings. This parody had been given fresh point by Berlioz' revival of Gluck three years before, and thanks to its cynical and sensual mockery of grandeur, it had introduced the henpecked Orpheus and ridiculous Jove to every capital in Europe. While such parasitism flourished, every antique subject—especially antique costume—was ruined for at least ten years. In this state of the public temper a Beethoven program was hissed at the Conservatoire. The *Fidelio* overture, though played with incomparable verve, was barely applauded. Berlioz could almost believe he was dreaming or that the screen of history was unrolling backwards. He philosophized with his characteristic willingness to face facts: "Nothing is sillier than death unless it be life, for what is the use of life? Oh, you will say, don't bore us again with your Shakespearean quotations and sepulchral philosophy: life is for the writing of comic operas."

This sally introduced *The Jeweler of Saint James,* a comic opera and thus a justification of life, though stillborn from natural causes. Fortunately another offspring, better compounded, was in existence and Berlioz had begun to conduct private rehearsals for its *première* the following August: *Beatrice and Benedict* was finished and Baden would have its play. At home, Berlioz was teaching the singers to speak. "It is infuriating to hear lines uttered contrary to sense, but by dint of making the actors parrot after me, I believe I shall succeed in making them talk like men."

"Berlioz," said a later critic after hearing the score of *Beatrice,* "worn down by fatigue and worry, obviously wanted to divert himself a little and to give proof that noise was not the mainstay of his art. Such proofs he had already put in evidence twenty times, but the world refused to credit it." The conjecture about diversion is doubtless accurate: the composer himself has told us how one of the most enchanting pages of his score was sketched during a colleague's speech at the Institute. The mood of the little opera, like that of Stevenson's Young Man With the Cream Tarts, is one of mockery. Wit is in perpetual contrast with the humor of gentle sadness, and Berlioz like Shakespeare in the *Tempest,* ends his career on a note of half-melancholy fantasy. *Beatrice* skims lightly over the conflict between sweet purity and Calibanism, and uses grotesque and airy figures and festive pageantry to half-conceal the purblindness of evil. The instrumentation is filigree work, tonal pointillism which acts upon us like champagne and prepares us for a drama of make-believe, a romance painted on a screen.

As if to answer the question, How could the harassed composer find it in himself to fulfill such an intent, he says that artists have "a fund of natural impressions, which rearise from their souls of their own accord, anywhere." The impressions which came forth as music when he worked at his comedy he organized around the familiar plot involving the two Shakespearean characters named in the title.[4] From the remainder of *Much Ado* he also borrowed the names of Hero and Claudio, but made them simply sentimental foils to the bickering pair. In addition, for the sake of *musical* humor, Berlioz created the figure of the grotesque *Capellmeister,* Somarone, meaning donkey, beast of burden. The dialogue, spoken throughout, makes frequent use of Shakespeare, and the poem, in Berlioz' purest and simplest vein, is well-nigh faultless.

In adopting the traditional alternation of song and speech it is as if Berlioz had wanted to re-emphasize, besides his kinship with Shakespeare, his undeviating principle that music should express none but musical situations. *Beatrice and Benedict* is once again a discontinuity of occasions brought about by words and allowing symphonic music full sway. Berlioz had shown in *Benvenuto* and *Les Troyens* how he conceived the broadening of the Italian tragicomedy and the antique tragedy. In *Beatrice* he took up French comic opera, seemingly staying within its tradition, but by musical inventiveness new-modeling it. With this score, the cycle of innovation begun by Berlioz upon the symphony, opera, oratorio, and cantata, was closed. Under his hand each had acquired flexibility from crossing with elements from the others, and responding to the needs of subject and mood, music was now free.

To Louis meanwhile, Berlioz expressed his firm determination not to undertake any other work. For Louis had at last written from Algeria. He was chastened and well, and Berlioz overlooked the wretchedness his long silence had caused him. "All is well—except me who have again spent 30 hours of agony in bed." In such bad health it was doubly distracting to have to move—and to move twice within a few weeks—but this was made unavoidable by the discovery that the apartment house rue de Calais was on the point of collapsing. Extensive repairs proceeded floor by floor and drove Berlioz out with his papers, manuscripts, proofs, books, and other tools of the man of thought. This contretemps gave added charm to the prospect which arose of being elected Permanent Secretary of the Institute, a post which carries official quarters. Halévy had died at Nice and the committee put Berlioz fourth on their list of nominees. He received fourteen votes but Beulé was chosen by nineteen. Rumor had it that the objectionable Mme. Berlioz precluded her husband's election. Two months later she no longer stood in the way: "I write you just a few lines in my desolation. My wife has just died, in an instant, struck down by cardiac failure. The fearful loneliness I feel at this sudden and violent parting cannot be told. Forgive my not writing at greater length."

Marie Recio Berlioz, who had barely turned forty-eight, had been chronically ill and subject to heart attacks for several years. She and her husband had been spending the day with friends in the country when death occurred without warning on Friday June thirteenth. Berlioz' efforts to be the first to reach her mother failed, and the poor woman, apprehensive at their lateness in returning, arrived to find her daughter dead. Berlioz declined the offers of his nieces and of Louis to come and comfort him. ". . . it is better for me to be left to myself."

After a few days, Berlioz' mother-in-law returned to Paris and he decided to continue living under the same roof. He did hope that Louis would go to Baden in August and meet him there, the young man's "family" not having been mentioned again, and having had, indeed, either a casual or an imaginary existence. "In the intervals of my work," pleaded Berlioz, "you would be my companion; I would introduce you to my friends, in a word you would be with me. . . . Of course I am rather nervous at bringing you into a gambling town, but if you give me your word of honor not to risk a single florin, I shall trust you and shall resign myself to the pain of separation when you have to go . . . ."

To Berlioz' surprise Louis, disregarding his father's choice of solitude, came at once to Paris and spent an all-too-short week that both enjoyed. After it, Berlioz wrote: "I find it so restful to chat with you. Yes, I agree that it was good, at night, to know that you were here, close by. But don't let the thought upset you. I would rather look on the fact that your new position is going to better your lot. You won't be making those endless trips that take you so far from me . . . We shall see each other oftener. . . .

"I had a letter from Baden this morning, telling me that the choruses now know their parts by heart and are found very effective. The manager is 'sure of a great success'—as if he knew the rest of the score! Everything in this world is ruled by preconceived ideas. Yesterday we began the actual staging in the Opéra-Comique, with every one present, for a change. . . ."

The Princess, by one of her messages of comfort, brought Berlioz' thoughts back to himself: "Your letter made me almost happy for a few hours, but such clearing of the skies is of short duration. . . . Like you I have one of the three theological virtues—charity—but not, as you know, the other two. . . . The insoluble riddle of the world, the existence of evil and pain, the mad fury of the human race, its stupid ferocity, which it vents, everywhere and at all times, upon the most innocent people and often on itself, have reduced me to the state of spiritless and desperate resignation which may be supposed to exist in a scorpion surrounded by live coals. The utmost I can do is not to sting myself to death. . . .

"You wonder how it is that you did not know of the existence of my two-act opera for Baden. It must be that I haven't written to you for a long time. . . . The intervals [of illness] during its composition were so long that on first rehearsing I became acquainted with music which I had lost all memory of. . . . I have my work cut out for me teaching the orchestra, for the thing is a caprice written with the point of a needle and it requires an extremely delicate performance. Farewell, dear Princess, I shall keep you informed."

At the new grave, which he frequently visited, Berlioz meditated on his lost loves from Estelle onwards; on his son whom he too seldom saw, on Liszt now twice remote. The mother of the late Mme. Berlioz had become a second mother to her son-in-law—or rather the first real one. He valued her affectionate care and she adored him, yet she could hardly be the domestic companion he had always sought. His second wife, of greater pretensions than merits, had embittered many a moment and alienated some of his friends. Was Berlioz a poor judge of womankind and doomed to the pangs of misprized love? Doubtless, as he made the lovers say in the verses of his Shakespearean comedy—

Love is a will o' the wisp which cometh none knows whence;
It flashes then disappears
That it may lead our souls astray,
It draws to him the fool and drives him mad.

Yet like them he concluded:

Tis better, after all, to be fools than clods
Let us adore, whatever says the world,
Let us taste folly for a day, let us love.[5]

But Berlioz' management of his feelings could not follow so simple a rule, complicated as they were by his genius for dramatization, that is to say, his desire to objectify his sensations, to see them have shape outside himself, and finally by his tenacious memory. He was like the pursuer of the Well-Beloved in Hardy's parable, who "was wretched for hours. Yet he would not have stood in the ranks of an imaginative profession if he had not been at the mercy of every haunting fancy that can beset man. It was in his weaknesses as a citizen and a national unit that his strength lay as an artist . . . But he was paying dearly enough for his Liliths . . . What had he done to be tormented like this? The Beloved . . . had taken up her abode in the living representative of the dead. . . ." Later on, Hardy's artist-hero has a malignant fever from which he recovers with a very strange result: "He became clearly aware of what this was. The artistic sense had left him, and he could no longer *attach a definite sentiment to images of beauty recalled from the past.*" [Italics added.] [6]

The man of imagination may be taking an unfair advantage in seizing upon some ordinary woman as the object of his creative attachment, yet the mishap is not wholly chargeable to him, for his very faculties exert an attraction often lasting into old age. Berlioz' spiritual energy certainly did so with precisely this result. At the cemetery Berlioz met a young woman of twenty-six, Amélie, whose last name is not known. Sharing kindred sorrows they came to talk, to meet, finally to love each other—though in different ways. He loved Amélie in the way that Disraeli at the same age loved the frivolous Lady Bradford;[7] Amélie loved like a Bettina to his Goethe, though without the éclat of a great estate to cast glory on the relation.

The affair could have none but an inward significance. They wrote letters; they were happy in a melancholy way for a space, though having agreed to meet no more. Then the letters stopped. Amélie too had died. After a time, Berlioz experienced other love imaginings, still more distant and chimerical, until the last concentration of his desire to love on the aged and uncomprehending Estelle. But this is to anticipate.

Meanwhile he worked. To coincide with the *première* at Baden, Berlioz had planned to issue another volume of music criticism. This would present the best version of his many reviews of Beethoven's sonatas and symphonies, of his articles on Gluck, Mozart, Weber, and Wagner; and of essays on religious music and other technical subjects, interspersed with shorter and gayer pieces to relieve the intensity. For the collection he had found the poetic play on words *A Travers Chants,* which appropriately suggested the long traverse he had taken through the realms of song: portions of the book dated back to his early *feuilletons* of the thirties. But the brief double motto expressed in six words his view of the journey's end—"Love's labor's lost" because (as in the Trojan tragedy) "the enemy holds the walls." [8]

On July 26, 1862 before leaving Paris, he invited the press and the musical world to a private dress rehearsal of *Beatrice and Benedict.* Two weeks later, alone in Baden for the opening, he climbed the podium in such pain that he could hardly hold himself upright.[9] Beautifully staged and played, the exquisite work was greeted with re-echoing applause. The "nocturne" concluding the first act was overpowering, magical.[10] The composer-conductor was called back again and again. And he had besides, in his pocket, a letter from Amélie—a true love letter, as Legouvé testifies.

But the consciousness of his age and exhaustion was for the moment too great—and yet too new. Though his vital energies were at dead center, he was not moribund enough to be reconciled to life. So for the time being the success of his last score, his last poem, his last reciprocated love, and his last homage in prose to the great dead, seemed disembodied, too far away for him to grasp and call his own.

CHAPTER 23

EMPIRE AND INDUSTRY

Faced with the penny paper, everyone trembled . . . the musician for his opera, the painter for his canvas. . . . The 1830 renaissance had created in France a great public . . . : the penny paper lowered this intellectual level . . . by making the smile of Mr. Worldly Wiseman the arbiter of French taste.— E. *and* J. DE GONCOURT (*1860 and 1868*)

To say that after *Beatrice and Benedict* Berlioz retired is true of him as a creator. "I am eager," he wrote Ferrand, "to cut the bonds that attach me to art, so as to be able to say to Death, 'at your service.' " He was weary and ill, but life and will power were not yet spent and he had not abdicated as man, critic, or musician. Indeed he was in these final years to experience his most resplendent defeat and his most gruelling victories. Tragic completeness demanded both, and only after tasting all the joys and miseries of action could it be said of him as of Nelson that "his death is not untimely whose work is done."

By 1862 the Second Empire had been in existence ten years and seemed flourishing in the thick of its special atmosphere. It had won a part of this reward by conscious effort, but the rest had come as a gift—the natural product of a new phase in the onward march of industry and democracy. The Paris that Berlioz returned to after the *première* of *Beatrice* in Baden was spiritually as different from the Paris that had heard the *Symphonie Fantastique* as the streets of that epoch were different from the new boulevards cut by Baron Haussmann. The Baron, also a graduate of the Conservatoire, had ideas on the grand scale like Berlioz, but working as he did in the tangible medium of cobblestones, his plans met more easily with official favor: the new Paris would glorify the regime and facilitate the mowing down of possible insurgents. The only acceptable revolution was now the industrial. The Second Empire bore the emblem of the bee like the original Napoleon, but its motive power was a steam-driven substitute: the very word industry had changed meaning. The imperial tone also was a dubious hybrid, like the operas of Meyerbeer, like the mind of Louis Napoleon.

Canny but not a great diplomat, warlike but not a warrior, jealous of his power but careless in its delegation, ruled by the consort he deceived, frivolous and apprehensive all at once, the Emperor was a living example of what happens to the heirs of genius when underbred and born out of time. It was only during his reign, out of the century following Waterloo, that France resumed the practice of national wars, and neither he nor the nation could manage them. It was only since his reign that it would have been conceivable for the titled leader of fashion—Eugénie—to give her favorite shade of red the name of a pointless and un-Napoleonic victory: it was peace and haggling that had added Nice and Savoy to the territory of France.

The decadence of mind which had begun after 1848 became oppressive after 1852 and well-nigh unbearable in the sixties. Machine industry fostered its characteristic social revolution, by which the lower middle class is perpetually extended yet never wholly acclimated, consisting as it does of those who know enough to want more but do not know enough to want the right things—"the generation born and bred in the backshop, reared on small tricks and frauds . . . on bad atmosphere and bad blood." [1] These were the potential mass men whom Flaubert insulted generically and vocally from the terrace of his house on the Seine as boatloads of them plied up and down in Sunday excursions. They were the indestructible butt of his anger in *Madame Bovary,* published and censured at law in 1857; they were the multitudinous sitters for the portrait of the druggist in the novel, which has made Homais the name of a cultural phenomenon.

In the arts, this new class had its counterpart in Bohemia—"a new race of intellects without ancestry, without mental luggage, without homeland in the past, free from any tradition . . . Bohemia brought the sharp demands of practical life into the pursuit of its aims: its appetites held its principles by the throat."[2] The outlet for these nipping, eager talents was the penny paper, offspring of Girardin's *La Presse* and progenitor of yellow journalism. By the time that Berlioz retired as critic of the *Journal des Débats* in 1864, the intellectual press he had been bred to and had helped make famous was already an anachronism. Not that newspapers as yet enjoyed the huge circulations we now expect—the London *Time's* 51,600 in 1860 was considered a record—but the style and contents of the new sheets were showing the effect of vulgarization. Invective itself became coarser and duller, and the careers of a Berlioz or a Delacroix ended in volleys of personal insults.

In the realm of physical things, rapid expansion was setting new standards of judgment by touch and quantity. The evidence of things unseen paled before those yearly tables showing always more mileage, more tons of coal, more bales of cotton. Between Berlioz' first and second visit to Russia, twenty years apart, European railroads had extended their network fivefold, and the mode of travel which had proved a wonderful conquest of mind as far as the Russian frontier was now a common carrier all the way to St. Petersburg. Comfort subtly usurped the place of pleasure—a passive for an active thing.

As the scale of success rose in these goods, so did the scale of required success in things of the spirit—a play or opera had to run hundreds instead of dozens of nights to be even noticed; it had to be played in six European capitals instead of one. Mankind had entered the age of numbers in which unity is necessarily the least; and as a consequence, while the channels of communication become clogged with things, the power of attention dwindles under an excess of stimuli. Repetition ranks as the chief intellectual force. Delacroix, also reading Taine in 1858, feels that here is "another of those who want to say everything, after which he says it all over again."

In a word, the aristocratic ideal was dead, and what replaced it was not so much the reign of democratic equality as the pressure of all to reach and to enforce identity. "There are epochs," wrote Baudelaire with some irony, "when the techniques of art are sufficiently numerous, perfected, and cheap for everyone to acquire them in roughly equal amounts." At first the tendency had seemed like a new wave of enlightenment, fulfilling the humanitarianism shared by Lamennais, Carrel, or Louis Blanc—clerical, liberal, and socialist alike. But there came a period of glut and apathy, as of the boa constrictor after an indigestible meal, and by the mid-sixties we find the men of three generations (Zola, Doudan, Sainte-Beuve) noting "a kind of general intimidation of the human spirit. . . . As time goes on, Mind becomes more cotton-woolly and insipid. This can be seen in things both large and small. Only the abnormal has any life in it."

This last remark helps to explain why *Les Fleurs du Mal* and *Salammbô,* Hugo's *Les Misérables* and Renan's *Life of Jesus* caused such perturbations. Nothing less than shock could distract the public of the sixties from the color of Eugénie's crinoline or the equally factitious bustle of the stock exchange. Even the expedition to Mexico and the World's Fair of 1867 fell upon dulled senses.

In this Empire, quite unworthy of any Tacitus, would Berlioz and his Trojans produce the kind of explosion, of vengeful satisfaction which the separately oppressed master spirits required? Baudelaire, who was not so sure a critic of music as he was of poetry and painting, preached Wagner, quite understandably, side by side with Delacroix and Hugo: *l'art romantique* was for him the repository of true glory, of protest and assertion by genius. But the one romantic composer who by chronological and intrinsic right should have occupied the open place in this French triad was obscured by the uniqueness of his own art and the evolution of his mind. The subject of *Les Troyens* falsely suggested a neoclassicism in the style of Ponsard or of the painter Cabanel. Besides, who had heard the music? *Tout Paris* thought it knew all about it and fashioned a queer reputation for it sight unseen. So dark is the day for kindred spirits and their common cause when the national circulation of ideas is stopped by a repressive government riding high upon a giddily prosperous public.

Flaubert could at least write and swear in peace, at home; he could publish and be read without his detractors' making it an auto-da-fé. Nor did he need the intelligent aid of a hundred men and the expenditure of a quarter million francs to exist as an artist. But without that prodigal prince, Bénazet, Berlioz' musical life would have been limited to occasional fragments at the Conservatoire or at Pasdeloup's Cirque d'Hiver. Bénazet's faith was such a tonic that when Berlioz returned to Paris in the fall of 1862, he expanded *Beatrice and Benedict,* adding the trio and chorus now found in the second act. This done, he wanted like his own Dido to mark by words the termination of his career. He wrote to the Princess toward the end of September: "Yesterday I set down the last orchestral note with which I shall ever blot a sheet of paper. *No more of that. Othello's occupation's gone.* [In English.]"

From this resignation a great artistic experience roused him: the reading of Flaubert's new novel, *Salammbô*. The book pleased Berlioz by its mixture of elevation and irony, by its antique setting and plastic prose. He thought for a moment of making it into music;[3] but he stuck to his resolve, urging Reyer to try his hand instead.[4] Besides *Salammbô*'s superficial similarity of setting with *Les Troyens,* which might be dangerous in the eyes of a skittish public, Berlioz feared that any new undertaking would seem quixotic in view of his unplayed score. He contented himself with writing Flaubert an enthusiastic letter and helping out the sale of the book with notices in the *Débats.*

At the Opera another *coup d'état* had taken place. Emile Perrin was the new director and his predecessor's promises were so much wind. True, the Opéra-Comique was toying with the idea of producing *Beatrice and Benedict;* foreign orchestras were playing Berlioz' symphonies of thirty years before; and in Paris, the first thought of a new but ephemeral society was to ask Berlioz to conduct two concerts, mainly of his own works. In March, moreover, the Conservatoire gave the nocturne of *Beatrice* and its cool impressionism stirred the audience to a vociferous *da capo*. But these were "victories without sequels, which exhaust an artist and discourage him as much as a defeat."

Not for vanity, which Berlioz had long outgrown, but for the sake of rounding out his musical life, it was imperative that he should make every effort to see his Virgilian score produced on home ground. *Beatrice* could not supply that sizable effect, that variety of means, and that serious public test which Berlioz' sense of form about his career made him desire. Accordingly, as he wrote to Davison on February 5, 1863, "if within a week the Minister does not put *Les Troyens* in rehearsal, I'll give in to Carvalho's urging and start getting ready for production at the Théâtre-Lyrique, risking fate in December. For three years I have been kept dangling at the Opera, and I want to hear and see my great musical affair before I die. . . . I live like a man who will die any minute, who no longer believes in anything, and yet who acts as if he believed in everything."

Earlier, Berlioz had accepted a call to direct *The Infant Christ* for the Strasbourg festival in June,[5] and meanwhile he was apprised that the Grand Duchess of Weimar would like to commission *Beatrice* for her birthday. He accepted again, and on March 30 set out for the old city where he had experienced so many artistic emotions. Physical pain beset him but as he told Ferrand, he "had no time for it." Seven years had gone by since Weimar's last "Berlioz Week"; Liszt and the Princess were no longer there to greet him, and the crowd of intelligent youth, now staider and less free, had also scattered.

From Rome, where his friends no longer sought marriage but surcease from care and the consolations of faith, Liszt would soon send a copy of the *Faust* symphony, just published and dedicated to Berlioz. After a first reading the recipient wrote to the Princess: "It is a great work." But in Weimar Berlioz had also heard a fine performance of *Tannhäuser* and had at once written: "It contains some truly beautiful things, in the last act especially. It is profoundly melancholy in tone and in the grand style, but why then is it necessary—no, there would be too much to say. Farewell."

His own little work pleased the distinguished audience. No applause was allowed because of the presence of the Ducal Highnesses, but they bade the composer to their box and fed him the most delicate flattery. Later, the artists and other celebrities from nearby centers gave Berlioz a banquet at which his praises were sung. A second performance brought enthusiasm to a peak and Berlioz was asked to give a reading of his *Troyens* poem before the sovereigns and their guests.

Housed by his faithful admirer and translator Richard Pohl, Berlioz was resting agreeably on his laurels when an invitation came from Prince Hohenzollern-Hechingen, now moved to Löwenberg in Silesia, who desired an all-Berlioz concert under the master's hand. The Prince had himself arranged the program and begun rehearsing. Neither man had forgotten the time twenty years earlier when at Hechingen proper, Berlioz had arranged without fee and for a minute orchestra a concert of his then unknown works. Now the Prince could put sixty men at Berlioz' disposal and, matching the artist's earlier care and thoughtfulness, he prepared for the composer the most exquisite pleasure in his career. When Berlioz arrived he found a small concert room of excellent acoustics, which connected with greenrooms, a musical library and an apartment for the visiting artist.

At four each day they come into my study to tell me the orchestra is assembled. I open a double door and find half a hundred players seated and *already in tune*. They rise as I step to the podium. I lift my baton, give the first beat, and we're on our way . . . If you can believe it, at the first rehearsal they went through the finale of *Harold* without a mistake, the adagio from *Romeo and Juliet* without missing an accent. . . . Seifriz, the capellmeister, told me after this [in French]: "Sir, when we listen this piece we ever in tears."

Do you know, dear friends, what touches me most in these marks of affection? It is the discovery that I must be dead. So much has happened in 20 years which I have the impudence to call progress: I am played almost everywhere [in Germany]. . . . My *Corsair* Overture is widely played though I myself have heard it only once. The others, *Lear* and *Benvenuto Cellini,* are often given and they are just the ones least known in Paris. Day before yesterday (laugh or smile if you like) I found myself unable to hold back a tear in conducting the *King Lear* . . . I was thinking that perhaps Father Shakespeare would not curse me for having made his old British King and his sweet Cordelia speak in those strains. I had forgotten the work since writing it at Nice in 1831. . . .

There being no harpist here, one was bidden to come 300 miles from Weimar. . . . The Prince is kept in bed by the gout . . . so during meals he writes me pencilled notes which are brought to me and which I must answer between fruit and dessert (for there is no cheese here) [6] . . . He knows everything I have written in prose and music. This morning he said, "Come and let me embrace you: I have just read your analysis of the Pastoral Symphony. . . ." [7] But I am exhausted. This is because a theatre orchestra is a slave stuck in a cave, whereas a concert orchestra is a king on his throne; and then these great symphonic passions upset me a good deal more than the make-believe sentiments of *Beatrice.*

The events and emotions of this Löwenberg visit bear the stamp of a valedictory. After the last concert on April 20, the Prince awarded Berlioz the Hohenzollern Cross as to a captain commanding troops; an officer climbed the stage and affixed the medal in military fashion. The next day, the Prince being still bedridden, Berlioz read *Les Troyens* before a small company gathered near the patient, who at the end called Berlioz to him, kissed him and said: "You are going back to France: to those who love you, say I love them."

Not long after, the Prince died, his orchestra scattered, and the name Hohenzollern attached to other deeds. But one of the visitors to Löwenberg during Berlioz' concerts had been Dr.

Leopold Damrosch, who had moreover played under the composer at Weimar and who, on emigrating to the United States in the seventies, brought with him an orchestral tradition that contributed not a little to America's musical awakening. Somewhat prematurely, no doubt, the elder Damrosch gave Berlioz' great concert works in this country. On a lesser scale his sons maintained Berlioz on the programs through the world's Wagnerian period, down to the present when others were ready to enlarge the repertory.

On April 24, Berlioz was in Strasbourg to start chorus and orchestra on their studies of *The Infant Christ,* and four days later he was back in Paris. The first news he heard was that difficulties were brewing with regard to *Les Troyens.* "When I turn my back, nothing goes right." Nor had the previous half year been without disquiet of the familiar kind. Louis had impulsively thrown up his land post in the merchant marine and come to Paris without means or purpose. His father's pleasure in seeing him was naturally mixed with the worst apprehensions. Slowly, Berlioz persuaded the "boy" of twenty-eight to resume his career. By March Louis was in Mexico, having signed on a ship with the promise of being master of his own vessel at the first opportunity.

By sympathetic identification Berlioz had also been shocked by the sudden death of Liszt's daughter, Mme. Emile Ollivier. His own romance with Amélie was over, though he did not yet know of her death—"a love which came to me smiling, which I did not seek, and which I even resisted for a time. But the isolation I live in, and the imperious, destroying desire for affection overcame me. I let myself be loved, and then loved in return, far more than I should. A voluntary break became necessary, compulsory, complete, without compensation—absolute as death. That's all. I recover little by little. . . ."

Humbert Ferrand, the friend of his youth, to whom he wrote these words was himself in wretched health and spirits. After a long period of intermittent correspondence, the two men had resumed their steady exchange, commenting upon one another's works and days, and matching philosophies like the aged Jefferson and John Adams. Ferrand's letters must have been still more confiding than Berlioz' for we find the latter excusing himself in case he seemed too reserved. Berlioz repeats that Humbert's letter has done him good, but that its praise is excessive; the sight of Ferrand's handwriting has made him happy the whole day, but "I can not so well as you express certain feelings we share in common; yet I feel them, too, do believe it. Moreover, I dare not yield myself too much. . . ." Without any break in friendship, there had been a contrary motion in their development as characters, Ferrand growing more direct about the simplicities of life as Berlioz came to shield them with stoicism.

The erstwhile poet was at this time half-paralyzed and greatly impoverished. He was easily distraught, and Berlioz expressed regret at causing him needless anxiety by reporting the musical goings-on in Paris. "Do not be at the pains to send me extended comments. . . . Writing must be for you as my feuilletons are to me . . . *Miseris sucurrere disco.*[8] It is enough if I have drawn your mind for a few moments away from your sufferings.

"At last Carvalho and I are harnessed to this huge affair of the Trojans. Three days ago I read the piece to the assembled personnel of the Théâtre-Lyrique and the chorus rehearsals are about to begin. The negotiations with Mme. Charton-Demeur are concluded; she is engaged to sing Dido. . . . But I had to consent to letting the work be cut down to the last three acts only; they will be re-divided into five and preceded by a prologue which I have just written, the theatre being neither large enough nor rich enough to put on *The Taking of Troy*. . . ."

Five months from the date of this letter, five years after the completion of the work, which is to say in December 1863, the mutilated *Troyens* was to have its *première*. But the half year's preparation for it was neither easy nor pleasant. Carvalho had banked on a subsidy of one hundred thousand francs from the Ministry of Fine Arts, which had been promised but not paid. Berlioz had to join in the campaign to get it. Then the contralto playing Dido's sister Anna turned out to be "non-music incarnate." She had a superb voice and face but Berlioz had to teach her the part one note at a time. Dido, on the other hand, was enamored of her role but terrified by its scope and power. She had bouts of weeping and the composer had to reassure her.

There was agitation backstage as well. To damp the extravagance of meddlers, Berlioz applied to Flaubert for an opinion on the Carthaginian costumes.[9] This was a pleasure to both men, but since the capital on hand was barely enough, recourse was finally had to the ready-made. The publisher Choudens, speculating on the chances of success, bought the score outright, with that of *Benvenuto Cellini* thrown in, for fifteen thousand francs. This was exactly twenty times the amount paid for the *Damnation of Faust,* but there was in this liberality a hidden joker which the composer could not foresee and which his admirers have not been able to circumvent.[10]

Meantime Berlioz had been at Strasbourg for the Lower Rhine Festival and returned. "I am back . . . , ground to powder, deeply moved. *L'Enfance du Christ,* performed before a veritable *people* made a profound impression. The hall had been built *ad hoc* on Place Kléber and held 8500 persons, yet everyone could hear. They wept and applauded, to the point of interrupting several numbers . . . You cannot imagine the effect of the final mystic chorus: it was the religious ecstasy which I had dreamed of and felt in composing it. An *a cappella* group of 200 men and 250 young women had rehearsed it for three months and they did not drop an eighth of a tone. . . . Carvalho's enthusiasm for *Les Troyens* is growing. The year began well: will it end the same way? Make a wish!"

The following month, when Berlioz had begun to expect a rather lonely three weeks in Baden (*Beatrice* to be played twice) Louis arrived from Mexico. They decided to go together and even planned Louis's return after a forthcoming cruise so that he might hear *Les Troyens.* While at Marseille Louis had gone to concerts and operas and now his interest in music, amateur though he was, partook of the intense ambivalent love he bore his father. The sight of Baden, its fashions, women and wealth, and above all the response of an audience of habitués to his father's work, acted upon the son as glory does upon a possessive mistress.

The Paris season at the Lyrique began very poorly on September 1 with the *Marriage of Figaro.* Money grew scarcer, which pinched still more the staging of Berlioz' work, but it was too late to cry halt. Rehearsals of innumerable "sections" went on daily, in a milieu Berlioz grew to dislike more and more. The creaky machinery for which his work had in fact not been conceived, irritated him in every fiber. "What a collection of tricks and traps! Benches that collapse amid supposititious flames; cupboards in which handsome youths are folded up once each way and that turn out to be empty; thunder that rolls deliberately, like a mayor in his scarf of office walking down the town hall steps; Albanian pirates, old Turks who can't walk, and old choristers who can't sing. Alas! concerts are a thing of the past; the theatre has swallowed up everything."

These autumn months also swallowed up friends, artists, notables. In September, Delacroix died, shrouded in that semi-neglect, semi-recognition characteristic of the epoch.[11] Similarly misknown, Vigny, the affectionate friend and admired poet, who had been godfather, so to speak, of *Benvenuto Cellini,* also died obscurely in his retreat. Then one of the two librettists of the same work, Léon de Wailly, a friend to both Vigny and Berlioz, also died. And lastly, the ever warm and cheerful Horace Vernet, who ended as he began, painting Napoleons and helping artists greater than he.

Carvalho's next productions, meant to recoup the losses incurred over Mozart, were Weber's *Oberon* and Bizet's first opera, *The Pearl Fishers*—both failures. Berlioz, who could tell a real musician by ear, tried to minimize Bizet's fiasco in the eyes of the public by a review in which he not only praised the young musician's merits but gave a prescient indication of his characteristic genius.

After this third bad investment, Carvalho's bank balance was seriously nicked and he became intransigent with Berlioz. The composer could not have the quite reasonable orchestra originally called for. He who thought he had "set down his last orchestral note" now had to reinstrument parts of his work. He had moreover composed a Prelude to replace the first "day" of his epic action: *Les Troyens* was being whittled down to the size of a stock-company budget. And not only whittled down, but puttied up. The know-it-all office staff led by Carvalho wanted words removed, measures added or cut to help an exit, not to mention other details to be altered for strong but incommunicable reasons. Berlioz changed none of the parts but granted the cuts and patiently argued the existence and attributes of the Roman gods.[12] Carvalho's last imposition was to set the opening date a month ahead—avowedly to start the intake of cash as soon as possible.

At the dress rehearsal on November 2 the preparation was visibly inadequate. Though some passages were magnificently sung—which stirred not Berlioz alone to deep feeling—many others required constant aid from the prompter. Nor had unity of presentation been achieved. The clumsy scenery on which the producer counted so heavily made the show last from eight o'clock to half past twelve. On the opening night, one of the intermissions lasted fifty-five minutes though nothing in the way of effect justified such a wait. Again, the actors forgot their parts, lost their place, floundered about; their costumes (it is said) made them self-conscious. The fact was that the music was as new to them as that of *Benvenuto* and the *Damnation* had been two and three decades before. Thirteen years later at Bayreuth, the *Ring* made a similar impression of disorder and incompetence, but here in 1863 there was no backing to sustain the piece through a bad start: it must make its own way.

The public was bewildered too, except at three or four places where the feeling expressed was so simple and the music so well performed that it carried immediately. The septet was encored. But the "Royal Hunt and Storm" was taken as an affront and an irrelevance: was it not symphonic music, which is always too long and has no business in an opera? The sailor's melancholy song was also too novel to be understood. Debussy had only been born the year before and the Russian school would not be heard in Paris for half a century. As for the sentries' dialogue, its imputation that quartered troops enjoy idleness, women, and good food shocked the pure taste of Paris. For opera, such naturalism was only a shade less objectionable than the statement in *Benvenuto* that at dawn in the country roosters crow.

In spite of these grave blemishes, when the curtain fell Berlioz' name was acclaimed, with one loud hiss to keep him from becoming conceited. The press the next day—barring a half dozen free lances—was respectful and even laudatory. Some had been deeply moved; others were beginning to understand; and as a group they felt the futility of further battle. Even the acrimonious Scudo was hushed, recognizing Berlioz' artistic power, misdirected though he felt it to be. At bottom everyone knew that the Romanticist generation was depleted enough to give no more trouble, and that Berlioz as its musical representative could safely be paid the next-to-last honors.

It was the funny papers and the pamphleteers who made the most of the occasion. They were bidding for that cynical laughter of which the Goncourts speak, and they descended to the coarsest personalities. One journalist described the burial of the Trojans at Père Lachaise; others combined their recollections of Wagner with the popular idea of Berlioz to caricature them as Beethoven's sons now spawning further abortions, *Tannhäuser* and *Les Troyens*. Even Offenbach, for all his admiration of Berlioz, could not resist composing a parody, *Il signor fagotto*.

The curious fact was that *Les Troyens* rescued Carvalho from his risky ventures in Mozart, Weber, and Bizet. The public came to hear Berlioz only twenty-two times, but it paid the boosted prices so readily that the composer's share, amounting to fifty thousand francs, freed him from his drudgery at the *Débats*. He asked to be relieved in December 1863, his last word having been written in support of one who was to continue a part of his own work, Georges Bizet.

To be sure, the last twenty-one performances gave the public no adequate idea of Berlioz' *Troyens*. Carvalho's single thought was cut, cut, cut. The sailor's song, Dido's imprecations in the last act, the Hunt and Storm, the Nubian dance, the sentries' dialogue, the workmen's processional and four other vocal numbers—in all ten large omissions in three fifths of the original. Even so, the run did not end because of slackening demand. The singers gave out first, for business reasons. Mme. Charton-Demeur had accepted a reduced salary for Berlioz' sake, and was booked for other engagements. Others followed and were replaced by poor understudies whom Berlioz rehearsed in vain. The orchestra relaxed its tempi, and the chorus, preoccupied with a new piece, could be heard in this one only intermittently—like the voices in Shakespeare's magic isle.

Still, most of the younger musicians came and Meyerbeer was present night after night, "for my pleasure," said he, "and my instruction." [13] One evening quite early, Berlioz was in the pit with a friend who observed the seats filling up and said: "They are coming." To which the composer dryly replied, "Yes, but I am going." He had, happily, moments of musical satisfaction. "It is beautiful, beautiful," he murmured at certain passages, and sometimes he wept silently.

At other times, disgust at the old practices which he knew so well got the better of him. What Choudens was publishing was not the full score mentioned in the agreement, but a hacked-up vocal score matching the current production. A few pieces were issued separately. "You can buy bits of me for ten cents, as at a butcher's stall . . . Ah! Trade and Art are mortal enemies." Besides, as he candidly told the Princess, the continuing stream of insults and mean-spirited jokes pierced his revivified sensibility: "Hard as I try, I am wounded by them, and ashamed of being wounded." [14] He was moreover distressed that some of his old friends had not come, notably Pauline Viardot, who may have been piqued at not being given the role of Dido. He had not had a free hand, and could not satisfy everyone. Roger, who had gradually come to appreciate Berlioz' melody, was hurt at not being asked to sing Aeneas—though he had lost one arm and his singing voice—but he did attend and he wrote a warm letter to the composer.

The finest testimonial, however, came from abroad—a sober, subtle, competent and reassuring message from the musician Daussoigne-Méhul, formerly professor at the Paris Conservatoire, then living in Liège and speaking with the accents of posterity:

> From the depths of my lair, whence I occasionally cast a glance on the men and things of our age, I have glanced at everything that the Paris press, big and little, has had to say about your *Troyens.* For my part—and I can only speak on the strength of the glorious precedents you have set—I put little faith in the praises of most reviewers and even less in their censure. . . . We Parisians, who pretend to lead the world in all things, actually rise up in arms against every innovation in the fine arts. Let an artist's eagle eye gaze steadily at the sun and seek to deflect one of its rays for the benefit of all—directly you see the inhabitants of the new Athens hide their heads like owls and curse the light that makes them blink.
>
> . . . We must deplore the evil result of so damnable a habit, for it might well be (such cases are not unknown) that a devout artist who should aspire to modify the conditions of his art would grow discouraged and give up his effort on the verge of its fulfillment. Of course *you,* my dear Berlioz, you who have fought victoriously for a quarter century, you will make light of all these stupidities. . . . With the help of routine and imitation we should still today be writing the music of Lully, Rameau, or Philidor! . . . All honor, then, to the men of genius who have enlarged our horizons. So forge ahead, Berlioz, and do for our nephews what others did for us. Music was born yesterday and art is boundless. . . . Courage! Germany awaits you and France will perhaps honor your fame in 1964. Does this not suffice for a man of spirit?

The last word on the partial staging of his music drama must be left to Berlioz himself, speaking in gratitude to his chief encourager, the Princess: "You were not there, nor Liszt either . . . But let me now put myself at your feet, take both your hands in mine, and thank you with all my heart . . . for your sympathetic words, your unforgetting friendship, your flights of soul, and your harmonic vibrating to the distant echoes of *our* work. Again my thanks, dear intelligence, believe in the deep and grateful feelings of your devoted Berlioz."

On December 20 all was over in Paris, but an English manager was interested, an English edition of the score had been arranged for, and Berlioz' ducal patrons at Weimar, besides sending congratulations, had ordered one of the scenes from the omitted Part I to be played at their theater. From St. Petersburg, Alexis Lvov also wrote, telling the sad news that he had lost his hearing and urging Berlioz to compose a new work for the stage. A Polish lady, unknown to the composer, sent him a bronze vase filled with flowers; and Auguste Barbier, the friend of Roman days, co-librettist of *Benvenuto* and now an extinct poet, dashed off a warm note beginning "Well-roared, lion!"

Berlioz was far from cold to so much personal good will, but he was once more alone. Louis, who had gone to every performance, had sailed again. Without the hurly-burly of public and private attentions Berlioz would have felt even more deserted. For the truth was that despite his resolve, music still held him thrall. It stopped his physical pain and restored his zest for life, his oneness of being. When Ferrand chose to write words for the processional in Gluck's *Alceste,* Berlioz sought out the original score and would not let the poet change a single note: "On such perfectly pure and beautiful music the words must fit like a drapery by Phidias on his nude statue. Try again patiently and you will find the right thing."

These passionate accents show us a Berlioz who might have called himself, like Hokusai in another art, "an old man crazy about music." Here lay the wonder and the tragedy. When Berlioz was busied with music he felt his expenditure of will to be self-justifying, soothing in its very tussle with the plastic material. But the work once finished, he was impelled not so much to exhibit it as to bring it conclusively to life by performance. In so doing his will struck other wills; his expense of energy was no longer selfless; it became ignoble, nauseating —and pain and pessimism returned. The conditions afforded by Prince Hohenzollern should have been his to command, for like the poet's imagined hero

> *His thoughts are so much higher than his state*
> *That like a mountain hanging o'er a hut*
> *They chill and darken it.*[15]

Thus when the post of conductor fell vacant at the Conservatoire, Berlioz, though turned sixty, put his name down among the candidates. In a sense the place was due him: for experience, reputation, and mastery he ranked first in the world. But he was considered too old—and too new—a possible danger to the gently ossifying tradition. Seeing this, Berlioz supported George Hainl, who was appointed and who at once called for excerpts of *Romeo and Juliet*. Lack of time postponed the concert, but Berlioz turned over all his musical scores and parts to the Society, knowing it and them in good hands.

In the spring of 1864, Pasdeloup played without permission the *Trojans* septet; and shortly afterwards, with greater courtesy, the Conservatoire obtained a warm reception for the *Flight into Egypt*. Berlioz' "indefinite leave" from the *Débats* being now a definite retirement [16] he had time to rest and contemplate—or so it seemed. But first he had to undergo in real life one of those Shakespearean scenes apparently reserved for the supremely conscious. A notice from the burial ground where Harriet lay informed him that either a transfer of her remains or a new lease would have to be made. Not imagining what it implied, he chose the transfer to the plot where Marie was buried, and where he expected to lie also. At the St. Vincent cemetery, Yorick's men opened not only the grave but the coffin as well, to convey the ashes in a different container. Berlioz, required by law to be present, had to endure the sight, noise, and other horrors of the operation, arriving shattered at the vault in Montmartre. He did not yet know that Amélie whom he had met here lay buried, perhaps nearby.

Toward the end of April, Berlioz was to dine with Meyerbeer—a late beginning of the social relations that the German composer had been circuitously seeking for thirty-five years. The meeting was put off. On May 2 Meyerbeer died. Symbolic as it may have seemed to Berlioz, it was for the musical world the greatest commotion of the year. Rossini is said to have burst into tears. The funeral was that of a prince—indeed finer than that of some princes, for although, like Don John of Austria, Meyerbeer was borne slowly across France, it was not done in secret, the corpse carried piecemeal by mules: Meyerbeer's return to Berlin was a public procession punctuated by speeches and performances of the master's own works. The common feeling was that the realm of music had lost its sovereign. Berlioz, Liszt, and Wagner were not to be mentioned in the same breath.

Berlioz could deem it a private compensation that his protégé Theodore Ritter was playing in a fortnightly series the five concertos of Beethoven, accompanied by "a delightful orchestra . . . I go and hear those marvels. Our *Harold* has again been given with success in New York . . . what can be the matter with those Americans?" [17] Hearing music, however, had to be paid for by enduring the increased ugliness and noise of the city. Berlioz longed at times to be with Ferrand. "Voice and look have a certain power that paper lacks. Have you at least some flowers and new shoots outside your window? I have nothing but walls opposite mine. . . . Fortunately I also have close neighbors [the Damckes] who are literate musicians and full of kindness toward me. I often spend the evening there. They allow me to lie on a couch and listen to conversation without taking part in it. Rarely do any bores come. When this occurs it is understood that I may leave without a word."

Through the summer, there was blessed calm. The only news was that Scudo of the *Revue des Deux Mondes* had gone insane. In August, when Louis came back from Mexico, he, his father and Stephen Heller took an excursion into the country outside Paris. At the close of day, finding a moonlit sky, they decided to return on foot. The sights of nature opened the sluices of the two musicians' hearts; they sang and wept, to the uneasy surprise of the young sailor. Yet Louis was beginning to give his father more unmixed satisfaction. "He is a good young fellow, whose heart and mind have developed late but abundantly." But his visits were necessarily short and the moment of his leaving never grew easier.

Berlioz varied his evening calls on the Damckes with longer ones to Spontini's widow and sister-in-law who resided in the Château de la Muette in Passy. On other days he went to the cemetery ("I know people there") or reread his favorite works —Virgil, Cervantes, Shakespeare, Molière, La Fontaine, Bernardin St. Pierre. He even took walks "into the vicinity of opera houses, so as to have the pleasure of not going in." After

Louis's departure of mid-August 1864 Berlioz yielded to a longing for the Dauphiné: Paris was in bloom and this made all the more enticing a sight of real country and of his sweet young nieces. Just before he left, he found he had been raised in rank within the Legion of Honor, twenty-five years after his first decoration. Legouvé had shared in the promotion, and they exchanged congratulations together with news of their respective ailments. At the official dinner, Mérimée shook Berlioz' hand, and with his usual cryptic raillery said: "This proves that I have never been Prime Minister." [18]

The stay in Dauphiné had a soothing effect, though it began with the shock of seeing Adèle's portrait and the discovery that her daughters were inevitably and healthily beginning to forget her death. Being the stranger and unoccupied, Berlioz could only live by recollecting. Just as his impulse to art had been remembered emotion, his life was now wholly memory; there was nothing to drain off the reservoir. It overflowed and covered everything—place, persons, ideas—obliterating time. It reached farther and farther back, mirroring the vision, the name, the valley home of Estelle, to whom—as someone has noted—Berlioz returned in a regular cycle of sixteen years.[19] Berlioz decided to make a pilgrimage.

Meylan revisited was like a balm. Not to act on the renewed emotion was impossible. He drafted a letter to his *Stella Montis,* more formal than the one which had been left unanswered in 1848 and, having ascertained her address in Lyon, called. She received him, an aged lady of nearly seventy. The interview narrated in the Epilogue to the *Memoirs* was outwardly calm and of significance (at first) only to Berlioz. Mme. Fornier was a simple good woman who was naturally amazed that an old gentleman, member of the Institute and wearing the rosette of the Legion of Honor, should be moved to such a visit by a childhood memory that she hardly shared. No doubt she had vaguely heard of Dante and of the poetic tradition, born in that same South, from which the *Vita Nuova* and the *Paradiso* sprang. But she could not be expected to feel the unspoken parallel. Besides, the modern world casts its black-coated literalism over the scene, since which even wiser heads than hers have failed to see that Berlioz' pragmatic testing of his love-illusion was an act of supreme faith comparable to the realization of his creative dreams.

His understanding of the position, long before Freud, was

perfectly clear and open: "She has no active recollections; she thinks . . . that my imagination is at work . . . and she never questions the conviction that what is imagined is *false*. But perhaps, unknown to herself, she is coming to feel that *the other one* [Berlioz as a child in love with her] is in control, and will remain master until the end, for he is not false but real. . . . And perhaps some day she will secretly admit to herself that it would be a pity not to have been loved so well."

She had indeed the grace to speak of him and her as "two children who had long known each other" (unless this should be Berlioz unconsciously supplying the fit phrase), and she accorded him permission to write. The remainder of the idyll is well known: she would not at first reply to his quite controlled effusions, then she tried to persuade "the other one" that they were really strangers, whom age and retirement from active life must keep from being anything else. This, said Berlioz, was a "masterpiece of grim reasonableness." But he quietly pressed his claims and she did not rebuff him.

Toward the end of the year he received from her newly married son and daughter-in-law a delightful visit in which he was affectionately scolded. He charmed them in return, and insensibly was established as part of their family circle. The next spring, he obtained Estelle's photograph; after this their regular correspondence was interrupted by only one rebuke on her part. He next visited her in Geneva, where she had removed, and again a second time—in answer to a confidence that she was in financial difficulties. Being still anxious about Louis, he was unable to help her immediately. Six months after this she lost one of her sons, and Berlioz went to condole with her. It was the last visit; when he went again to Dauphiné in August 1868 for a celebration in his honor, he was virtually dying and lacked the strength to make the side trip. In his will he left her an annuity.[20]

We return from our anticipatory glance to the fall of 1864 and find Berlioz again in Paris, where news awaited him that *Beatrice* was being produced at Stuttgart. At Passy on November 4, a surprise party was given him to commemorate the *première* of *Les Troyens*. Gounod sang the love duet with Mme. Banderali, and by himself Hylas's reverie. The next month the Viennese celebrated Berlioz' sixty-first birthday with a concert of excerpts from the *Damnation*.

Between times Liszt had come to Paris, and by avoiding the subject of music the two friends recaptured their old intimacy. The elder was moreover surrounded by affectionate friends who did their best to busy his mind and fill his heart. At the Château de la Muette, where he had read *Les Troyens,* the Spontini-Erard family asked him to read *Othello.* "I gave myself to it as if I had been all alone. There were only six people present and they all wept splendidly. Heavens! what a shattering revelation of the human heart! . . . And to think that a creature of our own species wrote it." [21]

Through the winter, Berlioz read proof on his *Memoirs,* which he had definitely ended on January 1, 1865. At the printshop his pale face, "carved as in marble, but reflecting every shade of thought" and surmounted still by abundant hair, all white, arrested every glance. His nervous accurate step and firm voice had the imposing air and aloof dignity that Balzac assigns, through the person of Marshal Hulot, to the survivors of the great age. Like the Marshal, Berlioz expected to die at any moment. He supervised the printing of Ferrand's words for Gluck's March from *Alceste;* he gave up for the second time the Baden conductorship; he sorted his papers. But spring came and Louis returned. This was revigorating and Berlioz went to St. Nazaire to meet him.

As master-on-probation, Louis had saved his ship in a severe storm and had been congratulated upon his making port at Martinique. His promotion to full rank was now a mere formality. Yet all was not well. Dissatisfied with life at sea, oddly lacking in self-confidence despite his ability and experience, wishing to marry (again? or for the first time?) the thirty-year-old captain needed fatherly help in money and advice. He had to be reasoned with, too, being in one of his shamefaced obstinate moods. When he sailed again, Berlioz was at once saddened and relieved.

In August, Berlioz revisited his nieces as well as Grenoble and La Côte—three weeks of restful coddling. By day he was only occasionally ill, but he could sleep only with the aid of laudanum and this he dare not use too frequently. In the autumn at the Institute, the customary eulogy was delivered upon the departed Meyerbeer by Berlioz' successful rival for the post of Secretary. The assemblage was informed that Meyerbeer was a supreme artist whose influence on the age surpassed that of either Byron or Chateaubriand. This, said the speaker, was because eclecticism was the mark of nineteenth-century art. He mentioned as a sign of virtue the fact that Meyerbeer never hesitated to make large outlays of money to insure his fame. Berlioz, who had attended the rehearsals of the posthumous *L'Africaine*—a financial success despite its unfinished and incoherent state—could be glad that he had neither to review the work nor to eulogize the great eclectic.

Though Berlioz himself was no longer a threat to Parisian music makers, he continued to be mocked and attacked, usually when news came of his being played in Russia, Denmark, Germany or the United States. At a Pasdeloup performance of the *Francs-Juges* overture, four thousand people cheered, but the hissing contingent was there too. Outside, indignant young men stopped him on the street and begged to shake his hand: "A strange experience—and it's you, my dear Humbert, who caused me to write that thing 37 years ago!" The rest kept saying that such music ought to be prohibited. Berlioz saw to this prohibition himself: when the creator of Dido's role was approached for a revival of *Les Troyens,* Berlioz begged her to refuse. He did not want to undergo "a new assassination"—an allusion not to the insults of the press but to the shabby means at Carvalho's disposal. "Why, for heaven's sake, mayn't I be left alone?"

It was asking too much. Even the Sultan of Egypt was after him, to know the reason why the *Treatise on Instrumentation* could not be made the official plan for reorganizing that country's military bands. A stubborn secretary had to be shown that the work taught the use but not the playing of instruments. The New Year (1866) brought a proposal from the Opera that Berlioz direct a production of Gluck's *Armide.* He accepted the new task, counting on the help of Saint-Saëns and feeling rejuvenated at the thought of real music. At the same time his stipend as Librarian of the Conservatoire, which had been reduced at the *coup d'état,* was now doubled. "Quite so!" exclaimed Berlioz to the Princess, "if one could only live to be 200, one would ultimately grow rich, learned, famous, and—who knows?—young besides."

Death was on the contrary still busy. Scudo was dead, and, closer to Berlioz, Vincent Wallace and Ferrand's brother. Berlioz became, if possible, more of a Shakespearean pessimist than ever; he quoted from *Hamlet* so often that his friends, the Massarts, urged him to give a reading of it to their circle: the wife knew the play but to the rest it was simply a name before which one gravely and ignorantly bowed. Berlioz could hardly credit it: "Not to know *Hamlet* at the age of 45 or 50—it is like having lived all one's years in a coal mine!"

The reading took nearly five hours, for he would make no cuts. On another occasion he read *Coriolanus,* yet these tasks did not fatigue him, rather the reverse. About this time also, he met again in Paris the English composer Balfe, whose *Maid of Honor* Berlioz had directed for Jullien, and who had meantime "discovered" Shakespeare and become an enthusiast. Equally exciting was the fact that Joachim was in Paris and playing Beethoven's chamber music. Berlioz heard the "Archduke" trio, the Quartet, Op. 59 No. 2, and a number of the violin sonatas.

Besides these pleasures there were interesting chores. For one thing the *Memoirs* took a long time to produce because of a printers' strike. For another, Ernest Reyer, who had replaced Berlioz at Baden and wanted to continue the Berlioz tradition, would call on him for help in program making. And finally the house of Choudens, which had bought *Les Troyens,* had begun their delaying tactics and Berlioz tried to bring them to book. He had several reasons for wanting the work published: the artist wants his *latest* great work to make its way; and he wanted to supplement the inscription to Virgil with a dedicatory epistle to the Princess.

His correspondence with her continued fairly active for a man who in his waking hours was subject to paralyzing pain. She kept badgering him affectionately and inquisitively, and he remained warm while sidestepping her encroachments. Like others of his friends, she did not wholly understand him, but knowing perhaps that she was thoroughly understood, she felt something akin to fear. When Liszt took holy orders in April 1865, she begged Berlioz not to make fun—as if his response to this foreseeable step could have been other than one of respectful regret. Had not Berlioz lived in long intimacy with the devout d'Ortigue? Apropos of Liszt again, she finally went too far. He had come to Paris in March to oversee the performance of his *Graner* Mass at St. Eustache—a work which Berlioz found antithetical to all his own principles, the "negation of art." Indeed, the work was designed to signalize Liszt's conversion by a change of heart with regard to expressiveness. Though Berlioz may have been blind to its musical merits, he was at least consistent with himself. By temperament, we know, he was repelled by a certain kind of religious mood which to others is the only one they recognize. Liszt, with the ardor of a neophyte, attempted to justify his work to Berlioz by a demonstration at the piano before a group of their friends.

Berlioz remained unconvinced. Rather than argue against his old companion, he left, and some time later the Princess chided him in terms that elicited a forthright reply:

"You propound in regard to music a paradoxical theory of 'ancestors' and 'descendants' which, if you will allow me to say so, is at once palpably absurd and a libel against me. It is as if you accused me with philosophic calm of being a liar and a thief. This made me indignant. I admire with passion many works by the descendants and I heartily detest many illustrious ancestors given over to what is false or ugly. . . . Times, periods, nationalities are all one to me, and nothing would be easier for me than to prove it. But let us drop these arbitrary systems designed to forward a special cause—one might as well dispute about theology.

"You have the kindness to wonder what I am doing, thinking, reading . . ."

This was the only time that Berlioz asserted, indirectly but unmistakably, his priority in the musical leadership of the century, and he did this not because his claim was being challenged—he had made no claim—but because the doctrine of "ancestors and descendants" was being used to dispose cavalierly of the one claim he did make about his music, the claim implicit in any work of art that it shall be judged for what it brings of new joy. The Princess, who had prodded Berlioz on the subject even earlier, can hardly have appreciated at its true worth the reticence he assured her of: "*Not one word* in my Memoirs' account of the last ten years has to do with Wagner, Liszt, or the Music of the Future." [22]

Berlioz was determined to let the future take care of itself—and of him. Though the two younger men were flushed with the hope of belated success—*Tristan* had just been produced—and their forgetfulness was therefore understandable, they could not expect Berlioz to blot his perfectly good memory of the chronology. We may be sure that he grasped the relation between his thirty years of singlehanded innovation and their relatively recent burst of "futurist" music.[23] He said nothing until the roles began to be depicted in reverse, and then only because the allegation made him out "a liar and a thief."

The rehearsals of *Armide* showed how long posterity takes to get a clear notion into its collective head. Gluck had been dead some eighty years, yet nearly everywhere his masterpiece was "blasphemed, insulted, disembowelled, resisted, and libeled—and by everybody: singers, managers, conductors and publishers." With music, aural tradition is everything: no one reads or heeds. "It is amazing to see the prima donna [Mme. Charton-Demeur] fumble around in these sublimities, the light of her understanding brightening up gradually."

In the midst of this conquest over darkness, the Opera decided to halt production. In all ways the musical world seemed singularly uncouth. When in April 1866 Pasdeloup again played the septet from *Les Troyens* to a cheering multitude, no one thought of sending Berlioz a seat. Hearing of the concert by chance he bought his own, and once there was forced to rise and take repeated bows. The next day, he received from a group of musicians a letter of homage identical in wording with one he had written to Spontini and later published in the *Evenings with the Orchestra*. That same month, *The Flight into Egypt* was given at the Conservatoire. The process of excerpting and serving up a "chef's special" had begun. It was touching and willful and amounted also to a "negation of art." Why create a unity only to have it broken up again and the fragments worn thin by repetition out of context?

After this relatively quiet period ending with the spring of 1866, Berlioz' musical concerns upsurged again. First he became Curator of the Instrument Collection at the Conservatoire, replacing Clapisson, though without stipend. In the two years of his tenure, Berlioz was to acquire ten pieces for the collection, and to reorganize both the Library and the Collection so as to make them actually serve the needs of students.[24] Then in midsummer, the Opera drew forth *Alceste* from its cache and again Berlioz agreed to direct it. On top of this a Belgian competition for religious music took him to Louvain, where he helped choose one of sixty masses. After a trip to Dauphiné and a few pleasant hours with Estelle, he came back for the opening of *Alceste*. It was a gala occasion. Fétis wrote to Berlioz: "You have fully entered into the mind of the great composer . . . In such an interpretation as yours, one discerns not only great musicianship but the skill of the poet and the philosopher."

Berlioz replied: "Your letter made me very glad . . . If anything could restore to me a courage which I no longer need, it would be your approval. I defend our gods." The gossamer irony of this message duly answered Fétis's variable attitude during four decades. Perhaps he was coming round for good: in the end they all seemed to come round—after Berlioz had worn them down by avalanches of proof. From Vienna, where twenty years before the *Damnation of Faust* had been called a travesty, there now came an invitation to hear it entire. It would be rehearsed before his arrival, would he direct the *Generalprobe* and the performances?

As Berlioz was rejoicing at the prospect, a sudden stroke carried off Joseph d'Ortigue. It was a bitter blow: his most faithful, understanding, and competent critic, who had always praised and blamed him with perfect freedom, with whom he could disagree about sacred music and yet treat as an equal in criticism, was gone—and gone in the same breath the companion of forty years whom he loved like a brother. Only a short while before, d'Ortigue had urged that Berlioz be commissioned to compose a symphony for the opening of the Exhibition in 1867. "Berlioz would give us a companion piece to his [Triumphal] symphony of 1840, that is to say, another masterpiece." It was d'Ortigue's last effort in behalf of art.

The rehearsals in Vienna proved almost too much for Berlioz. The strain of thirty hours by railway, the barrier of language and the excitement at rehearsing for the first time in thirteen years the whole of a work which the Parisians had doomed to extinction, made Berlioz irritable and even inadequate on the podium. He knew it and gave up the idea of conducting, saying "I am sick unto death." The performance, he felt, brought him the greatest triumph of his career. He was recalled eleven times, banqueted and toasted: "Glory to the man who has opened new ways to our art . . . who has fought dullness since the very morrow of Beethoven's death . . . I drink to the genius of Hector Berlioz." This was Herbeck, Master of the Imperial Chapel. Cornelius also was there, his faith undimmed: "To thee, knightly singer, great and daring artist, blessed with the spirit's fire, all German hearts must bring a tribute of adoration. . . ."

This validation of Berlioz' lifework was most welcome, most necessary to his peace of mind, for his diminishing strength let him sink into abysses of discouragement. Despite the tributes from younger men, even in France, he felt cut off and would say to himself: "It is somehow not right: I did not do what ought to have been done." Seeing his creation and feeling in every fiber how much he had put of himself into it, how much he had sacrificed for it, even to the sacrifice of his home and health and his son's happiness, he was wracked by the agony of self-doubting which is the traditional lot of martyrs, philosophers, and saints.

Yet as soon as Berlioz heard his music again it spoke to his spirit—as it does to ours—of precisely the vibrant life he buried within it. He knew his work was both beautiful and solid, blemishes included. He should have steadily remembered that, as Maclean puts it, "the works were indubitably *there*." But Berlioz had not the good fortune of being a thorough monomaniac. His obsessional dream, necessary for all creation, ceased when that function was accomplished, leaving in charge the critical intellect. This told him plainly that despite an enormous deal of launching his music caught on, as we say, only in fragments. True, he knew that Gluck and Weber survived mainly because he and a few others kept pushing hard, but this comparison brought no comfort; it told rather against a whole species of music to which his own belonged. With his quick insight into public psychology, he could tell that the growth of a Wagnerian cult did not so much raise a rival as confound a tradition.[25]

Berlioz had faced rivals all his life—Rossini, Meyerbeer, Mendelssohn, Schumann, even Félicien David, had certainly competed with him for public attention. But none of these could destroy him: the contrast was always clear cut and even Berlioz' exclusion or dismissal was undamaging. But with the rise of Lisztian Wagnerism, which was widely supposed to be the consequence of Berlioz' own handiwork, he was as it were kidnaped and made away with, the clinching fact being that the music of the future—evolutionary and prophetic—set Wagner atop a pyramid of musical dinosaurs whom it declared extinct: Gluck, Mozart, Beethoven, Weber—and Berlioz.

Only a godlike conceit could have ignored the evil omen. Berlioz had discouraged all advances to form a "school" around him; he hated coteries and slogans. Once he had given up his posts of critic and conductor to Reyer, he had no favors to dispense nor power to share. He wanted admiration to come from independent minds—as it did from Saint-Saëns, Gounod, Cornelius, Reyer, Bizet, Pohl, Massenet, Moussorgsky, and others. But critics would not have it so. He was regimented against his will. When Hanslick turned against the new music, he repudiated Berlioz and Wagner in one breath, as one tendency. Other wise heads described the pair as the offspring of Beethoven's demented latter years. An artificial neoclassicism was in the making which felt compelled to lump all the recent past in one reprobation.

Meantime it was 1867. Gluck was succumbing at the Opera under the productive pressure of Ambroise Thomas, just as the Wagnerians were sapping the reputation of Meyerbeer. This would leave, a decade hence, two admissible styles—the light French and the heavy German; for Verdi had not yet rearisen from the ashes of his early output and revivified the Italian school. Given Berlioz' position in art and in history, there was only one thing for him to do: undertake a new campaign, preferably in Germany, with his finest and least-known music. To this resolution, momentarily blurred by the death of the great painter and Gluck worshiper, Ingres, Berlioz gave his mind as the new year began.

CHAPTER 24

HOLY RUSSIA AND GIDDY FRANCE

Berlioz pointed the way for untold generations.—BUSONI

When early in 1867 Berlioz was planning a final mission to Germany, it was to combat with music the darkness he felt closing in. From his point of view, the music of the future was retrograde, the music of Ambroise Thomas stationary, the tomfooleries of Offenbach decadent. For the past half dozen years he had felt that art had taken refuge among the "new peoples"—in the United States and Russia. In Europe, it lay in hiding (in the realms of Bohemia and little coteries) or it wore a disguise. Saint-Saëns, the most gifted of the younger musicians was making his way with difficulty. Gounod, born to be a hyphen, was working on a Romeo and Juliet opera as he had worked on *Faust,* spoiling by sugared dilutions the taste for the originals that inspired him.

In the outer world, science excepted, everything seemed to stifle the forms of life that Berlioz stood for.[1] The strong men, Bismarck, Napoleon III, Francis Joseph—drew to themselves the attention which for half a century had been monopolized by men of thought. Napoleon's Mexican expedition (in which Louis Berlioz as captain of a transport was now involved) excited more public interest than Cyrus Field's laying an ocean cable. Scientific achievements were fast becoming a drug on the market. You could see a whole buildingful for one franc at the Great Exhibition in Paris that very summer; and even if the new Paris Guide had been composed by literary masters, the crowds behaved childishly, possessively, destructively. A wave of primitivism, senseless and aggressive, seemed to sweep over France.

Berlioz left. At Cologne, where he arrived by the end of February, his stout old friend Ferdinand Hiller had made everything ready. A room was reserved near the hall so that Berlioz could spend as many hours as possible reclining ("for I am one of the most horizontal men alive") and the rehearsals were so far advanced that Berlioz found the conducting easy and pleasant. The audience warmly applauded, from *Beatrice* Hero's nocturne, and the whole of *Harold in Italy*. The excellence of this execution, together with the revival of the *Damnation* at Vienna and the demand for a new edition of the *Requiem* by his Milan publisher, made Berlioz "almost quite happy."

He came back to find Paris turning itself inside out for the Exhibition in which, as a member of the Institute he was tediously involved. One hundred and four cantatas had been written for the competition which he and his confreres were to judge. They sat and listened. Berlioz made a successful plea for choosing the work of Saint-Saëns, and he ran to the young man's house to be the first with the news. "At last our musical world has done a sensible thing! It has given me fresh strength. I could not have written you [Ferrand] such a long letter without this joy."

Berlioz had other, remoter pleasures through hearsay: Cosima Liszt wrote to him that *Romeo and Juliet,* conducted by her husband Bülow, had been well received in Basel. From Copenhagen he had warm reports of *The Infant Christ*. And Louis from Mexico expressed passionate interest in the echoes of his father's success. Meanwhile Gounod's *Roméo et Juliette* had met with fair response, and the composer, who had discreetly failed to invite Berlioz to either rehearsals or *première,* took the first chance to seek him out at the Institute and give him a filial embrace. "I cannot imagine why," remarked Berlioz with his magnanimous candor.

By the late spring Berlioz was deeply worried at the lack of news from Louis. He lived torn between recollections of his son's childhood and anxieties about his future. As he had written some months before, "My dear Louis—if I did not have you! Just remember that I loved you even when you were little. And it was so difficult for me to love little children! There was something about you that drew me. Afterwards it grew less, in your middling years when you had not reached the age of reason. But it has since come back, enhanced, and I love you as you know that I do, and it will only increase more and more."

This was the truth mingled with the thin self-deception of guilt about those middle years, for which Berlioz was about to pay a price almost beyond his fortitude. Towards the end of June a few intimates invited Berlioz to a morning reception in the studio of the Marquis Visconti. On the richly hung wall of the room they had put Berlioz' portrait, decorated with leaves and flowers. On the other walls placards bore the names of his great works. Theodore Ritter, Stephen Heller, Ernest Reyer, the Massarts and the Damckes, who were the prime movers, would greet the master with music, and in front of other guests present him with personal tokens and remembrances.

The appointed hour came for the surprise party but Berlioz did not appear. Ritter was sent to find him. Berlioz, sensing something strange in his household—with good reason, as events proved—had decided to stay at home. With Ritter's arrival at the house there began a series of rash though well-meant attempts to continue hiding the truth in hopes of salvaging the party. First, Berlioz' mother-in-law admitted that something was wrong, saying that their neighbor Damcke had suffered a grievous personal loss. Berlioz at once left with Ritter to seek Damcke. He, knowing the real facts, played up to the deception by promising Berlioz a full account later. The three men now left for the Marquis's studio, but the conspiracy was doomed: a few steps away from the door an acquaintance came up to Berlioz offering condolences on the death of Louis, news of which was in the papers. Louis had died of yellow fever in Havana on June 5, aged thirty-three.[2] Berlioz reached home and collapsed. Reyer who stayed with him tells of his ceaselessly repeating: "It was for me to die." Callers found him lying mute, his head turned to the wall.

A week afterwards, he went to his office in the Library of the Conservatoire, drew out all the letters, notices, diplomas, decorations, batons, wreaths and other memorials of his career and, attended by his clerk, watched them burn.

He could not sleep; even large doses of laudanum brought no relief. He walked in a daze which his friends hardly knew whether to ascribe to grief or to the half-effective narcotic. His *Hymne à la France,* sung at the Exhibition, made a deep impression which they wished to tell him of. He no longer cared.

Business slowly drew him out, for Louis's affairs had to be wound up with his employers, and just then Ferrand, who had no son but a protégé of doubtful character, applied for help in an emergency. Berlioz ran at once to the Emperor's favorite legal counsel, who held the composer in high esteem, received advice and transmitted it. But Ferrand as was his custom made no reply, which compelled Berlioz to write twice more.

By this time Berlioz was in bad shape, and his doctor sent him to take the waters of Néris. He took five baths before the local physician decided that they were contra-indicated. He predicted laryngitis, which duly ensued, and bundled Berlioz into a train bound for Dauphiné where his nieces nursed him back to health. He recovered his voice, though when the throat affection left, the intestinal returned. He went several times to see Estelle, who had just lost a son also. On the ninth of September they met for the last time.

Two days later the elder of his nieces was married and insisted on her uncle's being a witness. The groom was "charming in every way, otherwise I would not have witnessed the least little bit" wrote Berlioz with a momentary flash of gaiety. From all over the county the Berlioz family, numbering thirty-two, had gathered. "We were all there but *one,* alas! It was the oldest whom I most enjoyed seeing again—my uncle the colonel, aged 84." The Marmion uncle who had dazzled young Hector with firsthand accounts of Napoleon, who had sung and fiddled for him, who had flirted with Estelle, who had initiated the young medical-musical student into Parisian fashions, who had tried to find the famous conductor-composer amid the crowds of the Crystal Palace—he and these multiple selves were face to face again. "We wept. . . . He seemed as if ashamed to be still alive: I am much more ashamed."

Hardly had Berlioz returned to Paris, his German mission cancelled, when the Grand Duchess Helen of Russia began a campaign of her own to have him come and direct five concerts in St. Petersburg. "I have done a reckless thing . . . she coaxed and flattered me so, herself and through her officers, that after consulting several of my friends I accepted." The terms were as flattering as the insistence: Berlioz was to receive fifteen thousand francs and his expenses. He was to lodge at her palace and have the use of a carriage, to make his own programs and receive help at rehearsals. "At least if I die of it, I shall know it was worth it."

At the same moment Steinway, on his own account or in

partnership with other impresarios, wanted Berlioz to come to New York at a fee of twenty thousand dollars. When he met with a steadfast refusal, "this good man was so angry that he had a bronze bust made of me . . . to put in a hall which he has just built. . . . You see that everything comes to him who waits—who waits long enough to be practically good for nothing." [3]

Musical visitors from everywhere—from Italy Boïto, from America, Theodore Thomas, who received a mint copy of the *Requiem*—hardly made life sweeter; the very endearments which the young and pretty singer, Adelina Patti, lavished on Berlioz in public emphasized his weariness. News of a brilliant concert of his works at Meiningen roused him but little. The paradox of eternal youth wearing out its bodily shell struck him afresh when he saw the Princess's daughter: "I found her so changed—there's Life for you!" And its purpose? "Absurdity now seems to me man's natural element, and death the noble goal of his mission."

Nature herself seemed throughout 1867 to have lost her balance. From March to August the world was shaken by cyclones, tidal waves, and earthquakes. Vesuvius and Aetna shook the land as far as the British Isles, Mauna Loa erupted, and Hawaii, Mauritius, Ecuador, Peru, and San Francisco suffered from the tremors. In October the earth was showered with five thousand meteors and the ensuing winter was so severe that many rivers froze: one could walk across the Seine. Berlioz who only a year before had been greatly interested in the Bad Lands and their paleontology now seemed indifferent to the upheavings of *Nature immense*. In the *Memoirs* he had ironically remarked that no sign had told his mother she was bearing a dedicated child; he was now free to think that the earth mother was presaging his death. But his mind dwelt rather on the Russian cold and the long hours on the train.

It was an arduous trip. At Berlin he stopped for three days, which he mostly spent in bed. In St. Petersburg he rested three days more. He declined all social invitations, saving his strength for work.[4] When music was in the air, the old Berlioz "came back to life" like Lélio. The orchestra was superb and the *Symphonie Fantastique* sounded as young as its composer for the moment felt. The work had been included by request, for the Grand Duchess considered that in his proposed programs his own works were far too modestly represented. To the first three he therefore added the *Benvenuto Cellini* and

Roman Carnival overtures and the *Symphonie Fantastique.* There was music for soloists by Bach and Haydn, Paganini and Wienawski. But the main courses were the Pastoral, the Eroica, the Fifth and the Ninth (three movements only, for lack of fit singers), choral fragments from Mozart, Weber, and Gluck, including the second act of *Orpheus* with one hundred and thirty choristers.[5] "The Russians, who knew Gluck only through frightful hashes committed by incompetent people . . . could hardly stop applauding. Oh, it is bliss for me to reveal to them the masterpieces of that great man . . . In two weeks we shall give the first act of *Alceste.* The duchess gave orders that I was to be obeyed in everything. I don't abuse her authority, but I use it.

"She asked me to come and read *Hamlet* to her one of these evenings. . . . Here they love what is beautiful, they lead a literate and musical existence; they have in their bosoms something that makes one forget the snow and the cold. Why am I so old and tired?" [6]

Berlioz' birthday (December 11) had been celebrated with gifts, banquets, and public tributes. He was allowed to recover, for he felt "as sick as eighteen horses," then was taken to Moscow for two more concerts. The local directors had commandeered the largest hall and engaged five hundred performers. "This idea, which had struck me as mad, produced the liveliest success." Twelve thousand four hundred listeners heard *Romeo and Juliet* and the Offertory of the *Requiem.* "I went through agonies when this last piece, which had been requested because of reports from Saint Petersburg, got under way. Listening to the 300 voices repeating their two notes, I suddenly feared the crowd might get bored and not let us finish. But they understood my idea; their attention grew, rather; and in fact they were gripped by this expression of resigned humility. At the last measure, acclamations broke out. I was recalled four times, the orchestra and chorus joined in, I did not know where to hide my head. It was the deepest impression I ever produced."

Back in St. Petersburg after the New Year 1868, Berlioz had two more concerts to give—the last in every sense. "What joy for me when I have beaten the final measure of the *finale* in *Harold!* . . . I shall go to Saint-Symphorien [to see Estelle, who had written to him in Russia] and thence to Monaco, to lie down among the violets and sleep in the sun."

The ultimate program had been ordered by the Duchess to

be all Berlioz. Just as after *Beatrice and Benedict* he could feel his creation done, so after this sixth concert he could feel his mission accomplished. He had met and played for the newest force in European music—the Russian Five. Balakirev, Cui, and Stassov were his special friends and admirers; Rimsky had attended rehearsals; Moussorgsky was deep in the *Treatise* and ebullient with enthusiasm.

The affinity the nineteenth-century Russians felt for the music of Berlioz is quite understandable. Their rising school of composers was inspired by a revival of folk melodies, coinciding with a flowering of legend, lyric poetry, and sacred music —the Romanticism of Glinka and Pushkin coming immediately after the great religious composer Bortniansky (1751-1825) had finished codifying and embellishing the native liturgy. Berlioz' tradition was, as we know, remarkably similar. This was shown in his early sympathy with Glinka. Even before that, he had been interested in Russian religious music and had arranged for the Tzar a number of sixteen-part chorales which have unfortunately been lost. On his first Russian visit in 1847 he made the acquaintance of Alexis Lvov, to whom he owed the knowledge of Bortniansky so admiringly recorded in his *feuilletons*.

But in 1847 there was as yet no Russian school. Tchaikovsky and the later Five were still children, whose true vocation was dormant for nearly two decades more. When in the sixties Balakirev, Rimsky, Cui, Borodin, Moussorgsky (and Stassov, who was the critic of this "Mighty Heap") [7] heard and studied Berlioz, they felt in the presence of a master whose lessons were at once congenial and free from any constrictive system. He brought them, as he had to his colleagues in other lands, the first modern orchestral style and a dramatic technique which served a Romanticism they could respond to: Moussorgsky's first important orchestral score, *St. John's Night on Bald Mountain* (1867) was a new working of the Faustian elements in the *Fantastique*.

What is more, Berlioz' melodies and developments fell gratefully on the ears of young men bred on Russian folk songs, for these, like Berlioz' tunes, tend to be modal, to consist of uneven groupings of phrases, and to combine in free rather than scholastic polyphony. The stars in their courses seemed to make Berlioz the predestined mentor of these ultimate creators of the century; and conversely, it was through them that he who had fought to a standstill on Western ground might have seen his musical principles sweep the world: Russian ballets, suites, monodramas, and symphonic poems were the offspring of the dramatic symphony; their light, transparent orchestration was his; and *Boris Godunov*—a *Cellini*-like conception—came forth in 1869, the very year of his death. Three years later, Moussorgsky, its author, was convinced that "in music there are two giants: the thinker Beethoven, and the super-thinker Berlioz. When around these . . . we gather all their generals and *aides-de-camp,* we have a pleasant company; but what has this company of subalterns achieved? Skipping and dancing along in the paths marked out by the giants . . ."

When Berlioz left, on February 15, 1868, he complied with the young men's request and deposited in the library of their new Conservatory a copy of *Les Troyens* and the autograph score of the *Te Deum.* This last gift was doubly symbolic; thanks to it, one of the most moving sections of the work was later saved from destruction; thanks to the genuine entente he had established, the continuity of Berlioz' fame was assured. As in 1847 he had blessed "Holy Russia, that has saved me," so twenty years later he could have repeated the grateful cry, for he had now forged the firmest link binding to him the next generation of creators.

CHAPTER 25

MEMORY'S END

I have known when there was no music with him but the drum and fife.—Much Ado

Berlioz' musical life was done. As if he knew that music was his life, his handwriting shows the sudden disintegration within. At the sight of it his friends could feel what one of his harsh biographers expresses with true feeling: "His hitherto admirable script—so decorative, artistic, imperious, and which had not changed in fifty years—is now painful to see. From [1819 to 1868] his hand stayed firm, tracing on paper without any faltering the visible and spontaneous symbols of a body and soul endowed with prodigious stamina, and giving proof of a character truly cast in bronze. . . . One shudders, one weeps at the sight of these autographs of 1868."

There was no need of Dr. Nélaton's verdict, given in Paris, to tell Berlioz that he was doomed. His handwriting alone recovered. On March first he left for the South. Nice drew him, as before, with its life-giving air, its memories of earlier healings, and its old tower where *King Lear* and *The Corsair* had been conceived. He paced the shingle and enjoyed the sea. He drove to Monte Carlo and clambered over the rocks. It was so magnificent that for a few moments he no longer wished to die. But without even the warning of dizziness he fell head first. Passing workmen picked him up, bruised and bled, and brought him to his carriage. He returned to his hotel in Nice, slept, and next day felt well enough to go out. This time, in going from one terrace bench to another, he fell again. Two young men escorted him to his room where he lay for a week.

When his mother-in-law saw his battle-scarred face, she had hysterics, for he had returned to Paris alone, having told no one of his two accidents, probably because he hoped that he would not recover from the second. Death was striking all around him—his old associate, Edouard Monnais, editor of the *Gazette Musicale,* then Pillet and Duponchel, one-time directors of the Opera, who must seemingly die as they have lived, in pairs. Worst of all, disaster struck again at Ferrand. This oldest of friends, crippled and impoverished, lived with his wife in a remote mountain hamlet, where they had adopted a child named Blanc Gounet. This was the protégé in whose behalf Berlioz had run errands to a Paris solicitor, for despite his foster parents' kindness the youth had grown into a vicious drunkard and a thief. In 1868 he was on parole under a sentence of ten years' imprisonment and living with the Ferrands. During the night of May twenty-fifth, he strangled Mme. Ferrand and disappeared with her few trinkets. Ferrand, equally devoted to his wife and to the boy, was shattered. Berlioz, who refused the consolations of glib philosophies for himself, could tender none to his friend. He became ever more silent and abstracted, pondering life and the blindness of those who call Shakespeare "morbid" or "exaggerated." On his way south Berlioz had avoided seeing his other dear friends, Lecourt and Morel, because they had known Louis so well. "I should have been broken up by your society more than by any other. Few of my friends loved Louis as you did. And I cannot forget—forgive me both."

In July, a little more than six months before Berlioz' death, Dauphiné woke up to the fact that the province had given birth to a great man. The town of Grenoble invited him to preside at a competition of local singing clubs, and to witness the dedication—also a bit tardy—of a statue to the first Napoleon. It was an excuse to fete the composer. In Grenoble, Nanci's husband, Judge Pal, took Berlioz in charge. "There were banquets and toasts to which I hardly knew what to reply. The Mayor gave me a crown of laurels made of gold. . . ." Though he was not far from Estelle and Ferrand, he could not summon the further strength to visit them. Poor Ferrand, whose foster son had been caught and condemned to death, was working to obtain a reprieve.

In his Paris apartment, rue de Calais, Berlioz was still badgered by the living, incorrigible as of yore; "They ask me for impossible things. They want me to say something favorable about a German musician—in which indeed I concur—but only on the condition that I shall also say something unfavorable about a Russian, whom they want the German to supplant, although the Russian is actually deserving. . . . What the devil of a world is that?"

The last months laid low other companions or enemies of early days. The murderer Gounet having been guillotined in September, Ferrand died a few days later. The next month, death took Stephen de la Madelaine, forty years a colleague in musical affairs; then Léon Kreutzer, a fellow student at the Conservatoire; and in November Rossini, who was buried in a mood of carnival gaiety, to refresh the jaded Parisians. Twelve days later, Berlioz went out for the last time. Charles Blanc, who had helped him keep the Librarianship during the troubles of 1848, was a candidate for the Institute and called in the regular way to solicit Berlioz' vote. Seeing him so ill, Blanc withdrew his request and was about to leave in some confusion but Berlioz bade him stay. "My days are numbered—the doctor has even stated the number. I can and will vote for you." On the appointed day, Berlioz had himself carried across Paris by his manservant (the aptly named Schumann) and cast his vote for Blanc, who was elected.[1]

In the last note we have from his pen, Berlioz told Stassov: "I feel I am dying; I no longer believe in anything." But he added: "I should like to see you; you might act as a tonic, you and Cui. . . . A thousand greetings to Balakirev." Through the winter he lingered on, silent but not losing his faculties, receiving his friends—the faithful Massarts and Damckes, Saint-Saëns and Reyer, his Dido, Mme. Charton-Demeur. Toward the beginning of March he fell into a partial coma. His tongue seemed to be paralyzed; he could only smile. At half past twelve in the afternoon of March 8, Berlioz died in the arms of his mother-in-law. A friend of hers and Mme. Charton-Demeur were also present. Reyer watched the night through.

The funeral on March 11 was of the conventional sort for a member of the Institute, Librarian of the Conservatoire, and Officer of the Legion of Honor. A company of the National Guard, to which Berlioz had once belonged, stood at attention rue de Calais. Trumpets blew for the raising of the coffin. The pallbearers included Gounod, Reyer, Ambroise Thomas, and Baron Taylor. At Trinity Church, Pasdeloup's orchestra and singers from the Opera played excerpts from Gluck, Beethoven, Mozart, and Cherubini; also the *Hostias* from Berlioz' *Requiem,* the septet from *Les Troyens,* and the religious march from *Harold.*

To the sounds of his own Funeral Triumph, the procession moved through the heedless streets toward the cemetery where Harriet and Marie already lay. The Institute delegation in uniform and a considerable following marched behind the hearse. Four speeches were to be made, the last of which, by Elwart as predicted,[2] infuriated Georges Bizet by its absurd references to the great dead as "our colleague." But before the body had reached the grave, a final Berliozian incident—never to be believed had it been recorded by a Romantic of 1830—took place. Not far from the goal, the pair of mourning-coach steeds, black and tame as Paris undertakers themselves, suddenly seized the bit in their teeth, plowed through the brass band in front of them, and brought Berlioz alone within the gates.

NOTES

TIME, PLACE, PERSONS

[1] Nanci or Nancy, as she was called, had been baptized Marguerite-Anne-Louise. She was born in 1806; Adèle-Eugénie in 1814. Prosper, the last child, was born in 1820.

[2] He wrote to Liszt's companion, the Princess Sayn Wittgenstein that so far as the musical expression of the feelings in the *Aeneid* went, "it was from the outset the easiest part of my task. I have spent my whole life with that tribe of demigods, and I have known them so long that I have come to believe they know me."

MUSIC ON THE MOUNTAIN

[1] The instrument in question was the classic guitar, played with the thumb and the first three fingers, not with a plectrum. It does not give the metallic percussive sound of the commonplace guitar, from which it differs in other structural respects. It is in fact a virtuoso instrument which, in Berlioz' day, still rivaled the piano as a means of serious musical study. Weber was another guitarist-composer, and Berlioz's contemporary—later his friend—Paganini at one time thought of giving up the violin in favor of a concert career as guitarist.

Berlioz' scoring for the instrument in his boyhood sketches show his mastery from the performer's point of view, a fact which, taken with his command of the flute, should modify the statement frequently seen that Berlioz "never mastered any instrument."

[2] Jean-Pierre-Claris de Florian was Voltaire's grand-nephew, a captain of dragoons, a great lover, and a very popular writer in many genres. The piece chosen by young Berlioz, it is worth noting, deals

at length with the kinship between the beauty of nature and the art of music.

[3] And so I am to leave forever/My native home, my darling love,/ Afar from both I shall wear out my days/In longings sad and full of tears.

[4] The *ranz des vaches* is a type of mountain tune, played on the *cor des Alpes* (Alpine horn) and so charged with feeling for those bred to its cadences that under the old regime it had to be prohibited within the royal precincts because the Swiss guard would desert or commit suicide on hearing it. The adagio of Berlioz' first symphony begins and ends with just such pastoral pipings.

[5] Weber: "How the funeral marches, rondos, furiosos, and pastorales whirl and somersault together when Nature is thus unrolled past my eyes!" Beethoven: "If you wander through the mysterious fir forests, think that it was there that Beethoven often poetised or, as it is called, composed. . . ."

OPERA AND CONSERVATOIRE

[1] "The dissecting-rooms of those days," writes the biographer of G. H. Lewes, "were far from inviting, even to the most enthusiastic student, and Lewes found he could not stand the strain; somewhat reluctantly, therefore, he abandoned physic and anatomy." Dr. Oliver Wendell Holmes records impressions very similar to Berlioz'.

[2] Only seven years older than Berlioz, Jean Zulema Amussat (1796-1856) had already acquired fame as a hero of the Napoleonic wars. Specializing in surgery, he contributed over one hundred memoirs on his subject and proved one of the most daring and successful practitioners of the century.

[3] *Azémia ou les Sauvages,* by Nicolas Dalayrac (1753-1809)—the same composer whose air had charmed Berlioz at his First Communion—had a libretto vaguely patterned after the plot of Shakespeare's *Tempest*. The other two works are by Boieldieu (1775-1834) and Méhul (1763-1817) respectively.

[4] This was a melodrama by Bernard Saurin (1706-1781), adapted from *The Gamester* by Edward Moore and Garrick, which in 1753 had proved to London that tragedy could be written in prose. The French version (1768) struck Berlioz as a genuine depiction of modern life; but he soon destroyed his score.

[5] To Delacroix, Berlioz, Hugo, Chateaubriand and other artists of the Romantic Period, the reality of Egypt and the Near East was the product of a discovery barely twenty years old—since the return of the scientists attached to Bonaparte's Egyptian expedition, the deciphering of the Rosetta Stone, and the use of Egyptian motifs in the Empire style.

[6] Compare Mozart's calming down of *his* father after the break with the Archbishop of Salzburg.

[7] In a later explanation of his conduct to his uncle Victor Berlioz, Advocate-General at Grenoble, Hector also shows his sense of the artist's social mission: "It seems to me moreover that through the arts one can pay to society the tribute it expects from us. This branch of human knowledge, and music especially, elevates the soul by giving it greater sensibility and this quality being the source of the generous emotions, the cultivation of the fine arts cannot deprave man."

[8] Victor Hugo expressed the feelings of the new generation in his "Ode to Chateaubriand," written immediately after the event.

[9] *I.e.,* the "Red" and the "Black" of Julien Sorel's dilemma in Stendhal's novel.

[10] "I love art and artists, but the trials to which talent is sometimes subjected cause it to triumph, and the day of success then repays it for all it has suffered."

[11] This performance did not take place.

[12] That is, the Emperor Augustus, for the claque were collectively called "The Romans" by analogy with the populace in the circus who decided the gladiators' fate. See in Berlioz' *Evenings with the Orchestra* (N.Y., 1956) a full account of this institution.

[13] François Henri-Joseph Blaze, known as Castil-Blaze (1784-1857) to distinguish him from the minor composer who was his father, was a miscellaneous writer and dabbler in many arts and trades. He composed quantities of"romances" (*i.e.,* parlor songs) and acquired a small fortune by rearranging the operatic works of foreign composers.

[14] Contrary to the usual statement, the historical substance on which the young men drew came not from Walter Scott (whose *Anne of Geierstein* came out five years later) but from a work published the previous year by the Franco-German writer François Loève-Veimars, about whom see below, Chapter 9.

[15] Of this wonderful French commodity, Amiel declares in his *Journal* that it is "a matter of supreme importance—the loss of it an irreparable evil, the acquirement of it a pressing necessity. What, then, is this good thing? The esteem of the public. . . . It is not exactly a good conscience . . . it is the witness from without . . . the homage rendered to a life held irreproachable."

[16] Mme. Berlioz seemed to have public opinion on her side. Not many years before, the body of a celebrated actress, Mlle. Raucourt, had been turned away amid jeers from the very church of St. Roch where Hector's Mass had been given. He could, in rebuttal, have argued that he did not intend to be an actor, and that inside the church Corneille and Diderot lay buried with honor.

[17] Gounod was later to suffer from the same cause, learning and unlearning these three systems. He reports Cherubini's impatient words and praises Lesueur as an admirable teacher.

[18] Balzac is referring to official competitions at large. The Rome prize in music had actually been established in the year of Berlioz' birth, 1803. It provided a stipend for five years, of which two must be spent in Italy, on the principle which had long brought painters and architects to Rome, the "mother of the arts."

[19] Jean-Baptiste Guiraud later came to the United States and directed the musical institutions of New Orleans. His son Ernest was born there, returned to France while still a youth to make his way as a composer, and was soon assisting Berlioz at the rehearsals of the *Infant Christ*. He lived to fulfill Berlioz' prediction of success (*Corresp.*, 222) and became professor of composition at the Conservatoire. As such he was Debussy's chief master.

FAUSTIAN MAN

[1] In England, her beauty was universally acknowledged; a critic sang:

> *"Can all be dark that life supplies*
> *Whilst earth can boast of Smithson's eyes!"*

See also the *Dictionary of National Biography* and a more recent study of contemporary opinion in *Musical Opinion* for Sept. 1946.

[2] Three years later, Juste Olivier, a young poet fresh from Switzerland, wrote in his diary (May 13, 1830): "At last! I have seen an actress! No, I saw a woman, a wife, a mother. I saw Madame Smithson in *L'Auberge d'Auray*. She is an English actress who does not know any French and who plays a role in this piece, or rather, she is the whole piece herself . . . After her exit, I did not want to see the rest of the show." (I owe this extract from an unpublished manuscript to the great kindness of the late Professor André Delattre.)

[3] The eyewitness sources for this account include Sainte-Beuve, Delécluze, and Charles Jarrin.

[4] The portion he kept may be heard, somewhat altered, in the *Tuba mirum* of the *Requiem*.

[5] François Habeneck (1781-1849), one of the last "violinist conductors," had been trying to introduce the works of Beethoven for two years. His first rehearsals, attended only by a few friends and colleagues, had sent most of them away disappointed, or—like Kreutzer—shutting their ears with their hands. Even under Habeneck, Beethoven's harmony was "corrected" here and there, and the movements of distinct symphonies mixed or reshuffled. He was not played "as written" until Berlioz and Liszt campaigned for this in the newspapers.

[6] Ill-mannered brusqueness was normal with Cherubini: Adolphe Adam tells of being, as a young boy, presented to him by his father who had long known the Director. The only greeting was "My! What an ugly child!" Liszt and César Franck had similar

experiences with him. But as often happens, this flint-fronted, gallows-faced personage was something of a sentimentalist who had, like the boy Berlioz, composed the *Estelle* romance.

[7] This rule harked back to the revolutionary fear of tyranny: the mixed votes were counted on to prevent any interference by the executive.

[8] Democratic man may need to be reminded that these begging letters are *de rigueur* in a centralized state, and are no index to character; Berlioz wrote them as modern youth fills out application blanks for fellowship awards.

[9] Although it has been called by Ernest Newman "the most astounding Opus 1" in musical history, Berlioz' *Faust* of 1828 is entitled to this numbering only in the sense that it was the first work the author deemed fit to publish. He soon had qualms even about this, withdrew the score after a very few copies had been distributed, and made every effort to recall the rest. The impulse which he regretted was contrary to his habit of keeping works for revision after hearing.

[10] Rossini, though himself a "modern," abused other innovators, saying that *Freischütz* gave him the colic. Because of this remark, when someone offered Berlioz an introduction to him, the younger man declined the favor.

[11] On Mozart in 1787: "He carries his effort at originality too far. . . . What a gulf between a Mozart and a Boccherini! The former leads us over rugged rocks on to a waste sparsely strewn with flowers. . . ."

On Beethoven in 1811: "His two illustrious predecessors [Haydn and Mozart] had long since occupied all the main avenues, and had left him only a few steep and rocky paths, in which good taste and the purity of tradition can easily come to grief. . . ."

On Berlioz in 1875: "We have been occupied with Berlioz; Rubinstein had to play us the *Symphonie Fantastique*. . . . There is a great wealth of ideas and melody in it, but they are like the good seed cast upon rocky ground. . . ."

[12] Ravel lost the prize by making just that mistake, and earned only a severe rebuke: "M. Ravel may take us for stuffed shirts [*pompiers*] but not for imbeciles."

[13] Known in English as *Masaniello,* the opera is based on the seventeenth-century uprising led by the fisherman, Tommaso Aniello, against Spanish rule in Naples. The music, much admired by Wagner, is indeed revolutionary for a member of the French school, especially in its instrumentation. Various conjectures have been advanced to account for this single burst of daring on the part of a delicate but tame composer, the best being that he caught the ambient fever.

REVOLUTION IN JULY

[1] Notice the order of the second and third movements, inverted in the final version: originally the waltz took the place of a minuet or scherzo third movement. Also, the "adagio" introduction of the first movement is now marked largo.

[2] Often cut from modern productions by actor-managers who know how sentimental ("romantic"!) their audience is.

The Romantic Chateaubriand, speaking of an eighteenth-century translation of Dante, quotes the climax of the Paolo and Francesca episode—"We let fall the book through which was revealed to us the mystery of love"—and dryly adds: "Perhaps this elegant turn of phrase does not quite render the simplicity of the Italian: 'We read no more that day.' "

[3] The work is thus Opus 4a in point of time, and 14a (as usually given) in order of publication.

[4] Berlioz was by then in Rome.

REVERIE AND PASSION

[1] See in Chapter 4, the note on this opera.

[2] Ferruccio Bonavia in the *Monthly Musical Record* for August 1929.

ROMAN HOLIDAY

[1] "We are going to have war! Wreckage everywhere. Men *who think they are free* will hurl themselves against men who are certainly slaves; maybe the free will be exterminated and the slaves will be masters."

[2] Meyerbeer's new opera was *Robert le Diable*.

[3] Ciro Menotti led an unsuccessful movement for the liberation of Italy and was executed in March 1831.

[4] Among other things, Vernet refused to have an "arrangement" painted of Michelangelo's "Last Judgment"—an auspicious point of similarity with Berlioz.

[5] Nice being then part of Sardinia, Berlioz had technically not left Italy.

[6] Stendhal knew the story and scribbled it in the margin of his copy of *The Red and the Black,* opposite the end of Chapter 65, adding the words: "Support *for me.*"

[7] Though Berlioz had no training as a singer, his Caruso-like range apparently enabled him to sing bass parts in choruses, and even to substitute for a missing cello in an emergency. Cf. his *Memoirs,* Chapter 53.

[8] Hiller, Du Boys and De Pons are already identified; some of the

others we shall meet again: Girard became an orchestra leader who conducted Berlioz's early works. Desmarest, a virtuoso cellist, remained a devoted admirer, as did Stephen de la Madelaine, a member of Choron's Choir School, who later became a theater manager, music critic, and office holder in the Ministry of Fine Arts. Richard was poet, musician and linguist, a translator of Hoffmann and of the Ode to Joy in Beethoven's Ninth Symphony. Prévost was a fellow pupil of Lesueur's class, who made his career in New Orleans; and Turbry, perhaps the most gifted of all, was a composer whose will power did not equal his musical talents. He also wrote a *Symphonie Fantastique,* but did not persevere and ultimately died destitute.

[9] "Long live your genius." The letter seems not to have been sent.

[10] Respectful silence during music was a recent innovation even in Germany, where Spohr and Weber took the lead in enforcing the demand, at the cost of personal unpopularity.

[11] It was at this time that Mme. Berlioz played her malicious trick on her son, sending him to deliver a note to a Mme. Fornier, who turned out to be his first love, Estelle. The mother doubtless thought that two subsequent loves had effaced the memory of the first, a mistake which shows how little she knew her son. (*Memoirs,* chapter 3).

RECOLLECTED IN TRANQUILLITY

[1] Berlioz' cousin, the physician.

[2] Altogether, 20 years out of 166. Lully ruled the house like a private monopoly from 1672 to his death in 1687. In 1830, the establishment had outstanding debts amounting to 1,200,000 francs.

[3] Berlioz destroyed the parts, as he states, but the full score, which he had sent as a Rome Essay, survived and is extant. It has been played a number of times recently by Dmitri Mitropoulos and the New York Philharmonic.

[4] His conclusion was: "Music is not made for the street nor for the open air."

[5] Owing to the vagaries of copyright practice, Schlesinger's arrangement gave him the German rights to any piece of music he bought in France, provided he issued it also in Germany. Hence he stood to gain large sums for an indefinite period, the sale of these works being outright and not on a royalty basis. At the same time he could say in his own defense that without the potential German market he could not have afforded to publish work as "advanced" as that of Berlioz.

[6] The English and Scottish Marys were enjoying a run, due to Hugo's play *Mary Tudor* (1833) and to Béranger's poem "Mary Stuart's Farewell," on which Wagner composed a song as late as 1840. The form "The Last Day of——" was much in vogue.

[7] Berlioz' cottage at Montmartre has been painted a number of times, notably by Utrillo, who seems to have lived in it.

[8] From the second of Moore's Sacred Songs, the one Berlioz had set in Rome as a *Méditation Religieuse.*

THE GOTHIC TRADITION

[1] Within a month, Berlioz wrote to his sister: "Do not worry; the boy is baptized. He is not named Hercules, John-Baptist, Caesar, Alexander, or Martial [Magloire] but quite simply Louis."

[2] François-Adolphe Loève-Veimars (1801-54), of mixed French and German parentage, was one of the translators of Hoffmann as well as the author of the history of the *Vehmgericht* on which Berlioz had based his first opera, *Les Francs-Juges.*

[3] It has been computed that for the year 1835 at least, by combining work on two newspapers with the remainder of the government stipend, Berlioz must have had an income of 7000 francs. This would probably equal 7000 *dollars* today, free of any but poll taxes.

[4] For a parallel, see Liszt's essay, "The Condition of the Artist and his Place in Society," which appeared in the *Gazette Musicale* from May 3 to Oct. 11, 1835. Some of Liszt's ideas reflect his earlier attachment to the socialism of Saint-Simon and the more recent religious liberalism of Lamennais and d'Ortigue, but the main arguments are those independently found in Balzac, Vigny and Berlioz.

[5] Symphonic concerts began usually at 2 P.M.

[6] Charles-Edmond Duponchel (1795?-1863), whom Berlioz was later to satirize as "the celebrated inventor of the canopy, the man who introduced the canopy into opera as the chief ingredient of success; the author of the canopy in *La Juive, La Reine de Chypre,* and *Le Prophète,* the creator of the floating canopy, the wondrous canopy, the canopy of canopies." (*Evenings With the Orchestra,* 4th evening).

[7] It is worth recalling here how Loève-Veimars "earned" his 100,000.

[8] George Sand had lately dubbed him a "Promethean genius" in the musically conservative *Revue des Deux Mondes.*

[9] The Irish revolutionist.

[10] Vigny was a competent amateur musician. He attended Berlioz' concerts from interest as well as friendship, and on this occasion he had the additional reason of being a former Army officer who had known and esteemed General Damrémont.

[11] The truth of this incident has been disputed. The balance of probabilities in its favor is supported by one eyewitness, who wrote the facts down at the time, the pianist Karl Halle, later Sir Charles Hallé.

[12] Despite his critical genius and his regard for Berlioz, Heine some-

times let his fancy bolt when he wrote of painters and musicians. His Paris news letters are filled with loose verbalism amounting often to error and always to exaggeration—witness the passage on Beethoven in *Lutezia,* Apr. 20, 1841.

THE HERO AS ARTIST

[1] "This prodigious and indeed sublime work." Letters of Jan. 26, 1868 and Apr. 21 and May 9, 1872. (*Briefe,* II, 115 and IV, 341, 345.) Compare other "discoveries" of it, by Hans von Bülow, Bruckner, Busoni, and Peter Warlock.

[2] Berlioz here repeats his allusion to the final scene of the opera. The score was printed but never published during Berlioz' lifetime; nor ever in France. To acknowledge his friend's help Berlioz was to inscribe first the *Benvenuto Cellini* overture, then a book of essays to Legouvé.

[3] Except perhaps by Spontini, Meyerbeer, and Paganini, who were present.

[4] J. Bornoff, writing in *The Nineteenth Century,* London, March 1940.

THE DRAMATIC SYMPHONY

[1] "He has been virtually hounded out of Prussia, and so I felt it my duty to write to him. In such a case one must miss no opportunity to put in a word that might restore a little calm to the lacerated heart of the man of genius, regardless of his faults or even of his egotism: the temple may be unworthy of the indwelling deity, but the god is a god." (To Ferrand.)

VOX POPULI

[1] Besides Liszt, Wagner, Chopin, and Heine, those likely to follow Berlioz' concerts included J. P. Pixis of Mannheim; Karl Halle (later Sir Charles Hallé, the founder of the Manchester Symphony); Sigismund Thalberg (Liszt's onetime rival on the piano); George Osborne from Ireland; the Alsatian Georges Kastner; Stephen Heller from Budapest; old Kreutzer's nephew Léon; François Seghers, the Brussels violinist who played in the Conservatoire orchestra; César Franck, another Belgian who was completing his last year in that institution; finally, musicians from the French provinces such as Auguste Morel of Marseille and Lambert Massart, newly appointed violin master at the Conservatoire.

[2] Heller should not be confused with Berlioz' intimate, also a pianist, Ferdinand Hiller.

[3] In his last days, according to Mottl, Wagner would brook no criticism of the *Romeo and Juliet* score.

[4] The year 1839 saw the opening of four important railroads, includ-the Paris-Versailles line. This evident mechanical progress was not discounted or disliked by artists and philosophers, but it widened the breach between "those who own and those who earn"—to use Vigny's words.

[5] The class nomenclature, by the 1840's, begins to change. It was in this decade that Louis Blanc first used the term *bourgeoisie* to mark off a class distinct from the people. (*Historie de Dix Ans, passim.*) In 1837, Jean Reynaud had defined the term as "those who were above want" (*Encyclopédie Nouvelle,* art. Bourgeoisie) which sufficiently shows the split in the formerly homogeneous Third Estate: the bourgeoisie was now regarded as an aristocracy but without taste or tradition.

[6] In a letter of March 1840 to his lawyer and friend Germi, Paganini says: "You may freely write to this same friend Berlioz, whom you must not confuse with the common scum of [musicians] but should look on as a transcendent genius such as rises but once in every third or fourth century; a man of perfect probity and worthy of our confidence."

[7] On the kinship between Bach's art and that of Berlioz, see Albert Schweitzer's *Bach.* On the relation to Handel, see Romain Rolland's *Handel.*

MUSIC FOR EUROPE

[1] *Sie sollen ihn nicht haben, den freien, deutschen Rhein* and *Le Rhin allemand.* The quarrel inspired many other poems, and the pathos of the situation is that quite a few of these utterances sprang from genuine liberal feeling. Such was the misused *Deutschland über alles* of 1841 by Hoffmann von Fallersleben, whom we shall meet again.

[2] [Italics added.]

[3] The humorist doubtless thought that a marine trumpet belonged to the brass family and made a loud noise. It is in fact a gentle *stringed* instrument, the so-called nuns' violin, which M. Jourdain in Molière quite sensibly likes to listen to, though the groundlings laugh at him on the principle of Berlioz' lampooner.

[4] Girardin was a pioneer in popular journalism. His chief innovation was the short editorial written in bulletlike sentences—the style of the late Arthur Brisbane.

[5] Possibly a sitting for his portrait, a project which was never resumed. This was unfortunate, for otherwise we should have had Berlioz' portrait in three styles, those of Delacroix, Courbet, and Daumier.

[6] What is more, the opera "belonged," in a performing sense, to the

Opéra-Comique, whose singers, managers, stage hands, and ushers rose as one man and swelled the opposition to the revival at the other house.

[7] "We deemed it proper to publish this essay because on all questions it is right to hear both sides and our readers will find pleasure in seeing *Freischütz* treated exclusively as a German work."

[8] Eight years later Wagner set his hand to revising the dialogue and recitatives of *Don Giovanni* for a performance in Zurich (1850), and he lived to re-instrument the Ninth for the dedication of Bayreuth (1872).

[9] When a few months later Wagner wrote to Berlioz asking him to use his influence so that a benefit might be given for Weber's widow, Berlioz replied cordially, saying he would try again to persuade the authorities.

[10] He termed reviewing "a dog's life—either biting or licking," and told his friends how to interpret some of his tactful reviews: "I said what I thought about Halévy's *Le Val d'Andorre* but the opposite is true of Clapisson's *Jeanne la Folle*." Again, he vents his impatience in a note to his editor: "The need is universally felt that I should express myself in writing upon *La Seraphina*. I shall therefore get to work and try to speak of everything except that emetic. . . ."

[11] Her real name was Marie-Geneviève Martin. She was born in 1814 near Paris. Her father, a captain, had married a Spanish woman, Sotera Vilas. Marie had studied singing with Banderali and was, when Berlioz met her, under contract at the Opera.

[12] In 1844, Vigny wrote one of his great poems, *La Maison du Berger*, in which he sings the passing of the Open Road and the mechanization of our individual destinies.

THE CONDUCTOR—COMPOSER

[1] Gustav Schilling (1803-1881) was a prolific musicologist and critic until about 1857. He then emigrated to the United States, for no known reasons, and died obscure in Nebraska.

[2] A top rate of 48 kreutzers (about 25 cents) was not uncommon.

[3] Berlioz was misinformed in this matter and his remarks have value only as an indication of his feelings.

[4] This opinion was probably due in part to ingrained habits of *reading*. Schumann had replied to a similar objection: "Pardon me, but you are judging without having *heard* the overture. *You have no idea* of his way of treating the orchestra."

[5] Between the long review of the *Fantastique* in 1835 and this meeting with Berlioz, Schumann had written notices of two other works and countered a number of violent attacks. His clear intuition is shown by his final words on Berlioz' sincerity being equal to Haydn's.

[6] Wolfgang Robert Griepenkerl (1810-1868) was the son of the editor of Bach's instrumental works, a teacher also, and a writer on musical and literary subjects.

[7] Isidore Justin Sevérin, Baron Taylor, was born in Brussels of English parents and died in Paris in 1879. During his busy life he was a man of letters, an engraver, a soldier, a sociologist, a public official, and a patron of the arts. It was he who succeeded in bringing back from Egypt the obelisk which now stands in the Place de la Concorde.

[8] It was after his concert of Nov. 19, 1843, that his enemies at the Conservatoire managed to deny him the use of the hall forever after by securing a ministerial ruling against its being rented.

[9] It took place on Feb. 11, 1844. Modern reference works keep repeating that the saxophone "made its first appearance in a symphonic orchestra in 1844." This is ambiguous: the first concert appearance was in Berlioz' piece. Toward the end of the same year, Berlioz' friend Georges Kastner scored a part for saxophone in his oratorio *The Last King of Judah,* which was played at the Conservatoire.

[10] Not to be confused with the North German violinist Ferdinand David, who had played for Berlioz as concertmaster in Leipzig.

FAUST AND PHILOSOPHY

[1] These are related in part in his articles in the *Gazette Musicale* for 1839. By the end of that year, the total sum collected among French musicians was 424 francs 90 centimes = 85 dollars of the period.

[2] Berlioz is hinting at the fact that there was some anti-French feeling among the Bonn patrons, which led to a few unpleasant incidents during the Beethoven week itself.

[3] It was during this interview that he was asked whether he always composed for 500 instruments and replied "No, sometimes I use only 450." Considering how often this has been quoted to prove Berlioz' lavishness by his own admission, it must be pointed out that the retort was ironic.

[4] The overture Mendelssohn had composed at seventeen, in 1826, but the remaining numbers of the suite, including the delightful scherzo, were new since he had met Berlioz again and rehearsed *Romeo and Juliet* with him.

[5] Compare Tocqueville: "I lose my mind trying to recall that maze of petty incidents, petty ideas, and petty passions; of private self-seeking and incoherent projects in which the public men of that time exhausted their lives."

SONG IN TIME OF REVOLUTION

[1] *Les diamants de la couronne* and *Gibby-la-Cornemuse* by these respective masters were among the successes of the year.

[2] Thirty-five years later, Roger candidly admitted that "in those days" Berlioz' melody did not seem melodic; now it was "a revelation . . . I used to sing under him, *but I did not understand him.*"

[3] Produced in 1839, by Romberg, it had earned 5000 francs for the impresario. A few years later the Imperial Chapel had commissioned Berlioz to prepare harmonizations for certain liturgical chants.

[4] On being hissed she tore her handkerchief with her teeth, shouted defiance to the public, and stalked off. Returning, she met the applause given to a colleague by threatening her with upraised hand.

[5] Humboldt, who liked Berlioz, was apparently the go-between for this request, with which Frederick William complied in a facetious tone.

[6] Apparently an Italian opera of Liszt's which was never produced.

[7] Cf. Stendhal's similar views and W. J. Turner: "Music is the imagination of love *in sound.* It is what man imagines of his life, and his life is love."

[8] In their reply, which has been preserved, they express appreciation for the "affectionate terms" of his disengagement notice. Though Berlioz wrote scornfully about the Paris situation to his intimates, he never abandoned diplomatic courtesy in the actual scrimmage.

[9] Louis Antoine Jullien (originally Julien) was born in 1812, the son of a Swiss bandmaster. He studied three years at the Conservatoire, then became conductor-manager of dance concerts for which he composed quadrilles on popular tunes of the day. Insolvent by 1838, he left Paris for London, where he soon established popular promenade concerts at one shilling. His orchestra of nearly a hundred pieces was excellent, and from 1842 on he gave annual series, winter and summer, as well as toured the country, presenting a mixture of popular and classical music. To draw the crowd he advertised "monster" shows on topical subjects and costumed himself gorgeously. His black hair and black moustache (a novelty), his velvet chair and jeweled baton, handed to him on a salver, were frequently caricatured, but they made him a national institution. *Punch* (just founded) dubbed him "The Mons." and Dickens and Thackeray wrote of him. When Melville arrived in England in 1849 he went to Jullien's concert the day after landing and greatly enjoyed himself.

[10] Balfe's *Maid of Honor* was a resetting of Flotow's *Martha.*

[11] He stayed in the United States from 1851 to 1854.

[12] Macready had acted with Harriet Smithson in Paris twenty years earlier and Berlioz probably knew, as he stepped upon the stage

of Drury Lane, that it was the spot where Harriet had made her London début at eighteen.

[13] Prince Albert's music director told him that everyone in London was delighted with Berlioz' presence except the native composers.

[14] Already the neighboring castle burns.

[15] *Lèse-art* = *les arts* = *lézard* (it is the crime of a reptile).

[16] One may take the seeming exception of the "Marseillaise" as indicative. Its maker, Rouget, was soon politically suspect and he had to wait thirty-eight years to be saved, accidentally, from destitution. What political revolutionists want from art is more neutral work like Cherubini's song entitled *Le Salpêtre Républicain.*

VISION OF A VIRTUOSO

[1] Delacroix: "Disgusting devastation . . . everywhere the signs of degradation, and an evil smell . . . everywhere the portraits have been hacked to pieces."

[2] Among other disturbing changes, the publishing house of Schlesinger had passed into the hands of Brandus, who at first ignored Berlioz completely. The former head, Maurice Schlesinger was the original of Arnoux in Flaubert's *Education Sentimentale,* and the publisher's wife actually the object of Flaubert's distant adoration —as transcribed in the novel.

[3] Delacroix, the following year: "After luncheon, I heard of the death of poor Chopin . . . What despicable rogues fill the marketplace while that beautiful soul burns out!"

[4] These difficulties were connected with his establishment in Weimar, where he lived with the Princess Carolyne Sayn-Wittgenstein —of whom more later.

[5] The conclusion of this note is as good as a self-portrait. It reads: "I love you enormously, as you know; but tonight I fear you even more than I love you, because of my wish that my score should make a good impression on you. A thousand greetings and a thousand thanks for having come to the rehearsal night before last."

[6] Singers and others have since told how Meyerbeer's handsome gratuities would induce them to prolong the run of his works. The press was similarly taken care of.

[7] Ten columns was a trifle compared with Fétis's five successive articles in the *Gazette.*

[8] Berlioz wrote fifty lines of warm and graceful praise, recalling Wagner's stay in Paris, his musical articles in French, and his subsequent removal to Dresden where his talents as poet and composer had met the success they deserved. One can measure the later Wagnerite frenzy by noting that the English translator of Wagner's Prose Works finds this encomium inadequate and too clearly due to Berlioz's friendship for Liszt.

[9] Pierre Dietsch (1808-1865) will be remembered as choral conductor

under Berlioz at the first performance of the *Requiem* in 1837. Much later he acquired a kind of *ex post facto* renown for having composed a *Flying Dutchman* opera on the text which he bought from Wagner. (1842.)

[10] Working by committee meant that Berlioz' experienced judgment was often overruled, while at the same time outside pressure was centered on him in the belief that he was in sole charge. For example, the patron of Mlle. Catinka Heinefetter had to be put off with tact and wit: "We shall see if there is some way to use her talents on a later program and we thank her meanwhile for her gracious offer. I was unable to attend her début but you were there and that is enough for me—but *were* you there? Best greetings."

[11] As Stendhal did for the musicians of 1820 one may list the composers who (besides those mentioned in the text) might reasonably claim attention in 1850: Auber, Adam, Carafa, Czerny, Draeseke, Flotow, Gade, Heller, Hiller, Kastner, Kittl, Lachner, Marschner, Moscheles, Nicolai, Pixis, Reber, Ries, Suppe, Verdi, Vesque de Puttlingen.

[12] Delacroix in 1847: "I have been making some bitter reflections on the profession of artist; the isolation, the sacrifice of almost all the feelings that move the majority of men. . . ."

[13] Berlioz had tried to help him by inserting notices of his musical qualifications in the *Débats*.

VICTORIAN LONDON

[1] Another guarantor of the enterprise was Thomas Brassey, the famous navigator and chronicler of ships.

[2] As early as 1837 (in *Contrasts*) Welby Pugin had enunciated the principles of functionalism in architecture, urged respect for new materials, and preached innovation as against archeology. And in 1845, William Vose Pickett (in *A New System*) had proposed metal construction and prefabricated parts.

[3] The detailed plan was found in Berlioz' papers and posthumously published. It exemplifies his grasp of all practical necessities, from the timing and housing of rehearsals to the financial provisions for the performers' travel allowances and the entrepreneur's profit. The site he chose within the Palace for placing his 1500 musicians and building the organ was the East Gallery, United States Section.

[4] He added a wonderful recitative in which Cellini, pointing to the glowing Perseus, reads out the Latin inscription upon it: *"Si quis te laeserit, ego tuus ultor ero."* (If anyone harms thee, I shall be thy avenger.)

[5] The largest of the four music rooms there ultimately contained the great piano-organ built by Alexandre. About this construction Berlioz busied himself on Liszt's behalf from 1852 to 1854, showing concern that not only its sound but its shape be beautiful.

[6] Joseph Joachim (1831-1907) had played before Berlioz in Leipzig and Vienna, and had been engaged by him as soloist for the concerts of the Paris Philharmonic in 1850.

[7] The *coup d'état* was "announced" by placards posted before six in the morning: everything had been done in the night. A brief insurrection on December 4 was quelled, some thousand being shot. A list of proscribed men, including Victor Hugo, Thiers, and Laboulaye, was published. Many others fled or were sent outside the borders or shot without formality. A plebiscite ratified the act of the Prince-President, whom Pius IX at once recognized.

[8] A paraphrase of Molière's line resolving the servant's doubt when he is faced with two masters who look exactly alike: "The true Amphitryon is the one where I dine." Péguy's notion is that Hugo found the genuine Napoleon to be the one he could turn into rhythm—*i.e.,* poetry.

[9] *Beethoven et ses trois styles,* St. Petersburg, 1852, 2 vols.

[10] A new translation by the writer of these lines has just gone to press: New York, Alfred A. Knopf, 1956.

[11] Wylde (1822-1890) was a pianist and organist, as well as professor of harmony at the Royal Academy of Music.

[12] In 1853 the directors followed Berlioz' original advice and moved to a smaller hall, but then Wylde did not draw like Berlioz and they still had a deficit; whereupon they renounced their capitalism and advertised that any profit would be turned over to charity.

[13] Trémont had been auditor of the Council of State under Napoleon and envoy to Vienna, where he had visited Beethoven, whose piano music he knew by heart. Taylor was identified on an earlier page. Between these two barons, the guilds of French writers, artists, and musicians were founded, nurtured, endowed, and given opportunities to come before the public in their professional capacities.

[14] This was the performance which electrified young Saint-Saëns and which he was still thinking of and writing about nearly seventy years later.

[15] Ernest Newman was the first to show the impossibility of Wagner's knowing what he was talking about, as well as the efforts of later Wagnerians to cover up the blunder by garbling texts.

[16] Liszt took Wagner severely to task about *Cellini,* and Wagner apologized twice, pleading that Liszt "must have misunderstood."

[17] The new title has nothing to do with Byron's poem of the same name. It alludes to Cooper's *The Red Rover,* Cooper having just died and the tale having remained in Berlioz' memory.

[18] Compare Rude's motto: "The great thing for an artist is to *do.*"

[19] In accordance with custom, a supper party had been arranged for the cast, the composer, and his friends. Berlioz appeared punctually, and so did J. W. Davison, but the rest stayed away, out of misplaced embarrassment. The two friends, showing signs of emotion at first, stayed to enjoy each other's company at one end of the glittering banquet table.

[20] The *Morning Post* wrote: "The work . . . was hissed with a determination which the major portion of the audience failed to overpower. . . . The conduct of a certain number . . . looked extremely suspicious. The sibilations were delivered with a simultaneousness, precision and perfection of ensemble which savored strongly of collusion. . . ."

[21] This prophecy began to be fulfilled in 1879. After a revival in 1883, the pianist-composer Marie Jaëll, wrote to a Paris critic: "It will live as long as French music itself; no one will write another *Cellini:* it is more Gallic than anything Gallic that has been written. There is in it Rabelais and Voltaire . . . this dazzling effervescence of mind and wit . . . no one has captured like Berlioz, and it will be his undying glory."

RELIGIOUS HISTORY

[1] The uniqueness of the new Baden is frequently described in the belles-lettres of the period. See the Goncourt brothers' *Charles Demailly,* Turgenev's *Smoke,* and such memoirs as Sir Horace Rumbold's *Recollections of a Diplomatist,* London, 1903, 2 vols.

[2] Compare Browning's similar use of the same myth.

[3] Brahms to Clara Schumann: "I have often heard it and it has always enchanted me. I really like it best of all Berlioz' works."

[4] Berlioz heard the Scherzo, op. 4 and the adagio of the Sonata, op. 5. Brahms tells Joachim: "On Sunday I even went to see Brendel in spite of the . . . Leipzigers . . . Berlioz praised me with such great warmth and cordiality that the others humbly followed suit."

[5] From his autobiography: *"Blassen Lisztianer, Bis zum letzten Ton und Hauch; Berlioz-Wagner-Weimarianer, Einen Cornelianer auch."*

[6] Later the slogan of the three B's was turned to different uses by Hans von Bülow.

[7] See the letter dated Jan. 7, 1854, which begins: "Sir: You read the libels, but you do not, apparently, read the refutations." (*New Letters of Berlioz,* N.Y., 1954, 112 ff.)

[8] Sainte-Beuve recalling those days after Berlioz' death wrote: "Miss Smithson was then ravishing all our hearts."

[9] Joachim: "Truly I never heard the woodwinds sound with so much sweetness and nobility as at this last concert . . . the vehemence of his invention, the breadth of his melody, the sonorous spell of his works have really enheartened me . . . You know, besides, the power of his personality."

[10] It was by no means so in Goethe's old age. See his conversations with Eckermann, Jan. 10, 1825 and Mar. 14, 1830.

[11] Berlioz could have pointed out that in order to compose the finale of the Ninth, Beethoven had mangled Schiller's "Ode to Joy."

[12] Antoine Louis Clapisson (1808-1866), a violinist and opera com-

poser whose *Gibby-la-cornemuse* was at that time his chief claim to renown. He collected musical instruments and taught harmony at the Conservatoire. Offenbach wrote an indignant squib in *L'Artiste,* expressing his admiration for Berlioz' genius and learning, which the Institute had passed over to choose an entertainer.

[13] Delacroix: "I am on probation to have it settled whether I am painter or dauber . . . [and] it will be just 30 years next year that I am in the dock." Delacroix's editor sums up the situation, precisely parallel to that of Berlioz: "In 1855, after three quarters of his life had elapsed, he was consecrated as a great painter. He won his victory, but at a price. He had defeated his adversaries but not disarmed them. He was to remain . . . as isolated as before."

[14] At this concert, dramatically enough, the two girls met their mother again after a separation due to Liszt's estrangement from her.

[15] The unison of the double chorus, supported by the trombones and declaiming the main theme, which chords on the woodwind punctuate. Above, a tremolo on the strings, and below the snare and kettle drums beat irregularly as in military salutes. Incidentally, the theme of this particular pomp and circumstance comes from the *Sardanapalus* cantata of 1830 where it ushered in the King of Kings.

VIRGILIAN MUSIC DRAMA

[1] Its only performance that I know of in recent times was given by the late Hubert Farren and his string orchestra in Coventry (England) on October 18, 1934.

[2] Long a professor of harmony at the Brussels Conservatory, Samuel became head of the musical institutions of Ghent.

[3] Fétis had the naïveté to write this fumbling judgment to Liszt.

[4] Just before these concerts George Eliot and Lewes, returning from Berlin, "sat at the same table with the composer Berlioz." They had all met in London three years before.

[5] It was three years since Wagner had said of Berlioz, again to Liszt: "He does not know me, but I know him."

[6] Berlioz reports this to Ritter in a light vein: ". . . we went to drink punch with Wagner after his concert, he renews his expressions of friendship, embraces me passionately, saying he had entertained many prejudices about me; he weeps and stamps his foot and hardly has he left when *The Musical World* publishes the passage in his book where he slates me in the most amusing and witty fashion, Davison roaring with delight as he translates it for me—the world's a stage, as Shakespeare and Cervantes have said."

[7] Liszt states unmistakably that this was the chief point at issue between him and Berlioz.

[8] *I.e.,* Berlioz began his score with the music of the love scene, the words of which, he tells Adèle, he "stole from Shakespeare and Virgilianized."

[9] This "mirage" was later replaced by a different scene.

[10] One may discern here the "new" doctrine, more or less based on Wagner's scholarly flirtation with Greek tragedy, that Liszt and the Princess preached to Berlioz at Weimar. However garbled, it conveyed clearly enough to Berlioz the one point on which he differed—the role of music in relation to drama, a role he refused to make subservient, let alone obligatory.

[11] Auguste Vivier (1821-1900), a Corsican virtuoso, one of whose specialties was playing full chords on the horn by singing one note and blowing another which yields a factitious third note. This feat would punctuate or illustrate some ludicrous improvised tale. Vivier seems moreover to have been Flaubert's precursor in collecting platitudes and publishing a repertory of them.

[12] Mérimée describes a similar prescription of "ether pearls" given him likewise as an antispasmodic.

[13] "I am aquiver from head to foot and from heart to brain with impatience, pain, enthusiasm, and superabundance of life . . . I cannot write my score fast enough. It requires a huge, a disastrous amount of time." (To Adèle.)

[14] Act IV, Sc. V, 191.

[15] To his nieces, Adèle's daughters, he writes that having five decorations to wear—two more than any other member of the Institute—his chest "resembles a hardware store" and makes a noise "like crockery in a high wind."

[16] "Heavens, but she is beautiful! If I had a Dido like her, my drama would be ruined: the pit would throw eggs at Aeneas for thinking even one minute of abandoning her."

[17] *Corresp.,* 250-1. The allusion is to the extravaganza Berlioz had written, ostensibly as a letter to the Tahitian Queen, after the Exhibition of 1855. It shows his curious knowledge of the South Sea islands and the native terminology, doubtless culled from a favorite book of travels. Berlioz also wrote as a *jeu d'esprit* the words and music of a *Salut Matinal* in the "native tongue and music." (See *New Letters of Berlioz,* N.Y., 1954.)

[18] Jules Pasdeloup (1819-1887) had been a drummer in Berlioz' Philharmonique and seeing both the merits and the defect of that enterprise, had begun one of his own.

[19] Delacroix's biographer: "Within the Institute itself he remained as isolated as before; he was deliberately held at a distance and was pained by it."

[20] The men of letters took the lead: Nerval published his *Souvenirs de 'Lohengrin,'* Gautier his report of a pilgrimage to Germany where Wagner was the new unknown. Within a few years, groups were formed even in the provinces to discuss the new art *in ab-*

stracto. Baudelaire's famous letter to Wagner after his first Paris concerts is typical of the mood of the times. (See *Pleasures of Music,* N.Y., 1951, 570-2.)

[21] This fact being that *Lohengrin* and *Tannhäuser,* though new to Paris, were by this time nine and twelve years old respectively. Hence Liszt's symphonic poems and Berlioz' last three works were newer and "technologically" more up to date.

[22] In the French theaters of Berlioz' day the composer was not allowed to conduct his own scores.

[23] Thirty-eight years later, in a novel called *Marie-Magdeleine,* Ollivier credits Berlioz, not Wagner, with initiating the true music drama. This was a trifle late and no help to the *Troyens* of 1858.

[24] Jacques Hittorf[f] (1792-1867) was a good classical scholar and archeologist, who had helped to establish the fact of polychrome architecture among the ancient Greeks.

ESTHETES AT WAR

[1] Joseph Michael Poniatowski, Prince of Monte Rotondo (1816-1873), a nephew of Napoleon's marshal, studied under Ceccherini and made his public debut as a tenor. He produced (and sang in) several operas of his own; he was an envoy from Tuscany; Napoleon III made him a Senator, and the Opera produced his *Pierre de Medicis* in March, 1860.

[2] Liszt would later write: "Berlioz was so good as to send me the printed piano score of his opera *Les Troyens.* Although for Berlioz' works piano editions are plainly deceptive, yet a cursory reading through *Les Troyens* has made an uncommonly powerful impression on me. One cannot deny that there is enormous power in it, and it certainly is not wanting in delicacy—I might also say subtlety—of feeling."

[3] Napoleon Joseph Charles Paul Bonaparte (1822-1891), Prince Jerome, commonly known as Prince Napoleon or else by the nickname of "Plon-Plon," was first cousin to the Emperor Napoleon III, the third son of Jerome, youngest brother of Napoleon I. He led the liberal opposition and incurred frequent displeasure for his outspoken criticism of policy.

[4] A niece of Nesselrode and the mother-in-law of Count Coudenhove, she had one of the most brilliant salons in Baden. She had been a pupil of Chopin's and her love of music was a passion, not an affectation. Gautier's poem, *Symphonie en Blanc Majeur* was written in her honor.

[5] Tocqueville: "The words one addressed to him were like stones thrown down a well; their sound was heard, but one never knew what became of them."

[6] At one time Balzac's mistress.

[7] An allusion to the time when Berlioz and Osborne tried to dissuade

the young singer from committing suicide after hearing Duprez's brilliant debut. See above, Chapter 9.

[8] Elisa Felix, called Rachel, the tragic actress who had died the previous year, aged 38. Berlioz respected as well as admired her, for she apparently always acknowledged the influence of Harriet Smithson on her own acting.

[9] Earlier, Berlioz had defended Mozart against this *mot* of Grétry's concerning *Don Giovanni.*

[10] The discussion imagined by Berlioz as overheard in the lobby also dates for us a change in fashions:

"Yes, I confess I had hoped it would fail."

"But why? Do you dislike M. Gounod?"

"I do."

"Why so?"

"Because he wears such a long beard. Has anyone ever seen a musician so heavily bearded? Do Meyerbeer, Auber or Halévy wear a beard? Do we live in Russia?"

"True, true, very true—Now that I understand your reasons, why, I myself . . ."

[11] Younger brother of Prince Chlodwig who, before his elevation to the Chancellorship of the German Empire under William II, was to be involved in the politics of Wagner's relation to King Ludwig of Bavaria. See his *Memoirs* (vol. I, 155, 166, 177, 296, 343).

[12] See above, Chapter 3, Berlioz' first denunciation of Castil-Blaze apropos of Gluck, thirty-four years since.

[13] H. J. Moser says in his book on Gluck: *"One* man deserves to be honored in this connection: Hector Berlioz." Berthold Damcke (1812-1875) a Hanoverian violinist, organist, composer and critic, settled in Paris in 1859. He soon became one of Berlioz' stanch friends and was named as his testamentary executor with Edouard Alexandre.

Fanny Pelletan (1830-1876) was the daughter and granddaughter of distinguished physicians, whose musical talents were cultivated from an early age.

[14] "Fantastic Ballet in Two Acts," known in Germany as *Der Förster.*

[15] The allusion is to the final scene of *Les Troyens.* As for the laudanum, it may be remarked that medication for gastric ailments had not improved in fifty years. Dr. Berlioz had taken laudanum; De Quincey's opium eating began as a result of the same prescription (ratified, it seems, by the authority of a Dr. Eatwell!) and Mérimée a little later was only shifted from opium to ether.

[16] *"Orpheus,"* said one kind of dilettante, "is the opera to see when you've just lost your parents—it's like a funeral." And a contemporary maker of opéra-comiques said: "There are not two singing phrases in the whole score. It's all recitative. If we wrote music like that, we would have eggs thrown in our faces."

[17] Looking back on the period, a French critic wrote: "What one discovered was a colossal system, at once musical, literary and

philosophic—a magnificent attempt to fuse all the arts—which filled with enthusiasm our poets as much as our musicians."

[18] A famous Wagnerian conductor and commentator, Maurice Kufferath, remarks how striking and musically exact this description is: "The motive . . . must be performed just so."

[19] The evidence of Wagner's and Liszt's and the younger Wagnerians' letters shows that "music of the future" was a phrase they used frequently and seriously as a description of the new product.

[20] Compare Henry James's description of Nash, the artist in *The Tragic Muse,* who inexplicably refuses to enter the "boats" (*i.e.,* doctrines and systems) of his amazed entourage.

PROSPERO'S FAREWELL

[1] On the right bank of the Seine opposite the Châtelet. The theater subsequently became the Opéra-Comique and later still the Théâtre Sarah Bernhardt.

[2] Rumor had it that the work called for twenty-two singers (actually nine) and that it required eight hours to play (actually four and a half).

[3] *The Queen of Sheba.*

[4] Berlioz doubtless did not know that the earliest English references to *Much Ado,* including one in the handwriting of Charles I, call the play *Benedick and Beatrice.*

[5] Act II, Sc. 15, duettino of Beatrice and Benedict. Writing at this time to his niece Josephine Suat about her sister, Berlioz stays consistent: "I am much relieved that Nanci turned down the suitor she disliked. One must not in such a serious matter allow oneself to be influenced by anybody or anything."

[6] *The Well-Beloved,* London, 1922, 101 and 209.

[7] Disraeli wrote her eleven hundred letters in eight years, but she found "embarrassing" the impassioned attentions which her far more intelligent sister, Lady Chesterfield, might have welcomed.

[8] *Hostis habet muros.*

[9] Readers of Turgenev's *Smoke* will remember that the novel opens in Baden-Baden, with a description of the promenade in front of the "Conversation." The date given, it so happens, is that of the day after the *première* of *Beatrice and Benedict,* August 10, 1862.

[10] Gounod was overwhelmed: "Here is all that the silence of night and the serenity of nature may do to imbue the soul with tenderness and reverie. The orchestra utters divine murmurings that find a place in this admirable landscape without taking anything away from the delicious cantilena of the voices: it is absolutely beautiful and perfect; it is immortal like the sweetest and deepest things ever written by the great masters."

EMPIRE AND INDUSTRY

[1] Goncourt: Journal, 163.

[2] One step higher, Sainte-Beuve observed that the generation of Taine, who was just leaving the Ecole Normale in 1851, seemed unpleasantly "bookish, absolutist, hurrying forward its raw intellect and tracking down ideas in the fashion of science."

[3] The "symphonic" passage in which the roar of the lions is heard above the human cries and confusion has since been called "analogous" to the close of the *Lacrymosa* of Berlioz' *Requiem.*

[4] Reyer's *Salammbô* was produced in Brussels in 1890 and in Paris in 1892. The subject also attracted Moussorgsky, who in 1867 began a setting of which ten numbers in piano-vocal score were published in 1939.

[5] The "tradition" thus established has lasted to this day. Like Manchester, Munich, Carlsruhe, and Glasgow, Strasbourg is a "Berlioz city." To this fact we owe the critical and directorial work of such eminent Berliozians as Albert Schweitzer, Abbé Hoch, and Charles Munch.

[6] As regrettable a lack, for a Dauphinois, as the absence of mountains in Paris.

[7] In *A Travers Chants,* which Berlioz must have just given him.

[8] I learn to aid the distressed.

[9] Flaubert insisted on being the one who should call on the other.

[10] Despite the contract Choudens never published either full score. He merely printed them and to this day, though in the public domain, they are unobtainable.

[11] The historian of Impressionism, Mr. John Rewald, writes: "Delacroix's isolation had increased during the last years of his life . . . The old and lonely painter closed his eyes at the very moment when many of those who . . . had benefited from his liberating influence were beginning to rally around Manet, a man of their own time."

[12] Carvalho is speaking: "Do you want to do me another favor?"

Berlioz: "What now?"

"Let us omit Mercury; his wings at head and foot will cause laughter. No one has ever seen wings except at the shoulders."

"So, human figures have been seen wearing wings at the shoulders? I never knew it, but no matter. . . . Since Mercury is not often seen in the streets of Paris, let us eliminate Mercury."

[13] There were other touching results Berlioz did not know, such as that Corot had become a devotee; he knew the score by heart, and sang it at his easel when he could not have his neighbor, Mme. Charton-Demeur, singing the airs for him.

[14] One critic, Albert Wolff, called on the French to kill Berlioz by ridicule and urged the composer to busy himself about ordering his tombstone: such were the witticisms published in Paris and re-

ported to Berlioz by sadistic friends. Incredible as it may seem, this same Wolff later blamed his contemporaries for having "vilified Berlioz' genius."

[15] Thomas Lovell Beddoes: "A Lofty Mind."

[16] D'Ortigue and later Ernest Reyer succeeded him.

[17] It had been first performed by Theodore Thomas's orchestra the previous year, on May 9, 1863.

[18] The meaning is, "or else you would have had the honor sooner."

[19] 1816, 1832, 1848, 1864. Since childhood Berlioz had actually seen her only for an instant in 1832.

[20] Twenty years later, Estelle's niece testified that this legacy "lightened the last days of a woman who had suffered grievous misfortune."

[21] It seems likely that the walls which echoed Berlioz' voice in these readings are now in the Boston Museum of Fine Arts. The paneling of two apartments from the Château de la Muette were acquired in 1924.

[22] The two references to Wagner go back to the 1840's and are altogether friendly.

[23] The decades run as follows:

	Berlioz	Liszt	Wagner
1830 —	*Symphonie Fantastique*	Works for Piano	*The Fairies,* an opera (1833)
1840 —	*Romeo and Juliet* *Funeral Symphony*	Bonn Cantata (1845)	*Rienzi* (finished in Paris, 1840)
1850 —	*Te Deum* *Infant Christ,* Part I	1st Symphonic Poem (*Bergsymphonie*)	*Lohengrin* (finished 1848)
1860 —	*Les Troyens*	12th Symphonic Poem (*Die Ideale*)	*Tristan* (finished 1859)

[24] From Berlioz' reports to the Minister of Fine Arts, Prodhomme concludes that "Berlioz' conception of a music Library was very modern and practical . . . his views have not even now [1913] fully prevailed."

[25] This was evident in the Parisian caricature showing *Les Troyens* as a grown boy asking his nurse to let him see his little brother *Tannhäuser*. (*Charivari,* Nov. 25, 1863.)

HOLY RUSSIA AND GIDDY FRANCE

[1] Berlioz was not nostalgic about olden times, on the contrary: "I admire our civilization more and more, with its post, telegraph, steam, and electricity—slaves to the human will, which permit the more rapid transmission of thought." But he wished that a way were also found for keeping the thought from being so generally dull and unhappy.

[2] The last of one Berlioz line unbroken for three centuries.

[3] Berlioz' bust (by Perraud) is still in Steinway Hall, New York.

[4] Rimsky-Korsakov does not seem to have understood how ill the composer was and imputes to self-importance the fact that Berlioz on this visit was hard to approach. Of the crowd of young musicians he saw chiefly Balakirev and Stassov.

[5] To Kologrivov, who had suggested a larger hall for the final concert of Berlioz' own works, the composer had replied: "It must not be. I cannot acquiesce in the idea that the public will be more eager to hear my compositions than those of the great masters."

[6] He did not seem tired during performance. "Berlioz' beat," says Rimsky, "was simple, clear, and beautiful."

[7] This is the meaning of *Mogrichaya Kuchka,* the name by which the Five were known.

MEMORY'S END

[1] The date is ascertainable from Charles Blanc's election: Nov. 25, 1868. Since the Revolution Blanc had made his name as a productive historian and critic of art; he had founded the *Gazette des Beaux-Arts* (1859) still in existence; and his election in replacement of Comte Walewski was fully deserved.

[2] Berlioz, who had foreseen so many things, had long ago chaffed Elwart, of the Conservatoire, "If you are going to be there and make a speech, then I'd just as soon not die."

INDEX *

The names of persons and titles of works are in one alphabetical sequence, except for the works of Berlioz, which have been gathered together under his name.

* Prepared by Miss Virginia Xanthos, to whom the author here expresses his gratitude. [J.B.]